MAKING WORDS MATTER

Haneef Ramay, *Muhammad* (ca. 1958)
By permission of Joyce Ramay

MAKING WORDS MATTER

THE AGENCY OF COLONIAL AND

POSTCOLONIAL LITERATURE

Ambreen Hai

OHIO UNIVERSITY PRESS
Athens

Ohio University Press, Athens, Ohio 45701
www.ohioswallow.com
© 2009 by Ohio University Press
All rights reserved

To obtain permission to quote, reprint, or otherwise reproduce or distribute material from Ohio University Press publications, please contact our rights and permissions department at (740) 593-1154 or (740) 593-4536 (fax).

Printed in the United States of America
Ohio University Press books are printed on acid-free paper ⊚ ™

16 15 14 13 12 11 10 09   5 4 3 2 1

Library of Congress Cataloging-in-Publication Data

Hai, Ambreen, 1964–
Making words matter : the agency of colonial and postcolonial literature / Ambreen Hai.
    p. cm.
Includes bibliographical references and index.
ISBN 978-0-8214-1880-2 (alk. paper) — ISBN 978-0-8214-1881-9 (pbk. : alk. paper)
1. Commonwealth fiction (English)—History and criticism. 2. Body, Human, in literature. 3. Colonies in literature. 4. Postcolonialism in literature. 5. South Asia—In literature. 6. Kipling, Rudyard, 1865–1936—Literary style. 7. Forster, E. M. (Edward Morgan), 1879–1970—Literary style. 8. Rushdie, Salman—Literary style. I. Title.
PR9084.H25 2009
820.9'3561—dc22
                    2009005524

IN MEMORY OF MY FATHER,
ABDUL HAI, 1927–2003

Speak, for your lips are free,
Speak, your tongue as yet is yours,
Your stalwart body is yours,
Speak, for your life as yet is yours.
. . . .
Speak, for truth is alive as yet,
Speak, say what needs to be said.

From "Bol," by Faiz Ahmed Faiz (1943),
who spoke against imperialism and injustice

Translated from Urdu by Ambreen Hai

CONTENTS

Acknowledgments ix

INTRODUCTION. The Unspeakable Body of the Tale 1

CHAPTER ONE. Children of an Other Language:
Kipling's Stories as Interracial Progeny 29

CHAPTER TWO. The Doubleness of Writing (in) *Kim*,
or, The Art of Empire 58

CHAPTER THREE. Forster's Crisis:
The Intractable Body and Two Passages to India, 1910–22 97

CHAPTER FOUR. At the Mouth of the Caves:
A Passage to India and the Language of Re-vision 151

CHAPTER FIVE. From a Full Stop to a Language:
Rushdie's Bodily Idiom 204

CHAPTER SIX. When Truth Is What It Is Told to Be:
Rushdie's Storytelling, Dreams, and Endings 265

EPILOGUE. The Body as the Basis for Literary Agency:
South Asia, Africa, and the Caribbean 312

Notes 327

Bibliography 361

Index 373

ACKNOWLEDGMENTS

Much of this book took shape while I have been teaching at Smith College, and I am grateful for Smith's generous leave policy, which allowed me to research and write new material and revise over the course of two separate year-long sabbaticals. I would also like to thank the office of the dean of faculty at Smith and the Jean Picker Fellowship Program, which granted me valuable course release time, and the National Endowment for the Humanities for the year-long fellowship that allowed me to make significant progress on this book. Parts of this book began as my dissertation at Yale University. I am also grateful to the Andrew W. Mellon Foundation for the year-long Yale Dissertation Fellowship that enabled me to write chapter 6, on Salman Rushdie.

An earlier version of chapter 1, titled "Children of an Other Language: Kipling's Stories, Inter-racial Progeny, and Questions of Censorship," was published in *The Journal of Commonwealth and Postcolonial Studies* as part of a special issue on Rudyard Kipling (vol. 5, no. 2 [Fall 1998]: 49–80), and I thank the editor for granting permission to reprint. Brief excerpts from my essay "Forster and the Fantastic: The Covert Politics of *The Celestial Omnibus*" (*Twentieth-Century Literature* 54, no. 2 [Summer 2008]) reappear in chapter 3, and I am grateful to the editors of *TCL* for allowing me to reprint them. Thanks also to Indus Chadha for finding the poem by Faiz. For her gracious permission to reproduce Haneef Ramay's early calligraphic painting *Muhammad*, and for her kindly sending me a scanned photograph, I thank his wife, Joyce Ramay.

Over the years while working on this book (and in the years that led to it), I have accumulated more debts from teachers, friends, colleagues, and family than I can possibly do justice to here. To the formative influence of my teachers Shahnaz Ahsannuddin and Roshan Muncherji at Karachi Grammar School, I owe my earliest joy and confidence in literary analysis. Durainow Mujahid's powerful words persuaded my parents to let me apply to an American college; without her I might never have left to study abroad. Of my beloved teachers at Wellesley College, Margery Sabin's astonishing generosity, example, wisdom, and prompt, thoughtful advice have continued to sustain me through the years;

Terry Tyler and Katheryn Doran, with their understanding and humor, intervened at a critical time and helped sustain my intellectual life.

At Yale, Nikhil Karani talked me into taking a graduate course titled "Anglo-Indian Rhetoric," something then unheard of, which launched my interest and career in the study of colonial and postcolonial literature. To Sara Suleri Goodyear's inimitable teaching and guidance and Paul H. Fry's generous advice, I owe the inception of this project in graduate school. Many fellow graduate students provided friendship, advice, and stimulating conversations and read early portions of my work: Cynthia Nieves, Anne Fernald, Kevis Goodman, Doug Mao, Edward Adams, Naomi Stephen, Margery Sokoloff, and Yoon Sun Lee. From my dear colleagues at SUNY-Albany, I learned a great deal as I moved into a crucial new stage of my career: in particular, Randy Craig, Gaurav Desai, Cesare Casarino, and Rosemary Hennessy provided invaluable support, friendship, happy conversations, and comments on portions of my work. My colleagues at Smith have provided a warm, nurturing environment and enabled in diverse ways the completion of this project. For their advice, support, active involvement, and willingness to read and comment quickly on sections of my work, I thank especially Michael Gorra, Betsey Harries, Bill Oram, Jeff Hunter, Rick Millington, and Michael Thurston.

Readers, colleagues, and friends elsewhere have also provided feedback, encouragement, and thoughtful responses, for which I am hugely grateful: Ian Baucom, Suzanne Keen, Mark Wollaeger, David Quint, Sharmila Sen, Josna Rege, Kristie Hamilton, and Jennifer Hall-Witt. I have also benefited a great deal from audiences at venues where I have had the opportunity to present my work: the Humanities Center at Harvard University; the University of Massachusetts–Amherst; the British Commonwealth and Postcolonial Studies Conference in Savannah; and the South Asia Conference at the University of Wisconsin–Madison. I am also indebted to the anonymous readers for the journals in which I have published and to the extraordinary readers for Ohio University for their astute and detailed comments, which have strengthened my work. And finally, I thank my editor, David Sanders, for his understanding, enthusiasm for this project, and remarkable facilitation of it through the publishing process.

To my parents' indulgence, I owe the development of my early passion for reading and literature. My father, in particular, always acceded—initially to my childhood insistence that I needed still more books and eventually to my need to leave Pakistan to pursue graduate work in literary studies. My parents had to put up with a great deal for my sake, from relatives and "friends" who criticized or humiliated them for being unable to control their daughter or dispose of her suitably in an arranged marriage. Despite the difficulties we had, I am grateful that my parents withstood those cultural pressures, unlike countless others who made other decisions for their daughters. I also want to thank my siblings, Aamer Hai and Mehreen Hai, for bearing with us during those times, especially my sister for her faith and support and for taking over for me at a crucial writing time when my father's illness necessitated us all taking frequent trips home. To my precious children, Anya and Amara Hai Rozario, I owe unprecedented happiness. Their presence shaped the final incarnation of this book, as they produced both the delays that matured my work and the urgency that led to its completion. I would also like to thank their teachers at the Smith College Center for Early Childhood Education at Fort Hill, in particular Polly Caron, in whose excellent care I could leave them and return to writing. Finally, to my companion and spouse, Kevin Rozario, I owe all else: his incisive readings; his thoughtful suggestions; his patience in living with this as a member of our family over the years; his co-parenting; his love, support, and enabling belief that one day this would be done.

MAKING WORDS MATTER

INTRODUCTION

The Unspeakable Body of the Tale

> All good art is provocative. . . . I do want art to stir you up, to make you think and feel. . . . That's what the work of art does to you. If it doesn't, it's inert.
>
> —Salman Rushdie[1]

IN HANEEF RAMAY'S abstract painting *Muhammad* (circa 1958; see frontispiece), a human figure sits facing sideways, silhouetted against blazing red flames, gazing meditatively at the curling tongues of a fire that appears to emanate both from him and beyond him.[2] A viewer unfamiliar with Arabic script may not realize that this geometrically shaped figure also is (or figures) the calligraphic inscription of a sacred word, "Muhammad." (Written in Arabic as محمد, with four letters: meem, heih, meem, daal.) This pictorial representation of a human body acts as a visual pun, coinciding with the verbal text that names that body. What relation does this startling convergence suggest between word and image, and word and body? How could one become the other? Which represents which? Quranic calligraphy has long been a subject of interest and reverence in twentieth-century

Pakistani painting and sculpture.³ By conflating word and image, however, Ramay's painting approaches what is forbidden to Islamic representation: the body of the Holy Prophet.⁴ Artful through his art, the artist replaces and simultaneously represents that body as a text. In so doing, he also suggests some crucial connections between words and bodies.

Ramay's painting presents the prophet Muhammad in the moment of *becoming* the Prophet: the messenger in the darkness of the cave, or *hira*, receiving the *wahi*, the illumination of the Divine Word. From this inaugural moment, the painting suggests, this body will bring word—eventually a sacred book—of a revolutionary new religion that will in turn become flesh, transforming peoples, identities, histories. Words thus are both produced by and act upon bodies with material, bodily force. Henceforth, the Prophet's words will act upon those who are converted by them to Islam, upon bodies that will literally take those words on their tongues, to recite, to bend in devotional postures, to adopt distinctive bodily markers. Yet words and bodies are not only interdependent but also analogous, for both can act or be acted upon, and both can be turned into an instrument of another's design. Muhammad's words and body have power to enact material, revolutionary change, but they are also vulnerable: his words can be misused or misinterpreted by others, and bodies can be constrained, hurt, or punished. By depicting both the word and the body (of) Muhammad as the same, as equally elemental, powerful, and fragile, Ramay disorders any priority we might assume of one over the other. By implication, this painting also invokes the bodily power of the word to evoke more generally the agency of art. What can art as a human construct—verbal or pictorial—*do* in the world of which it is a part?

I begin with Ramay's painting because it raises questions central to this book and exemplifies their convergence. Although it calls upon visual representation to evoke the verbal, it is fascinated with the relations between words and bodies, with verbal agency and art's material effectuality. Why should postcolonial art be preoccupied with its own agency; its political, material, social effectuality; its dependence on and exploitability in the world; its capacity to tell truth? What hubris, or anxiety, could drive both colonial and postcolonial literature to claim political agency, to imagine that words can matter, that language, so seemingly remote and abstract, can yet embrace, touch, and have material effects on the world? And why should the human body become central to such literary self-imagining, to the articulation of relations between texts and their world? Why do artists turn to the human body as the figure and site of literary agency: the condition of art's concomitant power and vulnerability?

Ramay's *Muhammad* depicts a pivotal historical moment when words enacted change; in so doing, it radically re-imagines that moment. By rendering ambiguous the source of those flaming tongues of light and fire, it introduces a staggering doubt: do they emerge from some divine source beyond representation, or from the Prophet himself? Is this human body/word a source or a medium, an autonomous agent or a tool of divine intent? Through those flames, at once suggestive of creation and destruction, of comfort and pain, surrounding his lone body or emanating powerfully from him, the painting hints subversively that Muhammad's flaming words may well be his own, engendered by *human* inspiration, illumination, and desire, calling upon its Muslim viewers to rethink their history and religion and the secular power of human/divine revelation. Thus, this painting also reflects upon its own agency as a human work of art: if Muhammad's "message" could change the world, how autonomous is art's message and what work can it do? Is its function to submit, revere, commemorate, or to question, critique, imagine alternatives for change? In a postcolonial nation such as Pakistan—founded as a secular homeland for Muslims seeking separation from India—what kind of agent can art be? From this religious and political context arises a secular art, interacting with its environment and asking how art may participate in the (re)making of its world.[5]

In a surprisingly comparable mode, Salman Rushdie's work also draws upon the human body to pose questions about its own agency. Early in *Midnight's Children* (1981), Saleem the narrator breaks off the saga of his life, family, and nation to reflect: "Family history, of course, has its own proper dietary laws. One is supposed to swallow and digest only the permitted parts of it, the halal portions of the past, drained of their redness, their blood. Unfortunately, this makes the stories less juicy; so I am about to become the first and only member of my family to flout the laws of halal. *Letting no blood escape from the body of the tale, I arrive at the unspeakable part; and undaunted, press on*" (my emphasis).[6] "Flouting" cultural and familial prohibitions to tell "unspeakable" truths, reconstructing a past that parental authority would erase, and evoking a shameful maternal sexuality, Saleem advertises his transgressions as a storyteller. Thus Rushdie flaunts his own daring, his fictive effort to tell dangerous yet salutary truths about the national and communal histories that he too casts as forbidden, forgotten, and familial. Yet why should this verbal act be cast as a bodily one of eating and sharing slaughtered flesh, as if stories (histories) taken in and given out, passed from mouth to mouth, were as necessary as food? Why should family history be "swallowed" and "digested" by the storyteller, assimilated and incorporated into his body, and then re-produced for his audience to consume? Unlike the storytellers who abide by the "laws" of their community, he, Rushdie suggests, will break the religious division between "halal" and "haram" meat.[7] *Not* letting the blood escape from his stories, Rushdie claims, he will present them whole, unpurified, and uncensored rather than "drained" of their blood, color, and life. To "press on to the unspeakable part" is to render his stories more sustaining and juicy (or "juicygory"),[8] to swallow the blood with the full "body of the tale."

Like Ramay, Rushdie calls upon the body to suggest both the vulnerability and the resistant, political potential of his work. His carnivorous metaphor suggests both the vitality and the violence inherent in narration and consumption: stories both nourish and can be subject to censorship or amputation. And like Ramay, reimagining a critical historical moment through this bodily language, Rushdie returns to the past to regain control of how that past is remembered and hence to recast how the present and future, both individual and collective, will be fashioned. But Rushdie's writing explicitly both raises doubts about and insists on its own agency. It valorizes its potential to enter other bodies, to change them and their world. *Midnight's Children,* his seminal novel of postcolonial nationhood, concludes with the well-known assertion that Saleem the narrator (and Rushdie too) has been "chutnifying history." Saleem conflates his writing of history with his manual work making condiments in a pickle factory, preserving in "words and pickles" his "memories, dreams, and ideas, . . . humors, messages, emotions," which are to be consumed by his readers (MC, 548–49). But this labor has political power: these "pickled chapters" are to be "*unleashed* upon the amnesiac nation" that will consume them (MC, 549; my emphasis). Thus, Rushdie proposes that his writing will infiltrate the unsuspecting bodies (and body) of the nation that consumes it, infusing them with healthy, vital alternative versions of national-as-familial history to contest politically sanctioned ones. His writing will remind that nation of what it may have forgotten, insisting only upon the truth that no history is truthful, educating its readers and changing how they see and are seen, what they remember of themselves, who they are and can be.

Rushdie's self-descriptions optimistically suggest that writing can be a material bodily act and have material, bodily effects, that the relation between his fiction and the world is not just one-directional: they link the body and language to advance a mutually transformative relation between language and the material to which it bears more than a referential relation. A trope of storytelling central to *The Moor's Last Sigh* (1995) proposes that the world is absorbed or taken *in* by the writer-protagonist (inhaled as oxygen), is incorporated into his flesh, transforming it, and then is breathed *out* in altered form (exhaled as carbon dioxide) so that what he sighs or (re)produces, as *word*, will in turn materially transform that world (*Moor*, 53–54). These bodily representations of language attempt to break down binary oppositions between language and material reality, between word and world, between inside and outside: both insist on the mutual reinforcement and inextricability of language and body, as well as the porous continuities between the self and its environment.

But such grand claims of material effectuality also reveal their own anxiety. Rushdie shows repeatedly how writers and writing are vulnerable to being co-opted or destroyed because of the truths that they might reveal. Because of this power, words can be destroyed or dismembered just as bodies can. In *Midnight's Children*, Saleem's communicative body undergoes the terrible "sperectomies" of Indian state repression, and his telepathic talents are co-opted by Pakistan's totalitarianism for genocidal ends. In *The Satanic Verses* (1988), the irrepressible Baal is executed for his blasphemous verses, while Salman, the more cowardly scribe, subverts but serves those whose authority he fears. By the time of his writing *The Moor's Last Sigh*, in the aftermath of the fatwa (1989), Rushdie's playful, audacious urge to tell forbidden truths, to name the unnamable, has turned into a sober insistence on the need to resist silencing. To sigh is literally to change the air through the action of one's body and figuratively to resist, to assert one's continued existence despite forces that may extinguish life: "I exhale, I overcome. . . . I sigh, therefore I am," announces the Moor, displacing the Cartesian mind with his body as the site of being.[9] If the Moor's "last sigh" refers to his long life story—Rushdie's novel—then to sigh is to continue to narrate, to insist on one's own version of reality, to give proof of coping with life, and to live responsibly in the world, because (especially after the fatwa) for

Rushdie the failure to struggle to change the world, to write, and to tell stories is indeed to die.

This book examines a preoccupation with what I call "literary agency," with how the capacity to act and to act for others, to affect and to be affected by their world, haunts and shapes both colonial and postcolonial literary texts.[10] More specifically, I examine how and why this preoccupation is centrally tied to evocations of the human body. For the purposes of this study, I focus on the work of Rudyard Kipling, E. M. Forster, and Salman Rushdie, three of the most influential and self-conscious writers to emerge from the history of British imperialism in India. Yet while the three share a certain set of cultural, historical, and political contexts and have a vertical if embattled literary relationship with each other (each subsequent writer is highly aware of, familiar with, and contestatory of the work of his precursors), they are also usefully different in representing three distinct political and historical positionalities—respectively, colonial, colonial anticolonial, and postcolonial—allowing me to chart both their similarities and their differences within a tight focus and to elaborate how, despite their differences, they articulate shared concerns with the agency of their work as they call upon the body to articulate those concerns. Through intensive readings of their fiction, essays, letters, and travel writings, I explore how this overriding concern about the function and status of art both manifests and works itself out by assuming central links between human language and the bodily. I argue that because they wrote in contexts of embattled power relations, and perhaps because they were situated between various cultural borders, these writers focus self-reflectively in their writing on the unstable capacity of words to be used and abused, to tell (or make) truth and to be censored. This central concern with literary agency is embedded in (indeed, definitive of) colonial and postcolonial literature. But I contend that for these writers (and indeed for many others, as I suggest in my epilogue), all of whom evoke distinctive and complex relations between words and bodies, the human body becomes central to the imagining of the text in the world because it uniquely concretizes a threefold instability about human agency: it is at once the site of autonomy, instrumentality, and subjection. What is distinctive about each writer is how he or she imagines this relationship and hence the power or susceptibility of art. Unlike many writers, however, Kipling, Forster, and Rushdie sustain this link between body, text, and literary agency throughout their work.

It is perhaps inevitable that political writing—fraught with dangers of censorship, prohibition, and retribution—should be acutely aware of its cultural and political potential and vulnerability. Anxiety, instead of necessarily being psychically disabling, can also be enabling when it shapes how a writer approaches his or her craft. Colonial experiences often produce what Trinh Minh-ha has called the "both-in-one insider/outsider," who is precariously located on the borders between unequal cultures, whose cultural (dis)location— or, in Rushdie's phrase, "at once plural and partial" identities—can enable both sympathetic and critical perspectives.[11] For such colonial and postcolonial writers with often multiple, conflicting allegiances—Anglo-Indian Kipling, born in Bombay, racially white, pro-imperial yet skeptical of English claims to know and rule India; English Forster, anti-imperialist yet not an advocate of Indian nationalism; and Anglicized Rushdie, born in India, a citizen of Britain, highly critical of Pakistan, to which his family migrated—the need for self-location becomes greater and the stakes of literary agency more fraught. If "it is the force of circumstance that triggers anxiety about agency,"[12] the self-examination and self-exposure of colonial and postcolonial writers reveals a complex cultural condition as well as concern about literature's raison d'être. All three writers studied here dwell upon the agency of their words (which take on an independent existence of their own), not outside of but *in* their art; indeed, their work is shaped by this concern. Though each calls *differently* upon the human body to center that concern about agency, they all seem to presume that art is not an inert artifact but something that *acts* upon others and upon the world, that *does* something, shaping subjectivities and actions, making a material difference in the world.[13] The doubleness of my title, *Making Words Matter*, thus suggests both the making of literature that matters in the world, and the making of it *into* matter, that is, making it material.

At the same time that it reveals unexpected connections, this study also reveals significant differences between the writers it examines, in particular showing how the issue of literary agency shifts tellingly over the literary-historical trajectory it charts (Victorian to postcolonial). As an imperial writer still subject to imperial censorship, Kipling is less concerned with enacting social change and more with the degree to which his writing can be damaged or evade damage, as well as with how he can encode an implicit though ambivalent critique of empire. Forster's work is perhaps the most marked by its concern with censorship (about homosexuality or empire), yet it is also far more intent upon finding ways to transgress, to speak the proscribed body, to have effect—though necessarily in covert form. Most dramatically of all three, since 1989 Rushdie has himself been threatened with bodily silencing and his book has been subjected to public burning, yet he, ironically, has been (both before and after the fatwa) the most defiant of censorship in his writing and the most overtly focused on how his fiction can affect national and global communities. This study is, however, not interested in merely comparing three significant writers. Rather, its purpose is to explore a broader problematic of the political agency of colonial and postcolonial literatures and the ways in which, even in highly different circumstances, these literatures are shaped by that self-consciousness. Establishing an interdisciplinary theoretical framework for these questions (and their relation to contemporary scholarship) here is thus key to my readings in the following chapters.

Why should writers preoccupied with the agency of their writing be drawn to the human body to ground their concerns? What does *agency* have to do with the *body*? The instability of the word *agent* is evident in its antithetical everyday meanings: one who acts autonomously, effectively, and intentionally, versus one who acts for another as a tool subordinate to someone else's will and design. The modern notion of agency includes being both "active initiator and passive instrument."[14] A basic reason why the human body draws writers concerned about literary agency is that the body uniquely concretizes the complexities of human agency. As philosophical action theory reminds us, human intention can be manifested and executed only through bodily action. Norman Care and Charles Landesman define action, something we *do* (as opposed to what happens *to* us), as involving "genuine physical interventions of a person in the world."[15] However, as A. I. Melden points out, though every action involves some "bodily movement, . . . not every bodily movement counts as an action," thus restricting action to bodily movements for which we are morally responsible.[16] Theorizing agency, the sociologist Anthony Giddens defines action as a "stream of actual or contemplated causal interventions of corporal beings in the ongoing process of events in the world."[17] Action and agency are thus fundamentally tied to bodily being. Our modern Western sense of individual and political autonomy is based on Hobbes's and Locke's definitions of selfhood as possession of one's own body, or bodily freedom. Hobbes's political theory in *Leviathan* depends on his "reduction of human beings to self-moving and self-directing systems of matter."[18] For Locke, the one thing every human owned was his body, hence his property was that which he acquired by bodily labor: "[E]very man has a property in his own person: this no body has any right to but himself. The labor of his body and the work of his hands, we may say, are properly his."[19] However, as historian Michel Foucault has shown, power is enacted singularly upon and through human bodies: bodies can be acted upon, or used, by others.[20] Mikhail Bakhtin argues that it is through representations of the grotesque or lower body that the oppressed (by class and also by race) have traditionally sought means of resistance to dominant authority.[21] Across disciplines, thinkers agree, the very fact of embodiment, the sense of inhabiting a body, is what both founds and confounds our sense of selfhood, autonomy, responsibility, and the ability to resist and to act in and upon our world.

Thus, the human body functions both symbolically and literally as the site of this threefold instability about human agency: it is at once the site of autonomy, instrumentality, and subjection. It is the primary vehicle for intentional action and responsibility; it can be made an instrument for another's intention; and as literary critic Elaine Scarry movingly describes, it can be made most abject when subjected to pain, punishment, or constraint.[22] The human body then becomes crucial for both colonial and postcolonial writers' representation of literary subjection, instrumentalization, and intervention in the public sphere because the body concretizes these instabilities of human agency: it is the site of subjectivity and subjection, of power and disempowerment, of vulnerability and resistance, of identity (usually encoded in racialized or gendered terms), and of separation from and interpenetration by the world, a seemingly stable constant of selfhood yet constantly subject to change. Moreover, the body centers the individual *and* relational experiences of inhabiting it, so that we are at once ourselves and ourselves in relation to others. This concomitant independence and interrelationality of the body and its multiple processes allows all of the writers I study here to explore the autonomy and material interrelations between literature and its environment.

In recent years, the broader problem of human agency has become a focus of renewed interest for scholars in a variety of fields. By replacing the humanist notion of the holistic "self" with the fragmented, multiply determined "subject," post-structuralism has complicated our understanding of individuality, selfhood, and intentionality as well as of acting with autonomy, responsibility, and will. At the same time, the disappearance of the "self" has been challenged by scholars concerned with historically suppressed or silenced subjectivities, who emphasize the personhood, resistance, and self-representation of women, subalterns, and ethnic or sexual minorities in and beyond literature. Literary and cultural critics have begun to explore the agency of characters and readers, as well as of language and texts. Literature and language act upon us, shaping our sense of ourselves and of our world. As Bruce Robbins puts it, "Novels both have and are agents. . . . One way in which they are agents is by producing and propagating fictions of agency and agent-characters which have worldly consequences in encouraging or discouraging various forms of action."[23] Jerome McGann contends that Romantic poets such as Blake and Byron show us that "poetry is a form of [social] action rather than a form of representation."[24] Likewise, postcolonial critics have emphasized how language can be a tool of both oppression and resistance. "Colonialism is an operation of discourse," state Chris Tiffin and Alan Lawson, "established initially by guns, guile and disease" but "maintained . . . by textuality."[25] Postcolonial writing, "with its signification of authority," seeks to "wrest" power back from "dominant European culture," assert Bill Ashcroft et al.[26] In his study of imperialism in eighteenth-century literature, Srinivas Aravamudan proposes the term "'tropicopolitan' as a name for the colonized subject . . . and agent of resistance" who "tropicalizes" colonial or metropolitan discourses as a "motivated" act of resistance, while Ketu Katrak's important study shows how postcolonial women's cultural texts underscore how women both experience and resist oppression through their bodies.[27] Thus, literary scholars working in a variety of historical periods have begun to examine how literature both addresses and affects the way human beings act in the world.

None, however, have explored how an anxiety about the agency of literature marks literature itself or why a consideration of the body is necessary to address that concern. And though literary scholars have amply examined the representation of bodies as sites of oppression and resistance, they have not considered how the body may be necessary to the *self*-representation of the text. This book contributes to these ongoing dialogues about agency and the body both within and beyond postcolonial studies and opens them up to the newer question of *literary* agency. It examines how texts are built on a consciousness of their own agency, an awareness of how words have an independent existence and can be independently (mis)read, used, or destroyed. Postcolonial criticism depends on Benedict Anderson's and Homi Bhabha's contentions that nations are "imagined communities," that narration is constitutive of nations, enabling communities to imagine and (re)invent themselves. But it has not addressed how writers involved in this cultural work of narration as nation making or empire making are aware of their role and responsibilities or how that awareness is reinscribed into the texts. This book shows how writers as diverse as Kipling, Forster, and Rushdie base their work on a self-awareness of its links to its world, seeking to use its power responsibly, as well as to delineate the limitations upon it. I draw on the work of postcolonial scholars who emphasize the ambivalence of colonial literature (for example, Homi Bhabha) and connect colonial and postcolonial texts to unravel the intimacies they share (in a manner similar to that of Sara Suleri), complicating the dichotomies identified by early postcolonial criticism (as exemplified by the work of Edward Said and Abdul JanMohamed).[28] But self-referentiality still tends to be regarded as a form of apolitical retreat.[29] I attempt to show how that turn inward can be a form of reflecting on the outward and, indeed, a form of political engagement.

In attending to important theoretical and political issues, recent postcolonial criticism has sometimes neglected the density or literariness of the language; the shifts, ironies, and contradictions; or the ways political concerns may be amplified and complicated by symbolic or formal choices. *Making Words Matter* takes a very different approach: I show how politics inheres in the aesthetics of the writings I examine, and I undertake methods of interpretation that attend to this inextricability. I avoid the tendency in postcolonial criticism to focus on politics as thematics; instead, I emphasize how reading formal or figurative features can also allow us to read politically. Having established its theoretical credentials, postcolonial literary studies now needs to shift toward what Gaurav Desai has called "a newer, historically, culturally and politically conscious literary criticism," that is, more subtle, attentive critical readings of both colonial and postcolonial texts that are informed but unencumbered by theory, as we draw upon other disciplines and read traditionally "non-literary texts."[30] In a similar vein, Derek Attridge urges " a mode of attention to the specificity and singularity of literary writing as it manifests itself through the deployment of form."[31] Attending to the formal properties of colonial and postcolonial texts is not to return to modes of reading that bracket off politics from aesthetics; rather, it can augment our political understanding of a text. The arguments of this book are made through such textual readings. One of my goals is to read these texts as complex and dense, existing in a fraught world, to explore the interrelations between a text's features and its contexts of power.

Focusing on literary nuances or regarding texts as supplemental (in the sense of carrying something extra) to dominant ideological imprinting assumes, however, that writers do not just passively absorb and reproduce the discourses and ideologies that surround them—that they engage actively in some way with their world to produce something new, to wrestle with questions of their time without being determined by those discourses. Margery Sabin argues for the critical need to read colonial and postcolonial writers as both subject to the ideologies of their times and able to question them. Hence she distinguishes the goals and methods of literary analysis from social studies: "I call my standard of selection and method of analysis 'literary' in that dissenters and mavericks are discussed here as authors, whose unorthodoxy manifests itself in distinctive qualities of language and design in their writing. . . . My sequence of argument tends to reverse the order now dominant in postcolonial analysis, where the stature of an admired text usually comes at the start of an argument that, in the end, presses the author back into the general cultural pattern. I tend to put the acknowledgement of a collective colonialist discourse first and then turn to what still remains distinctive and divergent in a particular text."[32] In attending to this "unorthodoxy," Sabin implicitly reminds us of the agency of writers who are not, in Anthony Giddens's telling phrase, mere "cultural dopes."[33] Writers can worry about the agency of their writing only if they have the agency to think about their agency. They can be concerned with the degree to which their work is imprinted by (or can contest) circumstantial forces only if they have the independence to think about their deviation from some norm.

As post-structuralist, Marxist, and New Historicist critics agree, multiple ideologies coexist in a culture at any one time, and their conflict provides the liberatory spaces for writers to develop resistances or individual positions within conflicting discourses. Hence Louis Montrose states, "The possibility of political and institutional agency cannot be based upon the illusion of an escape from ideology. However, the very process of subjectively living the confrontations or contradictions within or among ideologies makes it possible to experience facets of our own subjection at shifting internal distances—to read, as in a refracted light, one fragment of our ideological inscription by means of another. A reflexive knowledge so partial and unstable may, nevertheless, provide subjects with a means to empowerment as agents."[34] Sabin argues for scrupulosity and self-restraint in critical reading, allowing the text to guide the critic, instead of subsuming the text under a predefined argument or agenda or using the text to illustrate an argument of which the critic is already convinced. Such a schooled critical practice assumes that there is something unexpected to be found in a text if we as readers are willing to see it. Bart Moore-Gilbert similarly exhorts postcolonial critics to read colonial discourse with a view to its shifts over time, geographic location, complexities, ironies, and textual and "formal properties," which, he argues, might complicate our understanding of its ideology.[35] I locate my work in the postcolonial scholarship that is now returning to *reading* texts while grounded in historical, theoretical, and culturally aware questions and attuned to the elements of their *difference*.[36] But first I would like to elaborate on some of the broader theoretical underpinnings of this project which depends on three key concepts: agency, truth, and the body.

Literary Agency

> [A] person is not simply the *actor* who follows ideological scripts, but is also an *agent* who reads them in order to insert him/herself into them—or not.
> —Paul Smith, *Discerning the Subject*[37]

At a crucial point in Jane Austen's *Mansfield Park*, the quiet protagonist Fanny Price faces a difficult choice: either she must accede to the demands of her rich cousins and accept a role in the salacious play that they are rehearsing, or she must stake out a position of her own and refuse to do as they want. Her act of resistance (and of moral choice), however, is expressed through a very ambiguous metaphor: "I cannot *act*," she plaintively insists.[38] In this loaded episode,

Austen's pun on the verb *to act* pulls apart its antithetical meanings: of taking independent action versus playing a role given to one by another, being subject to another's words and will—indeed, being untrue to oneself, to some essential self. Fanny, a submissive, powerless, poor relation in the Bertram household, has as yet never been able to act for herself; she has had to play the roles given to her by her family and society. Austen's metropolitan novel (with its colonial geography, as Edward Said has argued)[39] traces the development of this individual who matures despite her circumstances; in its humanist assumptions of individual selfhood, will, and agency, the novel is concerned with Fanny's learning to act for herself and become an autonomous moral being. Yet as we can now recognize, even Fanny's final growth and stature remain limited in that she can act only within highly limited though less visible constraints, within a framework of gendered, racial, and national ideologies that she cannot or does not question.

This problem of human agency, of the degree to which individuals have a real ability to enact choices beyond the perceived and unperceived, external and internalized limitations of their circumstances, is evoked in a similar play on "acting" in Hanif Kureishi's 1990 novel, *The Buddha of Suburbia*. In an equally exigent crisis, Karim Amir, the "Englishman born and bred, almost" (3), son of a Pakistani father and English mother, gets his first job as an actor and discovers that the role he has been assigned to play is Mowgli, Kipling's Indian jungle-boy; he is then ordered to "act" on stage wearing only a loincloth and "shit-brown cream" and affecting an "authentic" Indian accent.[40] Satirizing the unintended racism of liberal 1980s Britain and its perpetuation of imperial legacies, the novel explores how the ineffectual Karim, at first unable to "act," *can* effect some degree of agency. Faced with the choice of submitting to the overdetermined role assigned to him (of reenacting anew the ridiculous native) or of giving up his aspirations for a theatrical career, Karim acts in both senses: he plays Mowgli but subverts the role from within, "sending up" the accent, exposing through postcolonial mockery and mimicry the colonial stereotype he is forced to play (158).

These colonial and postcolonial examples raise a broad question: to what extent are human beings free to act within or able to change the circumstances in which they are unavoidably placed? These examples also connect action with the issue of truth: to act, to combat the forces threatening one, is somehow to be true to oneself. Through the dual meanings of the term *acting*, they illustrate the conflicted modern usage of the term *agency*: an agent can (1) be autonomous, independent, choosing to act independently; or (2) act for another, in another's interests, subject to another's will or intentions, functioning as a tool or instrument. But agents can also (3) be *denied* agency and be acted upon, made into nonagents, left with no choice. This three-sided nature of agency is what interests me, as I extend the problem of human agency to literary agency, to the predicament of texts in the world, to their capacity (beyond their authors' agency) to (1) have effects; (2) be used as instruments for other interests; or (3) be silenced, suppressed, damaged, or censored.

Most discussions of agency use the term only in the first sense, as an index of autonomy. After Marx, Freud, and Saussure and our understanding of ideological formation and interpellation, of the split, unknowable psyche, and of the prison-house of language, it is no longer possible to think of the "individual" or "self" as whole, self-knowing, or self-determining or, in Paul Smith's words, as "the intending and knowing . . . conscious and coherent originator of meanings and actions." As "subjects," we are no longer sovereign over our thoughts or actions, the "bearers of consciousness," or "active mind(s) or thinking agent(s)";[41] rather, we are "subjects" in the sense of being subordinated, or subjected by forces within and without us, determined instead of self-determining. Our very sense of "self" is "other."

Human agency becomes a fraught issue, because how, then, can humans be autonomous, or claim credit or responsibility for their actions and choices? Smith contends that post-structuralist theory has overlooked the grounds for human agency and that "the human agent *exceeds* the 'subject'" (xxx). He defines *agent* as "the place from which resistance to the ideological is produced or played out . . . (even though that resistance too must be produced in an ideological context)" (xxxv). Sociologist Anthony Giddens identifies the opposition between "agency" and "structure" at the heart of rifts in contemporary Western thought: he shows how, on the one hand, Anglo-American philosophy has focused on intention and rationality to the exclusion of social institutions and frameworks; on the other hand, the social sciences have emphasized structure to an extreme degree of social determinism. Instead, Giddens proposes a dialectical relationship, arguing that even as human actions are produced by and within social structures, they in turn produce social systems and act within them. While acts are always "situated practices," he states, a necessary feature of action is that an agent "could [always] have acted otherwise." To Giddens, structure "is not to be conceptualized as a barrier to action, but as essentially involved in its production, . . . as both enabling and constraining."[42] Tellingly, most efforts to find room for human agency express a strong desire for at least a limited or mediated human agency. As literary theorist Meili Steele puts it, "We are both constructing and constructed subjects, and our deliberations need to be informed by both vocabularies."[43] Reflecting upon New Historicism, Louis Montrose writes, "I am aware of a strong stake, not in any illusion of individual autonomy, but in the possibilities for limited and localized agency within the regime of power and knowledge that at once sustains and constrains us."[44] Historian Perry Anderson critiques E. P. Thompson's famous attack on Louis Althusser by recasting the latter's pessimism about "the role of human agency in history" and proposes "self-determination" as a more reasonable term that acknowledges the limited yet real choices we have in everyday actions.[45] Such a concept of agency has had obvious importance for postcolonial critics, who have tried to locate at least a "peripheral" subaltern agency despite colonial suppression—both physical and discursive.[46]

This book recasts the question of agency in different terms: instead of the agency of the colonized subject or of the reader of colonial discourse, it explores the agency of literary texts produced in contexts of colonization and decolonization. If we were to understand agency in the terms set by action philosophy, in which agents are by definition conscious, rational intentional beings, to speak of texts having agency might seem a contradiction in terms. Obviously, I do not suppose that texts have consciousness or volition or that they "act" in the sense that humans do, with intention or rationality.[47] However, most literary and cultural critics now assume that texts do "cultural work," that they act in the world just as they are produced and limited by it.[48] Montrose observes, "To speak, then, of the social production of 'literature' or of any particular text is to signify not only that it is socially produced but also that it is socially productive —that it is the product of work and that it performs work in the process of being written, enacted, or read." Later, he elaborates, "In its anti-reflectionism, its shift of emphasis from the formal analysis of *artifacts* to the ideological analysis of discursive *practices*, . . . the emergent historical orientation in literary studies is pervasively concerned with writing as a mode of *action*."[49] Montrose's emphasis on writing as a "mode of action," on texts as being "socially productive" as well as produced, is crucial, recalling Kenneth Burke's argument that language is a form of "symbolic action," that it is not only denotative but also "suasive" by nature: it exhorts, it *does* something (though Montrose emphasizes the ways in which texts are equally subject to ideological and other forces).[50] Shelley famously dubbed poets the "unacknowledged legislators of the world," because through their words, writers act upon the world, to bring about social, political, and cultural transformation.[51] But as he recognized, those words remain in the world and act in it beyond their authors' knowledge or control. Reader-response theory has similarly contributed to our understanding that texts are not merely static objects that reflect the world but are instead "performative acts" that become "a way of world-making"; although "the text itself is the outcome of an intentional act whereby an author refers to and intervenes in an existing world," an author cannot anticipate what will happen between a text and its readers.[52]

Although texts do not act in the ways of humans and cannot be deprived of choice or volition, they do act in that they have profound effects on humans and social environments. Hence, because of their potential power, texts (like humans) are also subject to being used, misused, shaped by various ideologies, or subjected to silence and destruction. This is the sense in which I examine the agency of colonial and postcolonial texts, their capacity to act and be acted upon. Literary agency is thus related to, yet not the same as, authorial agency, for it exists independently of the author's agency, even though it is to some degree an extension of that authorial agency.

Truth and Unspeakability

> The secret of the imagination [is] that in its fictional forms it still deals in matters of truth and error.
>
> —Jerome McGann,
> *Towards a Literature of Knowledge*[53]

At a Royal Academy dinner in 1906, Kipling opened his speech on literature with the following parable:

> There is an ancient legend which tells us that when a man first achieved a most notable deed he wished to explain to his Tribe what he had done. As soon as he began to speak, however, he was smitten with dumbness, he lacked words, and sat down. Then there arose . . . a masterless man, one who had taken no part in the action of his fellow, who had no special virtues, but who was afflicted . . . with the magic of the necessary word. He saw; he told; he described the merits of the notable deed in such a fashion . . . that the words "became alive and walked up and down in the hearts of all his hearers." Thereupon, the Tribe seeing that the words were certainly alive, and fearing lest the man with the words would hand down untrue tales about them to their children, took and killed him. But, later, they saw that the magic was in the words, not in the man.[54]

Kipling begins by differentiating the man of action, or the doer of deeds "smitten with dumbness," from the storyteller, the man who records that action, as if his own storytelling were not action itself.[55] Exemplifying his habitual concern about the extent to which his writing constituted action, this parable also testifies to Kipling's sense that words are "alive" and act independently of their speakers, in part because they outlive and outdo them: if the primal storyteller is "masterless," so are his words. Hence the danger to both words and their users, he suggests, for it is because of this agency that words seem to have—their potential to tell (or not tell) truths—that words and those who use them are feared (and "afflicted"). The agency of literature is thus inextricable from its truth-bearing potential. Bodily themselves and having bodily effects, these words that are "alive" and "walk up and down in the hearts of [their] hearers" have power because they can shape the future of the tribe and how it is remembered. "We desire above all things to stand well with our children," Kipling explains (4); for their potential to pass on true or untrue histories that the tribe cannot control, words can be destroyed. Kipling's parable thus also suggests a primal relation between the agency or truth-capacity of words, and the storyteller, the destruction of whose body is equated with the destruction of his words. As a cautionary tale of the dangers (and attractions) of censorship, it expresses Kipling's anxiety as he addresses his own tribe about his writing.

This example illustrates how intimately literary agency is connected to the issue of the truth of (or in) literature. The capacity of imaginative writing to act in the world is bound to its ability, precisely through its fictionality, to convey some sort of truth that shapes readers' realities and influences how we perceive and act in the world. In however attenuated a form, literature addresses and refers to reality and carries effects of truth and falsehood. If it referred to nothing, or only to itself, it would have no relevance. For colonial and postcolonial writers, the capacity of their writing to act in the world is inseparable from its ability to tell dangerous truths, to push the boundaries of the unspeakable, or to participate in the making of new truths that shape reality. This study shows how these writers emphasize what can and cannot be said, the boundaries between language and the unspeakable and between external censorship and internal self-silencing, because truth is precisely what is at stake.

The unspeakable can be produced by at least two kinds of factors. First, truths of various sorts can be censored, or prohibited in public discourse by external authorities—social, cultural, or legal. These include colonial powers for Kipling; legal and cultural proscriptions against homosexuality for Forster; and neocolonial nations for Rushdie. But truths can also be unspeakable because language itself is limited, bounded by cultural or experiential parameters. Either it carries cultural values and prohibitions (such as when Forster struggles with the "obduracy" of language to "carnality" [*Letters*, 1:316]), or it is simply untranslatable in a particular language (as indicated by Rushdie's remarks about the South Asian concept of "sharam," poorly translated as *shame* [*Shame*, 34–35]). Each strives to re-create language, inventing ways to intimate alternative truths despite the resistance of language, through indirection, suggestion, or forms of negation.

The issue of literary truth is not often addressed in contemporary critical discourse, though it needs to be, at the very least because both colonial and postcolonial writers are explicitly preoccupied with it.[56] Kipling's fiction reveals truths about the British Empire in India that may not redound to the Empire's credit. As a self-consciously imperial storyteller, Kipling worries about not only actual censorship but also how much his writing is shaped by internalized prohibitions. (Kipling's anxiety about censorship—and self-censorship—was not unfounded, because even English writers in British India could be indicted for sedition, and his book *A Fleet in Being* was censored in 1898 for allegedly betraying naval secrets.)[57] For Forster, obliged to maintain silence about homosexuality in print and subject to surveillance by British censors in India, the (unspeakable) truth *is* the proscribed sexual and racialized body itself, the premise or condition for language. For Rushdie, truth is a fraught intellectual and political problem: as he openly indicts the falsehoods of official histories and the propaganda of corrupt governments, how can he claim to tell the truth himself, given his insistence that the truth of history or fiction is necessarily partial, relative, and constructed?

Contemporary efforts to address literary truth are affected by two kinds of histories. One is the tradition (starting with Plato's famous denunciation of poetry as a lie) that regards the truth of imaginative literature as literal correspondence to an external reality.[58] Defenders of poetry since Sir Philip Sidney have long claimed instead a greater *imaginative* truth for poetry.[59] Tzvetan Todorov has argued that fiction cannot lie, because it *presents* itself as fiction; a text can lie only if it claims veracity.[60] The problem with such defenses is that the referentiality of literature cannot be relinquished altogether. At some level, after all, the furor over *The Satanic Verses* was occasioned by the correct recognition that the novel challenges cultural dogma by offering alternative versions about how religious pieties are constructed, a truth that is deeply threatening to those invested in those pieties. (In other words, even the imaginative truths of the novel were referential and hit home.) Postcolonial critics frequently evaluate a fictive text's degree of verisimilitude—how a novelist or filmmaker discloses hidden truths about a society or political force, or represents a historical event—for the stakes of representation are high when audiences are unfamiliar with the cultural or political situations a text delineates or when the peoples it describes have suffered histories of asymmetric power and misrepresentation.[61] Thus, for postcolonial criticism in particular, it becomes crucial to retain some version of truth as correspondence that is not crude. Poetry has relevance or truth value for us because, as Graham Dunstan Martin argues, it has "some degree of correspondence to external reality. . . . Fictional referents do indeed refer, though indirectly, . . . [This] allows a writer the freedom to recreate the infinite detail of experience, and hence to refer to the real world more fully (and paradoxically) more directly than any work of fact or reportage can."[62]

More recently, trends in post-structuralism and postmodernism have discredited discussions of truth; with their emphasis on the constructed nature of truth, these theories seem to undermine the possibility of truth altogether. Following upon Nietzsche's assertion that truth is a matter of linguistic and cultural convenience ("a mobile army of metaphors . . . : truths are illusions about which one has forgotten that this is what they are") and Foucault's insight that truth claims depend on the power networks within which they are formulated, some scholars have concluded that truth cannot be regarded as a legitimate basis for literary or cultural interpretation, which is just a matter of language games, dependent on the consensus of interpretive communities.[63] Michael Riffaterre argues that narrative truth is solely a matter of the *appearance* of verisimilitude in accordance with given textual conventions.[64] Thus, in Riffaterre's view, "readers need not be familiar with the reality that the text is about in order to believe it true. The only reference against which they need to test the narrative's truth is language" (8). But by this token, orientalist or racist representations may appear true to some readers because they fit with those readers' ideological beliefs or language. In postcolonial fiction, film, or drama, the question of truth carries extremely high stakes, for contesting the misrepresentations of dominant imperial and neoimperial discourses as well as nationalist propaganda and histories.

It is worth here recalling the philosophical distinction between ontology and epistemology, between the existence of reality beyond language and the problems of knowing it. Even post-structuralist thinkers do not doubt the existence of reality—only of our truth-claims to know it, given the limitations of language and cognition. We can make distinctions between degrees of truth without giving up a belief in its existence. That does not resolve the problems of truth (because then we need to determine better or worse degrees of truth, by what ideological standards, what intellectual frameworks, and so forth), but it does mean that we need not give up on truth altogether. In an interview, while insisting on the need to understand how power relations in a society constitute its conditions of truth making, Foucault also demands a (limited) agency on the part of intellectuals. They must, he argues, strive to uncover the ways that truth is constructed in particular regimes and to change the "political, economic, institutional regime of the production of truth" itself, even when they are situated within those regimes ("Truth and Power", 133): "There is a battle 'for truth,' or at least 'around truth'—it being understood once again that by truth I do not mean 'the ensemble of truths which are to be discovered and accepted,' but rather 'the ensemble of rules according to which the true and the false are separated and specific effects of power attached to the true,' . . . a battle about the status of truth and the economic and political role it plays" (132).

Introduction

Thus, it is imperative for Foucault to uncover the truth of the *making* of truths, to believe that there is something to be unearthed and exposed—namely, the conditions that produce truth within a society.[65] Similarly, as Christopher Norris argues, the work of a post-structuralist such as Derrida, despite his unconventional approach, is guided by a principled belief that critical and philosophical inquiry seeks to find some truth about a text and the problems it poses.[66]

In this book, I use the term *truth* not in any singular abstract or absolute sense, least of all as "Truth," but as a deeply problematic though necessary concept for political writing, whose meanings vary with different contexts and writers. In my discussion of each writer, I approach the issue of truth in accordance with the particular concerns and assumptions each brings to it. I do emphasize, however, the critical need to maintain both a sense of the referentiality of colonial and postcolonial imaginative literature *and* an understanding of the constructed and contingent nature of truth-claims, while retaining a sense of the degrees of difference. Indeed, as we will see, Rushdie's understanding of these considerations is what makes his struggles with truth-telling more fraught than those of either Kipling or Forster.

The Body and Language

> The body furnishes the building blocks of symbolization, and eventually of language itself, which then takes us away from the body, but always in a tension that reminds us that mind and language need to recover the body, as an otherness that is somehow primary to their very definition.
>
> —Peter Brooks, *Body Work*[67]

If literary criticism has lately been wary of taking on "truth," it has been only too eager to embrace "the body": the body as subject and object, as experienced and observed; the body as racialized and gendered construct; the body as socially symbolic and literal thing; the body written upon or itself signifying, as silent and unreadable or as speaking its own language(s); the body as a whole or in parts; the body as surface and depth, exterior and interior. Perhaps this is because, as Elaine Scarry writes, "The turn to history and the body—the attempt to restore the material world to literature—has been in part inspired by a . . . collective regret at the very weightlessness, the inconsequentiality of conversation about literature."[68] Or, as William Jewett notes, "the eighteenth-century fear that we are (only) our bodies has been replaced with the postmodern fear that we are (only) our words."[69] Thus, criticism shares in a broader cultural desire to retrieve a concreteness or materiality that has been repressed in rationalist, post-Cartesian discourses. Several disciplines have sought to refocus attention on the human body as a key site for understanding human ways of constructing identity and social relations, as well as the politics of subjection and subjectivity.

But this fascination with the body has also produced debates on how the body is to be understood, on the degree to which we presume it to be a physical given or a social construction, since even our "experience" of it is mediated by learned ways of understanding our bodies and selves. Indebted to thinkers such as Mikhail Bakhtin and Michel Foucault, cultural historians and critics have begun to rethink the body as itself having a history and politics. Judith Butler argues that Foucault assumed a body prior to "cultural inscription"; instead, she argues for the body as entirely socially constructed.[70] Phenomenologists such as Maurice Merleau Ponty reject the Cartesian mind-body split and recast the body as the basis for experience, perception, and even thought, not secondary to but inseparable from the mind. Cognitive scientists, linguists, and philosophers have begun to investigate precisely how the mind is embodied or indeed part of the body, as manifested in our cognitive and linguistic schema.[71]

In this study, I do not assume that the body is either a natural given or only a social construct, nor do I advance a theory of the body per se. As Peter Brooks suggests, we need to grant a "broad semantic range for [the term] 'body'—biological entity, psycho-sexual construction, cultural product—since . . . it is all of these, often at once, to writers and readers."[72] I examine how different colonial and postcolonial writers draw upon and recast the human body in necessarily *different* ways to address their concerns about the political exigencies surrounding his writing. A central question for me is how we may understand the body in relation to language, since I am primarily concerned here with how and why these writers require the human body to represent or serve as a basis for their writing.

For Elaine Scarry, the body is a prelingual entity. In her account of torture, Scarry argues that the intensity of bodily sensation destroys language, returning us to prelingual sounds and to the unmaking of the world.[73] This assumption of bodily experience as prior to the onset of language is also central to Lacan's account of infant development, though Lacan assumes a hierarchy in which language replaces and displaces infantile experiences of the body. Peter Brooks acknowledges the primacy of bodily experience but argues for a dialectic between language and body. On the one hand, as the epigraph above suggests, language is precisely "other" to the body: one is a signifying, symbolic system, whereas the other is pre- or extralingual, the site of primal sensations that can only belatedly be translated into language. Our bodies are always felt, present to us, whereas language can only name that which is absent or removed from it. On the other hand, as psychoanalysis compellingly suggests, the body is what enables language to come into being and indeed is "the source of human symbolism"—for it is literally through the body that we produce a voice or writing, and the acquisition of language arises from infantile bodily sensation and (arguably) the understanding of sexual difference (Brooks, *Body Work*, xii). But Brooks contends that once language becomes a system that removes us from the body, it also needs to return to the body, as its own source and other, as a site of meaning or truth. Hence his chiasmic formulation that "the semioticization of the body is accompanied by the somatization of story": language becomes bodily as it tries to make the body signify and gather meaning (38). This may explain why writers as different as the ones in this study return to the body: from the fear that their language is too removed from reality; from the desire to borrow some degree of materiality for language; and from the urge to make their language renew contact with its source and ultimately its truth. However, whereas Brooks and others focus on the sexualized body or on the body as subject and object of erotic desire, I include in the realm of the bodily not only its sexual or erotic dimensions but also, more centrally, the processes of everyday experience and life functions such as eating, breathing, excreting, smelling, birthing, breast-feeding, suffering, and dying. In so doing, I identify three aspects of the body that are crucial to all three writers when they address literary agency: the body as a site upon which power converges, as well as a site of resistance to power; the body as the site of relations to others and to the world; and the body as a site of truth.

That the body is the site of both power and resistance is fairly obvious, for it is subjected to suffering, torture, imprisonment, punishment, and regulation, and through it we fight, evade, or assert resistance. What is less obvious is how subtly everyday forms of power operate upon us as and through our bodies. In a telling example from Rushdie's *Shame*, the illegitimate antihero Omar Khayyam learns that his three mothers refused to submit to certain Islamic rituals when he was born: they did not allow anyone to "whisper the name of God into [his] ear," have his head shaved, or "permit the foreskin to be removed" (15). All three are seemingly innocuous cultural rituals for newborns, but they are also bodily ways of marking individuals from the moment of birth and inscribing upon them a specific identity that carries the weight of (and inculcation into) a patriarchal religious order. For a child to become a proper Muslim, first, a powerful priestly male voice must literally enter the ears of a newborn as the first thing it hears in life, announcing the first tenet of Islamic faith (telling it to believe that God is great and Muhammad is his prophet); second, its hair must be removed because it is impure, given that it has been in contact with female (maternal) uterine matter; and third, male children must be circumcised, their bodies thereby marked as "pure" or clean. It is therefore upon the body that social power is enacted; but through the body it is also resisted, for the three "mothers," in their effort to build a matriarchal rebellion against the patriarchal system that has oppressed them, use their son's body to mark his (and their) difference.

Moreover, even though we tend to think of the body as defining the contours of selfhood, the limit point of responsibility and individual freedom, it is a site of both selfhood and relations to others and the world. The body is coextensive with the world; it exists and is defined in relation to specific environmental and physical conditions, and it comes into being and experiences itself in relation to others—through affects of love, desire, hostility, and so forth. Like Bakhtin, Francis Barker describes the modern body as a "related and relational" phenomenon: "[T]*he body . . . is not a hypostatized object, still less a simple biological mechanism of given desires and needs acted on externally by controls and enticements, but a relation in a system of liaisons which are material, discursive, psychic, sexual, but without stop or center. It would be better to speak of a certain 'bodiliness' than of 'the body.' . . . The site of an operation of power, of an exercise of meaning*" (italics in original).[74] Omar Khayyam's body is not "his" from birth: it is generated by not one but *three* mothers who control and mark it with their agenda; it is the site of his complex relations to them as well as to a broader cultural and social world that shapes him; it experiences itself in relation to others and the world. And finally, perhaps because the body seems so materially present, so undeniably a thing-in-itself, beyond the vagaries of language, the body is also taken to be the site or emblem of truth and reality: the touch of the caves in A *Passage to India*—a bodily emanation of suppressed forces—induces a revelation or realization of truth; in *Midnight's Children*, the touch of Amina Sinai's pregnant belly produces a magically "true" prophecy of the nation.

☐

This book consists of six chapters, two on each writer. Chapter 1 examines Kipling's Indian short stories (primarily 1886–1902) to trace how Kipling constructs a telling colonial imaginary in which he casts his own writing as a hybrid, interracial bodily product. Like the "Anglo-Indian" children in his stories (British but breast-fed by Indian women), these bicultural and bilingual products, he suggests, are capable of both perpetuating and subverting imperial power, for which they can be censored or killed. Historicizing Kipling's concerns in the context of censorship in British India, I argue that the obsessive recurrence of child-death and censorship in his stories bespeaks an anxiety about literary agency that becomes a form of muted and oblique, though not always consistent, imperial critique. Yet Kipling suggests that as a bodily living thing, his writing can survive by telling colonial truths under cover of lies. Chapter 2 reads Kipling's most important novel, *Kim* (1901), as a cautionary double narrative that tells two parallel stories at once: a tale about Kipling's text and a tale of the adolescent body of Kim, the interracial product of empire conscripted into imperial service. The novel begins with the child Kim in the same position as the text in relation to empire—with linguistic powers that can be both useful to and subversive of the Great Game. By the end, Kim is damaged, no longer autonomous, overwritten by imperial codes of signification. In charting this process, I argue, the novel separates itself, both articulating its anxiety about agency as a child of empire, and exposing that process of destruction. For Kipling, the body of the Anglo-Indian child—multiparented, imagined as at once preternaturally powerful and vulnerable—centers his anxiety about the predicament of his own fiction.

Chapter 3 examines Forster's fourteen-year hiatus in his novel-publishing career (1910–24, framed by his two trips to India) to argue that this crisis of writing was produced by a conjoint anxiety about the political efficacy of language and the desire to incorporate the body in that language. From his first short story, "The Story of a Panic," in which English bourgeois complacency is violently disrupted by the emergence of the god Pan who brings truth, to A *Passage to India*, Forster uses coded language as an agent of political intervention. To be effective, language for Forster must speak that proscribed body, make it materialize (in ways that may be covert), with the hope of changing language and of promoting social transformation. In this chapter I analyze his letters, Indian travel writings, and *Maurice* to trace a new mode of speaking the body that he developed together with an anti-imperialist politics in the course of his travels and writings from India. I show how Forster's understanding of interracial and (homo)sexual desire changed crucially over this period, so that although his Indian writings enabled *Maurice*, the change also led to a split in his unpublished and published work: in one, he allowed himself to explore this uncomfortable dynamic; in the other, he maintained silence. Chapter 4 then reads A *Passage to India*, his last and most renowned novel, as shaped and underwritten by the issues that produced his crisis. Unlike post-structuralist readings that cast its concern with language as a measure of the failure of language in general, or postcolonial readings that emphasize politics and history but ignore that concern, my reading argues that language is a central subject of the novel and is inextricable from its anti-colonial and sexual politics. Grounded upon Forster's belated understanding of interracial and sexual relations, the novel critiques colonial (specifically, Anglo-Indian) language and epistemology and incorporates the outlawed body and homoerotic desire into his language to suggest the resistant power of that conjoint racial and sexual force. I then show how that silenced but resistant body is mapped onto the Indian landscape—in particular, the Marabar Caves.

Chapter 5 examines Rushdie's recurrent concern with bodies, body parts, and bodily effluvia to suggest that through it he constructs a new idiom to render the agency of his postcolonial narrative, both to recast colonial legacies and to reimagine a postcolonial community or nation. It concentrates on his two foundational novels of nationhood, *Midnight's Children* and *Shame*, showing how Rushdie emphasizes the materiality and constitutive power of his language through three specific modes. Drawing upon the anthropologist Mary Douglas's argument that social hierarchies are built on the perception of bodily effluvia as "dirt" or "matter out of place," it argues that Rushdie's excremental language serves to disorder those boundaries as a form of political intervention within the social body politic. It concludes with a reading of the pivotal but neglected episode of the Sundarbans as Rushdie's rewriting of the repressed trauma of the 1971 genocide committed by the Pakistan army in Bengal, enabled through the three modes of bodiliness identified in this chapter.

Having established how Rushdie presents the bodiliness of his language to contend that his writing can act and have material effects, I then examine, in chapter 6, Rushdie's efforts at truth-telling (about the past) and truth making (of a viable postcolonial future) as ways of creating reality in and through his narratives. This chapter focuses on two (related) issues—truth-telling and dreams. First is a consideration of how Rushdie indicts national myth making as a form of bodily violence, as a "rite of blood," while insisting on both the partiality and the contingency of his more salutary truth-telling, as well as on the falsity of such nationalist histories. I read Rushdie's dreams as a mode of truth-telling, as another register of the bodily, to argue that Rushdie constructs dream-endings in all his major novels as a form of resistance to closure, not to heighten the end, as narrative theory predicts, but rather to defer the end and open up possibilities that often defy logic, thereby creating terms to make such postcolonial futures materially possible. It seems even more important for Rushdie as a postcolonial writer to build a language that can approximate the sheer fleshiness, materiality, relationality, and vulnerability of the human body. Only through such a language can he fulfil the ardent hope that underpins his seminal work: to make words *matter*, in every sense; to enable them to have powerful material, political, and social effects; to "leak" into nations and communities and hence transform organically how they imagine themselves as well as others.

CHAPTER ONE

Children of an Other Language
Kipling's Stories as Interracial Progeny

AT THE PEAK of his popularity in 1892, in a short reminiscence entitled "My First Book," Kipling describes his first publication as his firstborn child: "But I loved it best when it was a little brown baby with a pink string round its stomach; a child's child, ignorant that it was afflicted with all the most modern ailments; and before people had learned, beyond doubt, how its author lay awake of nights in India, plotting and scheming to write something that should 'take' with the English public."[1] The figure, "a little brown baby with a pink string round its stomach," re-renders Kipling's earlier literal description of the printed shape of this first book as a "brown paper bundle secured with red tape," which was "privately distributed by "reply-postcard" in India before it was published by an English publisher (176). However, this bodily image of a "brown baby" with a "pink" baby's umbilical cord suggests an interracial, hybrid production. If Kipling presents himself as one (white) parent, then who could the other unnamed parent be? India? Many critics have noted that Kipling's Anglo-Indian stories rarely allow the survival either of literal interracial marriages and liaisons or of their offspring in a world that he insisted had no place for them.[2] Yet it seems that for Kipling's colonial psyche, the progeny of a figurative or linguistic interracial liaison, a textual product *imagined* in physiological, otherwise forbidden terms, could be allowed to survive —even treasured with nostalgic affection—whereas a biological one could not.

Conflating sexual and textual (re)production in describing his book as his baby, Kipling replays a conventional metaliterary trope[3] but adds some striking features: interracial imagery; a suggestion of multiple parenthood; and a rhetoric of "affliction" or bodily injury. Kipling's child/book seems to have a second parent in India, the engendering space where his writing originates and finds its language and material. But his English and Anglo-Indian audiences seem to serve as additional co-parents, in accordance with whose demands his writing is shaped and reshaped, and these co-parents are imagined as agents of both production and destruction. This interracial offspring of letters is thus a multiply produced progeny of empire, conceived between Kipling (himself such a product), India, and England. Moreover, this "baby" seems capable in itself of engendering imperial ideas and perpetuating power—for, as Kipling also tells us, he "posted [it] up and down the Empire from Aden to Singapore, and from Quetta to Colombo," as if to disseminate it over an imperial terrain. If this book of poems is a "child's child," then Kipling represents himself as a precocious child-parent, abnormally, prematurely generative in the latitudes of colonial India.[4]

Kipling scholars are familiar with his reliance on the somewhat delusive rhetoric of family to describe imperial relations in British India—as if relations between colonizers and colonized could thus be euphemized. Zohreh Sullivan, for instance, suggests that the metaphor of "the impossibly extended family" of empire in India served to blur difference even as it articulated Kipling's need for the family he had lost at age six.[5] What has rarely been noted, however, is the extension of this rhetoric to include his own writing. The imperial family is not simply a site of love in which politics and power struggles are absent: rather, as Kipling seems to insist, this family both engenders and destroys, at once empowering and endangering both the writer and his writing, just as the writer and his work can in turn both subvert and perpetuate empire. To render the conditions of textual production and agency, therefore, this rhetoric of family supplies a language of bodily generation and destruction.

In "My First Book," Kipling's rhetoric suggests that this triangularly conceived "child's child" is also subject to destruction—possibly by its own "parents." It is "afflicted with . . . modern ailments" (177), damagingly restricted, tied down by string that "cut the pages and tore the covers" (176). Like his earlier poems, described in an idiom of brutality and mutilation (they were "burned apiece," "born to be sacrificed," and the "survivors . . . two thirds cut down" [174]), this "child's child" seems threatened by analogous destruction, if not extinction. Censorship, figured as death and affliction, may perhaps be one of the "modern ailments" that assail Kipling's children.

This passage from "My First Book" can be seen as paradigmatic of some of Kipling's concerns about his Anglo-Indian authorship, fiction, and verse.[6] Kipling's Indian stories, like this self-reflexive piece of writing about writing, are often *about* his Indian stories (his children), rendered as hybrid interracial linguistic productions; his obsessive returns to child-authors, children, and the deaths of children *in* his stories reveal many colonial anxieties *about* his stories, about their ambiguous status as stories of empire. These stories covertly suggest their potential power to subvert as well as uphold imperial myth making, as well as their susceptibility to censorship and the (self-)destructive powers of empire. Through this covert metafictiveness, the guise of child-family relations, Kipling articulates his concerns about literary agency in the context of imperial relations. Postcolonial scholarship has attended to the ideological implications of Kipling's child-figures (such as Kim and Mowgli), whose magical innocence and unquestioned superiority become ideological tools for reasserting colonial hegemony.[7] However, it has not examined how Kipling's Indian writings reveal a compulsive fascination for childhood and children's bodies as a way of evoking the relations between his writing and the British empire.

Whereas early twentieth-century scholars such as Edmund Wilson debated Kipling's politics or philosophy of art, subsequent scholars began to read his work as illustrative of the ideologies and discourses of empire.[8] George Orwell nominated Kipling as a "good bad poet" memorable for his rhythms and declared that, despite his imperialism, he was not a "fascist," because he had a sense of "responsibility."[9] Benita Parry's influential reading of Kipling's imperialism denounces the myopia of critics such as Alan Sandison, who attempted to save Kipling from his own politics.[10] From the 1990s on, postcolonial scholars such as Sara Suleri and Zohreh Sullivan have led the way in attending to the ambivalence of Kipling's colonial discourse, heavily embedded in a matrix of contradictory power relations and revealingly self-divided in both promulgating and questioning imperial and racial ideologies.¹¹ Enriched by these recent approaches, I read Kipling's Indian fictions as narratives of colonial anxiety and, moreover, examine how his work self-consciously explores its *own* complicated position of complicity and resistance, its own uncertainties, dangers, and subversiveness, by troping itself as both an enabled and an endangered child of empire. Heavily preoccupied with literary agency, Kipling is keenly aware of the degree to which as a colonial writer his work can serve to buttress or subvert imperial myths, for which it can be drastically censored.¹² I begin with some stories that exemplify the links Kipling made between linguistic production and Indian or Anglo-Indian children, focusing primarily on stories from Kipling's first collection, *Plain Tales from the Hills*, originally published between 1886 and 1888.¹³

The Milk of Human Language

In Kipling's experience, his family (parents, children, and *ayahs* [Indian nursemaids]) was the origin of linguistic and textual production. His autobiography, *Something of Myself*, begins with an account of his bilingualism, as if he had been created—indeed, parented—by two competing languages: "We were sent into the dining-room, . . . with the caution 'Speak English now to Papa and Mamma.' So one spoke 'English,' haltingly translated out of the vernacular idiom that one thought and dreamed in" (4). Having acquired language and consciousness via servants' Hindi songs and stories (his primary language) and his parents' English (the secondary one), Kipling frequently represents his sense of self as hybrid, fed by two linguistic and cultural sources.¹⁴ After his traumatic departure for England at age six and his return to India at seventeen, Kipling entered into an intense period of writing as a journalist, poet, and colonial storyteller that led to his early fame. This writing was fostered and coauthored within the tight intimacies of his nuclear family circle, with his parents often reading, approving, suggesting rhymes, or cutting his drafts. Thus, in both childhood and after his return, for Kipling India became a space associated with magically generative powers of linguistic fertility.

Perhaps for these reasons, Kipling presents Anglo-Indian children in his fiction as both products and producers of a special language. As if uniquely gifted with many forms of linguistic power, they have a creativity and magical inventiveness, as well as a polyglot fluency and ability to translate and mediate. They also have unique experiences that provide rare material for storytelling. In *Kim*, this fantasized linguistic prowess is reflected in the stories told by Kim's schoolmates, as the elite Anglo-Indian "native-born": "Their parents could well have educated them in England, but they loved the school that had served their own youth, and generation followed sallow-hued generation at St. Xavier's. . . . The mere story of their adventures, which to them were no adventures, on their road to and from school would have crisped a Western boy's hair. . . . And every tale was told in the even passionless voice of the native-born, mixed with quaint reflections, borrowed unconsciously from native foster-mothers, and turns of speech that showed they had been that instant translated from the vernacular. Kim watched, listened, and approved" (*Kim*, 172). Like the borrowed land that bore them, this language "borrowed . . . from native foster-mothers" is the source of their "quaint," "mixed" speech and hybrid powers: it has endowed these "sallow-hued" children with the unique gifts of a new language and new stories to tell. Kim, the quintessential product of Anglo-India (born Irish but raised by various Indian foster-parents), is distinguished from the beginning of the novel by his powers of language—able to curse better than any native in his own tongue, Kim can translate effortlessly and fabricate marvelous lies. This linguistic power becomes a measure as well as an instrument of his political and racial dominance. For this hybridity, a strange combination of his biological and foster parentage, is what enables his superiority both to new English arrivals in India and to Indians.

Similarly, in "Wee Willie Winkie," the six-year-old son of a colonel of a border regiment is able, through his command of their language (learned from a servant), to intimidate the dreaded Afghans who are about to kidnap him.[15] When a young Englishwoman foolishly crosses into Afghan territory, beyond the bounds of the British Empire, Wee Willie Winkie valiantly follows her and confronts the enemy in her defense: "People who spoke that tongue could not be the Bad Men. They were only natives after all. Then rose from the rock Wee Willie Winkie, child of the Dominant Race, aged six and three-quarters and said briefly and emphatically, 'Jao' [Go]! The men laughed, and laughter from natives was the one thing Wee Willie Winkie could not tolerate" (850). His knowledge of Indian languages, his childish innocence, and his ingrained habits of command together release Willie from fear. Recognizing by their speech that they are "natives" and therefore a part of his extended "family," he is able to intimidate them with the threat of British retribution and hold them off until help arrives. The narrator comments, "Speech in any vernacular— and Wee Willie Winkie had a colloquial acquaintance with three—was easy to the boy who could not yet manage his 'r's' and the 'th's' aright" (850). While demoting knowledge of Indian languages to a level less than that of English, Kipling suggests that this knowledge is crucial to a child of empire, for little Willie is able to do what neither the tongue-tied English girl nor his father's regiment can—extricate them all from a volatile situation without bloodshed on either side.

In a number of stories, Kipling suggests that this kind of cultural hybridity, this special status of the Anglo-Indian child, fed on a native wet nurse's milk or an ayah's nursery stories and love, is acquired via breast-feeding—as if language, stories, and cultural affinity were maternal fluids imbibed like milk. Such children become in this rendering not only producers of stories but also *products* of language—a language that is imagined as a bodily fluid. Thus, Kipling renders the phenomenon of linguistic engendering as a specific bodily relation—not as genetic or biological mothering but as what we may call "milk-mothering"— as if acquiring language from a native foster-mother were equivalent to acquiring her bodily substance and were as crucial to the construction of identity and ability. In this contradictorily essentialist logic, Kipling seems to assume that although the Indian women's language (and cultural knowledge) is somehow essential to her body, it can be passed on to, or physically acquired by, the Anglo-Indian children who imbibe it through (or as) her milk. This rhetoric reveals, on Kipling's part, not necessarily consistent or coherent assumptions that are nonetheless key to his imagining of his own hybrid authorship.

The much admired figure of Strickland, for instance, the Richard Burton–like Anglo-Indian who appears recurrently in Kipling's stories, is an early prototype of Kim.[16] Capable of infinite cultural cross-dressing and fluent in many native languages, he acquires otherwise inaccessible knowledge that is very useful for a police superintendent in British India. Reappearing in *Kim*, Strickland, as a "dark, sallowish, . . . faultlessly uniformed . . . Englishman," reveals that he and his ilk have been "suckled" by Indian women, in contrast to those "suckled by white women and learning (the Indian) tongue from books" (*Kim*, 123–24).

Language learned from the Indian breast seems to be the reason for their superior command of both idiom and environment. This inference is explicitly extended by the old lady of Kulu (in Kipling's colonial rationalization) to their superior ability to rule: "These be the sort to oversee justice. They know the land and the customs of the land" (124).

In "The Son of His Father," written decades after Kipling had left India (1923), Strickland's native subordinates say admiringly of his only son, Adam, suckled (like his father) by an Indian foster-mother, "Those who drink of our blood become of our blood, and I have seen, in these thirty years, that the sons of Sahibs once being born here, return when they are men."[17] Adam, named for "the first man," is indeed a first man, a paradigm for a new breed, a white child suckled by Indian women (like Mowgli suckled by wolves in *The Jungle Book*), who therefore has a greater capacity or "double wisdom" for ruling there (219). Strickland, scornful of a newly arrived "English boy," agrees: "I wish that government would keep our service for country-born men. Those first five or six years in India give a man a pull that lasts him all his life" (239). Strickland's infant son is rendered as having precocious linguistic and sagacious powers, as Adam retells native stories and legends (acquired from all his native friends and servants) to his bemused English parents. As the product and producer of a new or other language, he is described with a focus on his mouth, the site of this fluid intake and output: "He looked old as all time in his grave childhood, sitting cross-legged, . . . his forefinger wagging up and down, native fashion, and the wisdom of serpents on his unconscious lips" (232). Such a child of Anglo-India is presented as an inscrutable little Buddha, at once ageless and precocious, with a "serpentine" or dangerous knowledge of colonial India.[18]

Yet another story, "The Conversion of Aurelian McGoggin," provides a similar image of infant lips and of speech as mother's milk. McGoggin, an English adolescent recently arrived in India, is suddenly afflicted by aphasia, the abrupt termination of his linguistic powers, as if some unknown force of censorship has descended upon him. It seems to be a punishment from nowhere, a retribution for "playing bricks with words" (*Plain Tales*, 82): "Something had wiped his lips of speech, as a mother wipes the milky lips of her child, and he was afraid—horribly afraid" (85). In a curious inversion, as if speech was a result of inflow rather than outflow, this "something," this ominous maternal force of Anglo-India, seems to suckle McGoggin and feed him on language. But then, in a gesture both tender and terrifying, this mysterious force withdraws that language without warning or explanation, chastising this child for transgressing limits that remain unspecified.

While McGoggin remains permanently "cowed," possibly because he was not born or raised in India, Kipling's "native-born" Anglo-Indian infants seem to be succored by this alien milk. Kipling's 1894 poem "The Native-Born" invokes this peculiar hybridity, a product of Indian foster-mothering of Anglo-Indian children. The poem is addressed as a toast to Indian mothers, or to India as a mothering space, from whom this colonizing subject acquires a primary sense of being and language:

> To our dear dark foster-mothers,
>   To the heathen song they sung—
> To the heathen speech we babbled
>   Ere we came to the white man's tongue[.]

Again and again, Kipling's language daringly approximates his physical association with another color and race ("our dear dark foster mothers") and then retreats by turning that into a linguistic inheritance. Kipling understood what Frantz Fanon would later enunciate, that "to speak a language is to take on a world, a culture."[19] But for Kipling this translates into a new rationalization of entitlement based on a double inheritance: "Our fathers held by purchase, / But we by the right of birth." As if this "right of birth" also bestowed a cultural heritage and power, Kipling repeatedly suggests that English children born on Indian land and nurtured by Indian breasts have thereby acquired a new "other" language and thus greater abilities and rights of colonial rule than Englishmen whose domination by conquest is merely (and euphemistically) a "purchase."[20]

Such a familial inheritance was, of course, not free of contestation, as Kipling seems aware. In a nineteenth-century Anglo-Indian colonial household such as the Kiplings', primary mothering was often provided by a native wet nurse, or an *ayah*, a racially other foster-mother whose own baby may have died for want of the milk that the white baby would be supplied.[21] Kipling's metaphoric deployment of this exploitative cultural practice to imagine a white child's acquisition of Indian language as such a milk is also associated with guilt, violence, and death. Often, the gifts of this primary "other" language are linked for Kipling with theft, with a sense of being parasitically acquired at the cost of human sacrifice. The power of the hybrid child of language, is also predicated on familial violence.

Thus, Kipling constructs an elaborate imaginary in his stories whereby Anglo-Indian children are empowered by a language that is a bodily fluid, imbibed like milk or blood from an Indian body, and that structures his understanding of his own stories—his writing, his "child's child," which is imagined as such an infant produced between multiple cultural parents. In this imaginary, Kipling's stories are his children, but they are also children of language: indeed, they are *like* the children in his stories who are produced by language and simultaneously *are* the products of such children, exemplified by Kipling himself. In some sense, these Anglo-Indian children too are produced *by* that language, and then create their own hybrid mixture, an "other" language, just as Kipling produces a multivoiced language in his stories, full of words and idioms derived from Indian languages and carrying multiple meanings. But his is a double language also because it carries double meanings, reflective of a double allegiance, or hybridity.

Homi Bhabha's influential account has read the hybridity of colonial discourse as not univocal but double-voiced, an ambivalent internalization of challenges to colonial authority, a voicing of the unease and disunity of the colonizing subject: "Hybridity is a problematic of colonial representation and individuation that reverses the effects of the colonialist disavowal, so that other 'denied' knowledges enter upon the dominant discourse and estrange the basis of its authority."[22] However, as Robert Young notes, "in the nineteenth century [hybridity] was used to refer to a physiological phenomenon; in the twentieth it has been reactivated to describe a cultural one."[23] Young locates the origins of hybridity in quite literal biological terms such as fears of miscegenation, and he cautions against contemporary celebrations of cultural hybridity that rely on metaphoric models that may still carry implicit assumptions of heterosexuality and racialism (25). While my reading of Kipling is grounded in Bhabha's formulation of colonial discourse as multivoiced and ambivalent, Young's reminder of the racial and biological beginnings of hybridity are useful for understanding Kipling's specific imagining of hybridity and his contorted reappropriation of it to describe his linguistic production. Kipling makes a double move via an elision: first, to produce a model of hybridity as interracial reproduction, he elides the sexual production of progeny and instead uses the bodily relation of breast-feeding as a safer model for racial intimacy and familial connection; second, he turns this biological phenomenon into a cultural model for bilingualism and hybridity. Thus, he uses an unusual physiological model of interracial parenting as a figure for the linguistic and cultural parenting of Anglo-Indian children. Although he cannot imagine a (re)productive model of interracial sexuality or allow Eurasian children in his stories to live, retreating from the horror of miscegenation, he seems to need some concept of interracial physicality to imagine another kind of bodily interracial relationship for Anglo-Indian children that he sees as enabling and empowering: foster-mothering. So Anglo-Indian children can be imagined as physically mothered, breast-fed via their intake of milk, language, and cultural sensibility, by Indian women.[24] Kipling thus uses the permissible physical relation between white child and brown breast to figure such a child's acquisition of language as a physical liquid. But then, in a third move, he uses that cultural phenomenon as a figure for textual production—for the interracial hybridity of his linguistic "children," his stories, represented as fluid co-productions of a nurturing feminized Indian body.

While Kipling explicitly represents his stories or his books as his children, the children in his Indian stories can also be read as metafictive figures for his stories, that is, his stories of children are also stories about his stories. These children are not simply products of Anglo-India but are themselves associated with language and linguistic powers—as with his stories, their double-voiced hybridity, Kipling suggests, is a source of both their strength and their weakness. Many of his stories of children can be read as such metafiction, stories that self-consciously explore how Kipling's hybrid writing can be both powerful and susceptible to destruction, both an autonomous agent and subject to imperial repercussions.

Reading Kipling's Hybrid Children as Metafictive

One of the more memorable stories in *Plain Tales*, "Tods' Amendment," opens with the following scenario. Like most of Kipling's other Anglo-Indian children, combining an intrepid mischievousness with a habit of indulgence from all, Tods breaks up a "supreme legislative council" of colonial government to help him recapture his pet goat: "[A]fter an interval was seen the shocking spectacle of a legal member and lieutenant governor helping, under the direct patronage of a commander-in-chief and viceroy, one small and very dirty boy in a sailor's suit and a tangle of brown hair, to coerce a lively and rebellious kid" (144). In this comically subversive opening, Tods's ability to interrupt the "administration of Empire" and redirect its attention to his agenda (chasing after an escaped "rebellious kid") is symptomatic. He has intimate access both to the makers of imperial policy and to native languages and natives who trust him with their political views, an access that depends on his command of two languages. As a child of Anglo-India, fed on a foster-nurse's milk, he seems to have internalized in some deeply bodily way the knowledge of both groups, so that his understanding of each culture is superior to that of anyone belonging to only one. From the colonial familial household to the supposed family of empire, Tods mediates as a "buffer" not only between "the servants and his Mamma's wrath" but also between the British government and the Indian natives it rules. The story turns on how Tods's child knowledge of the native farmers' discontent with a proposed land bill (learned from his servants and bazaar talk), delivered in baby language to a group of attentive government officials at his father's dinner table, effects a crucial amendment in the making of a colonial law—and averts native resistance to colonial policy.

Playing in their midst as they discuss the problems of the bill, Tods interrupts and makes himself the privileged center of attention for these high-ranking colonial officials:

> Tods tucked his feet under his red flannel dressing-gown and said: "I must *fink*."
> The legal member waited patiently. Then Tods, with infinite compassion:
> "You don't speak my talk, do you, Councillor Sahib?"
> "No, I am sorry to say I do not," said the legal member.
> "Very well," said Tods, "I must *fink* in English."
> He spent a minute putting his ideas in order, and began very slowly, translating in his mind from the vernacular to English, as many Anglo-Indian children do. (147)

The passage functions as a scene of instruction, literally "out of the mouth of a babe," as the Anglo-Indian government and policy makers are educated on the needs, desires, and logics of the Indian people they rule, translated by this "other" child. Indeed, Kipling suggests, in India some hierarchies can easily be reversed: such children can be teachers, or guides, as Kim leads the lama and, indeed, as the young Kipling instructed his English readers.

Tods is thus rendered superior both to British adult officials (who in this fantasy of childhood power learn from him and make the crucial "amendment" that they name after him) and to the educated "hybrid, University trained" native, neither of whom can understand the "real native" (149). Again, this is because "of course he spoke Urdu" *and* "the *chotee bolee* of the women" (Kipling's literal translation of the English idiomatic phrase *small talk*—there is no such expression in Urdu), was "precocious for his age," and by mixing with natives had learned some "bitter truths of life" (145). As Tods's "amendment" to the proposed bill produces mutual satisfaction among natives and rulers, Tods, like Kim later, becomes another kind of Macaulayan interpreter, improving (apparently) upon the natives programmed for such a purpose.[25]

Tods becomes a figure both for Kipling and for his stories, because Kipling, the Anglo-Indian child who produced a "child," functioned in the same way, educating his British readers in their responsibilities both to the people they ruled and to the people they sent out to rule. If, as Gauri Viswanathan has suggested, the teaching of English literature in India became a way to inculcate the ruled in English values,[26] then Kipling, as a self-appointed bard of empire, also wrote back to the rulers, creating a new literature to educate them as well. Of course, in each case (of Tods, Kim, or Strickland, all raised in India), there is no doubt that these children work ultimately for the benefit of empire. Even though Tods earns the gratitude of natives, Kipling's celebration of the "amendment" is based on Tods's ability to enable the British government to rule more effectively, indeed, to minimize native rebellion. Analogously, Kipling suggests, his stories can work as agents in two senses: they too can mediate and work for empire, and they can educate their imperial readers to be more effective holders of power.

But in all these cases there are also hints of subversiveness, of suggestions that these hybrid children of empire (including Kipling's stories) may not be completely under imperial control, that they may follow an intrepid path of their own, that their voices are double in their allegiance. While they can support imperial power, they can also subvert it, and this is the peculiar property of their hybridity. Tods is unpredictably if amusingly intractable as he distracts imperial lawmakers to chase a goat or disrespectfully announces that the august "Councillor Sahib" looks like his Indian servant's "big (pet) monkey" (148). Wee Willie Winkie, discussed above, is guilty of childhood infractions that gather symbolic import, such as setting fire to his father's compound or, in accordance with his alternative loyalties, keeping secrets that he does not reveal to his father, the head of the regiment. Similarly, in "The Son of His Father," Strickland's son, Adam, remains beyond parental discipline and proves a source of some alarm as well as respect. He takes revenge on his father for an earlier punishment by withholding his knowledge of a native servants' conspiracy until his father has suffered equal "shame." After his policeman father has been properly fooled and beaten, Adam discloses his power: "[S]aid Adam in a loud and joyful voice. 'We *all* knew. We all knew. I and the servants.' Strickland was silent. His wife stared helplessly at the child; the soul out of Nowhere that went its way alone" (246). Even though this child eventually tells his parents what saves them from further mortification, he is unpredictable, "a soul out of Nowhere" whose loyalty cannot be counted on by parents who attempt to colonize their children—or their servants.

Analogously, Kipling's fiction also can question the establishment of imperial power in such delicately poised imperial allegories as "The Man Who Would Be King" or "The Judgment of Dungara" (which detail, respectively, the catastrophic attempts of two vagabonds to become kings and those of European missionaries to convert the colonized in a jungle).[27] Even though Tods is smacked and silenced by his father, Wee Willie Winkie put under "house-arrest" (which he breaks), and Kipling, as we will see, restrained and censored for some of his writing by other parental figures, Kipling's humor belies his serious and recurrent suggestion that such children's power is able to subvert the very authority it is expected to uphold. Such hybrid children and their unusual gifts, like Kipling's stories, can serve as both asset and threat to the establishment of empire. If these children can be dangerous to their imperial parentage, so too can empire, imagined as a familial force, threaten them: perhaps this is why Kipling's stories obsess over deaths of children, often occasioned by parents, and point to the destruction of their child-language as censorship.

Censorship and the Death of Children

Kipling's stories of children present British India as a familial place both unusually nurturing of and deeply malignant toward children. Every child or adolescent that Kipling writes about is haunted, if not overtaken, by sudden death.[28] Nineteenth-century Anglo-India was certainly renowned for its high mortality rate—from disease, accident, physical or psychological strain, or war.[29] In *Something of Myself*, for example, Kipling writes of his return to India as a teenage journalist:

> [M]y world was filled with boys, but a few years older than I, who lived utterly alone, and died from typhoid mostly at the regulation age of twenty-two.... Death was always our near companion.... Hence our custom of looking up anyone who did not appear at our daily gatherings.
>
> The dead of all times were about us—in the vast forgotten Moslem cemeteries round the Station, where one's horse's hoof of a morning might break through to the corpse below; skulls and bones tumbled out of mud garden walls, and were turned up among the flowers by the Rains; and at every point were tombs of the dead. (26–27)

Kipling seems haunted by this pervasiveness of death. *Something of Myself*, an autobiography that focuses on his writing and notably omits any mention of the deaths of his two children, opens with a telling metonymy that links death with silencing and censorship, congruent with the text's play of silence and disclosure.[30] This account of his artistic career begins with a gruesome childhood memory of a dead child, whose dismembered hand was dropped by a vulture from the Zoroastrian Towers of Silence near his house in Lahore: "I did not understand my Mother's distress when she found 'a child's hand' in our garden, and said I was not to ask questions about it. I wanted to see that child's hand. But my *ayah* told me" (2). For the child Kipling, the English mother's shielding and fearful censorship of such knowledge of death is superseded by the *ayah*, that other mother, the native supplier of language and stories, who ignores the prohibition. This lasting memory of two conflicting mother figures seems to have produced in the writer a sense that child death and fragmentary remains are synonymous with silence and censorship and, furthermore, that even brutalized remains can tell a story, that such silence can secretly be broken. Censored knowledge, like death, cannot be suppressed, either because it drops from the sky (literally) or because it resurfaces in other forms.

Kipling's Anglo-Indian fiction repeatedly returns to children's deaths, but with a resonance suggesting that death has become a metaphor for something else, something to do with these children's powers of language. Even "Tods' Amendment" begins with the casual remark "Most men had saved [Tods] from death on occasions" (144), as if death were a habitual visitor liable to drop in from time to time. Wee Willie Winkie is almost done away with by a brutally ruthless enemy, and his fragility is suggested by the broken lisp that accompanies his linguistic prowess. The magically gifted hybrid child, the producer of language and enabler of cultural mediation, is unexpectedly vulnerable to death. Unlike the jingoism of Kipling's later poem "The White Man's Burden" (1899), which seems to legitimate the sacrifice of white men and boys as the necessary burden of empire, these earlier stories protest this omnipresence of death, especially of white children, as evidence of the toll taken by empire upon its own people.

A good example is Kipling's short story "The Drums of the Fore and Aft" (1889), which describes a disastrous British raid against Afghans in which the two drummer boys who lead the British regiment are "killed dead" while the army they are leading runs away. As Andrew Rutherford notes, in the historical incident on which this story is based, this (expendable) vanguard of two boys was actually "black," or Indian.[31] Kipling makes two significant changes: one, the boys become white; and two, the cowardly British regiment that runs away and betrays them is repeatedly described as "young" and inexperienced—as if to suggest in both cases that the folly of empire was to kill its own unprepared and unprotected children. As the two armies rush upon each other, "'They are coming anew!' shouted a priest among the Afghans. 'Do not kill the boys! Take them alive, and they shall be of our faith.' But the first volley had been fired, and Lew dropped on his face. Jakin stood for a minute, spun round and collapsed" (*War Stories*, 34). Clearly, Kipling credits the Afghans with valuing the young, even of an inimical race, more than the British value their own. The tale opens with an epigraph: "And a little child will lead them" (Isaiah 11:6). With a suggestion of dark subversive irony, it leaves us with a terrible paradigm of imperial progress: of two boys unwittingly beating drums for their own death to lead an army that does not follow.

This destruction of English children in colonies abroad is a frequent occasion for Kipling's resentment and for instructing his British readers at "home," who must be taught through his fiction what they demand of and impose on their children. The very title of the story "Only a Subaltern," for instance, satirizes the expendability of a young British officer's life (who dies of cholera) by the familial and imperial forces that send him off to India.[32] Similarly, in his excoriating 1902 poem "The Islanders," Kipling addresses this insular British audience:

> Yet ye were saved by a remnant (and your land's long-suffering star),
> When your strong men cheered in the millions while your striplings went
>   to the war.
> Sons of the sheltered city—unmade, unhandled, unmeet—
> Ye pushed them raw to the battles ye picked them raw from the street.

Curiously, Kipling's stories of the deaths of children are often rendered in terms of the death of their language, as if the damage done to children were somehow synonymous with silencing or censorship. In psychoanalytic terms, as Sigmund Freud reminds us, silence or "dumbness" in dreams, fairytales, and literature can be a "familiar representation of death."[33] By figuring silencing or censorship as death while in the act of telling the literal story of death, Kipling also tells a story of imperial censorship. Perhaps a complaint against empire that he cannot lodge explicitly concerns its power to kill words, or stories—his children of language.

Kipling makes this link between the deaths of children in British India and the death of (their) language in disguised form, in stories that purport to be about something else. "The Story of Muhammed Din," for example, recounts an Anglo-Indian colonial official's growing tenderness for his Indian servant's child, whose artistic talents he indulges with a distant but paternal longing. Every day, to salute him in the compound, "a fat little body" rose respectfully to lisp *"Talaam tahib"* (for "Salaam Sahib"), and a "sensitive little architect's soul" was allowed to build "a wondrous palace" of "withered marigolds" and broken china, "for it was only the play of a baby and did not much disfigure [the official's] garden" (186). When the child suddenly falls sick, the event is represented by the absence of his endearingly broken language: "Next day there was no Muhammed Din at the head of the carriage-drive, and no *'Talaam tahib'* to welcome my return. I had grown accustomed to the greeting, and its omission troubled me" (187). The syntactic parallelism between Muhammed Din and "Talaam Tahib" suggests that the child-artist's physical absence corresponds —as if it is identical—with that of his language. The brokenness of that language, as of his never-to-be-completed project of building a "palace" from broken china, is symptomatic of the imminent brokenness of his life, for the sudden death of this child is prefigured by his language. His lisp not only suggests the fragility and incompleteness of the child's life but also becomes an oblique mode of associating the death of a child with the death of his language. This curtailment by an unnamed outside force becomes a figure for the self-censoring omissions in the narrator's transformed narration.

In a sudden switch from active to passive voice and from first to third person, the narrator abruptly reports that as a result of his sickness, the child "got the medicine and an English doctor." The syntactic shift seems to attempt to remove the narrator's agency, as it underlines his failure at rescue and perhaps a certain complicity in this silence—and the child's death. He concludes, "A week later, though I would have given much to have avoided it, I met on the road to the Mussulman burying ground Imam Din, accompanied by one other friend, carrying in his arms wrapped up in a white cloth, all that was left of Muhammed Din" (187). For Kipling, the explicitness of language cannot, *must not*, convey what is too horrible—even as he writes of it. The child's body wrapped in a white cloth becomes an emblem of Kipling's narrative, adverting to but unable to speak directly of death or of the covers that enfold the unspeakable in his own story.

"Beyond the Pale," like "The Story of Muhammed Din," suggests that a writer's tenderness for a native child, or his penchant for a native idiom, correlates to its horrible destruction. An Englishman, Trejago, finds his way to Bisesa, a "child"-widow, by decoding her secret "object-letter," a packet of domestic objects proposing a romantic assignation. "No Englishman should be able to translate object-letters," remarks the narrator sagely, as if the very process of this erotic interracial linguistic communication is doomed to call violent retribution upon itself. If she, as child and beloved, is associated with Kipling's native stories, both arrived at by the decoding of native life and encoded to avoid detection, then both are also rendered as liable to be brutally mutilated or censored. Bloodied stumps are all her lover sees of her once "flower-like hands" before he too is stabbed and injured for life. The graphic violence in Kipling's images suggests a register beyond the literal—mutely suggesting the disastrous consequences that may accrue to the act of writing: that neither writer nor text is immune.[34] The reality of imperial censorship notwithstanding, such a recurrent concern on Kipling's part, whether justified or not, is crucial to our understanding of his (meta)narratival anxieties and imagination.

In both these stories, the children associated with the death of language are Indian. In two other stories in *Plain Tales*, the "children" are English and do not actually die, but colonial punishment visits them in the form of linguistic damage, manifested as a form of disorder or rupture of speech. In a mirrored structure, both "The Conversion of Aurelian McGoggin" and "In Error" link a sudden speech disorder with "something" uncanny, reducing a young man to a helpless "child." McGoggin, as we have seen, is punished by an unaccountable, censorious force because he talked too much, because under the conditions of imperial rule, it is inadvisable to question and assert independence of thought. If anything, McGoggin's fault is his anarchic subversiveness, for he has become too clever and believes that "men had no souls, and there was no God and no hereafter . . . [and] that the one thing more sinful than giving an order was obeying it" (81). But as the narrator ironically suggests, such beliefs are out of place in Anglo-India, because there, above the "raw brown humanity" is an entire system of British hierarchy that requires uncomplicated belief. The questioning of such belief may open the possibility that "the entire system of Our administration [of Empire] must be wrong; which is manifestly impossible" (82). McGoggin is symptomatically punished, struck by an aphasic termination of his speech, as if implying that this could happen to Kipling's subversive irony too:

> [T]he speech seemed to freeze in him, and—just as the lightning shot two tongues that cut the whole sky into three pieces and the rain fell in quivering sheets—[McGoggin] was struck dumb. He stood pawing and champing like a hard-held horse, and his eyes were full of terror. . . .
>
> The stroke cowed [him]. He could not understand it. He went into the Hills in fear and trembling, wondering whether he would be permitted to reach the end of any sentence he began.
>
> This gave him a wholesome feeling of mistrust. The legitimate explanation, that he had been overworking himself, failed to satisfy him. Something

had wiped his lips of speech, as a mother wipes the milky lips of her child, and he was afraid—horribly afraid. (84–85)

This "[s]omething" that "wipe[s] his lips of speech" (86) remains necessarily unspecific. Like the forces that attack Bisesa and Trejago, inimical forces of silence cannot be named by a colonial writer. As I have shown elsewhere about Kipling's self-nominated "lies" that tell truth under the guise of fiction, Kipling can puncture the silence imposed by censorship only by writing about it in disguised and fictive form.[35] Stories of physical and linguistic disorder become ways of gesturing toward that imperial censorship, depicting it as an unnamable and *familial* force that wreaks havoc upon its own breed. As empire kills its own children, so too can it kill its own stories and storytellers. Yet by presenting the existence of this censorship, Kipling breaks the silence it imposes, drawing attention to what is not there or to something that has been suppressed.

In all of these stories, ubiquitous death dogs Kipling's children and is associated with the death of their linguistic powers. Indeed, in Kipling's narrative imagination of this period, death seems to have become synonymous with silencing and censorship. Where children represent Kipling's stories, and figures of bodily injury denote textual intrusion, death becomes a haunting metaphor for the damage that can be done either by external authorities or by Kipling to his own stories. Thus, Kipling can at the same time complain about imperial tyranny and acknowledge his participation in it.

Let me clarify, then, that in referring to censorship in Kipling's writing I include, but do not limit my definition to, external demands for excision or threat of retribution. Kipling's concern with censorship includes all forms of intervention that disrupt or derail the autonomy of his fiction, that impose omission or restrict textual liberties: informal familial or editorial suggestions, reader's responses, and, indeed, *self*-censorship. He seems to regard this authorial internalization of imperial necessity with a sense of conflict: as necessary but also a form of self-butchering (or infanticide) that may endanger the autonomy and viability of his production. In *Something of Myself*, Kipling offers many accounts of the necessities of self-censorship. An early lesson he claims to have learned well is that "crude statements of crude facts are not well seen by official authorities"—in other words, he had better not report on unsavory discoveries in British India (28). Claiming that his writing was the better for it, he describes his final revisions or "Higher Editing" as his "blacking out where requisite" with "Indian ink" (121). But such accounts are telling and double-edged: if his unwanted excesses were imperial secrets so black that they could only be covered, blotted out by the very ink that was acquired by imperial appropriation, such blots mark an untold story of self-inflicted silencing.

However, Kipling had good reason to be concerned about external censorship from the imperial government as well. As a journalist working for the *Civil and Military Gazette* (which dared on one occasion to criticize the government's Ilbert Bill of 1883, then allegedly changed its tune under pressure), he was well aware of the changing laws and "veiled pressure" that affected both the European and "Native" presses in his time.[36] Beginning in the late eighteenth and early nineteenth century, despite occasional periods of leniency, the European press and all printed matter in India were tightly controlled by the East India Company. Newspapers and editors could be fined, censured, or prosecuted or have their licenses revoked (all presses were required to be licensed by the government), could be deported from India, and, interestingly, were banned even from discussing the lack of freedom of speech.[37] (The latter may help to explain why Kipling so frequently calls attention to the necessities of censorship indirectly as that which is to be understood but cannot be discussed.) In the 1880s, East India Company servants were not allowed to be involved with the press. On many occasions, "seditious" editors or writers could be—and were—banished without trial (as in the 1823 famous and prolonged case of James Silk Buckingham, editor of the *Calcutta Journal*).[38] While uncomfortable with the more restrictive laws that curtailed the liberties of English subjects in India (compared to English laws), the company justified itself by claiming a special vulnerability because of its colonial rule, as in the following company statement of 1825: "Because the nature and circumstances of the British establishments in India have required, and the Royal Charters and Acts of Parliament, under which they have been regulated, have sanctioned, a control over the conduct and restraint of the freedom of British subjects while resident in the territories subject to the government of the East-India company . . . even the resort of British subjects to India, and their right to reside there, have with few exceptions been placed in the discretion of the East-India Co."[39] Though some of these restrictions were changed by Thomas Macaulay's recommendations in 1835, with the crisis of 1857, a more drastic "Gagging Act" was applied to all books, newspapers, and pamphlets printed in British India (Barns, 250);

the act prohibited "any observations or statements impugning the motives or designs of the British Government . . . [that might] excite disaffection or unlawful resistance."[40]

By Kipling's time, the East India Company had been abolished and Queen Victoria declared empress of India, but the legislation and history of control of all printed matter still held force. Informally, "disloyalty" or criticism was particularly to be avoided by the English press (and English writers), which was still under surveillance and held to have much influence and responsibility, especially when government anxiety was rising in response to a growing native press (in English and in many Indian languages), a rising literacy rate, and incipient nationalism (the Indian National Congress was founded in 1885). Stephen Wheeler, Kipling's first editor and supervisor, distrusted Kipling's "original writing" and refused to print his "Other Side of the Question."[41] Thus, although under much less restriction and suspicion than an Indian writer, Kipling was aware of the sensitivity and tact that he as an Anglo-Indian journalist and writer was expected to exercise because of a perceived need not to sabotage a beleaguered government. These constraints on the press in British India were even more applicable to Kipling's early fiction, most of which (thirty-two of the forty "plain tales") was first published in the *Civil and Military Gazette*, under the eagle eye of Wheeler.

Moreover, explicit measures could still be taken against an Anglo-Indian writer such as Kipling. Although Lord Lytton's controversial and repressive Vernacular Press Act of 1878 was the first to enact legal discrimination between Indian and European writing—and applied to everything printed in any vernacular language in British India, with penalties that included forfeiture of all equipment and copies, imprisonment, and fines—much formal legislation that remained was equally applicable to Anglo-Indian writers. This included Act XXVII of 1870, which for the first time made sedition punishable under the Indian Penal Code (section 124A): "Whoever by words, either spoken or intended to be read, or by signs, or by visible representation or otherwise, excites or attempts to excite feelings of disaffection to the Government established by law in British India, shall be punished by transportation for life or for any term, to which fine may be added, or with imprisonment."[42] In addition, Act XXV of 1867, "for the regulation of Printing presses and Newspapers, for the preservation of copies of books printed in British India, and for the registration of such books" (punishable by fines of five thousand rupees and/or imprisonment of up to two years), was what Gerald Barrier terms "the legal basis for a surveillance system" for both English and Indian writers.[43] It required the names of all authors, printers, and publishers to be printed on every book or paper for which they were responsible and a copy of every book (with maps, illustrations, and so forth) to be submitted to the government. In 1889, Kipling's last year in India, the Official Secrets Act, which had already become law in England, became law in India as well. For reasons of government "security," it was applicable to all subjects, British or Indian, and punished by fine, imprisonment, or transportation any breach of trust or disclosure of classified information. Indeed, under this act, in 1898 Kipling's book *A Fleet in Being: Notes of Two Trips with Channel Squadron* was censored for allegedly betraying naval secrets.[44]

Given this set of internal and external constraints, Kipling's oblique metaphors of child death and complaints against imperial censorship begin to make sense. If child death represents the effects of censorship, we should perhaps not be surprised that the children who die most often in Kipling's stories are either black or white, that is, either Indian or English/Eurasian—in Kipling's racial vision of inevitability. In contrast, usually *the Anglo-Indian children survive*, even though they are threatened by death. Unlike Muhammed Din, or Lew and Jake, or even McGoggin and Moriarty, the latter of whom have newly arrived in India as adolescents, the "native-born" Anglo-Indian children in Kipling's stories seem to pull through. This suggests the power of their milk-suckled hybridity and, indeed, of Kipling's stories—as Kipling represents it—making the body the source of strength or resistance and of vulnerability to reprisal. For Kipling suggests that although the threat of death and damage is an omnipresent and serious one, the hybridity of his children enables them to survive, perhaps because they have learned the languages of negotiation, translation, and surreptitious opposition. And if the hybrid child can survive, so too, Kipling suggests analogously, can his hybrid child-text, for it can likewise speak in a double voice, encoding a secret, muted critique, a critique that cannot be easily identified or punished. *Plain Tales* thus concludes with an important story that presents both these problems of authorship and the possibilities of subversion, offering unexpected insights into the problem of literary agency in turn-of-the-century colonial India.

Anxieties of Authorship and Strategies of Survival

"To Be Filed for Reference," the last story in *Plain Tales*, is told by a narrator who purports to be Kipling, breezily presenting himself as a writer and "collector" of Indian stories.[45] The tale can be read as a coda that looks back to this entire first collection, reflecting self-consciously on Kipling's stories. Even its title suggests its metanarratival importance, as if it was a key to Kipling's other tales.[46] Recounting how he befriended McIntosh, an Englishman-turned-native, the narrator ends with the following deathbed scene:

> I said "thank you" as the native woman put the bundle into my arms.
> "My only baby!" said McIntosh with a smile. He was sinking fast, but he continued to talk as long as breath remained. I waited for the end, knowing that in six cases out of ten the dying man calls for his mother. He turned on his side and said:
> "Say how it came into your possession. No one will believe you, but my name at least will live. You will treat it brutally, I know. Some of it must go; the public are fools and prudish fools. I was their servant once. But do your mangling gently—very gently. It is a great work and I have paid for it in seven years damnation." (241)

Like Kipling's own "child's child," the "baby" that McIntosh hands over to the narrator here is his book, earlier described as his "life's work," a book on "native life" supposedly unparalleled by any other. But this baby makes more explicit than does "the brown baby with the pink string" the multiparented interracial hybridity and sense of censorship as a kind of bodily harm that recur in Kipling's metafictive accounts of his Anglo-Indian stories. For like Kipling's "child's child," this "baby" too must be "mangled," as its father knows, before it will be accepted by the "foolish" public. That public, its anticipated audience, and Kipling, to whom it is entrusted, together become its co-producers, or parents, as well as agents of injury or destruction.

McIntosh, we are told, has converted to Islam, has "gone native" (even though he was once "an Oxford man" and knew his Greek and Latin); by cohabiting with a "native woman," he has fallen "past redemption" (235). Like the "child's child," McIntosh's "baby" is an interracial, multiply parented hybrid product. In handing his book to Kipling, McIntosh suggests that Kipling will become both its editor and its coauthor, the one who will achieve fame through it and, as surrogate parent, save the orphan from death. "Do not let my book die in its present form," is his dying injunction. In the kind of collaborative literary birthing that Wayne Koestenbaum has called "double talk," a homoerotic (re)production between men, the presence of the two writers suggests that this moment of death enables a transferal, a new birth between them.[47] However, in this account, the "native woman" appears as yet another parent and collaborator. Silently she transports the book from one man to another, passive yet crucial. In a curious gender inversion, she is the bedside helpmate who literally enables McIntosh to *deliver* his story (to Kipling). His liaison with her has given McIntosh access to the native "secrets" incorporated in his book, hence she is also the "mother" of his hybrid text to whom he calls in death. Like the Indian wet nurse, her role remains triangulated and diffused yet is necessary to the production of this "child."

This account of a multiply produced and reshaped interracial child-text suggests that somehow, as a consequence of its complicated genealogy, such a child (and story) may have preternatural potential. As McIntosh hands over his "treasure," he claims that it will supersede both Dante's *Inferno* and "all other books on native life, including the celebrated Mirza Ali Beg's" (240). In other words, it will outshine both European and Asian classical literature—perhaps because it is born of both and perhaps because, like Tods, its new powers may be of great help to the British government. The Kipling narrator regards McIntosh's claims with ambivalence: though skeptical, he suggests by his buildup the importance of this dangerous "gift."

This book is called *Mother Maturin*. In some sense, it is literally McIntosh's "life's work," since its pioneering inroads into native secrets have cost him his life.[48] But its title is also that of a lost (or destroyed) manuscript that we know Kipling worked on for years, reportedly about a brothel-keeping Irishwoman, the mother-in law of an Anglo-Indian government official, who became the channel through which government and native bazaar secrets were exchanged.[49] Kipling could relinquish that first book only by later replacing it—and the figure of the Irish intermediary in service of empire—with *Kim*. This story, then, seems to provide a metanarratival genealogy for Kipling's own writing, as if *Mother Maturin* were the textual mother of *Kim*, an early vehicle for conveying what Kipling's most acclaimed tale, *Kim*, would contain. In fact, the story suggests that Kipling's writing (like that much revised and transformed novel *Kim* that he would write in the future) *is* that great hybrid product of empire.

Thus, both McIntosh and the Kipling narrator function as figures for Kipling himself. McIntosh represents a peculiar vagabond artistry, transgressive of both British imperial interdictions and forbidden Indian secrets (like Kipling, who frequently represents himself as a young journalist in Lahore, McIntosh gains access to and reports on hearts of "native" darkness by supposedly risking his life). And the narrator is another "side" of Kipling's head, the respectable journalist who will "butcher" his own text, "expurgat[ing]" it to fit his "jerky jargon" (240, 241). Perhaps he will also take care to omit truths that it would not please imperial powers to be known. Kipling clearly understands the violence that such a writer can meet, for in another story he remarks about a book that Strickland (another fictive double) may one day write: "[I]f he chose to write all he saw his head would be broken in several places. . . . That book will be worth buying, and even more worth suppressing" (*Plain Tales*, 27).

The child-text that promises to be produced between these two men suggests a paradigm for all the tales in *Plain Tales*. Like Kipling's hybrid Anglo-Indian children, this writing is represented as importantly *dual*: as simultaneously capable of serving and threatening the power of empire, and in turn of being enabled and threatened by that power. Its "greatness" lies in the hybridity of its production: born of multiple parents, of many languages (like Kim later), his writing is able to gather and pass on crucial information; in its modes of disguise and its ability to mediate, to pass via cultural cross-dressing into both Indian and Anglo-Indian identities, it can thus be most useful for imperial service. But at the same time, in that very strength lies its weakness, for in so doing it may tell too much. Perhaps that is why, Kipling suggests, in the unpredictably inimical climate of colonial India, such a child is terribly subject to "brutality," to "mutilation," to censorship, or to death: "Do your mangling gently. . . . Do not let my book die," beseeches McIntosh repeatedly. And Kipling's stories are full of the deaths of children, both Anglo-Indian and Indian—"killed" sometimes, he implies, by their own parents.

At first, this authorial anxiety about censorship seems to have to do simply with a fear of reception—as we saw with the "brown baby"—an anxiety about generating something that will live, where the condition of survival is accommodation to readers' preferences. Certainly, Kipling was always aware that he was writing for two audiences, British and Anglo-Indian. This predicament, frequently recognized as a problem for postcolonial writers writing in a colonizer's language, addressing audiences in "metropolitan" as well as "home" cultures, was Kipling's as well. He had to address English readers both at "home" and in the colonies—readers separated by their ignorance or knowledge of the exigencies of empire. For the former, his material was alien; for the latter, much might be forbidden; and for both, some things might be too dangerous to be told. But under the constraints of writing for such an audience, of maintaining the necessary fictions of empire, the truth of which (as Joseph Conrad's Marlow knew) could not be revealed to metropolitan "Intendeds," much of what Kipling wanted to say had to be "killed."[50]

This anxiety about authorship and textual infanticide thus extends from audience reception to the greater political context of imperial power. Kipling concludes "To Be Filed for Reference"—and hence his first book—with this enigmatic comment: "If this thing is ever published, some one may perhaps remember this story, now printed as a safeguard to prove that McIntosh Jellaludin and not I myself wrote the book of Mother Maturin. I don't want *The Giant's Robe* to come true in my case" (241). With a stridency suggestive of guilt, Kipling declares that this story is "printed as a *safeguard* to *prove*" that he is not the author of his own stories, that he has simply transmitted what someone else created. This language of defense suggests at least two unusual functions for Kipling's writing. First, it must complicate notions of sole authorship, as if to deflect responsibility for what it reveals. Second, it must provide a legalistic safeguard, a protective armor against accusation of plagiarism, fraud, or betrayal of imperial secrets—gesturing instead toward others who remain unnamed. The Kipling narrator thus simultaneously claims and disclaims responsibility for his narration, layering with contradictions his own authorship—for reasons he will not specify. This may almost be a peculiar defiance of Anglo-Indian laws that required that the names of printer and author be printed clearly on every copy (and in the earliest version, on the first and last pages), should indictment be necessary.[51]

But why would Kipling choose to conclude his tale (and his first book) with the throwaway line "I don't want *The Giant's Robe* to come true in my case"? In his edition, Andrew Rutherford glosses *"The Giant's Robe"* as a novel "published in 1883, on the fate of a man who passes off a friend's novel as his own" (278). However, most nineteenth-century editions of *Plain Tales* do not capitalize or italicize "the giant's robe." This suggests another allusion—to *Macbeth*, when a spectator comments on the tyrant awaiting his condign end:

> Now does he feel his title
> Hang loose about him, like a giant's robe
> Upon a dwarfish thief.
>
> (5.2.20–22)

As an Anglo-Indian writer whose tales were "borrowed" from native sources (as the "native-born's" language is "borrowed" from native milk-mothers) and as a member of an imperial system whose legitimacy was very much questioned by Indians, Kipling may have found that Shakespeare's drama of usurpation, tyranny, and violence resonated with him on several levels.

On one level, clearly this allusive conclusion expresses Kipling's frequent anxiety and insistence that his stories are not original, that his fame is undeserving, that his power and privilege as a writer has been wrested from others to whom it is really due, and he must cite his debts to avoid paying Macbeth's price.[52] Thus, Kipling's dual impulse to account for his illicit authorship and to exculpate himself by confession speaks of a peculiarly contorted desire to have it both ways: as if the announcement of guilt and partial attribution could diminish the "theft" or protect him from its consequences.

On another level, however, the Macbeth analogy also suggests links between the power of writing and of empire. Writing is a form of empire making, a form of appropriation of power, because it is both analogous to and instrumental in the making of empire. For if, as Teresa Hubel argues, the ownership of India has depended on writing about India and the forms of constructing India—or, as Edward Said puts it, "the enterprise of empire depends upon the *idea* of *having an empire*"—so, too, in several stories Kipling suggests that empire is built by ideas circulated by storytellers.[53] Certainly, Kipling was well aware of his position both as a writer of empire—a purveyor and a perpetuator of the myths and self-enabling mythologies upon which the edifice of empire rested—and as a rival, a problem for empire.[54] As we have seen, this position of power was also a source of anxiety, for a writer's words could threaten that imperial power. It is no surprise, then, that imperial writers were under surveillance, subject to control and censorship.

Yet Kipling's allusion to *Macbeth* taps into yet another set of associations, for it speaks to a third implicit concern of that play: the problem of self-perpetuation in a situation of disputed power. If Macbeth's usurper's curse was the inability to produce children (which would render null his ill-gotten gains),[55] a similar fear seems to pervade Kipling's obsession with the death of children, as if the denial of imperial posterity is the vengeance of the future, as if somehow the British Empire too would have no children in India or that it would kill its own.[56] Intuitively, Kipling is telling a parallel story of the British Empire in India and of himself as a writer both subject to and invested in that empire.[57] Moreover, it serves as a warning to its imperial readers: an empire that requires the sacrifice of its children could, even as it engenders, destroy the promise and productivity of writers such as Kipling, ruining its mode of self-perpetuation if that writer should swerve from the demands of absolute allegiance. The illogic of empire might be precisely that, like Macbeth, Anglo-India would be doomed to destroy its own children. This is another way that the story speaks to Kipling's anxiety of agency, the desire to have lasting effect, of producing stories that will live. The bodily language of multiply parented children allows him to incorporate both the vulnerability and the promise of such imperial progeny as his fiction, to suggest its peculiar conditions of production, its capacity to produce and be produced and to be destroyed.

However, in the very act of telling this story, Kipling also addresses this anxiety, for his casting of censorship in terms of death and hybrid children itself constitutes an undermining of that censorship. The final twist to Kipling's self-revelations lies in his oblique raising of these issues, and his cautionary allusion to *Macbeth* suggests an oblique subversiveness. His stories can speak hidden truths, lodge critiques, and thereby evade repercussions because they speak in code. This ability to be evasive and subversive without appearing to be so is arguably the secret of survival for Kipling's hybrid literary progeny. "To Be Filed" is, then, ultimately a coded metanarrative of narratival survival. In figuring the death of children as textual destruction, this final story-as-afterword suggests that even when censorship as violent dismemberment is perpetrated on a baby by its parents, such a child might live. ("You will mutilate it horribly[,] . . . you will butcher the style to carve it into your own . . . ; but you cannot destroy the whole of it" [240].) These hybrid children, produced of multiple heritages, also have strange powers of survival despite the "mangling" that they must undergo. If these children can survive, as McIntosh has faith that his book will not be utterly destroyed, then Kipling offers the hope that his own writing (as we will see with *Kim* in the next chapter), even if censored and mutilated by imperial necessity, will be viable enough to live beyond that mutilation, that it will have powers of subverting that censorship even as it is subjected to censorship. As with Kipling's Anglo-Indian children, this may be because his stories speak in a dual "other" language, a language of doubleness and duplicity that combines multiple voices, heritages, and allegiances, speaking truths subversively via acquiescence and figuration, making inextricable the strands of co-optation and resistance—and that may perhaps be the secret of their survival.

CHAPTER TWO

The Doubleness of Writing (in) *Kim*, or, The Art of Empire

KIM (1901), Kipling's most important novel, begins with a pronoun that does not identify its subject by name: "He sat, in defiance of municipal orders, astride the gun, Zam-Zammah," a gun from which, we discover, "he" had triumphantly ousted both the native Hindu and the Muslim boys.[1] Why does it take Kipling a while to name Kim, the apparent protagonist of the novel, the Lahore street orphan who is as yet ignorant of his Irish heritage? Could "Kim" refer not only to the boy but also to the novel that bears his name? Critics have usually read this iconic opening scene as emblematic of colonial conquest, in which the gun stands for "the conqueror's loot" and reflects this white child's superiority and power as a representative of a young civilization colonizing with violence an older one.[2] But Kim also sits "in defiance" of colonial government and authority, occupying a position all his own, straddling the gun, in a position of in-betweenness. This initial posture of simultaneous power (over natives) and subversion (of colonial rule) suggests that the text *Kim*—for whom Kim may be a figure—may adopt the same stance. The name "Kim" may indeed refer not only to the child but also to Kipling's novel.

From the beginning, Kim's power, even as a vagrant, stems from his fantasized linguistic (and not physical) superiority. He keeps Hindu and Muslim children alike off the gun because he has greater control over their language and history (52). He survives—indeed, thrives—amidst the conspiracies and dangers of the streets primarily because of the dexterity and readiness of his language: his ability to switch disguises and understand many different (Indian) dialects; his capacity to speak in and apprehend coded messages; and most of all, his fearless fabrications of instant, outrageous lies. When a native policeman, Kim's token enemy and stand-in for governmental authority, orders the lama away from the gun, Kim jumps in first: "'Huh! Owl!' was Kim's retort on the lama's behalf. 'Sit under that gun if it please thee. When didst thou steal the milkwoman's slippers, Dunnoo?' That was an utterly unfounded charge sprung on the spur of the moment, but it silenced Dunnoo, who knew that Kim's clear yell could call up legions of bad bazar boys if need arose" (61).[3] Kim's energetic, inventive linguistic prowess does not for a moment conceal its powers of tyranny, and Kipling's text remains well aware of that dangerous potential in itself: of how it, as a text, may replicate this power of misrepresentation and how its modes of fabrication may also subvert governmental authority. An implicit comparison is set up between Kim and the text: both can lie or tell truth, to the benefit or detriment of those they may serve. If the lie signifies for Kipling the fictive capacity to tell tales, to offer a coded critique or exposé of empire, what good or harm, *Kim* seems to ask, can these linguistic powers of both text and character do in the world they inhabit?[4] And how can this novel cast its own relationship to imperial power in this narrative about the making of imperial power?

The novel's title implies its dual focus. In telling what appears to be one story, in fact it tells two stories at once: overtly, the story of an orphan boy; covertly, the story of the text *Kim*. Both are engaged in the Great Game of empire.[5] Character and text become figures for each other, suggesting how one can mirror the other: how a human subject, a character, may function like a text and how Kipling's text confronts the same predicaments as does Kim. Kim's body is an overdetermined site of signification, a surface that is literally written upon, disguised, and read, a source of loaded meanings that are only at times under Kim's control. As such a body, the text *Kim* draws analogies and distinctions between itself and the character Kim, as it foregrounds the capacity of language both to have and to suffer material effects.

The novel begins with the child Kim in the same position as the text in relation to empire. Like the children of empire in Kipling's Indian short stories, both Kims are products of (or parented by) two cultures and two languages and are themselves producers of multiple languages, combining Hindi, Urdu, and English, or coded and apparent meanings in a single utterance. Empowered by their gifts of language, their hybridity and inventiveness, both can be put to use in the Great Game.[6] And both can be subversive, because their language and its multivalence cannot be controlled. As the narrative outlines first Kim's joyous powers of language and creativity and then his fall into the hands of empire, the trajectories of the two Kims separate: whereas Kim may end up losing altogether the power he begins with, as he is used, silenced, and overwritten by empire, the text *Kim*—even as it outlines Kim's indoctrination, and even as it knows that it cannot extricate itself from complicity in the processes of power—explores the possibilities of escaping Kim's fate.

This chapter explores this doubling of text and character, body and text: how Kim's body becomes a defaced and damaged text and has to cede his original powers of reading and linguistic fertility to the dangerous arts of empire; and how the text *Kim* implicitly tells a tale of its own absorption in the Game, even as it seeks to develop a certain agency in telling that tale. The story of Kim as an imperial text enables Kipling to explore the agency of his text in the context of empire. How can his novel also be conscripted into the service of empire and how can it, as a child of other languages, speak in a double voice that may undercut that service? By casting the relationship of text and empire as ominously familial, Kipling considers how such a relation can be both mutually generative and threatening. As it covertly expresses fears of its own conscription and loss, the novel *Kim* also suggests its powers of subversion. Presenting the dangers of imperial control in the guise of the adolescent Kim's encounter with empire—a disguise reflected by Kim's frequent resorting to cultural cross-dressing—*Kim* itself attempts to evade control through subterfuge, naming in double language what it cannot name directly.

Postcolonial scholarship on *Kim* has largely focused on Kipling's skill and complicity in creating a discourse of empire and on the hidden ideologies of Kim's work of colonial espionage. Citing Victor Turner's anthropological research, Edward Said reads Kim as a "liminal" figure who helps to "maintain societies" by his very marginality and then consolidates the hold of the British Empire on India as he moves from "liminality to domination."[7] S. P. Mohanty's important essay on *Kim* proposes that the childlike innocence of Kim and Mowgli serves to idealize and camouflage their role as surveillance experts for the empire.[8] Zohreh Sullivan delineates the contradictions inherent in Kipling's ambivalent representations of India: the oppositions between familial desire and imperial control; and between Kim's exotic fantasy of an India as a space of magic, love, and freedom as well as a space of danger and mystery, in need of imperial mastery. But for Sullivan, too, Kim ultimately emerges a winner on the side of colonial power, albeit at the cost of his earlier freedom. The rhetoric of "love" for the lama and for India versus the reality of Kim's work for the secret service creates a split, she argues, revealing a paradigm of "bad faith" (Sullivan, 150), within which, in Althusserian terms, "Kim's real relationship to India [is] of spy, protector, British interests, colonialist, imperialist. But his imaginary relationship to India [is] as 'The Friend of all the World,' . . . a sort of one-man United Nations" (166).

For all their differences, these readings share the premise that Kim represents—and is allied with—the empire for which he becomes a pawn. But they do not address the possibility that he may also represent the colonial artist or text.[9] By focusing on how Kipling uses Kim as a figure for the text produced by empire, I consider how colonial writing like Kipling's, though clearly in concord with most colonial ideologies, may still be self-referential and self-questioning on its own terms. Without gainsaying Kipling's imperialist and undoubtedly racist mind-set, we can, as Sara Suleri proposes, credit his ability to "read the details of colonial loss without necessarily proceeding to a larger abnegation of the whole."[10] While sharing Sullivan's diagnosis of Kipling's torn allegiances, I would add that his work carries some awareness and tension about its subjection to the needs of imperial culture. Even Said's appreciative account, for example, does not allow for such self-awareness within Kipling's text: "Language for (Kipling) was not, as it was for Conrad, a resistant medium; it was transparent, easily capable of many tones and inflections, all of them directly representative of the world he explored" (*Culture and Imperialism*, 157). Homi Bhabha has shown how colonial discourse may be internally split or divided, rendered dialogic because of its awareness of the mimicry or voices of the colonized.[11] But that still locates the source of anticolonial resistance *outside,* not *within,* imperial discourse. What I am suggesting is that Kipling's colonialist idiom is internally split by its own doubts, anxieties, and resistances to dominant ideology, even as it largely subscribes to this ideology. This is what creates the instability of Kipling's writing; to express those doubts and disguise those resistances, Kipling creates a coded, double-voiced language, such as, in *Kim,* the doubling of text and character.

The first chapter of the novel establishes how Kim's body may function as a text or site of signification. Born into the underclass of whites in India, Kim was orphaned at three and has been reared in the streets:

> Though he was burnt black as any native; . . . Kim was white—a poor white of the very poorest. The half-caste woman who looked after him . . . told the missionaries that she was Kim's mother's sister, but his mother had been a nursemaid . . . and had married Kimball O'Hara . . . [of] an Irish regiment. . . . His [father's] estate at death consisted of three papers—one he called his *"ne varietur"* because those words were written below his signature, another his "clearance certificate." The third was Kim's birth certificate. Those things, he used to say, in his glorious opium hours, would make little Kimball a man. On no account was Kim to part with them, for they belonged to a great piece of magic. . . . Nine hundred first-class devils, whose God was a Red Bull on a green field, would attend to Kim. . . . [A]fter his death the woman sewed parchment, paper, and birth-certificate into a leather amulet case which she strung round Kim's neck. (49–50)

For all his initial freedom of linguistic inventiveness and autonomy, from the beginning of the novel Kim is marked by writing. Placed upon his chest, "strung round his neck," is an amulet that contains writing that he cannot read, crucial papers that identify Kim's father and his father's regiment in the British army. This heritage, which establishes Kim's superiority over the other boys, is his racial genealogy: he is white. As long as it remains hidden and unread, Kim maintains his freedom and fluidity of identity, camouflaged by his sunburnt skin color. Like McIntosh in "To Be Filed for Reference," Kim's father "died as poor whites die in India," and his "baby" (in this case not his book but his biological creation) has been salvaged and delivered to the world by a native "foster-mother." Like the native woman who "delivers" McIntosh's baby, she preserves the papers in the amulet (and Kim) and hangs them around his neck. With allusive reference to Kipling's oeuvre, Kim the character and *Kim* the text seem to have replaced, like a palimpsest, an earlier writing: Kipling's own "baby," or the lost book described in his short story as *Mother Maturin*.

More important, the amulet suggests that Kim is also written *upon*, for what he bears around his neck, albatross-like, is the name of his father, the first burden of many that he will carry: the writing of a patriarchal colonial order that will deliver him into the hands of the Great Game. Kim's body thus becomes at once the page upon which his father's signature lies and the product that his father authors. For the child Kim, his amulet is a totemic reminder of his father, apparently unallied to spoken language, which is his forte. Unread writing, it impels him into adventure—as it impels the narrative of *Kim*—pursuing his "quest" with the lama: to find the prophesied "Red Bull on a Green Field" that, unknown to him, is the mascot of his father's regiment. But the amulet bears seeds of trouble. A veritable Pandora's box, this first instance of writing within *Kim* needs only to be read to unleash imperial forces that sweep Kim into losing both his physical mobility and his linguistic freedom.

This writing that lies on his body effects Kim's capture in the first place. Traveling with the lama, Kim is caught eavesdropping outside the priests' army tent. As he bolts for the door, Father Victor grabs his neck, and with it the precious amulet. The rupture occasioned by this tearing of writing from Kim's body is reflected in the transference of writing from magical token to intelligible meaning. As the priests read Kim's father's papers, incredulous that a "native" should possess this certification of British paternity and speak a broken English, the text emphasizes the opening of Kim himself—as a text and as a body to be read. For not only does his body *bear* writing, it is literally a site of racial signification. Father Victor steps forward "quickly" and rips open "the front of Kim's upper garment" to observe, "'You see, Bennett, he's not very black. What's your name?' 'Kim . . . Will you let me go away?'" (134).

Kim's chest—upon which he bears the writing of his various fathers throughout the novel, from his father's papers to Mahbub's coded letter and, later, to all the hidden letters of espionage for the empire—functions here as a text in two senses: it is a site of (hidden) writing and a site of bodily identity, the page that is opened and read by this new "Father." Like his speech, it is a source of strength and vulnerability: capable of being read, only too transparent, *and* of being the *cache de lettre*, the hiding place of writing, of secret messages. No tabula rasa, the whiteness of Kim's chest signifies. It locates him in the taxonomy of race, as a child of his father. It carries a message: his racial identity.

Peter Brooks, in his introduction to *Body Work*, examines the relation between identity and the body in the European literary tradition by focusing on the moment when Odysseus in disguise is recognized by his old nurse by the scar on his thigh:

> [T]he moment of recognition is a dramatic climax, a coming into the open ... through a mark on the body itself. It is the body marked in a significant moment of the person's past history that enables recognition—a scenario that will be replayed throughout literature, and given its most formulaic version in ... the token affixed to or engraved on the abandoned orphan which at last enables the establishment of identity. It is as if identity, and its recognition, depended on the body having been marked with a special sign, which looks suspiciously like a linguistic signifier. The sign imprints the body, making it part of the signifying process. Signing or marking the body signifies the passage into writing, its becoming a literary body, and generally also a narrative body, in that the inscription of the sign depends on and produces a story. The signing of the body is an allegory of the body become a subject for literary narrative—a body entered into writing.[12]

This movement of the body into writing is precisely what occurs in *Kim*. Both the token hung on his chest and the whiteness of his skin serve as markers that convert his body into a readable (and usable) text. And, of course, they impel the narrative of *Kim*. Even though Kim is not literally marked by writing, the writing on his chest develops into a burden that by the end of the novel collapses the distinction between bodily surface and depth. The letters he carries for the empire become a "load of writings on his heart," as if they had inscribed themselves upon his being (319). But Kim's scenario also differs significantly from what Brooks describes. Kipling inverts the convention of epic recognition, for the revelation of Kim's "identity" does not lead to triumph. It occurs early, not at the end of the narrative, bringing about the end of his freedom—and of his body—to signify. Moreover, the sign of whiteness (his covered skin) read by the priests is not a result of life experience (as is the sunburnt color of his exposed body). Rather, it is the identification of race that is passed on as inheritance, through blood.

On another occasion soon after his "capture," Kim's chest is read again by Mahbub Ali, the Afghan horse-dealer who secretly works for the Game.[13] After his "capture" by his father's regiment, Kim tries to persuade Mahbub (another father) to help him escape by reminding Mahbub of Kim's earlier faithful delivery of Mahbub's coded letter to Colonel Creighton—carrying secret information that has enabled the British to identify and "punish" some rebellious kings (85). (Kim here manifests his awareness of the codes and double meanings of imperial writing and of the Game.) As Kim now asks Mahbub, in coded language, to help him, he reveals his excellent candidacy in the games of empire. But instead of being a compliant "tool," Kim also suggests his potential power to expose the workings of the Game, appropriating his knowledge of coded language for his own purposes. In response, Mahbub places his hand on Kim's heart, as if reading Kim as a text through his body, testing him for his reliability for the Game (155–56). Kim's chest here becomes a bodily text that enables Mahbub to read Kim himself as a coded letter: to find out whether Kim knows the significance of the message he delivered and whether he can conceal his dangerous knowledge. Ironically, Kim shows himself proficient in both, for he succeeds in concealing from Mahbub his knowledge of Mahbub's involvement, while revealing his proficiency in creating coded messages. "Who cares to tell the truth to a letter-writer?' Kim answered, feeling Mahbub Ali's hand on his heart" (156).

This chest, which Father Victor rips open his shirt to reveal and which Mahbub tests, is both the site of signification, enabling the reading of Kim, and the site of reinscription in the letter(s) of the Game. From here on in the narrative, Kim's chest will carry messages for the empire and be used to disguise his identity for that service. And with typical duality, like any of Kipling's texts, this chest can be disguised (used) by Kim himself to escape the surveillance of the Game. On his first vacation from school, as Kim prepares to escape (briefly) into India and Indianness from his telling whiteness and its burdens, he pays a courtesan to darken his face and chest, making up a story of a lover's rendezvous: "'Spread it also on the breast. It may be her father will tear my clothes off me, and if I am piebald—' he laughed" (174). Clearly, fathers are associated

65

with a violent and disturbing ability to denude and decode—and their reading is an invasive activity, an imperialistic enactment of power with potentially violent consequences. At the same time, at this point in the novel, Kim is also able to some extent to control those readings, to reinscribe his own meanings (and agenda) upon the text of his body.

Throughout the novel, Kim remains marked by writing. The amulet bearing the name of his father is replaced later by another amulet on his chest, which carries the secret code of his membership in the Game. The name of his biological father is overwritten by the name of empire, which reinvents Kim and literally reinvests him in a new identity. Invented with pride by Hurree Babu (yet another father), this amulet encircles Kim's neck, literally and figuratively: its exposure can cost him his life, and it is a burden from which there is no escape. Upon returning from his vacation, during which he submits to further training at Lurgan Sahib's, he contemplates telling his schoolmates of his doings—knowing that he may then get a reprieve of a few days of life but no more. By the end of the novel, Kim carries the Russians' letters on his chest, but this writing of espionage seems literally to infect him. The increasing literal and figurative burden of letters on his chest—the writing of empire—leads to a series of breakdowns, and at the end of the novel Kim is severely damaged, a text whose meanings are severely constrained and possibly destroyed by the dictates of power.

When Kim is conscripted into imperial service and his linguistic and cultural facility is harnessed into the service of colonial espionage, he is reinscribed in other languages, re-produced by his double education as an imperial spy (both at his school and by his multiple fathers: Mahbub Ali, Lurgan Sahib, Colonel Creighton, and the rest). As his initial ability to signify autonomously is controlled and channeled by imperial powers, Kim becomes a discursive product, produced by language and by writing, often literalized in the struggle between English and Urdu.

In *Kim*, there are thus several ways in which Kipling explores the problems of language and agency, paralleling the character Kim with *Kim* the text, exploring the question of how, in an imperial context, language can be used to exert control and to build autonomy. Language in this novel includes not only verbal codes but also nonverbal ones. In the first section of the novel, Kim's prowess in language consists of verbal and nonverbal skills, for his body is also an active participant in the game of multiple signification. Kim's body is not only a surface that carries writing, readable by others, but also a text whose meanings he can deliberately change for specific purposes. Indeed, Kim seems to have equal prowess over the language of his body, over a system of signification that extends beyond the verbal, over a body that enters into multiple disguises that employ both clothing and knowledge of bodily gestures. As he, a consummate actor, shifts from one guise to another, changing clothes and skin color, the play of his body constructs multiple selves, working against the fixity of a single label.

Early on, we are told that Kim's "half-caste" foster mother "insisted with tears that he should wear European clothes" as she attempted to fix a certain identity upon him, in the external mark of the gear that covers his body (51). But Kim has the inner flexibility to "act" as any kind of boy—Hindu, Muslim, or European—and possesses an actor's wardrobe, "his costume" or "his properties," the accouterments that enable that magical flexibility (51). Thus, his body is not confined to a single place, racial identity, or form of cover. As he begins his travels with the lama, he changes into the garb of a low-caste Hindu boy (63). Later, as Mahbub Ali's horse-boy, he changes yet again, into a "Mohammedan" disguise (179). As Lurgan Sahib later tells him, this mobility is not just a form of revelry or an exercise of freedom: it is literally a matter of life and death when Kim is employed in the Great Game, for if he makes one false step of bodily gesture or cultural knowledge, those among whom he is spying would kill him. After his capture, this mobility is halted, as Kim is forced to wear army clothes that fix his identity. Still later, as a well-schooled player of the Game, Kim relearns how to utilize that cultural mobility in the service of the Game but does not have the same autonomy as before. He can no longer disguise himself and requires help from others, as we will see. In the first section, however, neither skin color nor clothes can control his body's ability to signify or fix the cultural mobility of Kim. His body participates actively in various systems of nonverbal signification. As long as he has the independence to signify as he pleases, Kim has the power of hybrid disguise, of multiple cross-dressing, of controlling the readings of those around him.

In *Something of Myself*, Kipling describes *Kim* as a "plotless" narrative (82). In fact, the novel is carefully organized into three very discrete sections: chapters 1 through 4, the precapture idyllic section, in which Kim meets and then roams free in northern India with the lama; chapters 5 through 10, the middle section of his capture by the British army priests and "education" by Colonel Creighton and Mahbub for the Great Game (even during his vacations, Kim remains under surveillance, under the rubric of his secret training in espionage by Mahbub and Lurgan Sahib); in the third section, chapters 11 through 15, Kim rejoins the lama, supposedly to continue the latter's quest for the lost sacred river but in fact to embark on his first official project for the Great Game. This has led numerous Kipling critics to read *Kim* as a conventional tale of adolescent development, with the first segment signifying "discovery"; the second, "training"; and finally, "testing" in the third section.[14] But this three-part structure also reveals an increasingly tightening grid under which Kim is placed, each marked by the predominance of a different kind of communication, one of three orders of signification: speech, the letter, and the map; or the oral, the written, and the visual-spatial. The insouciant, verbally dexterous Kim is replaced after his capture by the letter-sending, message-intercepting Kim, who is then succeeded by the new map-making "player" of the Game. As I argue below, through each stage, Kipling explores the different interconnections between each form of language or textuality and empire in relation to his own text.

The Fantasy of the Uncaptured Kim

The first section of the novel, before Kim's "capture," is characterized by a free-flowing, unhampered autonomy that is reflected both in Kim's linguistic abilities and in the movements of his body. It is a fantasy of a world where language carries power—for Kim, its expert deployer—and no untoward consequences: agency without subjection. Like the fantasy of young Tods, who is gifted with a polyglot ability to translate to and from all tongues, Kim (the Anglo-Indian child par excellence) is presented as an effortless and comfortable inhabitant of a variety of worlds of signification. Apparently self-authored and an author of endless linguistic and bodily inventions, Kim seems to know no equal. His ingenious curses, his impudent insults, his flattery of women in the train (which procures him food and money for a ticket), his production of native proverbs with inimitable promptness, his inexhaustible fund of stories told to children and adults—all arise from a miraculous linguistic facility, a fertility or power of invention that establishes him as a dauntless, almost tyrannical producer of language and meaning. Likewise, his ability to change clothing, vernacular idiom, and hence identity suggests his capacity to produce and control bodily forms of meaning. By analogy, in the first section, the text *Kim* offers a fantasy of its own potential freedom from authoritarian control, its own ability to signify freely and to produce multiple stories unhampered by constraints of location or of racial or political affiliation.

In this prelapsarian world, Kim inhabits language in several complex ways. A generator of words and stories, Kim is also a translator and a bearer and interceptor of messages, enabling both the continuity *and* the break of signification. Like a signifier himself, carrying an author's meaning, he mediates the transfer of messages. Because of his unique linguistic talents, Kim is first able to connect with the lama. The constable, who "spoke Punjabi," turns to Kim above all the other bazar boys for help: "'O Friend of all the World, what does he say?' 'Send him hither,' said Kim, dropping from Zam-Zammah. . . . 'He is a foreigner, and thou art a buffalo'" (53). Similarly, Kim appeases a suspicious villager whom the lama blesses in his own language: "Pardesi" (a foreigner), he explains (63).

This function of translation or transport of the spoken word is extended in Kim's role as message bearer or secret apprentice for Mahbub Ali, who employs him without explanation many times almost as a form of testing and training: "Sometimes he would tell Kim to watch a man: . . . to follow him for one whole day and report every soul with whom he talked. Kim would deliver himself of his tale at evening, and Mahbub would listen without word or gesture" (66). Kim's "tale" here depends not upon fabrication but upon truth, upon accuracy of imitation, upon dependence on its original. He uses both his body and his speech to replicate the suspect he has been tracking, deploying his knowledge and ability to mimic cultural idioms and gestures. Mahbub, meanwhile, knows not to give himself or his game away by deploying either "word or gesture," both of which Kim is only too adept at reading. But Kim can also make up tales on the spot. His value to Mahbub lies in his ability to lie and not to lie—selectively: "Kim was the one soul in the world who had never told him a lie," which would have been "a fatal blot" if Mahbub did not also know that "for his own ends or Mahbub's business, Kim could lie like an Oriental" (71).

The Doubleness of Writing (in) Kim

At the same time, Kim can also function as an obstruction, interfering with or changing the direction of intent and meaning. He is an interceptor of messages, an artful eavesdropper, able to intercept spoken and written messages with increasing potency: he saves Mahbub's life by overhearing and disrupting a conspiracy against Mahbub, effectively dispatching its authors to death or jail; later, Kim intercepts the Mahratta—himself a letter of sorts, pursued by death and in pursuit of a letter—literally to rewrite and transform him, averting his death or his falling into the wrong hands, delivering him safely to Strickland (another adept player of the Game); and at the end, Kim intercepts the Russians and their incriminating letters in the final coup of the novel.

In addition, Kim is also an expert at reading messages. At this stage of the novel, Kim remains in an order of the spoken, excluded from the written. Able to signify with his body, Kim has not yet learned to write or to read writing, an order of signification that he enters only subsequent to his capture. He can read just enough not to be cheated by unscrupulous natives (75) or to "puzzle out English Police notices . . . because they affected his comfort. . . . He had been kicked as far as single letters, but did not think well of them" (147). At one point, Kim teases Mahbub Ali, reminding Mahbub how Kim hid a key letter from an enemy who was searching Mahbub's lodgings: "At that hour had I chosen, thy head was forfeit. It needed only to say to that man, 'I have here a paper concerning a horse *which I cannot read.*' And then?" (182; my emphasis). Although Kim can read the situation, guessing that this important coded letter is in fact not about a horse, he literally cannot read that letter. For the young Kim, writing is as yet a magical object that he must carry upon his chest, in an amulet tied around his neck, or something pleasantly mysterious and valuable, but it is also *unreadable*, hidden in multiple layers, in "a small wad of tissue paper wrapped in oilskin" that he bites out of a piece of bread that Mahbub flings him (69). It is something to be delivered; it earns him money and the smell of intrigue but is not something that he can decode, though he learns its power as he watches Creighton decode five pinpricks on a map of India to identify five renegade kings.

But Kim is still a highly adept reader of the world around him. This ability to read both enables his survival and makes him attractive for the Game. S. P. Mohanty has argued persuasively that both Kim and Mowgli, by "their ability to read the world around them," are crucial to a "desire" in Kipling's texts "to be invisible, to belong, to contain the threat of any real encounter, to observe without being observed—in short to rule colonial India without seeming to do so."[15] Reading the world is continuous with imperial surveillance and rule: "There is a continuity . . . between learning to observe carefully, to observe without being observed (as Kim often does), to interpret people and situations, to move stealthily and unnoticed, and to assume roles. Both Mowgli and Kim learn through their narratives the value of doing these things—to inhabit perfectly without being tied down to the place of habitation; like their roles and disguises, they discard their places at will" (Mohanty, 32). Only later are Kim's talents suborned for imperial service. To begin with, Kim's capacity to read is multivalent and dangerous to those in power.

Endlessly curious without any particular purpose in a way that is suggestive of Satan in paradise, spying on Adam and Eve, Kim eavesdrops on the lama and the curator of the museum or watches Colonel Creighton read Mahbub's coded message. Kipling's language here suggests that Kim is almost serpentlike. "Instead of slinking away, he lay close to the grass and wormed nearer to the house. . . . Flat on his belly lay Kim, almost touching the high wheels" (84–85). Even when he can neither hear what these colonial officials say nor read their letters, Kim is able to "learn what he wanted" because he is an unmatched reader of the human body (86). As Creighton reads the letter from Mahbub, Kim reads the reader's face and body language. The "darkening of his countenance," the omission of his "attempt to look for the speaker, showed Kim that he knew," and "Kim . . . took good note" (84).

At this point in the novel, while Kim is a reader of the body or of the world as text, he poses a danger to the order of empire, for his freewheeling is too uncurtailed in its brilliance. His powerful energies and abilities to lie and tell stories and to read what is not meant for him to read are focused not on the Indian world but on the English one, from which he gathers information that he then disseminates carelessly among the natives. Innately crafty, he knows not to tell too much, but his loyalties are not tethered to any cause or race. Indeed, he regards those of his race with suspicion. Only when they appropriate him in the name of his father does Kim become subsumed to the service of empire. When critics denounce Kipling for Kim's disguised imperial service, they ignore the possibility that the text—or the author—may share their chagrin at this induction. By analogy, the novel suggests its own power to disseminate information, "true" or otherwise, its own power to enable or hamper communication and to decode signs in the world it occupies. Indeed, by describing some of the operations of the secret service, the forms of their disguises, or the methods of their message bearing, Kipling opens himself to risk, for he exposes some of the secret workings of empire.

Thus, before his capture, Kim is established as in control of the power of signification: able to generate stories, to transport messages or translate, to intercept and change meanings, to read bodily languages. Moreover, Kim is apparently uncontrolled by linguistic signs. His lack of a name is then quite significant. Nicknames such as "The Friend of the World" and "The Friend of the Stars" suggest his lack of geographical identification. No one (except the narrator) until his capture calls him Kim. He names himself when it suits him, as the lama's "chela," but we are left in no doubt of the fictiveness and transience of that name. In Althusserian terms, we are given names, or labels, placed in the world, so that we can be interpellated through our given identities. By evading the signification that, unknown to him, is tied around his neck, awaiting its fulfillment, Kim is free from the fixity of identity, for no one knows his name. When the lama is asked to confirm Kim's story, he can say only,

> "But I remember now, he said he was of this world—a Hindu."
> "And his name?"
> "That I did not ask. Is he not my disciple?"
> "His country—his race—his village? Mussalman—Sikh—Hindu—Jain—low caste or high?"
> "Why should I ask? There is neither high nor low in the Middle Way." (68)

Only the lama seems able to accept the unimportance of that lack of fixity, of place, in the system of signification.[16]

Later, when Kim has been given a name and escapes the army only to be inducted into the Game, he longs for his lost namelessness and for the seeming glamour of the Game's players, of having "like the Babu . . . [or the Mahratta, E23] the dignity of a letter and a number—and a price upon his head!" (209–10). Likewise, Hurree Babu, when Kim first encounters him, is identified by his namelessness: "He is a writer of tales for a certain Colonel. His honor is great only in Simla, and it is noticeable that he has no name, but only a number and letter—that is a custom among us" (208). But Kim's namelessness at the beginning of the novel is of a wholly different nature from that of the Game's players, which constitutes a form of branding, a dehumanizing substitution of letter and number for the human. The loss of the Game's players' names reinscribes them as imperial tools, erased from the records if killed in their work. When Kim becomes a player of the Game, he becomes subject to its new chains of signification, a "chain-man" indeed, entoiled in a system of power that he may at times manipulate but cannot escape.

Unlike Kipling's stories of children, in *Kim* the move from speech to writing corresponds almost exactly to the shift from childhood to adolescence. Once Kim falls into the hands of his captors, he enters a new order—of writing—marking the onset of his adolescence and the curtailment of his freedom. But Kim does not simply have to learn writing and use it instead of speech; he is also increasingly written upon. Writing becomes an emblem of his conscription to empire, a form of signification wholly different from speech or body language, imposing new constraints but also enabling new modes of resistance.

Kim's Capture: The Fall into Writing

Once his name is discovered and his identity has been fixed upon him, Kim is required to speak English instead of Hindi, and his body becomes constrained both in its movements and in its ability to signify. Now Kim turns to the stratagem of the letter. In his first letter, dictated to a native scribe, he begs Mahbub to rescue him. "A priest clothed me and gave me a new name," he writes, as if the two were coterminous (150). Instead of the ease of hybrid "costume" and the freedom to "squat as only natives can" (149), Kim has been forced into a rough school uniform, military clothes that "rasp" his body and "silence" him like "a wild animal" (144). Disabled by his new clothes and name, both instruments and signs of his capture, Kim knows that he cannot run away, not only because the clothes would identify him but also because they would "tire him out" (148). Literally weighed down, barred from the ease of movement and changeable identity he once enjoyed, Kim's body transfers its powers of signification to the form of the letter, which suddenly begins to proliferate in the text. In some ways an obvious consequence of Kim's imprisonment, this new mode of the letter embodies the mediation that has become necessary to contact potential rescuers, going where Kim cannot go.

The instrument of his capture, writing is also Kim's first act of resistance. In composing and sending his first letter, Kim evades the surveillance of his new captors and invents a coded language that may be read by others but not understood except by its intended recipient. This resistant aspect of writing seems to be effected precisely by the fact of obstruction, the halting of flow — of Kim's movements, of his body's ability to signify, and of his speech. Of course, Kim's main desire in writing is to return to those earlier forms of signification. But because he literally cannot write, being cut off for the first time from language, he has to rely on the services of a letter writer. He summons one by indulging in a vigorous exercise of the very power of language that is under threat: "Kim hailed a sweeper, who promptly retorted with a piece of unnecessary insolence in the natural belief that the European boy could not follow it. The low quick answer undeceived him. Kim put his fettered soul into it, thankful for the late chance to abuse someone in the tongue he knew best. 'And now, go to the nearest letter-writer and tell him to come here. I would write a letter'" (148). Having undergone the rigors of military silencing, Kim's powers of language must now be schooled and transformed into another mode. Created by necessity, this new mode is one of silence and coded double meanings. "At Umballa I carried the news of the bay mare's pedigree," he writes, carefully recoding and concealing Mahbub's code of the "white stallion" but also covertly reminding Mahbub of the dangerous service Kim has rendered — and thereby asking for help. His second letter (also to Mahbub), sent after he has "escaped" from further surveillance and training for his first school vacation, craftily asks "the Hand of Friendship to turn aside the Whip of Calamity," in other words, that Mahbub should mediate for him with Colonel Creighton, whose authority he has temporarily defied (176). Kim's letters thus represent the coexistence of constraint and evasion: actuated by the necessity of resistance and self-disguise, they cannot be pinned down like his body. Not only is his language veiled and full of hidden meanings, but his writing remains unsigned, unmarked by his name. Indeed, by not signing his letters, he also avoids being bound by his "new name."

Unlike speech, writing defers the delivery of meaning, suggesting a difficulty that is different from the immediacy of speech. It is a delayed mode, born of constriction and dependent on mediation. It is also the result of materially different circumstances. Although Derridean theory has renewed the links between speech and writing, contending that all language is predicated on loss or absence, nevertheless, in an everyday sense, writing still marks a greater sense of absence (of speaker or audience) and desire than does speech, as well as the potential misconstrual or miscarriage of meaning. In Kipling's canny story of the invention of writing in *Just So Stories*, for instance, a Stone Age child, Taffy, invents writing because she is literally absent from her audience—her mother—and needs a form of communication that will carry messages across space and time. But in the process, the messenger to whom she entrusts her letter is almost killed, and the message is miscarried, because this new form is far more difficult to understand and to convey.[17] For Kim, writing is similarly treacherous, not a source of pleasure, as speech is, but the result of need in a situation of loss. It also carries a cost, which he tries to defer (as in the first letter that he sends through the letter writer) but eventually has to pay—in more ways than he can foresee.

Through the predicament of Kim, Kipling's text alludes to the necessities of its own self-disguise, to the difficulties that shape the act of writing and the secret resistances that writing may enable. It presents writing as inherently double: as able to evade control and prohibition through its capacity for secret meanings but also as a mode of power that can be used to inscribe (indeed, imprint) the subjects that are placed under its control. From this point of Kim's capture onward, *Kim* elaborates this twofold aspect of writing. While suggesting these possibilities of resistance and subversion, it also shows how writing can be used by the Game, for the purposes of empire.

As an art of empire, writing becomes the mode of Kim's indoctrination for the Game, suggesting how, as Kim learns to write, he is written upon. His schooling at St. Xavier's is paralleled in his schooling in the Great Game, which reshapes him as a user of language, both verbal and bodily. Empire is a possessive, dictatorial parent; it wants to have—and to (re)produce—Kim in its own name. Kim is retrained in abilities that he first has to lose and then relearn according to the specifications of the Game. Central to his new education is literally learning to write and read—in English. Indeed, for Kim, learning writing seems synonymous with learning English, a language in which, unlike the many Indian languages he knows, he has been deficient. Earlier, when Father

Victor grabs his amulet, Kim protests in a broken English "the tinny, saw-cut English of the native-bred" (132). The fact that he speaks English at all makes him stand out as not wholly a "native," but its brokenness also marks him as lacking the requisite fluency of the master race. The subsequent struggle for Kim's allegiance is fought in terms of his language, figured as the struggle for priority between English and Hindi. Kim thus becomes a palimpsest from which a prior language must be effaced in order for a new language to rewrite and redefine him.

Zohreh Sullivan has identified this middle section of the novel as a Lacanian fall into language, a shift from Kim's earlier mode of the imaginary into the symbolic, from the maternal comforts of Indian freedom into the prohibitive regime and disciplinary laws of white fathers. "It is here that Kim recognizes his loss of something nameless, a sense of self that was once autonomous, free, 'Imaginary.' . . . His entry into 'the Gates of Learning' is also an entry into language and into an understanding of the rules of culture that he must master through language" (Sullivan, 161–62). While my reading shares this recognition of Kim's loss, I would disagree that Kim enters language at this point, for he has already exercised a powerful capacity for language prior to his capture. In a more complicated shift, the order of British paternalism inserts Kim not simply into language but into a new kind of language that requires the suppression and demotion of his earlier languages and skills.

After his capture, English (as opposed to Urdu) comes to represent this new mode of signification in which—as it is the language of his father (and of empire)—he will be indoctrinated. In fact, Kim is now literally rewritten (upon) in a new language. This new language is not literally the English language but is represented by his turn to English, and away from his Indian languages. After three months at St. Xavier's, Kim is found reveling in his newly learned skill, which allows him not to depend on letter writers: "Moreover, this was magic worth anything else—he could write. In three months he had discovered how men can speak to each other without a third party, at the cost of half an anna and a little knowledge" (173). Repeatedly he boasts of it, as in his reunion with Mahbub: "I have learnt to read and to write English a little at the *madrissah*. . . . I shall soon be altogether a Sahib" (178). As Kim wavers between English and Urdu, the Game teaches him to subordinate and utilize his knowledge of the latter (and of India) for the purposes of the Game. Though English is not Kim's preferred language, he learns to define himself as a "Sahib," and therefore as superior to Mahbub Ali or Hurree Babu, by virtue of his possession of English. Others validate this: Lurgan addresses him as "O'Hara" only when Kim proves his worth — by using English to fight off hypnosis (202). But literal English is only a metaphor for the language of the Game, the codes of signification that are inscribed on its players, who must commit themselves wholly to the Game, believing unquestioningly in its founding assumptions of the right to rule; in British cultural, racial, and linguistic superiority; and in the utter necessity of what must be done, at all costs, for the empire.

Kim's first instructor in this system is Colonel Creighton, who, on the train to St. Xavier's, Kim's expensive new school, tells Kim "to be diligent and enter the survey of India as a chain-man" (166). At first, Kim does not follow Creighton's English, and he is happier when Creighton turns to "fluent and picturesque Urdu" (166). But Creighton makes it clear that although Kim should retain his knowledge of Indian languages for the purposes of the Game, ultimately, Kim's allegiance must be to the British Empire. And Kim proves himself worthy. Delighting in the challenges of danger and espionage, Kim remarks that unlike him, the "half-caste boys" (the term Kipling uses for the despised children of interracial alliances) try to dissociate themselves from Indians, pretending to know nothing about the "black men" or their language. Creighton approves, confirming that Kim's whiteness is precisely what enables him to acknowledge and utilize his knowledge of natives and native languages, for he can have no such fear of being misread as Indian:

> "There are many boys [at school] who despise the black men."
>
> "Their mothers were bazar-women," said Kim. He knew well there is no hatred like that of the half-caste for his brother-in-law.
>
> "True, but thou art a Sahib and the Son of a Sahib. Therefore, do not at any time be led to contemn the black men. I have known boys newly entered into the service of the Government who feigned not to understand the talk or the customs of black men. Their pay was cut for ignorance. There is no sin so great as ignorance. Remember this."
>
> Several times in the course of the long twenty-four hours . . . did the Colonel send for Kim, always developing this latter text. (167)

What Kim is learning then is not simply English but a system of racial and cultural hierarchies, a coding of human worth according to Creighton's "text."

Prior to his capture, Kim was a translator between various Indian languages, all of which no single native could speak. As he becomes able to translate between English and those Indian languages, he learns a new kind of power, for he is programmed to ally himself with the ruling race. Even though he has to retain his old expertise, the Game requires a certain distancing from his earlier loyalties. On his first "vacation," Kim is subjected to a test endured by few—Lurgan Sahib's powerful hypnotism, which he resists only when he switches from thinking in Hindi to multiplication tables in English (202). The order of mathematics (in which Kim has come to excel) and the English language together seem to release him from a form of tyranny—hypnosis—enabling him to read for himself. Hindi, his language of first proficiency, cannot effect that independence.

Urdu/Hindi remains with him, resurfacing at crucial moments of crisis. There are times when Kim forgets that he is a "Sahib," when he has to switch consciously from Hindi or Urdu to English. It still represents his childhood and the gifts of creativity, magical inventiveness, and linguistic generation. But slowly, the novel documents how Kim is schooled by the writing of the Game to lose those earlier strengths, especially his wild, subversive linguistic energy. Not only is he "educated," but he is also tamed, reined, and broken in. The continual metaphor of Kim as a colt that peppers the text from his "capture" onward suggests the "breaking-in" to which, in an earlier story, Aurelian McGoggin, also described as a young "colt," had to submit.[18] Whereas McGoggin is struck by colonial aphasia, Kim is struck, as Sara Suleri points out, by a psychic aphasia that results in his repetition of his name: "Who is Kim—Kim—Kim?"[19] As Kim is instructed in the Game, he acquires a new ability to *act* from Lurgan Sahib. But this is not acting on his own behalf or action in the sense of autonomy. Increasingly acting for others, Kim gradually loses the autonomy he began with.

Kim thus embodies the functions of not only reader and writer but also of the text, a text that attempts to control how it is read though it may, as in the struggle over the lama's map, get badly torn. He becomes the letter that may or may not signify, the letter that may become emptied of signification or upon which only a certain significance may be pinned. Like a letter himself, he is delivered literally from door to door—Colonel Creighton delivers him from the army camp to St. Xavier's; Mahbub delivers him to Lurgan Sahib's; and Hurree Babu, in pursuit of the letters that Kim carries on his chest, dogs his travels with the lama.

The costs of this new form of writing and rewriting on Kim become increasingly apparent. Soon after his "capture," he begins to misread. In an incident he often recalls later, Kim misreads Mahbub Ali's refusal to take him away from the army camp as Mahbub's "betrayal" of Kim (156). In fact, Mahbub enables Kim's deliverance from the army camp, albeit to deliver him instead into the Great Game. Although Kim retains his ability to curse, it becomes a relief from frustration. And whereas the earlier Kim had complete autonomy over the changes of his costume and the language of his body, subsequent to his capture Kim has to ask for help. To get away from St. Xavier's, Kim goes to a courtesan to change him into a native again. Later, he is taken to Huneefa, the old blind woman who hypnotizes him to transform him into a proper player, leaving him as inert and helpless as a puppet.

The paradigm that overshadows Kim's education most ominously in this middle section is of colonial silencing, epitomized by the incident of the voice-box. On his first night at Lurgan Sahib's, Kim is left to sleep in a dark room: "That was no cheerful night; the room being overfull of voices and music. Kim was waked twice by someone calling his name. The second time he set out in search and ended by bruising his nose against a box that certainly spoke with a human tongue, but in no sort of human accent" (198). Lurgan's efforts to test Kim evoke his new pride at being a sahib, but that is a precarious state, to which he has to "cling." The boy who once thought his amulet was magic is now able to undo this machine's magic by destroying its voice: "He slipped off his jacket and plunged it into the box's mouth. Something long and round bent under the pressure, there was a whirr and the voice stopped" (199). The incident confirms Kim's candidacy for the Game, as Kim demonstrates his ingenuity and force of will, even though the disembodied voice terrifies him because it knows his "name." It also indicates Kim's powers of subversion, for he can interrupt and destroy the workings of a mechanism like the Game. Yet this incident can ultimately be read as a dark omen of colonial silencing, in which Kim's complicity in imposing that silence in no way reduces its extension to himself, as a machine in the making that is itself to be silenced. It becomes a curious emblem of a struggle in darkness against an enemy that one does not know.

When Kim returns to St. Xavier's, he has stories that he cannot tell (210). Whereas the child Kim was unable to suppress his contraband knowledge of imminent war, disseminating it as a magical "prophecy" over the Indian countryside, the new Kim has learned the necessities of colonial silence. Later, when Kim is about to leave the school, a jealous schoolmate insinuates that Kim's appointment to a governmental post is a nepotistic benefit of Creighton's illegitimate paternity. Kim swallows the insult, subsuming personal pride to the interests of empire: "Kim, instead of retaliating, did not even use language" (224). The language he could delight in earlier to exert his superiority over all and sundry must now be subordinated to the secrecies of the Game.

This middle section of *Kim* charts how writing can be a resistant form (for both Kim and for Kipling), a response of necessity to obstruction or difficulty, and simultaneously a tool of subjection. As the Game "educates" Kim, it transforms him into an instrument that can no longer exercise autonomy over its meanings. Analogously, *Kim* the text, subject to the dictates of imperial expectation and censorship, may be similarly circumscribed in what it can say or do. At the same time, Kipling suggests, writing can enable Kim to resist, to develop covert meanings, as *Kim* the text does, more so than Kim the boy. In the last section, as *Kim* traces the further damage and circumscription of Kim through the complicated issue of map making, the text *Kim* begins to separate itself from the story of Kim, distancing itself from the modes of signification that surround him.

Map Making, Medicine, and Magic — The End of Kim

The third section of the novel inaugurates Kim's supposed release from "schooling," to enter the greater bondage of the Game under the guise of the lama's *chela*. It also marks a point at which Kim moves from adolescence to manhood. We are now told repeatedly of his "beauty," his attractiveness to women. As the lama observes proudly, "It is no longer a child, but a man, ripened to wisdom, walking as a physician" (238). The text, however, does not support this sense of "ripening," for although he carries medicine with him that he applies to others,

Kim is no "physician." Himself in need of a cure, Kim is shadowed by an increasing sickness, as if debilitated by the burdens of the Game.

If the first and second sections of the novel can be characterized roughly under the tokens of "speech" and the "letter," respectively, then the form that dominates the last section is the "map." The map becomes a central, more complex metaphor for the kinds of writing that imperialism imposes on Kim, as well as for the kinds that may offer a challenge to it. Speech, the dominant form of the first section, allowed the greatest freedom and autonomy for Kim, while writing, the dominant form of the second section, both enabled a mode of resistance and represented the system that reinscribed him in new imperial codes. The map, the dominant textual form of the last section, reveals the increasing tightening of the forces upon Kim and sharpens the contrast in the choices open to him. It is at once a sign of his abilities (and debilitation) and an alternative form of signification.

Equipped with a map maker's tool-kit—compass, paint box, brushes—Kim resumes his travels with the lama, now trained not only as an imperial scribe but also as a map maker. Maps epitomize the art of colonial surveillance: combining writing, drawing, and calculation, they function as crucial forms of information about a land and peoples, about ways literally to invade and control, just as they subject the terrain that they record to the grid of a foreign signifying system. Ian Baucom writes, "Within [the imperial] archive, the map occupies a position of privilege. Its fiction remains the one most seductive to the imperial state: the fiction of fixity, of ordered, visible, and bounded space."[20] Map making is a form that reveals how adept—and how subject—Kim is to the order of empire. Even before he leaves school, he is taken by Mahbub Ali on one of Mahbub's vacations to "the mysterious city of Bikanir . . . where, in defiance of the contract—the Colonel ordered him to make a map of that wild, walled city" (218). Bikanir is a fortified city ruled by an independent king beyond the purveyance of the British Empire. Kim's secret entry into it, disguised as a horse-boy, involves risking his life. It also involves producing a "written report" that would be of use to an invading British army. This map making and writing are clearly valuable work for the empire. But this work is instigated as both a command and a violation of Kim's period of traineeship. Willing though Kim may be, he has no choice but to do as he is told. Moreover, it involves the direct conscription of Kim's body. Because he cannot use survey instruments in this city, "Kim (is) forced to pace all his distances by means of a bead rosary" (218), using both his feet and his rosary to count, becoming himself literally an instrument of imperial surveillance.

Kim proves himself so well at this task that Mahbub rewards him ceremoniously with coming-of-age gifts—lavish clothes and a gun. But then, in a strange lapse, the narrator's voice disrupts narrative time and convention, to leap into a future moment: "The report in its unmistakable St. Xavier's running script, and the brown, yellow and lake-daubed map, was on hand a few years ago (a careless clerk [mis]filed it . . .), but by now the pencil characters must be almost illegible" (218). Reaching into a time in which Kim is absent or unlocatable, this comment carries darker implications. If Kim's writing and map making are subject to such disrepair and devaluation, then how long Kim himself can be preserved is yet more uncertain. Like Kim, these instruments of the imperial Game are easily misfiled and lost, obliterated once they outlive their use.

In contrast to Kim's imperial map making, another kind of cartography described by Kipling represents a rather different worldview and discourse: the lama's. In the third section, when Kim rejoins the lama, announcing happily that he has become a "scribe" for the empire, the lama pulls out a map of his own:

> "And also," the old man chuckled, "I write pictures of the Wheel of Life. Three days to a picture. . . . I will show thee my art—not for pride's sake, but because thou must learn. The Sahibs have not *all* this world's wisdom."
>
> He drew from under the table a sheet of strangely scented yellow Chinese paper, the brushes, and slab of Indian ink. In cleanest, severest outline he had traced the Great Wheel with its six spokes, whose center is the conjoined Hog, Snake, and Dove, (Ignorance, Anger, and Lust), and whose compartments are all the Heavens and Hells, and all the chances of human life. Men say that the Bodhisat Himself first drew it with grains of rice upon dust, to teach his disciples the cause of things. Many ages have crystallized it into a most wonderful convention crowded with hundreds of little figures whose every line carries a meaning. Few can translate the picture-parable; there are not twenty in all the world who can draw it surely without a copy: of those who can both draw and expound are but three. (240)

Set up as a rival and parallel to the art of empire (the sahib's "wisdom"), the lama's map is presented as something extraordinary, an alternative form of "art" that Kim may also learn. But instead of mapping a geographical terrain, it maps literally another world, another reality, the "Wheel of Life," which is representative of quite different values, desires, and goals. "Crowded with hundreds of little figures," this "picture-parable" is saturated with meaning, a text overdetermined with significance. Its "figures" are dual, suggesting both representations of human bodies and abstract numerals or linguistic signifiers. In creating the phrase "I write pictures," the lama's language draws attention to the combination of the written and the visual that his map making represents. Even in Urdu, "to write" (and not draw) pictures is an incorrect construction. But the lama's conflation of letter (writing) and picture (drawing) suggests a more advanced order of signification that reaches beyond the spoken or written, as well as beyond the writing and map making of empire. At the same time, through this duality, instead of establishing control over the space it codifies, this map making insists on the mystery of that which it attempts to approximate.

Gazing upon it, Kim pays a tribute that seems quite sincerely to recognize something superior to his imperial education:

> "I have a little learned to draw," said Kim. "But this is a marvel beyond marvels."
> "I have written it for many years," said the lama. "Time was when I could write it all between one lamp-lighting and the next. I will teach thee the art— after due preparation; and I will show thee the meaning of the Wheel." (171)

Throughout the novel, the depiction of the lama alternates between absurdity and dignity: on one hand, childlike, gullible, and loved but duped by Kim for the benefit of the Game; and on the other, as an alternative, otherworldly father for Kim, promising unqualified love and bent upon a spiritual quest. But here he seems elevated to a new position as an artist who not only rivals but also holds out a possible alternative for Kim and for the making of art under the constraints of empire. As he draws out this map, the lama begins to represent a mode of signification that might draw Kim out of the modes that bind and overwrite him.

At the very beginning, when we see the lama conversing with the curator of the Lahore museum, this map making is foreshadowed as an alternative to imperial epistemology and cartography. At first the curator is clearly dominant, as he shows the lama what the lama has long sought: historical (and holy) relics of Buddhist art. He curates a museum that, by definition, maps (or categorizes) and houses native artifacts and, in so doing, produces the paradoxical demise of the culture it preserves.[21] In having documented and taxonomized the products of the lama's culture, the curator's scholarship exerts its power, its capacity to know and control that knowledge. His famous gift—the new glasses he offers for the lama's battered old pair—suggests the imposition of vision, the bestowal of sight that will frame—and contain—what the lama can see.[22] The lama in turn is full of wonder and gratitude: "For the first time [the lama] heard of the labors of European scholars, who by the help of these and a hundred other documents have identified the Holy Places of Buddhism. Then he was shown a mighty map, spotted and traced with yellow. The brown finger followed the Curator's pencil from point to point" (56–57).

However, the brown finger soon stops following the curator's pencil, when the lama asks a question the answer to which cannot be located on any European map. "There are things which [the European scholars] have not sought out," he says (57). Recounting the story of the Lord's River, created by the Fallen Arrow, "the lama drew a long breath. 'Where is that River? Fountain of Wisdom, where fell the arrow?' 'Alas, my brother, I do not know,' said the Curator. . . . 'If I knew, think you I would not cry it aloud? . . . I do not know. I do not know.'" (58). In this repetition of "I do not know," the control and supremacy of the curator suddenly gives way, as the lama turns to him as an equal. "We are both bound, thou and I, my brother," says the lama; "we are both seekers, thou and I" (58). The tables are now turned, as the lama quite innocently points out limitations of European epistemology, gaps in what the Europeans have not sought or found.[23] As a corrective to this imperial geography, the lama's map making seems to offer a superior form of artistry: "'When I return, having found the River, I will bring thee a written picture of the Padma Samthora such as I used to make on silk at the lamassery. Yes—and of the Wheel of Life,' he chuckled, 'for we be craftsmen together, thou and I'" (60). This is the map that the lama presents to Kim upon their reunion, almost as if Kim were the surrogate for the curator, to whom the lama made that promise. But Kim is not yet settled into his role as curator or ethnographer for imperial service, and he is favored with the lama's map not as an act of fealty, for the map to be added to artifacts in a museum, but to be educated otherwise. Even in the scene with the curator, in return for the glasses, the lama reciprocates with a more telling gift: his pen case, "of ancient design, Chinese, of an iron that is not smelted these days" (60). In exchange for vision, the lama offers the curator a frame, highly wrought, that will contain instruments of writing. Itself a rare form of art to which Europeans can only aspire, this pen case may symbolically frame the writing of the pen it encases. By extension, what the lama has to offer may frame the writing of empire.

This promised map triggers the penultimate crisis of the novel and, indeed, the moment when Kim is drawn (at least momentarily) out of the imperial Game. It also provides a critical turning point for the plot: the Russian that Kim has been shadowing demands the lama's map; when refused, he strikes the lama, evoking the vengeance of Kim as well as the local coolies. In the ensuing confusion, Kim and Hurree Babu are able to grab the incriminating papers they seek. In this sense, it is easy to read the lama's map, like the lama himself, as merely an instrument for the success of Kim's imperial mission. But that does not account for the symbolic weight of this incident or its mode of representation.

In the moment of fury when Kim flings himself upon the Russian and batters the man's head on the rocks, he is not thinking of the Game or strategizing how to serve imperial power: his act is an unthinking one that prioritizes the insult to the lama over any effort to play spy. Later, when he breaks down, "hysterical" with exhaustion, Kim laments his involvement with the Game, regretting that he had "walked [the lama] too far" (after the Russians), using the lama as a cover for Kim's own purposes (320). It marks the point from which Kim's loyalty to the Game wavers, as he becomes increasingly sick—of the Game—loaded down by the Russians' packet of letters and books that he carries: "If someone duly authorized would only take delivery of them the Great Game might play itself for aught he then cared" (320). By the end, Kim, unlike any of the other players even at their most wounded or tired state, and even though he responsibly completes his mission, has no desire to continue the Game.

But why should this map produce this crisis, a crisis both for the plot and for the future of Kim? The struggle over the lama's map occasions a crisis over two opposed modes of seeing, reading and writing, both embodied by map making. One is the European imperialist one, which violates as it desires and imposes itself on others. Represented here by the Russians and also by Kim's imperial map making, it is the mode that seeks to appropriate and supersede the other. The Russian and Frenchman are spies and experts at map making. They carry precious instruments and tools of espionage: a theodolite, "books, inkstands, paint-boxes, compasses, and rulers" (303). They want the lama's map to add it to their museum of colonial (and colonizing) knowledge, their collection of native objects. "What is he doing? It is very curious," they ask (288). But what really draws them is the desire to "make their mark," to compete with and overwrite what they regard as a threatening form of art and cultural value.

When the Russian and the Frenchman gaze upon the ancient lama, who, oblivious to them, continues explaining his map to Kim, they read him as a text, "a picture," that they already know and must depreciate as a representative of a culture older than their own.

> "Look!" said the Frenchman. "It is like the picture for the birth of a religion—the first teacher and the first disciple. Is he a Buddhist?"
>
> "Of some debased kind," the other answered. "There are no true Buddhists among the Hills. But look at the folds of the drapery. Look at his eyes—how insolent! Why does this make one feel that we are so young a people?" (289)

In accordance with a tradition of European discourse that decried the "rude antiquity" of Indian culture (in favor of Europe's more evolved modernity),[24] the Russian enacts his sense of youthful inadequacy through irrational violence. "He struck passionately at a tall weed. 'We have nowhere left our mark yet. . . . *That* . . . is what disquiets me'" (289). Like a schoolboy, the Russian "scowled at the placid face and the monumental calm" of the lama, poring over his treasured map. It is this ancient culture and landscape, represented by the lama's text and body, upon which this representative of the "young people" feels the need to "make his mark." For one problem seems to be, Kipling reiterates, that "the lama was an artist, as well as a wealthy Abbot in his own place," whose art is beyond the Russian: "The lama warmed to his work, and one of the strangers sketched him in the quick-fading light. 'That is enough,' the man said at last brusquely. 'I cannot understand him, but I want that picture. He is a better artist than I'" (290). The Russian first reduces the lama to a picture and then tears his map, before hitting the lama full upon his face. This imperial desire to map one's own presence and superiority upon another culture, to know and to appropriate it, is represented here as also an oedipal one, an anxiety of influence that is both violent and violating. It is the key, as Forster too would later suggest, to the British imperial desire (a cultural anxiety of influence) to mark the face of the Indian landscape with an "intersecting" system, a "net"—of roads, trains, telegraph lines, bridges—that would make it navigable, knowable, and controllable: a writing of empire that would overwrite and efface to make its own mark instead.[25] In a recent essay, Suvir Kaul notes, "*Kim* is a remarkable colonial novel in that it features virtually no violence."[26] But this climactic moment of violence underlines the systemic symbolic violence—with material consequences—with which the novel is in fact concerned.

When the Russian tears the lama's map and then slaps the lama, the two acts are rendered as almost synonymous. "Oh, sar! sar! You must not hit holy man!" cries Hurree Babu. "Chela! He has defiled the Written Word!" responds the lama, as if the blow upon his face is indistinguishable from that upon his map (291). Like Kim's body, the lama's body and writing are conflated in their vulnerability to the inimical mode of reading and writing that confront them. Later, the lama makes explicit this continuity between himself and his map. The tear in the map, he tells Kim, represents the torn past of his life, "rent" across the house of birth and childhood to "the empty House of the Senses"; the remaining untorn part, "the Breadth of a fingernail," augurs the short remaining part of his life (310). The map, in turn, is described as "brutally disfigured," as if it were a bodily thing, subject to injury, like the lama, who becomes sick from this point on (311).

The lama poring over his map, then, suggests another way of reading and seeing: a mode not of imposition on others but of self-scrutiny and self-interrogation. It is symptomatic of turning inward, of mapping interiority, not of imposing oneself upon others. Mohanty writes that the lama is a poor reader, for unlike Kim, he has no desire to "dive into" the world around him.[27] But the lama is a different kind of reader: not of the external or social world but of the internal psyche in relation to the world. When Kim is captured by the English priests, the lama reads their faces, and the lama's own unconscious desires, better than anyone else: "I see now that the sign of the Red Bull was a sign for me as well as for thee. All Desire is red—and evil. I will do penance and find my river alone" (141). His mode of reading seems to shut out the world, because it is directed toward self-questioning, not surveillance; it also is sanctioned by Kipling's novel. The lama is right to question his own desire (unlike anyone else in the novel) and its effects on others, for in his attachment to Kim he has become reattached to the world that his quest requires him to abandon. Only the lama reads the crisis with the Russian as connected to his inner state—as a rebuke for his pleasure in the physical world—unlike the players of the Game, who cannot question their role in the system they inhabit. "Had I been passionless, the evil blow would have done only bodily evil.... But my mind was not abstracted" (301). When Kim breaks down in tears, he exhibits some of this self-questioning, blaming himself for the lama's illness (320). The tearing of the map, then, also tears Kim along the fault lines that the novel has exposed. It represents not only a choice between two loyalties or fathers (the worldly Game versus the unworldly lama) but also two opposed modes of reading and seeing, or forms of hermeneutic ethics and conduct. The lama's map making and reading are only implied and not further elaborated in Kipling's text, but they represent an alternative principle that may or may not be available for Kim the character or *Kim* the text.

From here on, Kim becomes increasingly sick, as if he were also a damaged map, overwritten by empire and sick of his work. Most critics tend to read the end of *Kim* as Kim's textually validated return to imperial service. In her comparison of Kipling's and Dickens's deployment of gender and race, for instance, Deirdre David ignores Kim's sickness at the end: "Toward the end of his journey on the road to perfected white male identity, Kim ... [comes] into full possession of his role as sympathetic sahib.... In Kipling's novel, we see an embrace of origins, of empire, of life, of curiosity."[28] Similarly, though cognizant of Kim's losses, Zohreh Sullivan concludes, "Although Kim has been transformed from a youthful, reckless, happy adventurer into a cog in the imperialist wheel, the ending blesses and sacramentalizes this change by investing it with the displaced glow of the lama's transformation."[29] In contrast, I read the end of *Kim* as far more ambiguous. Given the cumulative losses that Kim sustains and the growing references to his sickness of mind and body, the text proposes a much less sanguine picture of his future and conscription to imperial service.[30]

In the third section, the novel links with map making two other forms of art that the imperial game practices on Kim (and requires him to practice): magic and medicine. Although claiming to be curative, each underlines Kim's increasing sickness and wreaks damage upon him. Kim's formal entry into the Game is inaugurated by his sinister encounter with Huneefa, the blind courtesan-magician. Overwhelmed by darkness, smoke, incense, and the chanted names of devils summoned to "protect" him, he is sent into a trance so that

Huneefa, Mahbub Ali, and Hurree Babu can work on his body. But constituting the core of this magic and preventive medicine are ominously manipulated voices (as in the voice-box episode) and a sinister form of touch: "Huneefa, now whispering in his ear, now talking from an immense distance, touched him with horrible soft fingers, but Mahbub's grip never shifted from his neck till, relaxing with a sigh, the boy lost his senses" (227). These "ventriloquial necromancies" are followed by Huneefa's own loss of consciousness. As Kim turns into an unconscious body that has no control over itself, Huneefa too becomes a receptacle, a medium that "lay spent and motionless beside Kim, as the crazy voices ceased" (228). Spoken through by terrifying unknown powers, dispossessed of her voice, and "hauled aside" by Mahbub Ali and Hurree Babu when her usefulness is spent, Huneefa, though clearly reinforcing orientalist stereotypes, suggests a curious mirror for Kim himself. As with Kim, her use of voices (or her curious "native" art) has been conscripted to the service of the Game. But her art is also presented as a minor version of the art of empire. "Magic," regarded by Kim at the beginning of the novel as the "magic" of the written object, now becomes a figure for the art of empire. The "players" who control Huneefa's trance are Mahbub Ali and Hurree Babu, who dispose of her limp body to work on the naked and senseless Kim's: one undresses and "changes his [whitened] color" and the other dresses him in the guise of the lama's chela. In returning Kim to the lama like a doll whose internal machinery has been transformed, yet with its outer attributes apparently unchanged, this transformation that the Game wreaks upon Kim bespeaks a grotesque magic, which works devil-like invisibly for its own ends, taking the outward shape or guise of that of which it takes "possession."

This magic is then practiced by Kim in his encounter with the Mahratta, in an episode that confirms Kim as a successful player of the Game. Here Kim combines map making, medicine, and magic, as if they were coextensive arts of imperial game playing. Encountering the Mahratta fleeing from deadly pursuers, at first Kim proves himself an excellent reader, for he sees through the man's story of having suffered a fall. The Mahratta's body tells a different story—it bears no "signs of gravel rash," its cuts are clean, and it is literally shaking with terror (246). Clearly, this player of the Game is wounded in more than one sense, for he has lost the ability to coordinate the signification of his body and of his voice—they tell conflicting stories. But he also functions as a sinister double for Kim, because like imprinted birds, both bear identically marked amulets on their chests, created for them by Huneefa's "magic": "Kim made as to scratch his bosom, and thereby lifted his own amulet. The Mahratta's face changed altogether at the sight, and he disposed the amulet fairly on his breast" (246). After this mirrored moment of mutual recognition (which, like Freud's moment of self-recognition in "The Uncanny," happens on a train and reflects Kim's own wounded status), Kim proceeds to redisguise the Mahratta, using "invocations" to convince his audience that he is using a magical "charm" to cure a sick man (253). Paradoxically, he effects this new disguise not by means of new clothes but by dis-investment, by a baring of the body, by turning the Mahratta into a near-naked Saddhu covered only by ash, turmeric, and paint. As Kim pulls out the paint box that he uses for his maps, the body of the Mahratta becomes the new map that Kim paints: "He drew from his bosom the little Survey paint-box and a cake of crimson lake" (251). Kim thus literally maps onto the Mahratta's body the disguise that would be best suited for his survival in the Game. In the past, Kim has also used this paint box to paint himself, so that his painting of the Mahratta further suggests his attempt to repaint himself, as if to cover his own wounds. But this is not a form of magic or medicine that might enable for either player a real "healing" or freedom from the Game, for this art is itself the source of the problem.

The ruptures in the Mahratta's body reflect the ruptures in his disguise, and Kim uses "medicine" literally and figuratively to effect a cure in this breach of signification. Twice he tells his fellow passengers that this disguise is a "healing": "A healing against the shadow of death" (250); "The child will be fortunate all his life. He has seen a great healing" (252). Indeed, re-covering the Mahratta's body with paint *is* the process of his recovery, as the rupture in his disguise is healed by Kim's new "medicine." Kim literally *doctors* the Mahratta, in the sense both of cure and of "tampering [with evidence] in order to dissemble."[31] The doctor of the Game conflates medicine with the interception and transformation of signifiers, for empire is contingent on such forms of doctoring. The "cure," the text suggests, is then part of the problem itself, as it reduces each individual to a dispensable instrument for the Game. Kim has become fully a "chain-man," one in a chain of changing signifiers, Game players who include the Mahratta, pursuing a stolen letter and himself pursued by mysterious enemies who want to make *him* a letter, a cautionary "example" for his co-players, to whom the Mahratta is finally delivered. As the Mahratta chillingly reminds Kim, each is interchangeable with the other and subject to simple erasure when no longer serviceable: "We of the game are beyond protection. If we die, we die. Our names are blotted from the book" (248).

The text thus surrounds Kim with figures who shadow his condition of increasing sickness. In addition to Huneefa and the Mahratta, Kim is accompanied part of his way by a sick child and the child's father, the Jat-farmer. The child mirrors the sickness of Kim, traveling with the lama. But unlike the child, Kim cannot avail himself of imperial medicine, for that is the source of his sickness. Earlier, Kim was not susceptible to disease or physical weakness. Upon entering the Game, however, he receives a box of drugs from Hurree Babu, as if to prepare him: "You see, you are so young you think you will last forever and not take care of your body. It is great nuisance to go sick in the middle of business" (211). And Lurgan Sahib, who "cures" sick pearls, instructs Kim "as to the care of his own body, the cure of fever-fits, and simple remedies of the Road" (217). Clearly, the activities of the Game are associated with sickness and cure. Sara Suleri argues that Kim's new susceptibility to disease is a "casualty" of empire: "Whereas the pre-educated Kim was both a voice and a body that commanded comfort wherever it found itself, the posteducated Kim is suddenly vulnerable to the pains of mind and body" (*Rhetoric*, 130). This is a casualty that the text recognizes and deplores, which surely mitigates the complacency that many critics find in the ending.

In the crisis with the Russians in the hills, these tropes of medicine, map making, and magic coalesce, marking the course of Kim's final collapse. As the lama sickens in the hills, Kim "remembers that he [Kim] was a white man" and had access to the "medicine" in the *kiltas*, the baskets that the hill men have been carrying for the Russians (293). The same *kiltas*, however, also contain "the Written Word," the trove of maps and incriminating papers for which Kim and Hurree Babu have pursued the Russians. This writing again is figured as "magic," as a ruse that Kim uses to take it from the hill men. Yet this white man's "magic" carries negative associations: "I can draw out its magic. Otherwise it can do great harm," Kim tells the hill men (297). However, when Kim obtains the precious red *kilta*, it seems to underline his inadequacy. Each object he finds in it marks its distance from him. Even though he tries to "review" each item "from a Sahib's point of view," he seems alienated from both the objects and the "point of view": "The books I do not want.... The letters I do not understand.... The maps—they draw better maps than me of course" (302). Kim has enough knowledge to know what to keep and what to discard, but he cannot possess these things himself. He works for the empire with "delight," but the language of negation bears another message, especially when the narrative comes to the point at which Kim (with reluctance) has to dispose of the valuable cartographic tools that he cannot carry: "He repacked the *kilta* with all he meant to lose.... The wheeling basket vomited its contents as it dropped. The theodolite hit a jutting cliff-ledge and exploded like a shell; the books, inkstands, paint-boxes, compasses, and rulers showed for a few seconds like a swarm of bees. Then they vanished; and though Kim, hanging half out of the window, strained his young ears, never a sound came up from the gulf" (303). This rejection of "all he *meant* to lose" is figured as "vomit" (by association, the upside-down Kim's), as if a sickened body wanted to regurgitate violently all it has taken in, to evacuate itself in a relief-seeking paroxysm. The red *kilta*, like the voice-box earlier, becomes associated with Kim's body—another object of use in the Game.

Kim's sickness, however, is not emptied into the hills, for unlike the tools of contagion, the contagion itself is not so easily disposed of. As he carries it down to the plains, Kim becomes increasingly sick, as if the magic of the charm he bears has not been "drawn out" but is instead doing him "great harm"(297). Now he is weighed down by the "load of writings on his heart" (319). The letters and maps that he carries hung around his neck do not make a distinction between surface and depth, for Kim is inscribed in no easily locatable way, and that very inscription is the disease. "Kim thought of the oilskin packet and the books in the foodbag.... He was tired and hot in his head, and a cough that came from the stomach worried him" (320). It is a sickness of both mind and body: "For some absurd reason their weight on his shoulders was nothing to their weight on his poor mind" (324). He has lost interest in the Game and cannot wait to be relieved of his burden: "The present need on his soul was to get rid of the loot.... [H]e had been annoyed out of all reason by the knowledge that [it] lay below him through the sick idle days" (327).

One of the most dire effects of this disease is the curtailment of Kim's language. "His tongue itched for free speech again, and but a week back the lightest word clogged it like ashes" (325). Aphasia strikes Kim with increasing force as, in his three crises and his repeated question "Who is Kim, Kim, Kim?" (166; and again on pages 233 and 331), Kim seems to become increasingly deranged. Kim's return to language is related in some way to the work of the lady of Kulu, the inveterate "talker" who has a joint power of language, generation, and nurturing. She effects a new magic, an art that is figured in terms of her femaleness and domesticity, through her "mysterious" brews and her ability to cook and massage Kim into a mysterious sleep. Even her maternal feminine arts, however, cannot overcome the writing that lies upon his heart. When Kim awakes and hands the papers to Hurree Babu, the latter remarks (twice), "I shall embody your name in my verbal report" (272, 328). Kim seems to have become interred in the language of empire. For him, these maps and letters remain "a burden incommunicable" (328), writing that is literally undeliverable—he cannot relieve himself of it, even though he may pass the papers over to Hurree Babu. The language that once represented a power of generation has become one that stultifies him.

As Kim makes his way weakly out of the house, seemingly awakened from sickness, he breaks down again, shifting into another crisis that is rendered as a fetal turning inward from the world, a womblike return to "Mother Earth" (332):

> The unnerved brain edged away from all the outside, as a raw horse, once rowelled, sidles from the spur. It was enough, amply enough, that the spoil of the *kilta* was away—off his hands—out of his possession.... All that while he felt, though he could not put it into words, that his soul was out of gear with his surroundings—a cog-wheel unconnected with any machinery, just like the idle cog-wheel of a cheap Beheea sugar-crusher laid by in a corner. The breezes fanned over him, the parrots shrieked at him, the noises of the populated house behind—squabbles, orders, and reproofs—hit on dead ears.
>
> "I am Kim. I am Kim. And what is Kim?" His soul repeated it again and again. (331)

The promising colt who was inducted into the schooling of the Game is now broken, not just broken in—along with his language. Kim is lost, a part of a machine that recognizes that he is just a part of, while also apart from, language, so broken that "he could not put it into words." As a reader, he cannot respond to the world to which he was once so alive—sounds, the language of the human and natural world, fall on "dead ears." His futile repetition of his name marks that loss of selfhood in that world.

What follows has usually been read as Kim's return to health, to the ability to participate in the Game again, as he seems now to "click" into place, to recognize the order and hierarchy on which the empire he works for subsists:[32] "He did not want to cry—had never felt less like crying in his life—but of a sudden easy, stupid tears trickled down his nose, and with an almost audible click he felt the wheels of his being lock up anew on the world without. Things that rode meaningless on the eyeball an instant before slid into proper proportion. Roads were meant to be walked upon, houses to be lived in, cattle to be driven, fields to be tilled, and men and women to be talked to" (331). Yet this "return" is not a return to health. It is only a return to submission, to acceptance of a totalized system, in which all things are defined by their functionality. The wheels of his being are "lock[ed] up" anew, as the discourses of empire reclaim him.

Now Kim falls into another sleep, a sleep that would not be needed if Kim had returned to his original state of health: "Mother Earth was as faithful as the Sahiba. She breathed through him to restore the poise he had lost lying so long on a cot cut off from her good currents. His head lay powerless upon her breast, and his opened hands surrendered to her strength. The many-rooted tree above him, and even the dead manhandled wood beside, knew what he sought, as he himself did not know. Hour upon hour he lay deeper than sleep" (332). Kipling's language is deeply ambiguous here, presenting both the regenerative power of a return to vitality through the medium of a female nature ("good, clean dust . . . that holds the seeds of life") and the suggestion of death that is presented through denial ("[the dust was] no new herbage that, living, is half-way to death already") (332). Kim's options are rearticulated in the "many-rooted tree" and the "dead manhandled wood": whether Kim has access to those roots or whether he has become the "dead manhandled wood" remains an open question.

At the end of the novel, both Mahbub Ali and Hurree Babu assume that Kim will return to the Game, as a mature player of the Game who has proved his mettle. But the lama believes that he has not only fulfilled his own quest (thanks to Kim) but also has repaid that obligation by winning spiritual freedom for Kim: "[T]his very night he will be as free as I am from all taint of sin—assured as I am, when he quits this body, of Freedom from the Wheel of Things"

(333). However, though these dissonant readings find concord over Kim's future (he will be a "teacher" and a "scribe" for the state; "sure of paradise, [he can] yet enter Government service," as Mahbub and the lama agree [334]), the text provides no such concurrence with either point of view. It splits off into greater ambiguity. The "freedom" that Kim may win in death from the Wheel of Life is no comfort for the lack of freedom he has under the wheel of empire. Moreover, through subtle hints, the text also calls his fitness for the Game into question.

As a result of his sickness, Kim's deterioration as a player has increased to the extent that he cannot maintain the flawlessness of his native disguise and is rebuked on separate occasions by both Hurree Babu and Mahbub Ali for his slips. Hurree's last words to Kim in the novel are "Good-bye, my dear fallow, and when next you are under thee [sic] emotions please do not use the Mohammedan terms with the Tibetan dress" (330). Kim has made what could have been a fatal slip—to use the language of a Muslim when in the guise of a Buddhist. Hurree Babu's malapropism "fallow" for "fellow" indicates, indeed, that Kim has become fallow—in all the senses of unusable, unproductive, inactive, and obsolete—at least for a time. Similarly, Mahbub Ali's last sight of Kim is of a boy who has lost his old vigilance, exhausted and collapsed in deep sleep in the open countryside, manifesting a carelessness that is hardly appropriate for a player of the Game. "'Allah! What a fool's trick to play in open country!' muttered the horse-dealer [before he leaves Kim to his fate]. 'He could be shot a thousand times—but this is not the Border'" (332).

The last words of the novel are given over to the lama, who asserts his conviction of "salvation for himself and his beloved" (338).[33] But this is undercut by the lama's continuing inability to see through Kim's deceptions in using him as a cover for the Game. Moreover, Kim's view of the lama's fall into the river undermines his "master's" vision; his entirely practical concern for the lama casts the latter in mundane and bodily terms either as in need of food or as having barely escaped death by drowning. Why, we may well ask, does Kipling conclude with the lama's patently false conclusion? Sullivan has suggested that this is the worst moment of evasion in the text (*Narratives of Empire*, 176–77). But another way to read this end is to see the text as cautioning against certainty in assigning a definite future for Kim—while refusing to provide a definitive account of what that future may be.

Yet though *Kim* leaves ambiguous the possibility of Kim's successful return to the Game, suggesting only how incapacitated he has become, it suggests something different for itself. Whereas Kim the character ends up a secret agent in the sense that he is an agent for empire, *Kim* the text suggests that it may itself be a secret agent in another sense. As it depicts the working of the imperial system, it also depicts, without being entirely subordinate to the system, the negative effects of the induction of Kim. Moreover, in presenting the multiple coded languages through which this text, as another child of empire, may speak, *Kim* hints at its own subversiveness, its capacity to expose and obliquely critique the effects of imperial conscription. To what extent this text is successful in such an attempt is perhaps a moot point. What it does reveal is the way in which this text's fears and anxieties about its own agency, and its efforts to assert some agency, are written into its making.

CHAPTER THREE

Forster's Crisis

The Intractable Body and Two Passages to India, 1910–22

> I know what I *want* and will epitomize it. I want greater freedom for writers, both as creators and as critics. In England, more than elsewhere, their creative work is hampered because they can't write freely about sex, and I want it recognized that sex is a subject for serious treatment and also for comic treatment.
>
> —Forster, *Abinger Harvest*[1]

BY 1910, at age thirty-one, E. M. Forster had published many short stories and four novels, in a brief span of six years.[2] Yet at this point of high acclaim and expectation, Forster hit a block. Between 1910 and 1924—when he published *A Passage to India*, his most successful but last novel—there remained an unexplained gap in his novelistic career, a peculiar silence, a knotty difficulty that seemed to stymie this strangely promising writer. In 1911, he tried (unsuccessfully) to write plays, and he began a new novel, *Arctic Summer* (which he never finished). Hoping to recharge his energies, in 1912 he traveled to India and returned in 1913 to begin *A Passage to India*.

But after having drafted eight chapters, he came to a standstill, halted—rather like Adela Quested—by a resurgence of the unspeakable at the mouth of the Marabar Caves.[3]

In 1914, Forster wrote some short stories explicitly about homosexuality (which he later burned) and *Maurice* (published posthumously, in 1971). During the First World War, he worked in Egypt for the Red Cross (1915–18) and had his first sexual experience and love affair (with Mohammed el Adl, an Egyptian bus-conductor who died after his experiences in a colonial prison). But Forster's efforts to continue "the Indian novel" brought despair. From England in 1919 he wrote to Siegfried Sassoon, "Abysmal depression all today. . . . While trying to write my novel, I wanted to scream aloud like a maniac."[4] He resumed *Passage* after his second Indian trip (1921–22) but could not complete it until 1924. This fourteen-year gap in Forster's published fiction thus frames another gap (1914–22) in the writing of his last novel, itself structured around a central gap—the mystery of the caves—echoing in its very form the hiatus that underwrote it.

What produced this crisis? How did it shape what he *did* write? Biographers have cited the "paralysis" of the success of *Howards End* (1910);[5] Forster's difficulties with his mother, with whom he continued to live; his "idleness, sexual frustration and sense of ineffectiveness"; and dissatisfaction with the limiting form of the heterosexual bourgeois romance.[6] But as his letters and diary make clear, Forster understood that it was not sexual frustration but the inability to *write* about that frustration—something publishable about dissident sexuality and desire—that preoccupied him and produced his sense of ineffectuality. The unspeakability of love between men (and of the body more generally) and the urge to craft a poetics and politics that overcame it lay at the heart of both his crisis and his subsequent writing.

A Passage to India, Forster's most powerful novel, must then be understood in the context of this crisis. The result of intense authorial frustration and revisions, it was finally produced by the years of reflections on the very questions that obstructed its author's capacity to write. In those intervening years, Forster wrote voluminous letters, travel reports from India and Egypt, journals, and unpublished fiction that have been generally neglected by Forster scholars. Written in part as self-conscious rehearsal for a future novel, these interim writings both dwell on the concerns that produced Forster's crisis and constitute the effort to find a solution. Addressing broader questions about literature, social justice, and ethical action, they center on three related concerns: (1) how could his writing explore same-sex desire and emotional fulfillment in a climate of severe prohibition and surveillance;[7] (2) how were domestic proscriptions on alternative sexualities systemically connected to imperialist prejudices about nonwhite races; and (3) how as a writer could he participate politically in the public sphere regarding matters at home and abroad—that is, how could his writing make a difference or act to intervene and impel positive social change?

In this chapter, I read Forster's Indian letters, journals, *Maurice*, and travel and other writings from 1910 to 1922 to trace Forster's concerns with the sexual and racialized body and literary agency as they developed over the course of his contact with India. I begin with his reflections on the problem of the unspeakable body and the tensions he saw between language and body, action and reflection. Until he went to India, Forster was able to articulate the problem but not solve it to be able to write a publishable novel.[8] I show how these Indian writings became a crucible for solutions he crafted as he reflected on his experiences of travel and imperialism. Through them, I show how Forster's understanding of the body, bodily desire, and interracial sexuality changed over time and transformed his understanding of his writing and its agency. These lesser-known writings are crucial not only in the light they shed on his final novel but also in themselves as revealing the development of a complex, even contradictory anticolonial bodily politics consequent upon Forster's experiences in India. Indeed, they speak to broader cultural concerns, as they reveal how issues of homosexuality, literature, and agency in England dovetail with those of imperial power and race relations in India to produce a late-imperial dissidence and critique through self-implication. In chapter 4, I read *A Passage to India* as drawing upon and self-consciously rewriting this prior writing, making the problems of colonial language a subject of the novel, even as it attempts to bring the forbidden body into language. A novel written with so much angst and self-conscious reflection on the difficulties of writing is, not surprisingly, deeply concerned with language and the question of what it, a construct of language yet existing in the material world, can *do*: what agency or efficacy it can have.

After the posthumous publication of Forster's explicit writings about homosexuality (*Maurice* and *The Life to Come*) and the disclosure of his sexual orientation, the critical pendulum swung from the initial condescension of homophobic critics to the denunciation of post-Stonewall critics who denounced Forster for his political cowardice in not coming out in his lifetime.[9] Subsequent scholars have crafted ways of reading and recuperating Forster's work that are more nuanced, recognizing the inextricable linking of race, sexuality, and gender within his oeuvre as well as its necessarily muted politics.[10] Even so, they have not attended to the significance of the Indian travel writings or to the ways in which these help us recast Forster's crisis and novel-writing career as well as help us understand his better-known novels. Informed by recent developments in postcolonial, queer, and gender studies, I examine how issues of sexuality, censorship, race, and travel intersect in Forster's work, showing how, together, they produce a self-conscious politics of writing.

A Letter to Masood

In July 1916, during the First World War, while Forster was working for the Red Cross in Alexandria, he wrote a letter to his friend Syed Ross Masood in India.[11]

> Dearest S.R.M.,
>
> I have a long unfinished letter to you somewhere. I remember the chief points: (i) I had been dreaming of you and longed to see you—and indeed woke up in the night to write. (ii) I was telling you how much I disliked the Egyptians and how inferior to the Indians I have found them, both in charm, intellect and morality. Now what shall I tell you in this letter? My longing to see you remains, but I grow frightfully pessimistic, frightfully. First the war must end, then freedom to travel must be re-established, and God knows how long this will take. I have had a long cable from Dewas asking me to be his private Secretary and Right Hand. I should have accepted in normal times, partly because it would have given me the chance of seeing you. But it is impossible to leave the Red X at present. As it is they tried to hoof me into the Army, a disaster that I have hitherto avoided. I hope I shall be medically unfit, but they take everyone who isn't actually diseased I fancy. Except for my nerves, which have got bad (owing to this enlistment worry) I am looking and feeling pretty fit. (Quoted in Furbank, *A Life*, 2:27–28)

Characteristic of his epistolary manner, this letter reveals the complexity of Forster's relationship with Masood: the easy familiarity, the unself-consciousness in speaking of his love, the knowledge that Masood both understood and was not discomfited by it, and the acceptance that Masood could return only affection. It bespeaks the difficulties of speaking of the love that had no name even as the letter speaks it, albeit in this very private mode. Unlike his published fiction, this letter also candidly expresses Forster's political opposition to an imperialist war, his reluctance to be conscripted, his unpatriotism in describing the British imperial authorities as trying "to hoof [him] into the Army," his humorous "hope [that he] shall be medically unfit," and his unconcern about seeming "unmanly" as this was defined by dominant gender codes. (His friends were able to have him removed from the list of those to be conscripted, without his having to "attest" to being a conscientious objector.) Hence this letter also reveals an anxiety and inability about making a public political statement, as made by his friend Siegfried Sassoon later, about an inwardly determined stance.

However, this letter is particularly arresting because it was itself the subject of arrest, emblematic of the environment that conditioned Forster's conjoined anxieties about writing, political agency, and sexual and colonial surveillance. Like others earlier, this letter was "intercepted by the postal censor in Bombay, who was scandalized and forwarded it to the Bombay political department" (for the British colonial authorities) (Furbank, A Life, 2:28). Here is the censor's report: "I took up a letter by the same writer to the same addressee last year to Special Officer. The letter was passed into the post. It was much of the same type as the present one, only it showed up the writer still more as *a decadent coward* and apparently *a sexual pervert*. I think the Political Secretary, Government of India, should see this letter as *the writer does not seem to be fit to be employed in Dewas*" (quoted in Furbank, A Life, 2:28; my emphasis). In the ensuing correspondence, the British political agent responsible for supervising the "independent" Native States assured the colonial authorities that Forster, "a novelist of some repute," was "evidently a poor creature" but not "a sexual pervert," and that he would "take steps to ensure that the Raja's offer of an appointment would not be renewed" (Furbank, A Life, 2:29). Thus, Masood finally received Forster's letter, and neither recipient nor writer ever knew of the shadow that this cheery epistle had cast upon them. (The offer was later renewed, and Forster went to Dewas in 1921–22.)

This episode is significant in a number of ways. First, it indicates the degree of colonial surveillance and potential censorship of individuals subject to imperial power, who may be positioned racially and politically very differently. Masood, an affluent Indian Muslim; the Maharaja, a ruler of an independent Hindu state; and Forster, a middle-class English novelist: all are all brought under the purview of this network of suspicion. It is also a barometer of the homophobic monitoring of homosexuality across the empire. This official—and officious—reaction (which, given the crisis of the First World War, might now be understood as homosexual panic) has the political consequence of a British agent telling the Maharaja whom to employ.[12] Barring the entry of such an Englishman from colonial territory seems also necessary to the construction and maintenance of a masculinist (and homophobic) colonial authority.

This censoring—and censorious—colonial discourse categorizes any avowal of love between men as homosexuality and castigates it as "perversion." In so doing, of course, it fails to recognize any continuity or intersection between normative (homosocial) forms of male bonding or friendship and sexual desire.[13] It thus also defines itself defensively by opposition, as *not* that unspeakable thing, as manly in monitoring such unmanliness. In the censor's letter, Forster is cast as at once a "decadent coward" and a "sexual pervert"—as if the two were coincident.[14] An added, even queer, twist to the situation is that this threat of perversion, weakness, and corruption comes not from "outside" the parameters of Englishness as understood by colonial notions of selfhood, not from the racial other, but from a writer *within* the bastions of Englishness—from the very knowledge of which both colonial authority and colonial subjects in India must be kept safe.[15]

Forster's letter and the disturbance it aroused are thus powerful indicators of the colonial context of the conjoint control of sexuality and race relations, censorship, and the constraints that a writer such as Forster faced. It is an unusual moment of intersection of the public and private that Forster sought to keep separate in his writing, exemplifying the consequences of exposure (and misapprehension) of unspeakable desire. Similar to the moment in A *Passage to India* when Aziz's letters are appropriated and read by colonial authorities as evidence of his sexual/racial decadence and political seditiousness, it suggests both the political consequences of a private signifying system appropriated and misread by a more limited and judgmental one, and the coexistence of a racialized and sexualized understanding of the body under colonial surveillance.

This incident, then, offers a paradigm for the intersection of concerns that were key to Forster's crisis and that he sought to address repeatedly in his writing. This letter to Masood is a rare example of Forster's indiscretion, but his published and unpublished writing, both fiction and nonfiction, negotiates precisely these constraints, clustered around two main issues. First, there is the centrality of the (male) *body* as at once a site of proscription and a site of desire: the body as racialized, sexualized, and rendered unspeakable; the body as the source of Forster's ambivalent desire to exercise caution and to write about the forbidden; the body as the palpable site of alterity, hence the means of addressing sexual (and by extension racial or class) oppression. Second, there is the problem of crafting a form of political *agency* in and through writing: how to enact a politics of the body in writing; to voice protest when the body is subject to power and language about it is proscribed; to combat the forces of silence and to foster tolerance for difference. These two issues are inextricably linked for Forster, for they pose related problems. The slow effort of writing *A Passage to India* yielded a recognition of this inextricability and eventually a conjoint solution to both: a realization that finding a way to speak the body might become a mode of enacting writerly agency.

Both Forster's letter and the censor's bring into focus the proscribed sexual body that is racialized in a context of imperialism and war. To the censor, it matters not only that the letter writer may be homosexual but also that he is white—and English—that his words and body, his verbal and physical arrival in the carefully controlled space of India, would produce a disruption in the desired order of colonial authority and the construction of colonial identity.[16] To Forster, the letter enables a covert expression of forbidden homoerotic desire, as well as of forbidden interracial intimacy. This is not to suggest that the difficulties of sexual orientation were analogous to those of colonialism and racism. But Forster's understanding of one produced empathy for the other and, eventually, an understanding of how English nationalism, racism, and imperialism were systemically connected to English bourgeois morality and sexual and gender codes. As Forster came to see these connections between both forms of oppression and intolerance, forming an ethical opposition to one may have contributed to his ability to oppose the other.

Forster's letter thus illuminates his need to work out a strategy of noncooperation, to enact a form of agency with regard to the systemic links between race, war, imperialism, sex, and homosexuality. It expresses the problem of working out an appropriate channel (or passage) for the expression of the as-yet-blocked desire for agency as a novelist regarding imperial and sexual politics. These interrelated concerns—the body in writing and the political agency of writing—developed in Forster's writing from 1910 to 1922. They were situated at the heart of his crisis and became the grounds for growing convictions that shaped the rest of his career. Indeed, Forster's reflections in his letters and diaries suggest how self-consciously he understood these questions in his own terms.

Obdurate Carnality: Art and the Unspeakable, Intractable Body

Even with good friends, Forster could not discuss his difficulties, as in a letter to Forrest Reid: "You ask about my work.... I am dried up. Not in my emotions but in their expression. I cannot write at all.... [H]ave a shot at helping me for I need it. Please do not mention this, as few people know. It often makes me very unhappy" (February 2, 1913; *Letters*, 2:187). But a diary entry as early as June 1911 makes clear his understanding of them. In addition to ill health and his mother's depressing and repressive presence, he lists as a basic cause his "weariness of the only subject that both I can and may treat—the love of men for women and vice versa. Passion and money are the only two main springs of action ... and I can only write of the first and that imperfectly."[17] Explicitly recognizing physical "passion" as the "main spring of action," Forster suggests that his own "main spring" has been wrenched: he writes "imperfectly" because he is limited to writing only of heterosexual love. The entry thus expresses the desire to write of another kind of bodily and romantic desire, that of love between men, along with a weariness of his old resort of disguising under the acceptable dynamics of heterosexuality the same-sex dynamics that he really wanted to explore. It suggests that passion is the requisite and suppressed *subject* of narrative, the main interest of the plot, as well as its dynamic *agent*, or driving energy, for passion is also the source of his impetus to write, of his own action as a writer. As if the continuous use of the wrong fuel has brought him to crisis, the prohibition against homosexuality even as a subject of fiction halts his ability and desire to write and also disables him from taking action as a writer by speaking the unspeakable.

The unspeakable body became for Forster at once the implicit subject of his writing, the obstruction to his writing, and eventually the means of escape from cultural dictates, of carving out his own agency. In the years 1910–24, he developed a conviction of the centrality of the repressed body and the need for writers to bring that body into writing, to make it materialize into language, indeed, to transform language itself. As Forster became increasingly committed to including the "carnal" in writing and in intellection as a matter of political and artistic integrity and as a form of resistance, this became a touchstone for his reading of other writers as well. In a diary entry of October 25, 1910, for instance, Forster ponders the relation between bodily desire and literary production and reception: "To work out: —The sexual bias in literary criticism, and perhaps in literature. Look for such a bias in its ideal and carnal form.... What sort of person would the critic prefer to sleep with, in fact."[18] Conscious or not, the reception as well as the production of art is infused by erotic interest. This becomes a new goal, a way of re-seeing art. In an unfinished essay written circa 1911, he discovers that artists "are all writing to the body with the body, in language however delicate, and it is only in degree that they differ." An audience that does not share the artist's interests may be disgusted: "[F]or though we all love, objects of loving are numerous, and those who do not sympathize with the artist's passion are repelled by it: there is no middle way" (quoted in Heine, introduction to *Arctic Summer*, xvi). In his writing, he tries to craft that "middle way," to incorporate the truth of his interests yet also appeal to different audiences.

Debrah Raschke has shown that an important shift occurred in Forster's thinking around the time that he wrote *Maurice* (1913–14), a shift from a Platonism that opposed the body and the soul, to an integration of the two. Indeed, far from distrusting the body, Forster came to regard the bodily as integral to intellectual and artistic aspiration. "Paradoxically, Platonism gives voice to homoerotic expression, but because it situates truth away from the body, it thwarts the physical fulfillment of this alternative expression.... In the end, it is the body as position of nontruth that *Maurice* attempts to revise.... Maurice ... embrac[es] a different sexuality and a different metaphysics, one that does not 'dissever the soul from the communion of the body.'"[19] But as early as 1910, Forster was already making the body central to his intellectual and social politics, as exemplified by his comment on Matthew Arnold: "He's not as good as he thinks, but better than I thought. His central fault is prudishness—I don't use the word in its narrow sense, but as implying a general dislike to all warmth. He thinks warmth either vulgar or narrow" (August 12, 1910; *Letters*, 1:111). What Forster finds lacking in Arnold is "warmth," the register of the bodily and the emotional, a lack that is symptomatic of elitist and intellectual separatism. Arnold's "prudishness" is not simply distaste for sexual pleasure but a more political association of the bodily and emotional with the lower class and of the intellectual and rational with middle-class aspiration. What might be "narrow," then, according to Forster, is not warmth but precisely Arnold's lack of it.

In a letter to Siegfried Sassoon about *Maurice*, Forster makes an important comment: "Nothing is more obdurate to artistic treatment than the carnal, but it has to be got in I'm sure: everything has got to be got in" (October 11, 1920; *Letters*, 1:316).[20] In one sense, of course, the carnal is obdurate because, after Oscar Wilde's trial and death, writing about sex between men was difficult, not only because of potential criminal action but also because there were few prior models to work with, few templates to follow.[21] One would have to invent anew. However, the carnal is also obdurate in other, more contradictory ways. On the one hand, it is obstinate, resistant, refusing to be malleably inducted into the purposes of art. How could the materiality of the body be subsumed into language? In an earlier letter, Forster writes about Keats's poetry as failing to conduce the body into language in the right way. "I think [Keats] would have become a great poet, but he wrote during the years when the sex impulse is naturally strong . . . and unluckily with Keats sex chanced to be unaesthetic. . . . Always fatuity, vulgarity, as soon as human passion is touched" (to Malcolm Darling, December 1, 1916; *Letters*, 1:247). In other words, Keats fell into the trap of excess. The integration of the carnal and the aesthetic requires a lighter touch.[22] When finally Keats succeeds in *Hyperion*, Forster remarks, "[T]hat is the palace round whose door we all grope" (*Letters*, 1:247). Such a phrase suggests that the right blend of language and carnality would ultimately be the greatest fulfillment—the crowning destination—of Forster's own artistic desire.

However, Forster's letter to Sassoon intimates that if carnality is obdurate because it is hard to bring *into* art, it is also obdurate because it cannot be kept *out* of art, because suppression of the body damages art. This is the source of Forster's notorious remarks about James's exclusion of the body from his writing:[23] "I never find Henry James difficult to understand, though it is difficult to throw oneself—flat flatter flattest—to crawl down his slots. Intellectually the exertion is slight. Bring muscle or blood to bear, and you stick at once, and put down your failure to deficiency of brain" (to Robert Trevelyan, January 29, 1918; *Letters*, 1:283). Forster's metaphor suggests that reading James requires flattening oneself into narrow self-deprivation, squeezing out life to restrict oneself to the bloodless asceticism of intellect without the robustness of the body. "Intellectually the exertion is slight," he comments, in a telling metaphor of physical action. For a reader of (manly) "muscle or blood," there is literally no room in James's narrow book. That this language of blood and muscle is linked to (a gendered) sexuality is clear in *Aspects of the Novel* (1925–26), in which Forster describes James as "declining to think of homosex" (171) and as preferring "vegetables with no reproductive organs" (164).

Thus, the term *obdurate carnality* suggests a double problem that Forster confronted: first, how to bring the carnal into writing—what relation could be built between the materiality of the body, the ineffability of desire, and the apparent immateriality of language? How could language be an effective medium for the carnal, the bodily, the sexual, without effacing that materiality? But second, how could the carnal to be kept out of writing, without making that writing bloodless? How could one be honest and write of the legally forbidden, when the alternative was to choke off one's creative impulses and damage one's writing?

This dilemma is linked with the desire to tell the truth, with Forster's lifelong conviction that art must be true to one's inner vision and political convictions. His insistence on the inclusion of the body evinces his desire to tell the truth of the denied body. In "The Curate's Friend," a surprisingly revealing tale first published in *Putnam's Magazine* in 1907 (republished in *The Celestial Omnibus*), Forster offers a thinly disguised account of sexual self-realization and release from the bonds of heterosexual marriage and society. The curate-narrator describes how one day, to his horror, a large naked "Faun" suddenly materialized at a family picnic. Trying to explain why he was the only one able to see this giant male body, the curate links bodiliness with truth, obliquely suggesting his affinity to the Faun's otherness: "How I came to see him is a more difficult question. For to see him there is required a certain quality, for which *truthfulness* is too cold a name and *animal spirits* too coarse a one, and he alone knows how this quality came to be in me" (*Collected Tales*, 113–14; my emphasis). Invisible and inaudible to conventional bodies, the Faun—a mysterious presence in the English countryside and a materialization of that which exists beyond ordinary vision—represents both bodily and sexual truth, understood not only as the earthy fairy world or (in a knowing pun) the hidden world of homosexual society[24] but also the impulse of truth that ruptures convention to reveal repressed desires. His magic touch triggers the revelation of the curate's fiancée's passion for another man and the curate's realization of his own real desires. To be the only one of a group of English picnickers to perceive the Faun, as the curate does, and to hear, in an echo of Caliban, that the "place was full of noises" (117)—"the voices of the hill beneath me, of the trees above my head, of the very insects in the bark of the tree" (119)—is to possess an other, magical sense. It is important that this other sense in the curate combines an impulse for "truthfulness" with "animal spirits," that it is at once carnal and ephemeral, like Puck both animal and faery, *and* that he cannot find words in the English language to explain that combination of the bodily and the true— for that must by definition lie outside the boundaries of the conventions that are threatened by and built to shackle it.

This truth-inducing touch of the Faun, which constitutes both sexual invitation and spiritual conversion, forces the recalcitrant curate out of self-denial: denial both of the self and of what the self desires. The Faun's "sunlit" presence, which for the first time enables the curate to hear the poetry of the earth, "the singing" of the downs (123), becomes the secret source of the curate's joy and creativity, of his efficacious capacity to preach better sermons and help his parishioners—though that success must depend on his silence about its source. The transfiguring joy of the Faun's massively homoerotic presence is thus linked with the body, the earth, and England's pagan history. Unlike most of the other stories in the collection, in which the protagonists escape society, the curate stays to help others, to use his secret power to affect (and infect) his unknowing community of parishioners through his writing and speeches. He thus enacts agency, but only under conditions of secrecy, for he is unable to change the conditions that impose silence upon the real source of his skills. In this strangely self-exposing paradigm, Forster suggests that true creativity and agency come from bodily and spiritual consummation but that such fulfillment must remain silent about itself to be effective. Indeed, if, as Forster's joking signature "self and Faun" in a letter suggests, the Faun is a dimension of Forster's own split self, the daemon perhaps of his own creativity, then the tale is also metafictive in articulating both Forster's sense of painful restriction and his artistic desire to produce material effects.[25]

If, as Elizabeth Heine argues in her introduction to *Arctic Summer*, Forster's difficulties with that attempted 1911 novel stemmed from his inability to write about homosexuality, which is where he found its narrative heading, then his crisis may be understood as arising from the conjoint desire to tell the truth and the inability to do so, as he is caught between the need to speak and the need to disguise truth. If he must keep silent, he could not continue with untruth either. After *Howards End,* Forster struggled to find a publishable form that would tell the truth of the body and balance the tensions of his aesthetic and political leanings. One temporary solution he found was the form of the fantastic, in short stories published in the collection *The Celestial Omnibus.*[26] But that did not work for longer fiction, nor was fantasy taken seriously by his readers. Only after his trip to India was Forster able to craft another way, through the voicing of anti-imperialist sentiment and the articulation of the sexual as racial body.

Out in India: Writing the Racial and Sexual Body, 1912–13

> As he had looked outside his own class for companionship, so was he obliged to look outside his own race for wisdom[.]
> —Forster, "Edward Carpenter"[27]

Upon returning from his first trip to India, Forster reported jubilantly, "I am so fit myself—blatant. Everyone ought to go to India. There is a desert of purple stone and cold air in Rajputana where I caught some germ that will stop me ever being ill again" (to Lady Ottoline Morrell, October 4, 1913; *Letters,* 1:206–7). This change in tone registers Forster's sense that his trip had been somehow invigorating and restorative, an antidote to a bodily and perhaps writerly malady. Suggesting something sexually invigorating about India (synecdochically cast as the "purple stone" of Rajputana), he slips into the cliché of an exotic other space but then subverts another colonial cliché of contamination by implying that the "germ" he caught out there would actually be a protection from metropolitan or English ailments. As his writing from this first trip indicates, this protective "germ" may have been "caught" from an Indian atmosphere of increased politicization, providing Forster with a psychic liberation and political education in anticolonial sentiment as well as in alternative modes of constructing gender and sexual identities.

Forster's first trip to India in 1912–13 was designed to provide a change, an escape from the suburban English bourgeois ethos that stifled him, and help produce fresh thoughts and material for a new novel. Over six months, he traveled with college friends across mostly northern and central India, visiting Syed Ross Masood and the Rajah of Dewas. Forster's letters and travel journal from this first trip reveal a renewed effort to address the concerns that had produced his crisis as a writer and intellectual: the twin difficulties of integrating the bodily with the artistic and of crafting a form of literary agency in relation to dominant cultural norms. These letters convey two main kinds of reactions that attest to a dual political education: first, a tremendous, though ambivalent, pleasure and excitement at the sheer difference of cultural constructions of sexuality, gender, same-sex relations, a sense of freedom from English norms, and growing awareness of the constructedness of English as well as Indian sexual identities; second, an education in Indian nationalist anticolonial politics and an awareness of how the effects of racial, economic, and political subordination infiltrate every interaction. Indeed, the two combined to produce a subversive, politicized voice at once critical of imperial and racial hegemony and of English cultural, gender, and sexual codes. In and through these letters and travel writings from India, Forster constructs a mode of political agency, both through explicit imperial critique, showing that he was learning political dissent from the nationalist politics of the Indians he met, and through an implicit sexual dissidence developed from his growing understanding of the constructed nature of sexual and gender regulations.

Even before he undertook this trip, Forster imagined India as a second "home," an alternative space to restrictive England. In a letter to Malcolm Darling, his colonial administrator friend in India, he wrote, "Since reading your letters and the articles I have supposed myself to feel at home there [in India]. The Alps and other mountains that I know feel like boundaries—barriers between two countries rather than worlds by themselves—but the Himalayas . . . can hardly give the sense of anything behind, across, them—they must feel like the 'sea that ends not till the world's end.' May I see them before I die" (January 20, 1910; *Letters*, 1:103). If the Alps, representative of Europe, "feel like boundaries," then the Himalayas, "worlds by themselves," seem to represent India as a capacious space of liberation and difference. When Forster finally did see the Himalayas, he reported this as a fulfillment of a romantic dream, in which, unlike Wordsworth in the Alps, arrival exceeds expectation: "[T]he last four miles were the most impressive I've ever walked," Forster noted, and went on to observe, "I'm in love with the Himalayas" (*Letters*, 1:160–61). In December 1915, he would write with yearning to Masood that Egypt was "vastly inferior to India, for which I am always longing in the most persistent way, and where I still hope to die" (*Letters*, 1:233).

Concurrently, Forster's letter writing in preparation for his Indian trip also proclaims a growing anticolonial politics, an opposition to imperial policies and colonial discourse that developed out of a delicately negotiated position in-between his Indian friend Masood and British administrator friends such as Darling. Describing Masood's annoyance with missionaries, for instance, he wrote to Darling, "I should be grievously sorry if the whole world became Christians, but within certain limits missions have their value. E.g. in Northern Nigeria the missionaries would do something to raise the population, while the government (if I may judge from a friend) resents all attempts to make the native think or feel, because it may increase the difficulties of administration" (June 29, 1910; *Letters*, 1:109). While opposed to the religiosity of Christian missionary work, here Forster welcomes the possibility that it might have unwittingly subversive effects. By providing a colonial education, it would arm natives with the tools to build anticolonial sentiment, to "raise the population" against imperial governments.

In his letters and journal from this first trip, this incipient anticolonialism develops into a stronger sense of the problems of racial and cultural oppression, of the analogous structures of alterity to the proscriptions of homosexuality, and of the potential of resistance in his own writing. Writing about racial bodies allowed him to engage in a certain homoeroticism, to bring the body into language, while understanding embodiment in a different culture enabled him to question and loosen the hold of English cultural taboos. Moreover, the politics of anti-imperialism and antiracism allowed a concomitant though concealed homosexual politics in his letter writing, which eventually enabled him upon his return to write *Maurice*. Thus, two forms of political opposition—to sexual/cultural/gender constraints and to national/racial/colonial policies—work in tandem; indeed, they grow to support each other as Forster discovers how they are both analogous and mutually reinforcing. His literary agency would lie in how his words could work against both—to expose and undermine one would also enable him to undermine the other.

Aware that not many English people were invited to stay with Indians as friends, soon after his arrival Forster wrote, "Altogether I am charmed with India, and have had the rare privilege of dropping straight into native life" (October 31, 1912; *Letters*, 1:145). These letters are surprisingly crafted, as if self-conscious drafts for future writing. Early on, he tells his mother to preserve them so that he could reread them upon his return (*Letters*, 1:145). Full of details and deft turns of phrase, they reveal an excited, astute, and sensitive observer, responsive to sights and sounds, to birds, animals, landscape, and architecture, though undoubtedly also tinged by the orientalizing fascination, puzzlement, irritation, and self-doubt that are recognizable features of colonial travel writing. One of his earliest letters, for instance, conveys pleasure and tranquility: "I sit in the verandah of the house of Masood's friend, with now a chicken running past and now a squirrel, and listen to the doves and green parrots making conversation in the garden.... At Aligarh I was a guest at a village feast. We banqueted in the public view on dishes of strange food, and slept afterwards, equally publicly, on beds that were drawn up in a row on the loggia" (October 31, 1912; *Letters*, 1:144–45). Later, on December 15, he writes of his desire to collect and play with Indian clothes, both unsure of how they will fit his body and sensuously relishing how they transform his identity: "Clothes are so lovely that I always want to buy them, but don't know where I should put them except in a drawer, not being one for fancy dress balls. As it is, I bought a little round cap at Peshawar, quite useless, which dances on the crown of my head."[28] From Dewas he describes the elaborate spread of Indian food or the Indian clothes he wore to a wedding, partly to amuse his mother, maintaining contact, but also at some level establishing difference, suggesting that he is no longer the body she produced and fostered but a creature of new influences, beyond her control.

In part, these letters convey a sense of the sheer physicality of the transformations wrought by travel. Aware that travel is itself an intensely bodily experience and that bodies are physically changed by new environments (they are physically dislocated; put under stress and inconvenience; subjected to new terrain, spatial arrangements, food, and drink; and bodily rhythms of sleep and food are disrupted), Forster draws attention to the ways that travel literally wrenches him out of himself. Moreover, his fascination with the bodiliness of his experiences and observations also suggests his growing understanding of how identity—cultural, racial, sexual—is constructed through the body. He becomes interested in the body in its various social configurations—in its occupation of space, in its movements, in its clothing, in its relation to others, and as a site for the construction of gendered, sexual, racial, and class identities. He observes other bodies, those of Indians in everyday movements, in habits of sitting and standing, and in bodily postures of traditional dance, song, and drama—and then how his own body adapts to these new spatial and social relations. At once happy and uneasy about this, his letters express a sense of himself changed and thus, through him, his Englishness.[29] Thus, they also carry an unusual strain that testifies to something political—suggesting that he saw in India a happy alternative to the English suburban ethos of heteronormativity and imperialism, an alternative that he would repeatedly describe as "queer."

Initially, this sense of queerness has to do with the strangeness and novelty of India, particularly with the ways that human bodies are situated differently in relation to the world and with ways that male-male relations and sexuality are organized. But soon this "queerness" slides into something else, tingeing both observed and observer. During his stay in Delhi, Masood's friends arranged a performance of a Nautch, a traditional dance by women who were not considered respectable enough for "ladies" of the house to be present. Forster describes this event twice, in a letter to his mother as well as in his private journal. Here is the version written for his mother:

> It took place in the middle of the Old City, a most romantic place—and on the roof of a house. . . . The ladies—two—salaamed us on arrival—one with queer but charming manners; the other less charming, in white knickerbockers. . . . [S]he wore a nose ring. There were five attendants who robed the dancers. We sat cross legged or as cross as we could on the floor. . . . The noise was often excruciating—the musicians seemed out of tune and playing in different keys, I could seldom follow the rhythm, and the ladies' voices went into my ears like battering rams; but the dresses & gestures were so lovely, and the singing so clearly emotional that I did get a great deal of pleasure from it. For instance, the charming one did a peacock dance; very slow, scarcely moving her feet, but gradually a shawl of scarlet and gold over her head. This was the peacock's tail, and at the climax of the dance she let a wonderful gold border appear at the end of the shawl, and made it quiver between her outstretched hands as though it were alive. Then she did a dance in which she flew imaginary kites . . . most delightful. (November 6, 1912; *Letters*, 1:149–50)

Witty, droll, and sardonic in tone, the letter seeks to entertain, to maintain intimacy, as well as to record for his future reference. The details suggest that Forster is interested in this event on one level as an orchestration of the body in its relation to other bodies and in space—the forms of dress, the intimacy of attendants dressing the singers in public, the elaborate artifice situated in an outdoor space. To his mother, he describes it as a "romantic place," but he omits significant details that, in his *Indian Journal*, amplify the sexual nature of the event. The journal reveals, for example, that the nose ring of the junior dancer signifies her virginity, and Forster notes, "[S]he didn't attract me" (November 2; *HDI*, 136). Once the love songs began, he notes to himself, he "realized what a Nautch must be to Indian [men]"—a sanctioned form of communal sexual incitement. There he describes how his host attempted to make him "kiss the singers." Thus, the journal makes clear another aspect of the Nautch: that men could act as sexual procurers for each other to consolidate their friendship. Ansari, his Indian host, unknowing of Forster's sexual preferences, attempted to entertain him as an English visitor, to bind them in a homosocial exchange of shared mischievous prurience. Unlike the letter to his mother, Forster's journal registers some discomfort with the heterosexuality of the Nautch, though also a fascination with the homosocial camaraderie it generates and amusement that the performance, though socially licensed among middle-class men, was too scandalous to be held in a respectable middle-class Indian house.

But the journal also indicates how the sexual permissiveness of this privileged male space extends into producing an analogous fluidity of racial and national identity. Although he tells his mother that sitting cross-legged was difficult, as if to reassert his hold on his Englishness in this un-English bodily posture, in his journal he notes, "One could easily 'lapse' into an oriental; I found myself discussing [the performing women's] points dispassionately" (*HDI*, 136). Nor does he tell her of his bodily response to the music, which is quite the opposite of the usual colonial horror of drums ("The drum would thunder in on the last note; this excited us"), or how, despite its strangeness, the music took him over ("[E]motion came to me through the harsh voice and the music"). (If Forster's Englishness is shaken in this encounter, so is the Indianness of those he meets: he leaves with a handshake from the senior performer, which he imagines is their unusual concession to him as chief guest.) Both the letter and the journal show how the experience produces a meditation on how the body and bodily human relations are socially and culturally coded, which in turn enables him to rethink the coding and construction at home. India per se does not allow him freedom, but the contrast allows him to rethink the very fact of construction and hence to release him from any one set of cultural codes.

Repeatedly, Forster notes how masculinity and same-sex relations are constructed in India in different ways than in England. He describes the way men walk around half-naked, enjoying a different bodily freedom and lack of bodily self-consciousness. In closer proximity, men can serve other men while "naked to the waist" without arousing discomfort.[30] Occasionally, he registers unease, a sense of foreignness and difficulty, in the midst of this delighted sense of novelty. He often describes the lack of privacy in India, especially in bed or in sleep. In the course of a hunting trip, for instance, they stop at a village near Aligarh, where, he says, "[W]e fell asleep on the beds, with the whole village looking on" (*Letters*, 1:142). In another letter from Delhi, he writes, "The house is small, and full of people who come in without being announced and sit over the room, and even on one's bed. . . . All the time I was half undressed, and the curtain being drawn—exposed to the view of other guests" (*Letters*, 1:146). The space of the bedroom, which by Western bourgeois norms presumably signified for Forster both the private retreat of an individual self and a suggestive space of sexual privacy, is startlingly recast for him in India as a public space of communal friendship, conviviality, hospitality, and reception. (This is an experience he would describe repeatedly: in *Passage*, for instance, Aziz's friends crowd into his bedroom and onto his bed when he is sick with flu.)

But Forster is attentive not only to the different meanings of bodily and spatial arrangements and their effects on social and erotic relations but also to a different discourse of sexual desire. He describes the Rajah of Dewas's male gatherings during which musicians and boy actors would dress as women and jokes about homosexuality were a matter of course, since Indian disapproval of homosexuality was cast in a different language, not tinged by the sense of horror and silence that had developed in Edwardian England. In India, Forster found that the form of sexuality that was monitored much more closely was heterosexual, not homosexual, thus enabling an atmosphere in which men were comfortable making jokes about homosexuality, because, paradoxically, doing so made it less threatening, less palpably real. In "Kanaya," for instance, an important fragment from his locked diary written during his second visit to Dewas in

1922 (which I discuss below), Forster describes how he became embroiled in a scandal with a homosexual servant the Rajah had secretly procured for him. To ward off suspicion at the court, the Rajah advises Forster that the course of innocence was to play along with the jokes about his homosexuality, to "assent to every innuendo" and to accuse his accusers of jealousy, because while silence or embarrassment would give him away, as long as he could respond with overt jokes and counterinsinuations, he would not be suspected (*HDI*, 321). Hence Forster was able to rethink the gender and sexual coding he had escaped from, because he was able to re-see it via a system that coded gender and sexuality quite differently. This is not to say that he saw no constraints on sexuality in India, but even recognizing a different kind of legislation highlights the constructedness and relativity of specific cultural prohibitions and destabilizes the dominance of any one set, throwing it into question as neither inevitable nor natural.

This initial sense of the "queerness" of India soon begins to shade into another kind of queerness—of his own writing. At an early point in his travels, Forster writes to his closest female friend, Florence Barger, from Delhi: "I am in the middle of a very queer life, whether typically Oriental I have no means of knowing, but it isn't English"—as if to be "queer" was to be strange and Indian, or not-English (November 2, 1912; *Letters*, 1:145). Benares is a "queer city"—both holy and an "unbelievable mess" (January 9, 1913; *Letters*, 1:177); even the sunset in Bombay's Victoria Station is "queer" (October 23, 1912; *HDI*, 126); and the Himalayas have "queer crinkled outlines . . . , coloured purple and brown" (*Letters*, 1:160). Writing to his mother about his stay with Masood's Muslim friend in Delhi, he describes the house ("the garden was full of queer carriages & the sitting room full of queerer people who came in unannounced"), the courtesan who had a "queer but charming face and delightful manners," and then his midnight train-trip to Lahore ("Is it not a queer life!") (November 6, 1912; *Letters*, 1:150, 151). The final comment conveys a sense of being himself changed by India, so that what he presents is not merely India as "queer" but himself queered by it. Even the Englishmen in India have become—or already are—queer: "I had expected to find queer Englishmen in power, but this man [the political agent appointed by the British government to oversee the native state of Chhatarpur] is a stumper" (December 16, 1912; *Letters*, 1:171). As the queerness of India slides into the queerness of Forster's presence in India and then into the queerness of his writing, it suggests implicitly that to be "out" in

India means being un-English in many ways, repudiating the pressure to conform to dominant definitions of Englishness or masculinity.

In their introduction to *Queer Forster,* Robert K. Martin and George Piggford distinguish between the term *gay* as "minoritizing and sanitizing" and the politically and theoretically preferable term *queer,* which they define as "seek[ing] to disrupt the economy of the normal" (4). Similarly, Yonatan Touval has suggested that we may take queerness to suggest not merely a sexual identity but that which is subversive of the norm: "[I]f we take 'queer' to mean the mapping out, and . . . demystification of, relations and identities that a hegemony of the normative would rather keep unquestioned."[31] In Forster's repeated use of the term in *A Passage to India,* Touval argues, "queerness is the stuff [that] things Indian, [or those *gone* Indian,] are made of," for queerness is "constituted by its *difference* from the English" (Touval, 242–43). Hence, *queer* in Forster's usage carries two overlapping registers: homosexuality as a politically chosen subversion of dominant social norms; and a racially or culturally different ethos that may undermine, question, or reshape Englishness itself.

After his sojourn in Egypt during World War I, Forster introduced his friend, the poet C. P. Cavafy, to English readers as situated "at a slight angle to the universe."[32] A Greek from Constantinople, a cosmopolitan, bilingual, and homosexual poet living in Alexandria, Cavafy wrote about homosexual love and about freedom from cultural and political imperialism. Describing Cavafy's cultural and sexual politics, Forster denotes a "queer" politics that seeks to shift the normative axes of seeing the world. The phrase is applicable to Forster as well, for his disruption of the normal also signifies a convergent sexual, racial, and imperial politics. This redefinition of *queer* can alert us in reading Forster's 1912 letters as linking homosexual and racial alterity, as both disruptive of English cultural hegemony. In them, Forster found a way to articulate a politics of dissident sexuality coded within, because integrally linked to, a racial and antiimperial politics that originates in a critique of Englishness.

According to the *Oxford English Dictionary,* in 1912 the word *queer* did not yet carry associations of homosexuality. Yet Forster and his contemporaries' use of it does suggest such an association. P. N. Furbank describes a clergyman who saw Roger Fry's post-Impressionist portrait of Forster (which Forster himself described as "queer") and remarked to his mother, "I hope your son isn't *queer?*" (1:206–7). (The painting was then removed from his mother's drawing room.)

Although the homosexual overtones of "queer" may not have acquired common currency, "there were groups of men—such as Henry James and E. M. Forster—who, in the 1890s and early 1900s, discreetly gave this epithet a homophile inflection."[33] By 1914, in *Maurice*, Forster had clearly come to associate *queer* with homosexuality and, indeed, with a certain (male Oxbridge) dissonance from normative bourgeois Englishness. In the first happiness of their union, for instance, Maurice and Clive talk about the discovery of their feelings at Cambridge as a "queer business."[34] When he embraces heterosexuality, Clive repudiates Maurice and the milieu Clive associates with his former "outlaw" self: "He hated queerness, Cambridge, the Blue Room, certain glades in the park"—as if "queerness" was defined by its relation to the homosocial intimacy and homosexual eroticism of the rest (175). As the novel progresses, the term *queer* is reclaimed from Clive's derogation of homosexuality and is associated instead with the subversiveness of Risley, who reveals to Maurice the irony of "respectable London" idolizing Tchaikovsky's masterpiece inspired by the nephew with whom he had "fallen in love" (162).[35]

In Forster's 1912 letters, these homosexual overtones of "queer" include a broader sense of cultural questioning. On the boat to India, Forster describes himself and his group of Cambridge friends (many of whom were homosexual) as "queer" because they rejected the group racism of the Anglo-Indians on board: "They think us very *queer* on board, but are not uncivil and term us the 'professors.' The women are pretty rotten, and vile on the native question: their husbands better. The only person I am intimate with on board is a young officer. Sounds *queer*, doesn't it, but not as *queer* as he must sound to the army, for he reads, writes rather decadent stories, knows Pushtu, Urdu, Russian, Arabic, Italian &c, and hates society, God, and authority" (to Florence Barger, October 17, 1912; *Letters*, 1:140; my emphasis). To be "queer," according to most English people bound for India, is to be outside the sphere of ordinariness and acceptability; to resist nationalist, bourgeois, cultural solidarity; to be too intellectual. But Forster transforms the epithet into a self-celebrating political position that combines homosexuality, antiracism, and a polyglot facility in different cultural and linguistic systems with a refusal to being tied to one system or allegiance. (Searight, the "young officer" in question, was also homosexual and wrote a "voluminous confessional diary" and "minorite" stories, some of which he lent Forster to read.)[36] For Forster, the word *queer* gathers multiple registers that are key to his unprecedented pleasure in things Indian: it suggests an alternative to the dominance of middle-class Englishness that is both racial and sexual—overtly signifying the extraordinariness of India and covertly also a signifier of homosexuality. It constitutes a challenge, a mark of difference that could not be rendered openly. Moreover, it puts the dominant notion of "Englishness" in question, subjecting it to the pressure of other ways of being English, disrupting the possibility of a stable norm of Englishness. To "que(e)ry," then, is not only to engage in a politics of sexual dissidence but also to estrange, to disrupt given societal norms.

In such a mode of "que(e)rying," Forster later queers Englishness in *Maurice*, showing explicitly how Englishness is constituted upon denial. As Maurice looks at himself in the mirror, he reflects ironically on the deceptiveness of his normality: "What a solid young citizen he looked—quiet, honorable, prosperous without vulgarity. On such does England rely" (that is, both at home and abroad, homosexual men are part and parcel of Englishness) (154). Forster's India trip enabled him to recast and re-see England as built on an imperial consciousness that suppressed knowledge of its constitutive fractures. *Maurice* ends with Forster's quietly ironic statement: "Clive on the bench will continue to sentence Alec on the dock. Maurice may get off" (255). In both cases, the homogeneity of a presumed "normality" is disrupted by the fact of a pervasive "outlaw" reality. As Risley (risibly) suggests, the pretensions of "respectable" English society rest on ludicrous ignorance: they "flock" to absorb bodily a music that is, in fact, the product of Tchaikovsky's deeply homoerotic desires (162).

While the privacy of Forster's travel journal—written only for himself—allowed for explicit reflections, the letters to his mother and aunts enacted a much more public function. Forster's 1912 letters were written mostly to a family of women, the feminine bourgeois suburban circle that bound him by laws of both affection and social and sexual restraint: his mother, aunts, and family friends. Although not to be published right away, they were written as *public* letters, in that they were shared, cross-referenced, and even read aloud to household help.[37] (When he finally published some of these letters in *The Hill of Devi* in 1953, he chose the ones written to his mother, not the more intimate revealing ones addressed to close friends.) This audience curtailed his voice—as he wrote in his 1953 preface, in 1912 he tended to turn "remote and rare matters into suburban jokes" (*HD*, 8)—but it also allowed him to subvert cultural, sexual, gender, and racial norms via the apparent novelty of the travel account. Thus, these letters reveal both Forster's preoccupations and his efforts to create a new kind of writing, a new form of agency, by undermining the norms that his English readers took for granted. These letters are thus more political than Forster's private travel journal, because they seek to effect a change in their readers' minds.[38]

As a result, Forster's Indian journal must be distinguished from his letters home. In the journal, used for private jottings of first impressions, Forster could be less guarded than in his letters, using it as a record for himself and a means of reflecting on his reactions. On his second day in India, for example, he measures the strangeness of what he sees against the familiar: "The Egyptian East has been Royal Academized [that is, painted to excess and deadened in museums], but not the Indian. Sometimes everything was strange . . . , sometimes a Surrey landscape of heath and blue distance would have buffaloes wallowing in a pond or scarlet lumps in the middle of the field" (October 24, 1912; *HDI*, 127). Like the colonial travelers that Forster had been reading, he aestheticizes what he sees as picturesque. But then this gaze shifts to a different kind of observation, as the "scarlet lumps" become moving bodies with a new body language: "Dawn revealed people walking beautifully, and it is these motions that strike me even more than their colours or clothes. Whether a man washed his legs or a child its whole body in the Railway Station fountain, whether a porter carries two trunks . . . or Baldeo [his servant] strides . . . , I am struck by the *individuality* of their movements. No two bodies function alike" (October 24, 1912; *HDI*, 127). Fascinated by different cultural codes and ways of constructing, limiting, or inhabiting the body, Forster seems to be compelled not only by bodies per se but also by their place in their environment, their different modes of enablement. Again and again he makes notes for reflection, such as his observation at a lake: "Many naked washermen on its margin" (January 3, 1913; *HDI*, 171). What repeatedly fascinates him is not just the nakedness but the unselfconsciousness and permissiveness of nakedness, the pleasant contrast (to England) of the nonscandal of the unclothed body. Noting frequently in his journal the worship of the divine phallus that for him links Hindu religiosity with unabashed sexuality, Forster does not mention these "lingams tipped with garlands" in his letters to his female readership at home (*HDI*, 172, 175, 177).

Notably, it is often the peasant or lower-class native whose body draws Forster's attention. When he meets college students at Aligarh, he notes to himself that they "are of all types, but one that is thin, dirty and bearded predominates. I was not attracted by them" (Aligarh, October 25, 1912; *HDI*, 128). Another entry reveals both revulsion and interest, as at a visit to a school: "Behind me a mass of little boys in blue turbans, smelling rather. Not a good type. Handsome specimen from A's school had come for the show—broad-shouldered, straight bright eyes, scarf, dhoti" (January 9, 1913; *HDI*, 176). Self-revealing and self-examining, Forster's private travel journal is as interested in what he sees as it is in seeing himself seeing, in observing himself as observer.

In contrast to this self-addressing diary mode, Forster's letters to his female relatives are more purposeful: they reveal greater caution and self-censorship but also contain subversive jibes at English ethnocentrism. Often Forster makes overt comparisons to critique Englishness both at home and abroad. In a letter to his Aunt Laura, he writes of a village near Aligarh: "The manners of our hosts were perfect—courteous and grave—and one thought with shame of their social equivalents in modern England" (October 31, 1912; *Letters*, 1:145). In the same letter, he describes a young Indian doctor, perhaps an early study of Dr. Aziz: "He seems as competent as he is charming, and I think I would as soon rely on him as on certain paler skins at home, whom I might mention by name but will not!" (*Letters*, 1:144). Again and again, Forster seems keen to undo colonial stereotypes and emphasize both the attractiveness of things Indian and the racial prejudice of the English. A letter to his friend Florence Barger concludes, "I'll end by remarking that I have enjoyed myself in India ever since I landed. It is quite different from anything anyone says.... When I happened to say on the boat that I was going to stop with a native, my table-neighbour was so horrified that after one gasp she changed the conversation. One was also told that Indian food is impossible—quite untrue" (November 2, 1912; *Letters*, 1:147). In another letter, describing one of Masood's friends as "thoroughly English in appearance and mind, but really a Eurasian—Hindu father and Irish mother ... a nice intelligent youth with a great deal of character and not at all what one expects Eurasians to be," Forster ruptures both the colonial silence about English women marrying Indian men and the stereotypes about Eurasians that were created by colonial fictions (January 21, 1913; *HDI*, 182–83).[39]

This explicit effort to counter colonial prejudice and racial stereotyping, to question English claims to cultural superiority and knowledge, extends into an attack on English assumptions of sexual propriety and desirability. When writing to his mother, he repeatedly describes as "beautiful" the often naked or half-naked men he saw, knowing that he can use the seemingly distanced language of aesthetic patronage and racial difference. In so doing, he can also convert that discourse into one of same-sex attraction and thereby query the English horror of unclothed bodies. After a visit to Peshawar, he describes the mountain people of the north: "The people, especially the men, were most beautiful and walked like kings. They dressed in every kind of garment or its absence, and always successfully" (*Letters*, 1:153). As if inverting Kipling's famous imperial allegory, "The Man Who Would Be King," in which two English vagabonds try to crown themselves kings of the Pathans, whom they consider to be white "savages," Forster presents Pathan men as already "kings" themselves, regal in their enviable self-possession of their bodies and space, unencumbered by clothing or its "absence." This replacement of clothing with bodily self-possession becomes a repeated refrain in these letters, as if exhorting his readers to see with his eyes, suggesting an unspoken desire both for those bodies and for their comfort in their bodiliness. The same letter describes a visit to Hindu temples in Lahore, where he "saw the priest, naked to the waist, singing hymns to Krishna" (*Letters*, 1:156). Racial, cultural, and class difference allows him to describe these bodies as "beautiful" when he may not have been able to use the same language for English male bodies (in writing to his mother)—yet that very difference allows a covert articulation of same-sex eroticism.

Later, on March 25, he describes an odd scene to his mother from Aurangabad: "Such a funny expedition this morning to the jail and to an old tomb near it. Saeed, myself, and the jail inspector, who knew no English, sat on the edge of the tomb-platform and took light refreshments. Naked men ran up trees and shook them and down fell things like catkins, which were picked up by policemen; they didn't taste bad" (*HDI*, 221). Under cover of a seemingly innocuous, amusing anecdote, Forster presents a self-knowingly incongruous picture of himself as both spectacle and spectator, a beneficiary of class and racially inscribed power, gazing on naked imprisoned men who labor for his benefit and are compelled to offer a suspiciously dangling unnamed fruit for his edification. Part of the irony of this description consists in the unwittingly official legislation of this scene: the homoeroticism of these men shaking this fruit off the tree is authorized by the presence of policemen, signifiers of violent authority, who monitor their movements. But Forster's irony revels also in the suggestively "catkin"-shaped fruit (probably mulberries), its strangeness contrasted to something English and familiar and offered for as seemingly innocuous a consumption as he offers this scenario to his readers. The image of the half-naked Indian man, which recurs also in *A Passage to India* (the silent man who emerges from the pond in Fielding's grounds with his scarlet tongue, or the punkah-wallah in the courtroom), thus suggests a paradigm for what India signifies for Forster: an opportunity for partial concealment and partial exposure, a dynamic not only of eroticism but also of writing.

This "que(e)rying" political edge in Forster's letters develops also in response to a political education in Indian racial and anticolonial struggles. Forster's critique of English sexual and racial prejudices borrows from and develops into acerbic, informed commentary on British colonial policy in India. Among the first Indians that Forster met were Masood's Muslim friends in Aligarh, which was then the center of the Muslim League and eventual separatist nationalist movement.[40] Early on, Forster learned about their frustration with the ongoing Balkan war, "which they [saw] as the death-struggle of Islam." In his letters, this Muslim nationalism is linked with an anti-imperialist critique of the British in India. "Why should Sir Edward Grey have been the *first* to recognize Italian rule in Tripoli?" he reports them asking. Forster's initial response is skepticism and uncertainty, finding the Indians at once "charming" and "grumbly," melodramatic yet "pertinent" (October 25, 1912; *Indian Journal*, HDI 128). But by December 2, with a deeper understanding of Indian-British relations, he has come to express irritation with British arrogance: "Nowgong a small Cantonment and a bore; polo; officers' wives with hideous voices and faces of that even pink. Though not more attracted to Indians than I was, I'm irritated by my countrymen more. They made dogs beg" (*HDI*, 156). As in *Passage* later, Forster's animus is directed toward Anglo-Indian women as gatekeepers of an Englishness that he disavows, along with their representation of racial and national homogeneity. Articulated in terms of color ("faces of that even pink"), his comment exposes whiteness as a construction, as a literally made up artificial unity.

Writing to his mother on December 16, 1912, from Chhatarpur, he criticizes the abuse of power by the British political agent appointed to watch over the Hindu Rajah, "bullying" him "in his own palace" (*Letters*, 1:171). When a bomb is thrown at the British viceroy in Delhi, Forster wearily refuses to repeat the rhetoric of English self-righteousness: "I needn't go into details as you will have had only too many in the papers" (*HD*, 27). Instead, he reports the bloodthirstiness (not reported in those papers) of "several Englishmen—officials of high position," who wanted their soldiers to fire into the unarmed crowd and "seemed really sorry that the Viceroy had not been killed, because then there would have been a better excuse for doing such a thing" (*HD*, 27–28). A precursor to the notorious 1919 Amritsar massacre, the event seems to inspire in Forster a counter desire to rupture the English claim of superiority and to ensure that readers back home knew of the ugliness of those acting in their name.

As Forster saw more of British-Indian tensions, he was called upon to take sides, to display loyalty and conform or be accused of sedition. Uneasy about taking a position thrust upon him, he adopts a guise of neutrality but feels compelled to report the ill behavior of the British and how it upsets him (191). Writing to his mother from Bankipore (January 15, 1913), Forster describes first how (educated middle-class) Indians were not allowed at the English club and could not play tennis and then, to his surprise, that he found himself defending the British empire to a respectful group of young Muslim nationalists: "[I]nterests of British Empire so complex, policy based not on hatred of Islam but on fear of Germany. It is very easy to talk politics when you meet someone who knows less than you do" (*HDI*, 180). The occasion is instructive, revealing both how Englishness infiltrates him and how it might be disavowed. Ironizing in his letter how his phrases poured over an impressionable group of admiring Indians, Forster registers his awareness of his glibness, undercutting the force of his own words, much as he would later undo the borrowed phrases of colonial cant uttered by Ronny Heaslop (*PI*, 52–53).

More often, he is impatient with English pretensions and tactics. To his friend Frances Barger, he grimly describes people who were rude to him for staying with Indians, pressuring him to conform and warning him of sedition when he tried to do anything "that wasn't done" (January 14, 1913; *HDI*, 182). In February, his stay with an assistant magistrate, R. B. Smith, produces depression and revulsion. "R.B.S. typical civilian. Protects ryots but hates any class that can criticize him. Invited Ahmed Mirza to lunch, but could not talk to him. Declared that Germany could make a fortune out of India by torturing natives till they gave up their hoards. Is curt and insolent to the pleaders in his court. Very bad—worse than I feared. Grew too depressed to sit with them" (February 2; *HDI*, 191). To Josie Darling, on February 4, 1913, he wrote, "I am so depressed by this hatred between the educated native (barrister type) and the ICS. I have always told the former that they were touchy and suspicious, but it is now borne in on me that they see no more than there is to see—much of the rudeness is studied and all of it springs from conscious superiority. . . . I don't repeat native gossip, but what I have myself heard and seen" (*HDI*, 193). At the end of his trip, after a conversation in Hyderabad with a young man whose fiery remarks about driving the English out become the template for Aziz's final outburst in *Passage*, he concludes in his journal that both are unjust to the other—but the English more so to the Indians (March 27, 1913; *HDI*, 223).

This understanding of British-Indian tensions made him heavily aware of how the effects of racial and colonial power infiltrated interpersonal encounters. In a letter to his mother, Forster describes his attendance at an Indian wedding ceremony set up by the Rajah of Dewas for his recently married English friends, Malcolm and Josie Darling. "There was a cry of 'May I come in' and enter the Rajah, bearing Indian raiment for me also. A courtier came with him, a very charming boy, and the two aided Baldeo [his servant] to undress and redress me" (*HD*, 31–32).[41] In the scene of cultural cross-dressing that follows, Forster seeks first to reassure his mother:

> At first nothing fitted, but the Rajah sent for other garments off people's backs until I was suited. . . . My legs were clad in jodhpurs made of white muslin. Hanging outside these was the youthful sirdar's white shirt, but it was concealed by a waistcoat the colour of Neapolitan ice—red, white and green, and this was almost concealed by my chief garment—a magnificent coat of claret coloured silk, trimmed with gold. I never found out to whom this belonged. It came to below my knees and fitted round my wrists closely and very well, and closely to my body. Cocked rakishly over one ear was a Maratha turban of scarlet and gold. . . . I carried in my left hand a scarf of orange coloured silk with gold ends, and before the evening ended a mark like a loaf of bread was stamped on my forehead in crimson, meaning that I was of the sect of Shiva. (32)

But the scene suggests more about Forster's new (queer) understanding of gender and sexual construction. His self-description proffers a figure whose identity is multiply acquired, created literally through the varied colors and articles of raiment borrowed from unknown individuals; the description reveals a fascination with the intimacy of wearing other men's clothes "closely to [his] body." It hints that a new kind of masculinity can be donned by the donning of clothes that signify the masculine in another system: the "rakish Maratha turban," possibly regarded as opulent or effeminate by Westerners, here both transforms Forster and is transformed by him (for his English readers) into a signifier of the masculine warrior. Moreover, it suggests more generally that masculinity in any system may itself be a garb, a matter of accepting culturally defined borrowed plumes. Then, as if to suggest that he was not the only one singled out, Forster continues: "Meanwhile the others too had been surprised with Indian costumes, Malcolm looking very fine in pink with a sword, and the other man in purple. The ladies went as themselves" (HD, 32–33). The phrase "the ladies went as themselves" suggests that even the English ladies did not have an essence, that their gender and racial identities likewise were performative, constituted by other "costumes" and role-playing.[42]

This deceptively light-hearted account is, however, further complicated by Forster's awareness that the contexts of colonial power and history of race relations heavily inflect these games of cross-cultural friendship. Forster knows that these exchanges of excessive amiability, the almost overeager tone of cordiality between this Hindu Rajah and his English friends, are laced by their knowledge of the ugliness between Indians and Britons around them and can only be understood within that broader framework. To disavow to themselves and to each other the tensions and politics of the British Raj, both groups—the Hindu Rajah as well as Forster and his liberal friends—try to emphasize their cordiality, graciousness, and mutual trust. When Forster notes how excited people are when he arrives—bowing, serving food, and so forth—he is well aware that it is because he is a white English man, inevitably a representative of his race and nation, that he is welcomed and treated well. (In a letter about his departure from Dewas, for instance, Forster describes how the "train waited 40 minutes for us [Forster and his companions] because we were white" [*Letters*, 1:173]). Because elsewhere, as with the visiting political agents, there is the tension and pompous formality that reminds each where he must belong, here, between H. H. and his English friends, there is an overly intense desire to please, to have fun.

Thus, in a typically astute observation, Forster notes in his journal from Dewas, "Land of petty treacheries, of reptiles moving about too cautiously to strike each other. No line between insolent and servile. . . . Is there ever civility with manliness here?" (*HD*, 41). Forster's sensitive antennae pick up the intrigues and power struggles at the Rajah's court, but his comment also suggests that he is thinking about gendering systems and how political and racial subordination affect the construction of manliness. For a well-bred Englishman, civility is a function of power—he can afford to be gracious where an Indian at this court cannot. If British manliness is defined by self-control and civility in the face of irritation, in the "independent" Rajah's court, where obeisance is expected of native subjects and civility toward an Englishman might be taken to signify disloyalty to the native regime, Indian men have to choose between opposite extremes. Subject both to their monarch and the British Empire, they have developed a cultural system of expressing servility to Britons, coupled with a mitigating insolence that simultaneously expresses resistance. Forster's comment thus also reveals his understanding of the inextricability of racial, gendered, and sexual oppression: that racial disempowerment is concomitant with a gendering and sexualizing process.

Forster's dual political education thus produces a new kind of writing in his letters from his first trip to India. In que(e)rying British racial and imperial policies as well as gender and sexual norms, Forster's letters to his female suburban audience try to educate, to find ways to bring the forbidden into language, and so to enact a form of action. A letter to his aunt Mary Aylward strikingly exemplifies this complex of concerns: the effort to compare Indians favorably with Britons, to undermine assumptions of English superiority and Forster's authority as a colonial traveler, and to incorporate an interest in male physicality as a tacit sexual politics. Describing a hunting trip with Masood, and the hospitality of a village near Aligarh, he remarks, "They had—the old men especially—such beautiful manners, and thin fragile faces that seemed full of intelligence; though I suppose they are the equivalent of a yokel on Salisbury Plain. Shaking hands was curious—they put both of theirs in yours, but without the slightest pressure; it was like saying how dye' do to a Greek statue" (*Letters*, 1:142). The letter evinces a fascination with these male Indian bodies, their manners, actions, faces, hands, as he tells his female English readers of their precious and rare quality. But then he shifts to the opposite strategy of making these Indian country men seem familiar—as familiar as the English country yokel—as if to reassure his readers (or himself), to assert similarity, not difference, between the English yokel and the Indian one. In both cases, his effort is to counter his reader's racial prejudice, even though he does so by placing these Indians by comparison lower in a hierarchy of class. But then Forster unsettles it again, as if needing yet another form of reference. His comparisons shift to the Greek statue. Notably, he is fascinated by the Indian body in a particular form of social contact—touching, or shaking hands—that he interprets as better than the English handshake. The Indian man seems to give himself wholly to another, "without pressure," without demand of reciprocation: "[T]hey put both of their [hands] in yours." But in an odd aestheticizing move, he also monumentalizes that Indian body, freezing it into a classical remnant ("a Greek statue"), whitening that black Indian body but also distancing it by locating it in an earlier time. Recalling Keats's similar fascination with a Grecian urn, this Indian body becomes both desirable and remote. Yet this, I would suggest, is a very complicated move. Forster expresses an ambivalent admiration, oscillating between diminishment and magnification. The reference to the statue suggests, as always with Forster's references to classical Greece, a nostalgic yearning for a homoeroticism not yet proscribed, and also a sense of himself being dwarfed, of being ludicrously inadequate, trapped in his Englishness, in this encounter with an altogether other and desirable but inaccessible being. It emphasizes the incongruity of modern English civility, ludicrously "saying how dye' do" to a Greek statue when confronted—and dwarfed—by something other.

Forster thus educates his suburban readers, reminding them that travel involves a two-way interaction, consisting not only of his reactions to the other but also of the other's reaction to him. A sense of his alienness, of a knowledge that his enthusiasm for these Indian villagers was not reciprocated, is apparent as he comments, "Hookahs were passed round but not to me, because not being a Mohammedan, I should have defiled it and the village would have had to throw it away" (*Letters*, 1:142). Although a colonial traveller, Forster is not trapped in his own vision of what he sees; he reports how others see him, disrupting the hegemony of a single gaze, or the one-directionality of subject looking at object. The self under the gaze of the other becomes representative of an English I/eye turned inside out, inviting his readers to rethink their positions, to become conscious that they are seen as well as seeing. Repeatedly in these letters he makes himself the object of others' gazes, a figure of ridicule, subjecting Englishness, via himself, to fracture.

In her important study of colonial travel writing, Mary Louise Pratt has described the self-aggrandizing discursive and epistemological strategies of writers such as David Livingstone and Richard Burton, as well as the self-undercutting and ironic stance of more ambiguously positioned colonial women writers such as Mary Kingsley.[43] Forster's later colonial epistolary travel writing does more: it provides a critique of Englishness both at home and abroad, to demonstrate that Englishness is not unified but constructed; it questions its hegemonic constructions of gender and sexuality and understands this questioning as both a political and a sexually dissident act. And in this, finally, is constituted the literary agency of these early Indian writings, in their effort to subvert and to change, through a language of the body, the dominance of imperialistic ways of seeing and of acting. Using the (pre)text of travel narrative, Forster rewrites (his own) colonial discourse to incorporate a coded articulation of travel as an alternative to imperialistic and heteronormative suburbanism at home. This would bear fruit in the fiction he wrote upon his return to England.

The Inestimable Gain of a New Language: Re-writing India in Maurice, *1913–14*

In April 1913, Forster came back from India invigorated, ready for a new novel. He began *A Passage to India*, only to stop after eight chapters. Between October 1913 and June 1914, he wrote *Maurice* in a burst of creativity, as if the energy released by his trip had to be diverted into the writing of this other (unpublishable) novel. Critics who connect the two novels usually read *Passage* as a completion of *Maurice*.[44] But perhaps it is really *Maurice* that secretly completes what *Passage* began: the fulfillment of male friendship across barriers of race, class, or sexual prohibition. Undoubtedly this novel, as Forster states, was the "direct result of [his] visit to . . . the home of Edward Carpenter and [Carpenter's] partner Merrill"—of their inspiring "touch," their comfort with their "inversion," their radical class politics, and his reading of Carpenter's work.[45] But another enabling factor may have been the trip to India, or what Forster learned from traveling and writing there. Though *Passage* was halted, Forster's Indian writings achieved something else: they informed and enabled *Maurice*.

The completion of *Maurice* brought Forster immense relief, joy, and approbation from the few friends with whom he shared it.[46] In a letter to Edward Dent, he writes confidently, "I wrote it neither for my friends [n]or the public—but because it was weighing on me.... I do feel that I have created something absolutely new, even to the Greeks" (March 6, 1915; *Letters*, 1:222). Forster's happiness came from believing he had pioneered a genre, putting into language what had so far eluded him, that he had overcome internalized prohibitions to achieve a self-recognition that even writers such as Walt Whitman and D. H. Lawrence denied themselves.[47] In *Maurice*, Forster describes the first "love scene" of Maurice and Clive, their jubilant mutual acknowledgment of their feelings for each other, as the "inestimable gain of a new language." His phrase well describes his own sense of gain as a writer. "No tradition overawed the boys. No convention settled what was poetic, what absurd. They were concerned with a passion that few English minds have admitted, and so created untrammeled" (93).

In his landmark essay, Robert K. Martin argues that in writing *Maurice*, Forster moved, like his protagonist, from one understanding of homosexuality to another, that of "the *fin de siècle* aesthetes to the robust political homosexuality of Whitman and Carpenter" (109). *Maurice* does not trace a simple movement from repression to awakening but instead marks—and endorses—a shift from an idealized, nonphysical sense of homosexual identity to one charged with a sense of political agency: "In this final stage [Maurice] begins to accept the social and physical consequences of homosexuality.... [H]e realizes that the outlawed state of the homosexual provides the privilege of a radical perspective on society ... indeed to the possible connections between homosexuality and democracy" (108–9).[48] Forster's reading of Whitman and Carpenter led him to consolidate his sense that the homosexual body could be written about; that a politically aware homosexuality entailed a broadening of political concerns to social justice of many forms; and that his writing could articulate these convictions. However, Martin does not include a crucial event that contributed to Forster's changed understanding of the link between homosexuality, political agency, and social divisions: namely, his first trip to India and his understanding of the link between not only class and sexual hierarchies but also between racial and sexual oppression. *Maurice* also depends on Forster's experiences in writing about India; it resonates with a new conviction of the need to intervene, in and through one's art, in pressing political matters.[49] Forster's renewed politicized view of homosexuality not only led to his racial and imperialist politics but also owed something to it.

Maurice is peppered with sardonic critiques of English society that echo Forster's 1912 Indian letters: the English lack of empathy with difference, the compulsion to conform, and the building of national identity upon an imperial imaginary. Maurice has to be educated out of this form of Englishness and learn to inhabit another. In the central crisis of the novel, Forster casts Maurice's inability to understand his friend Clive's turn to heterosexuality as an *English* failure of imaginative sympathy: "Maurice had the Englishman's inability to conceive variety. His troubles had taught him that other people are alive, but not yet that they are different" (161). The novel opens with an ironic account of a consultation between two English schoolmasters about their boys' sexual education. Mr. Ducie, the kindly senior master, believes in introducing the boys to the facts of heterosexual life. His bumbling "good talk" combines periphrasis with graphic anatomical drawings that baffle the young Maurice (13–15). But Mr. Read, the headmaster, is oblivious even to the need for such knowledge, and for his denial of the body is reserved Forster's more biting critique: "The Principal neither knew nor would have wished to know. Parting from his pupils when they were fourteen, he forgot they had developed into men. They seemed to him a race small but complete, like the New Guinea pygmies, 'my boys.' And they were even easier to understand than pygmies, because they never married and seldom died" (*Maurice*, 10). To this headmaster, "his" boys are a different "race": like a colonial anthropologist whose knowledge of his natives is purely instrumental, to be used to possess, police, and civilize those understood to be entirely distinct from himself, this ruler of powerless little male English lives fails to acknowledge any further responsibility to them.

Indicting the stunted nature of this schooling, this opening suggests that the novel will alternatively understand and explore this new "race" in directions that are closed to Mr. Abrahams (named possibly as an archetypal father figure who sacrificed his sons). It will concern itself with Maurice not simply as a boy but as one of an invisible "race" of English men whose preference for men must remain secret—a race of men who (as Forster told Florence Barger), like the pygmies, inhabit a "new and painful world," "a tiny world that is generally unknown to all who are not born in it" (March 28, 1915; *Letters*, 1:223).[50] The comparison suggests that for Forster a homosexual community had become analogous to "remote" colonized peoples such as those he had lived among in India, whose difficulties, desires, and codes he had attempted to learn and understand. As if enabled by his ability to write of one form of alterity (race), Forster begins *Maurice* via this comparison to address another (homosexuality), both subject to a similar system of forming and policing identity. Without drawing an equivalence between race, sexual orientation, or class, Forster understood the systemic links between these different forms of disenfranchisement and that a politics of resistance needed to integrate its opposition to them all.

Thus, Clive's mother links racial and sexual alterity when she tries to distance her son from his homosocial Cambridge associations. She expects him to "take his place," she tells Maurice, to marry, produce an heir, and travel to "the Colonies," not Greece (95). As a proper English aristocrat in an imperial and heterosexual system, Clive must, in other words, relinquish his interest in deviant suspicious activities (Greek history, homophilia, and philosophy) and participate in two forms of mastery: the colonial travel and knowledge represented by Mr. Abrahams, a distant survey of those whom he governed; and the perpetuation of an imperialistic country house tradition through marriage.[51] To both of these, this English mother intuits, Maurice, as Clive's middle-class "friend" and Platonic lover, represents a threat. As in his letters from India, here too Forster interrogates the Englishness constructed by this English matron, as built upon conjoined imperialist and heteronormative assumptions.

"Words *are* deeds," asserts Risley the "queer fish," Maurice's friend from Cambridge (32, 34). As if fixing the problem of *Arctic Summer*, Forster's abortive 1911 novel in which "battle" (material social action) is imagined as separate from "work" (writing and thinking), Risley's words resonate through *Maurice*, expressing Foster's newfound faith in the agency of writing. Thus, *Maurice* also provides some answer to Forster's crisis, enabling him to speak the unspeakable and to bring the body into his art. For the first time in his fiction, Forster names homosexuality (51). Not surprisingly, it is raised by the voice of prohibition. At Cambridge, another instructor interrupts a student's translation in Greek class: "Omit: a reference to the unspeakable vice of the Greeks" (51). Later, in a terrible scene of despair and self-disgust, when Maurice seeks a "cure" from his family doctor, turning against the truth of his own body, he can find no language to describe himself except to declare, "I'm an unspeakable of the Oscar Wilde sort" (159). But this prohibition opens up the "delicate subject," so that

Clive can counter-educate Maurice by exposing the criminal "hypocrisy" of this censorship of "the mainstay of Athenian society" (51). Thus, Maurice learns both that it was possible to speak of the unspeakable and that speaking brought freedom and the cementing of their relationship: "No more was said at the time, but [Maurice] was free of another subject, and one that he had never mentioned to any living soul. He hadn't known it could be mentioned, and when [Clive] Durham did so in the middle of the sunlit court a breath of liberty touched him" (51).

This unspeakable body, Forster suggests, is also the site of truth. When Maurice forces himself to engage in heterosexual dalliance, he plays a role out of touch with his own truth and forces his attentions upon a guest. "It was not that Miss Olcott objected to having her hand pressed. Others had done it and Maurice could have done it had he guessed how. But she knew something was wrong. *His touch revolted her.* It was a corpse's" (54; my emphasis). In this dramatic trope, "something" remains unspecified, but she knows from Maurice's touch a bodily truth—that he may well be dead to her. Like Adela in a similar outdoor moment of physical contact, Miss Olcott flees in panic from a sexual knowledge that she cannot acknowledge in words. "The body is deeper than the soul and its secrets inscrutable," remarks Forster (54).

Maurice ends with Forster's redefinition of Englishness, learned from his travel writing in India, incorporating both race and class divisions and a new ability to speak the body. It suggests that Englishness is not immutable but can be changed and complicated. Locating it in an earlier tradition of the greenwood, moving from the national museum to the woods, Forster offers not just a nostalgic retreat, as many critics have read the ending.[52] Escape from England to the colonies would be too easy, relinquishing the definition of Englishness to the imperialists who exclude the likes of Maurice and Alec. Instead, to reconstitute Englishness in the heart of England is to reassert class and homosexual difference within it, to insist that England is itself other. Unlike "The Other Boat," also begun in 1913, in which homosexual desire and social standing are split literally between the worlds above and below deck, and between England and the boat to India, in *Maurice*, there is no other boat for Maurice.[53] Instead, he reclaims England. As he bids farewell to the steamer that would have taken him and Alec abroad, Maurice turns with a poignant wistfulness to a braver alternative: "For a long time he gazed after her, then turned to England. His journey was nearly over. He was bound for his new home. He had brought out the man in Alec, and now it was Alec's turn to bring out the hero in him. He knew what the call was, and what his answer must be. They must live outside class, without relations or money. . . . But England belonged to them. That, besides companionship, was their reward. Her air and sky were theirs, not the timorous millions' who own stuffy little boxes, but never their souls" (238–39). At the novel's conclusion, Maurice claims possession not of his lover but of "England," and hence of his own "soul." Paradoxically, England belongs to those who are free within it, who refuse to submit to its "stuffy little boxes." Maurice rejects the option of escape; he chooses to transform England from within. This choice is presented as "heroic" and "manly" not only because it will require the sacrifice of all that shaped his prior identity but also because it spells a new form of radical agency. In so doing, Forster redefines Englishness as the heroic capacity to grasp one's freedom. Such a revision must take place in the heart of England, not outside it. Thus, Forster takes what he has learned in India about power and its effects, and he applies it at home.

India Again (1921–22) and Interracial Desire

The completion of *Maurice* brought Forster immense happiness as well as despair. As Furbank explains, "[T]o have written an unpublishable novel, he found, was no help at all towards producing a publishable one" (Furbank, 1:259). To Goldie Dickinson, Forster wrote, "What's to occupy me for the rest of my life, I can't conceive. I am very glad to have got [*Maurice*] done though it exhibits the emptiness of all literary achievement in rather an acute form. . . . [E]ven if it could be published, in 20 years all would be as it is today. Really why does one write? And feel that despite all that writing's important?" (December 13, 1914; *Letters*, 1:216–17). Yet such doubts about the social or political efficacy of art, written at the brink of war, reveal the desire for that efficacy. For the Bloomsbury group, the war spelled the demise of civilization and democracy, but it also exacerbated Forster's concern about taking action in a public sphere. The Indian travel writing and *Maurice* had provided a new fuel, and war, as a crisis of another sort, compelled the taking of strong positions and action through writing. Forster's wartime writing (1915–19) reveals new and important features: he took a public stand on war, censorship, and British imperialism; and he adopted a direct mode—essays, reviews, travel journalism—eschewing the indirections of fiction.

When D. H. Lawrence's novel *The Rainbow* was seized by Scotland Yard, Forster wrote a vehement letter to Sir Henry Newbolt, insisting that precisely during war, when censorship was rationalized in the name of national security, rights had to be protected: "[T]he right to literary expression is as great in war as it was ever in peace, and in far greater danger, and I write on the chance of your being willing and able to protect it" (November 7, 1915; *Letters*, 1:231). Thus began Forster's lifetime battle against censorship—literary or otherwise.[54] He wrote strong letters to the *Manchester Guardian* and the *Daily Herald* on imperial policy in both Egypt and India: "Europe is starving. In Egypt the native population is being arrested wholesale. Similarly in India. At home prices are rising, unrest is increasing. . . . Are we downhearted? No. Do we clamour for facts, for the removal of censorship, for the repeal of DORA? No" (quoted in Furbank, 2:59). Taking a political stand was thus intertwined with protecting men he loved: protesting their racial and colonial predicament as well as the English imperial system that constrained him as a similar "minority" or "outlaw" within England. Racial and sexual oppression are thus conjoined and implicated for him in the same system.

Between 1919 and 1921, Forster wrote two kinds of nonfiction—as if the political agency he desired for his fiction had to be rehearsed in these forms. One, at the request of Leonard Woolf, was a history of the British occupation of Egypt and a pamphlet on the Egyptian question ("for Mohammed's sake" [Furbank, 62]). "How easy it is to write impressively about politics," Forster commented (Furbank, 62). Second, he wrote *Alexandria: A History and Guide* (1922) and collected his wartime journalistic pieces from Egypt under the title *Pharos and Pharillon* (1923).[55] As travel journalism, each guide to Egypt attempts to build understanding, to function as a humble lighthouse amidst the shoals and rocks of cultural misapprehension.[56] Each also rehearses ways to rewrite British colonial discourse and to craft a language of agency and transformation that he would draw upon for his Indian novel.

But from 1921 on, Forster's writing is split into the visible and invisible, the public and private. While he published urgently motivated letters, essays, and reviews, privately he wrote homosexual stories that he could not publish and which, unlike *Maurice*, did not even win the approbation of friends. What Forster desired, as he struggled to resume *A Passage to India* in 1921, was the conjoining of the two. But something else seemed to intrude, something new that obstructed the fiction he desired to write. This is intimated in the writing from his second trip to India.

Forster's letters and journals from this second trip to India (March to November 1921) reveal considerable differences from his first: less exuberant, more exasperated, more prone to cultural and racial generalizations. Nine years after his first trip, Forster returned to India with more experience of writing, travel, and sexuality, not touring with friends but in the capacity of secretary to the Rajah of Dewas, and he found Indian-English relations noticeably worsened.[57] Yet his change in tone cannot be accounted for entirely by these factors. In contrast to the public versions of his letters that Forster later revised and published in *The Hill of Devi* (1953), the private writings—journal entries and letters to intimate friends such as Florence Barger and Goldsworthy Dickinson—reveal a deeper unease and an ambivalence about interracial relations that arose from a new and different understanding of same-sex interracial desire in the context of unequal power.

To be sure, the 1921 letters that Forster selected for *The Hill of Devi* in 1953 still express many of the anti-Anglo-Indian sentiments and efforts to subvert stereotypes as those of 1912–13. His first letter to his mother describes a party to which he went wearing Indian clothes and watched the singing and acting: "I crossed my legs as long as they would bear it, then sat behind on a chair and reflected with pleasure that there was not another European within [a] radius of twenty miles" (*HD*, 85). In another letter, he reflects on his privilege and British misconceptions: "People talk about Oriental seclusion: what strikes me is Oriental publicity. Here I am among Maratha nobles, a conservative and lofty race, yet I eat with them, sit in their bedrooms and visit their womenfolk" (*HD*, 94–95). He criticizes imperial government and administrators, as in his ironic account of the "Insult" he got (as an Englishman serving an Indian king) from a visiting British official (*HD*, 144–47) or of the foolishness of the "Political Department" for its "bad manners," which he saw as out of touch with the changing realities of Indian nationalism (*HD*, 113).

But at the same time, these letters also express a surprising irritation with the disorganization and "muddle" in Dewas, which extends to Indian aesthetics, religion, and sexuality (HD, 115). There is less effort to reassure or amuse and a greater exasperation, weariness, and sense of difficulty. His first letter begins with an almost symbolic account of cultural miscommunication: no one arrived to greet him, because Masood had not received any of Forster's letters and the nobles from Dewas had misread his address. Inaugurating a central concern of *A Passage to India*, he begins with the problems of language and writing, misapprehension and misplaced letters (HD, 82). Throughout, Forster repeats the difficulty of literally not knowing the language, a difficulty magnified into a larger sense of confusion and miscommunication across different codes of signification. "Everything that happens is said to be one thing and proves to be another, and as it is further said in an unknown tongue I live in a haze" (HD, 93). A more recurrent refrain, especially felt because of his responsibilities as secretary, concerns the extravagance, waste, and disorder of Dewas: "You would weep at the destruction, expense, and hideousness, and I do almost. . . . I look into a room — dozens of warped towel-horses are stabled there, or a new suite of drawing room chairs with their insides gushing out. I open a cupboard near the bath and find it full of teapots. . . . And so on and so forth. I don't know what to do about it all and scarcely know what to feel. . . . [I]t is as profoundly Indian as an Indian temple" (HD, 86–87). To Malcolm Darling he is more blunt: "I am glad the arrangement is temporary only. . . . To check the idleness, incompetence and extravagance is quite beyond me" (HD, 99).

Unlike Rushdie, who would later celebrate the multiplicity of Indian Hindu culture against the austerity of Islam in Pakistan, Forster becomes gradually horrified by the excess of what he regards as Hindu culture and aesthetics, against which he sets the clarity of Islam. To one (unidentified) friend, he writes, "I am coming round a little to your view of the Indian or anyhow Hindu character — that it is unaesthetic. One is starved by the absence of beauty" (HD, 131). Unable to understand religious rituals — Holi or Gokul Ashtami — which he describes in sardonic detail, he comments, "What troubles me is that every detail, almost without exception, is fatuous and in bad taste" (HD, 159). "There is no dignity, no taste, no form, and though I am dressed as a Hindu I shall never become one" (HD, 161). Upon leaving Dewas, he comments, "I do like Islam, though I have had to come through Hinduism to discover it" (HD, 193) and "I have passed abruptly from Hinduism to Islam and the change is a relief" (HD, 235). Reading the architecture of each culture symbolically, he prefers the singularity of a mosque or the Taj Mahal to the "mess and profusion and confusion" of the Hindu temple (*HD*, 192–93).

This disenchantment with Hindu religion and culture seems to stem from an unease about sexual and bodily codes that undoes the sense of liberation of the first trip. He expresses discomfort, as before, about the lack of privacy: "I cannot get over the constant publicity," he writes, of servants' "creeping forms," the intrusion that extends to surveillance (*HD*, 105). This dislike of personal invasion is linked to a distaste for what he sees as a certain bawdiness in daily life and forms of entertainment. He deplores the Rajah's (that is, H.H.'s) "vulgar" uncle Scindhia (*HD*, 126), who epitomizes the worst faults of Dewas: "the tiresome practical jokes, the growing dread of education, the bawdy talk which is subtly wrong" (*HD*, 130). To Florence Barger, he writes that the singing parties would appear a "debauch to the superficial observer. But there is much verbal and histrionic indecency which amused me at first, not now, because I see that it takes the place of much that I value" (185).

The letters of 1921 that Forster excluded from *The Hill of Devi* reveal a yet stronger distaste for this purportedly bawdy Hindu sexuality. A comparison of two versions of one incident is illustrative. The first occurs in a letter to Goldsworthy Dickinson, the Cambridge mentor with whom he first went to India, who was one of his circle of homosexual friends. Unlike the sanitized account to his mother (*HD*, 85), here Forster gives a detailed account of the musical farce that he saw performed under the auspices of Holi:

> I'll pick from the confusion a few impressions of Holi, the Hindu Dionysia that coincide with our Easter and that few Europeans can have seen much.... Troupe of dancers & actors from the Deccan—only one of the girls a girl, the others boys. There was a farce which I saw again at the Palace the next night.... Husband & wife. She: "Can I go and see my people?" He: "Dangerous for you—and for me—and morality generally." She persists, and as soon as she goes the husband says "I want a eunuch—*at once.*"—A tall scraggy man with a moustache then came on, in a pink sari, and paid attention to such members of the audience as His Highness indicated. (This is a recognized turn: the boy dancers did it too.) The "eunuch" squatted beside his victim and sang "do not hurt me"—or "I am not too old yet to remember what we did as boys"—and tried to kiss him amid laughter from the court. Resuming the drama he danced indecently before the husband, made terms with him,

bought him sweets, and was coming to a conclusion when the news is brought to the ill-advised wife. She returns from her parents. "How can you ruin your health by such a proceeding?" is her argument: and I think that is where this particular indecency ended. (April 10, 1921; *Letters*, 2:3–4)

Revealing his concomitant unease and sense of liberation in the upsetting of sexual and gender norms, Forster casts Hindu India here as a "confusion," while also linking it with the carnal and carnivalesque—the overturning of social hierarchies and order by the bodily—in the "Dionysian" Greek tradition that he upheld. He notes first the gender cross-dressing and (role) playing allowed among men: as he adds later, if the actor playing the cross-dressed eunuch had been really a girl, it would have been "too much," but a boy-actor was allowed to play the eunuch who can entertain the husband while the wife is away. Second, he seems struck that the boy actor can disrupt the boundary between performance and reality, breaking out of the putative "play" to engage in real play with actual members of the audience (selected by the all-controlling Rajah), so that the performance becomes a joke, a setup to engage in the real teasing of chosen male members of the court, including (presumably) Forster himself. And third, the letter notes another element of what Forster took to be Indian sexual permissiveness: the joke that men will "naturally" turn to eunuchs to satisfy homosexual urges as soon as their wives leave, suggesting that their heterosexuality is merely a concession to the cultural imperatives of procreation, whereas a woman's role is to ensure and monitor that norm. But wives *know*, and they take this disruption of the norm in stride. The wife in the play is warned in all comic seriousness by her husband; upon returning, she can only protest weakly, "How can you ruin your health?"—as if her primary concern were to ensure that his homosexual dalliance not jeopardize their heterosexual productivity.[58]

Then Forster describes his reaction, rather different from that of his first trip:

I was struck with the remoteness of their sexual gestures: in most cases I didn't know what was up. One "girl" lay on her face and extending her hands before her clasped and unclasped them alternately. This indicated the act of copulation. "If it had really been a girl" said H.H. "it wouldn't have done, it would have been too much. But they have a boy which makes it all right." I wonder! All very odd. I shall never feel the surety of matters here that I felt in Egypt. The sphere of "naughtiness" seems wider, and perhaps this it is that makes it faintly distasteful to me. And I rather fancy religion queers it. For a few days later, I came in for more Holi in a village. . . . We rested outside while the villagers sang and tried to cover our clothes with red powder: and the women issued from a rent in the mud wall and sat twenty yards off. When we passed them they abused us ritually like the women at the bridge in Ancient Greece. And I expect that queer superstitions are mixed up with the merriment and sex generally, & that's why we can't follow either. (April 10, 1921; *Letters*, 2:3–4)

Like his remarks about language earlier, here too Forster finds Indian bodily codes unreadable and "remote." What seems strange to him is that heterosexuality is more tightly policed than homosexuality here—a girl could not engage in this sexual teasing while a boy can. Forster finds this Indian carnivalesque disturbing and repellent; hence he deems the Hindu religion and its sanctioned liberties unpleasantly "queer." At best, he can link the women's ritualistically "obscene" abuse with the primitivism of a known ancient culture, but one that remains remote.

What are we to make of this unexpected change from the tenor of the letters from his first trip? Does this bespeak an internalized sexual disgust displaced upon racial otherness, as some scholars have seen it?[59] But such readings do not account for its newness, the shift from Forster's initial delight in India's "queerness," or for the self-awareness of his racial and sexual distaste. For if Forster was aware of his new negative feeling, then how could it be an unconscious displacement of sexual self-disgust? And why did Forster conceal this acknowledged unease when he revised these letters for publication? A comparison with the version he sent his mother shows that Forster was unwilling to reveal this sense of racial distance and repulsion in his public persona. In the version rewritten in 1953 for publication in *The Hill of Devi*, Forster tells his readers that after his mother's death, he can be more open about describing court ribaldry. Yet this later version is actually more cautious and concealed than the original letter to his friend Dickinson:

> *Arriving as I did during Holi, I found Dewas at its most Dionysiac. That play which I witnessed the first evening at the cavalry party was so characteristic of the riotous season that I could not describe it when writing to my suburban home. It was a ribald oriental farce.* Husband and wife. She: "Can I go and visit my parents?" He: "Dangerous for you—and for me—and for morality more

generally." She persists, and as soon as she goes the husband cries, "I want an eunuch . . ." [ellipses in original] A tall scraggy man with a moustache then appeared, dressed in a pink sari, and paid *grotesque and unwelcome* attentions to such members of the audience as H.H. indicated.—This *seemed to be* a recognized turn. Squatting beside his victim, the *hideous creature sang and mopped and mowed while the court applauded. Returning to the farce, he behaved similarly* to the husband and was offering him a present of sweets when the news was brought to the ill-advised wife. She returns from her parents hastily. "How can you ruin your health by such a proceeding?" was her argument, *and it prevailed. Since both the performers were male, H.H. considered that the proprieties had been observed.* (HD, 95–96; later additions indicated by italics)

In this revised and abridged version, Forster both adds distancing remarks and excises crucial explicit details. He omits what the eunuch says to his "victim" and the audience's active encouraging participation and enjoyment, describing the scene as entirely a one-sided performance; most crucially, he leaves out his reactions of unease or ambivalence or generalizations about Indian culture. He adds seemingly impersonal but overt judgmental adjectives—"grotesque and unwelcome attention" and "hideous creature"—that apply to the actors, not to their reception, and help establish his position as a gracious but distant English observer.

This split between private and public versions of Forster's Indian travel writing is symptomatic of a more general split in Forster's writing from 1921 on, between his published essays and *Passage* and the unpublished fiction and letters.[60] In print, Forster continues to express his liberal politics, advocating interracial friendship and understanding. But in the unpublished writings, he reveals serious doubts about interracial sexuality and explores complex dynamics of same-sex desire and repulsion as refracted by the hierarchies of colonial power. This is where he articulates a different, otherwise unspeakable understanding of both sexuality and racial difference that is not apparent in his published work yet is necessarily the dark underside to that work. Forster's ambivalence about the sexual codes he found operative at Dewas are part of a broader irritation with the pernicious effects of the colonial situation on both Indians' and Britons' sense of self and interpersonal relations. Moreover, as we learn from his locked diary, his change in tone is also attributable to something he could not make public: his experiences in 1921 with Kanaya, a royal servant procured for Forster's homosexual pleasure, which embroiled him in frustration, disappointment, betrayal, courtly intrigues, and finally humiliation. This led, I argue, to private (posthumously published) writing in 1922 that reflects on that experience and reveals a new, highly self-aware understanding of interracial desire as inherently molded from the asymmetries of power and consequent power struggles.

Christopher Lane makes an important distinction between "homophilia" (the ideal that Forster overtly promoted, of friendship and understanding between men of different races or classes) and "homosexuality" (the reality, in which same-sex male desire across difference became volatile and violent) (*Ruling Passions*, 165). Lane argues that Forster was overcome by his unconscious racism and sexual self-disgust and that his publicly proclaimed politics was undermined by the ambivalence revealed in the unpublished fiction. Aiming to "foreground the ambivalent sexual and unconscious fantasies that underpin relations between colonizer and colonized in Forster's work," Lane claims that, "far from resolving political distance into personal connection, interracial sexuality usually compels Forster's characters to disavow or redefine the precise meaning of their national and sexual identities."[61] However, between such an aim and a claim, Lane creates a slippage between Forster and his characters. I contend that the more mature Forster is fully *aware* and *self-critical* of the contradictory nature of interracial same-sex desire and that he in fact explores its slippery dynamics in his unpublished writing. After his experiences in Egypt with Mohammed el Adl and the war, he understood not only, as Robert Young has argued, that racial "disgust always bears the imprint of desire" but also that interracial colonial desire was often conjoint with, indeed even exacerbated by, racial antipathy.[62] Indeed, the difference between Forster's published and unpublished writing is attributable to his attempts to work through the very difficulties that he confronted in the unpublished writing, which provided an occasion to explore what Forster was unwilling to make public. Lane also tends to homogenize Forster's "public" writing—from "only connect," the optimistic plea of *Howards End* (1910) to the vigorous assertion of "What I Believe" (1939).[63] However, Forster's understanding of the complexities of interracial same-sex desire came later in his career than his avowed politics, and he struggled to resist the interference of this knowledge with the writing he meant for publication. In 1922, upon returning from India, Forster wrote two important pieces, the short story "The Life to Come" and an autobiographical fragment in his locked diary, "Kanaya," that both self-consciously explore this dynamic and work through what he could not articulate concurrently in *Passage*.

Before turning to these posthumously published writings of 1922, however, I would like to look at an earlier manifestation of the self-critical consciousness that underpins them. In 1916, Forster wrote to Malcolm Darling, then a colonial administrator in India, from Egypt:

> My idealisation . . . of India mounts and mounts. . . . Egypt feeds it by contrast. I hate the place, or rather, its inhabitants. This is interesting isn't it, because I came inclined to be pleased and quite free of racial prejudices, but in 10 months I've acquired an instinctive dislike to the Arab voice, the Arab figure, the *Arab way of looking or walking or pump shitting or eating or laughing or anythinging*—exactly the emotion that I censured in the Anglo-Indian towards the native there. What does this mean? Am I old, or is it the war, or are these people intrinsically worse? Any how I better *understand* the Anglo-Indian irritation though I'm glad to say I'm as far as ever from *respecting* it!! It's damnable and disgraceful, *and it's in me*. (August 6, 1916; *Letters*, 1:238–39; my emphasis)

In this astonishing passage, what Forster identifies as repulsive are signifiers of bodily difference ("the Arab way of looking or walking"), or modes of inscribing cultural and racial alterity. Written before Forster had met Mohammed el Adl, this outburst was triggered by an incident that Forster goes on to describe: an Egyptian acquaintance had invited Forster to an illegal "Hascish [hashish] den," indulged himself there, assured the owner of secrecy, and then turned him over to the police. Forster's comment needs to be understood not as an expression of unconscious or latent racism but as a more complex, conscious tussle with that latent racism, or as a resistance to the hegemonic, an engagement with the ideological indoctrination that Forster both recognizes in himself and seeks to repudiate. Horrified to discover that he is infected with exactly the kind of racial prejudice toward Egyptians that he had censured in British attitudes toward Indians, Forster invites his reader to contemplate—with him—his divided reaction ("This is interesting isn't it"): first, he makes clear that he condemns it—"It's damnable and disgraceful"; second, he recognizes that "it's in me." This discovery of alterity within the self, this distinction between "understanding" and "respecting" that deeply inculcated racial antipathy leads to a particular kind of late anti-imperial self-critique that operates through self-exposure, by revealing the effects of imperialist cultures on the implicated subject.[64]

"Kanaya," a more startling piece, develops this self-awareness into a radical understanding of interracial sexuality in the context of empire as violent and self-annihilating, as fundamentally different from the anti-imperialist antiracism that Forster overtly opposed. Written in 1922 not for publication but to be read to his friends and critics in the Bloomsbury group, "Kanaya" is a highly crafted piece, and though autobiographical, it is no less self-conscious or deliberate than any of his fiction.[65] It describes with extraordinary explicitness, upon Forster's arrival at Dewas, his sexual frustration, his fear of the Rajah's discovery of his homosexuality, his guilt at having betrayed H.H.'s (the Rajah's) trust, and his final confession to the Rajah. The result of this is that H.H., who had publicly condemned sodomy, declares Forster an exception (because he is English) who must not be allowed to suffer from unfulfilled lust. H.H. then functions as a royal pimp for his English secretary and procures a male prostitute, a servant boy named Kanaya.[66] However, Forster is then put in the even more difficult position of having to conceal his encounters with this boy not only for his own sake but also for that of the Rajah, whose complicity, if discovered, would undermine his already fragile power in the double context of British colonial surveillance and local rivalry.

A remarkably self-disclosing and self-knowing document, "Kanaya" can be read as the unspeakable underside to the published version of Forster's Dewas sojourn in *The Hill of Devi*, explaining his increasing seemingly gratuitous racial irritability and disenchantment, which coincides with his mounting tension and declining prestige. Far more explicit in sexual details and racial generalizations than the published letters are,[67] "Kanaya" charts a narrative of Forster's disillusionment with interracial homophilia and his resignation to a darker understanding of interracial homosexuality. It begins with Forster's account of his sexual urges, intensified—in a recognizable colonial idiom—by the heat and geographical location, and reveals his undaunted desire for friendship or "conversation" to extend beyond the merely carnal (312). When he meets Kanaya, he hopes for friendship as well as sexual gratification: "As is usual with me, I at once felt interest and tenderness towards him and hoped we might become friends" (319). But India would teach him another lesson, he suggests, in the erotics of disappointment. Kanaya proves to be "a pretty boy," an absurd, "effeminate," diminutive creature, "skipping away through the sunshine holding an umbrella to protect his complexion" (318), with "the body and soul of a slave" (319). Lost in a garden at night with Kanaya guiding him home "hand in hand," Forster reflects on the disappointing disjunction between emotional and bodily need: "[T]his is the companionship one really seeks, although it presents itself as a physical urge. I couldn't know this barber-boy, for the reason that there was nothing to know" (320).[68]

Crisis occurs when Kanaya boasts indiscreetly of his relations with Forster and attempts to blackmail the Rajah. H.H. decides that to quell rumors, Kanaya has to be retained, because his dismissal would confirm the scandal. Forster describes how, upon discovering Kanaya's perfidy, he boxed Kanaya's ears and enacted the oriental despot at whose feet Kanaya wept for mercy:

> [Kanaya] had been such a goose—had done himself and the rest of us in because he *couldn't hold his tongue*, and the cooli [an earlier aspirant to Kanaya's position] had been the same. *What relation beyond carnality could one establish with such people?* . . . I resumed sexual intercourse with him, but it was now mixed with *the desire to inflict pain*. It didn't hurt him to speak of, but *it was bad for me, and new in me,* my temperament not being that way. I've never had that desire with anyone else, before or after, and I wasn't trying to punish him—I knew his silly little soul was incurable. I just felt he was a slave, without rights, and I a despot whom no one could call to account. (*HDI,* 323–24; my emphasis)

Caught in this bizarre situation of betrayal and enforced intimacy, Forster renders carnality (or interracial and cross-class homosexuality) as deplorable, a lesser substitute for friendship (homophilia) established through conversation, trust, and understanding. Yet this passage is tricky. In describing the sudden turn from ideal friendship to the sexual and psychic pleasures of inflicting pain, Forster is well aware of his metamorphosis into sadist and despot. His statement "it was bad for me" is disingenuous, disregarding the body on which he inflicts pain, but it also refocuses his readers'—and his own—attention on the transformative effects of colonial power. Like the letter from Egypt, "Kanaya" becomes less an account of the folly of Kanaya, or even of Forster's disillusionment with interracial homophilia—and more a deliberately self-exposing account of Forster's reaction and metamorphosis. Providing an account of the violence inherent in erotic desire and the degrading self-destruction incumbent upon the abuse of power, Forster exposes what he has become thanks to the larger structure of racial and imperial hegemony in which he is located.

Whereas some critics have read this as Forster's substitution of racial for sexual disgust, I would contend that the disgust expressed here is *colonial* self-disgust, cognizant of how imperial power refracts erotic desire, and desiring to reveal from within, to attest to the lived truth of such metamorphosis upon the colonizing psyche. Forster's writing here seeks to unravel and expose the effects of imperial conquest and racial superiority in and through his experiences. Every encounter is loaded by the tensions produced by British-Indian relations. When Kanaya's indiscretions realize Forster's fears of exposure and hostile courtiers revel in Forster's humiliation, he writes knowingly of their anticolonial triumph: "I had to bear a good deal of impertinence and ill-breeding.... They weren't openly rude but there was an air of rollicking equality: 'You're no better than we are, after all,' and probably a little racial vengeance" (321).

Back in England, as he struggled to resume *Passage*, he reported in his diary, "Have this moment burnt my indecent writings or as many as the fire will take. Not a moral repentance, but the belief that they clogged me artistically. They were written not to express myself but to excite myself.... I am not ashamed of them.... It is just that they were a wrong channel for my pen."[69] But both "Kanaya" and "The Life to Come," the story of interracial homosexual desire that he wrote that same year, survived this bout of destruction either because they did not "clog" the writing of *Passage* or because Forster could not bear to burn them. Perhaps both did enable the novel, rehearsing in some form what could not explicitly be said there. Even more so than "Kanaya," "The Life to Come" (1922) elaborates the belated understanding of the dynamics of power and sexuality that emerges in his writings from his second trip and shadows his last novel.[70] Indeed, it articulates a reluctant knowledge that Forster reached after his second visit to India, which remains a constitutive though unspeakable premise of *Passage*: that homoerotic attraction may arise not *despite* but *because* of the differences of power across racial or class divisions, and that its frisson depends on the asymmetry and potential of violence and abuse that are inherent in such inequalities of power.

A highly ironic and crafted tale, "The Life to Come" opens with an account of how Paul Pinmay, a young English missionary, attempts to convert

Vithobai, a native (possibly Indian) "inland chief" to Christianity but is instead seduced by Vithobai's flower-bedecked body into a passionate fulfillment of same-sex desire. Punning on "the love of Christ," the story satirizes the process by which Vithobai is seduced as well, by Pinmay's promises of continuation of their ardor in "a life to come," and then exploited and dispossessed of his kingliness, in a typical evocation of colonial deception. But to any easy reading of this story as a simple denunciation of the invasion and destruction of an indigenous community by capitalist imperialists in the guise of chauvinistic civilizers, the depiction of Vithobai and the violent ending prove a problem, apparently confirming stereotypes about native inscrutability, unreliability, and vengefulness. While Pinmay is clearly cast as an abusive colonial official, slowly losing his conscience as ten years pass to consolidate his power, Vithobai, who lies dying of tuberculosis (disease brought by the colonialists) turns upon Pinmay (who has come to assure him again, ambiguously, of "love" in "the life to come"), stabs Pinmay through the heart, and jumps to his own death.

But if read closely, this ending suggests how the power and racial differences between the two men exacerbate their attraction for each other, suggesting that their sexual desire for each other is itself a function of the desire for power over the other. Vithobai's final act is impelled not simply by a romantic desire to reunite with his lover in death or afterlife or by a vengeful desire to reverse the exploitation and servitude he has suffered for ten years, but by the inextricability of both. Hence it is neither inscrutable nor unmotivated, as some critics have suggested. As Vithobai's wasted body struggles for its last breath, Paul is moved to touch Vithobai in what he considers a "human" gesture, a spiritual effort to elicit Christian "love." But the touch elicits a surprisingly mixed response: "Vithobai shivered, then looked at him with surprise, pity, affection, disdain, with all, but with little of any, for his spirit had mainly departed" (80). No one emotion is uppermost. In the last paragraph, after he stabs Pinmay, we are finally given access to Vithobai's thoughts:

> [Vithobai] survived for a moment longer, and it was the most exquisite he had ever known. For love was conquered at last and he was again king, he had sent his messenger before him to announce his arrival in the life to come, as a great chief should. "I served you for ten years," he thought, "and your yoke was hard, but mine was harder and you shall serve me now for ever and

ever." He dragged himself up, he looked over the parapet. Below him were a horse and cart, beyond, the valley which he had once ruled, the site of the hut, the ruins of his old stockade, the schools, the hospital, the cemetery, the stacks of timber, the polluted stream, all that he had been used to regard as the sign of his disgrace. But they signified nothing this morning. . . . [B]eneath them, solid and eternal, stretched the kingdom of the dead. He rejoiced as in boyhood, he was expected there now. Mounting on the corpse, he climbed higher, raised his arms over his head, sunlit, naked, victorious, leaving all disease and humiliation behind him, and he swooped like a falcon from the parapet in pursuit of the terrified shade. (81–82)

Spurred ironically by Paul's promise of the life to come, Vithobai sends Paul ahead of him as a servant in their joint afterlife, thereby regaining his lost identity as "king." This is both revenge for betrayal and humiliation and a reversal of lost power: he is king again, "sunlit, victorious," as his colonial master becomes his servant. Thus, his final survey of his land is important, for it includes the "signs of his disgrace" that he has now repossessed, and suggests his reappropriation of the territory that has been colonized. Within the system that Paul Pinmay set up for him, his act is entirely rational. But Vithobai's fantasized return to boyhood also recalls the beginning of their story, the love that he found with Pinmay, and complicates the irony of "the real and true love" that he promises Pinmay in "the life to come" (81). Together with power, Vithobai also promises and seeks sexual intimacy from his lover at the end; the emphasis on his nakedness suggests his readiness to embrace and acquire the body that will now be entirely subservient to his. "Wait for me in it" is the last thing he tells Pinmay as he kills him, as if he has caught Pinmay's habit of equivocation, suggesting in his turn a doubleness of language that promises both erotic reunion and mastery, an ironic counter to Pinmay's false promises of "Not yet" and "Never." In the eternity of recompense that he envisages, Paul is to be both overcome and kept with him, not simply banished or annihilated. Thus, the story ends with Vithobai jumping not to self-annihilation but to a better future, in "pursuit of the terrified shade." The "shade" that he pursues suggests the ghost of Pinmay, waiting for him, terrified indeed, the prey after whom Vithobai triumphantly swoops like a "falcon," bound to Vithobai for ever in the life to come.

This story, while undoubtedly participating in the racializing discourse that it seeks to decry, finally points to a realization that Forster could not make public: that colonial interracial homoerotic desire is constituted by power asymmetry, not by sameness or equality, and that the potential for abuse and violence is integral to its formation and fulfillment. Unlike *A Passage to India*, which attributes the failure of well-intentioned interracial friendship to the external forces of colonization, this story suggests that desire for otherness is more complexly constituted, that power is not separate from or corruptive of desire but is instead constitutive of it. Like "Kanaya" and Forster's letters from his second trip to India, "The Life to Come" reveals two important points. The first is that in a context of empire, Forster saw interracial desire as doomed by prohibitions of racial and same-sex sexual intimacy that are so deeply internalized as to collapse any opposition between external restriction and internalized repulsion. As in the letter from Egypt, this is not an unconscious interruption of his politics but a conscious recognition even in himself of what assails those subject to imperial history. The second is that these difficulties arise also from the problems of language. One of the central problems of Paul and Vithobai (and Aziz and Fielding, as well as Maurice and Alec) is language—created both by the differences of culture and by the unavailability of a language for that which "has no name." Unlike *Maurice*, which offers the "inestimable gain of a new language," these postwar writings are far more skeptical about the possibilities of human communication across barriers of difference.

In his unpublished work, Forster thus chose to explore and expose the effects of such pernicious socialization upon the English psyche, even as he sought in his published work to undo it. Desire was something that Forster came to understand, ahead of his time, as not simply a natural force prior to or suppressed by civilization but as itself inextricable from and produced by the political unconscious, constituted by both attraction and repulsion, exacerbated by the inequities of power and not suppressed by them. His unpublished writing allows us then to radically to reread the ending of *A Passage to India*, where Aziz and Fielding's friendship is thwarted not by the external constraints of colonizer/colonized power relations but by a more complex dynamic that Forster understood but could not make explicit: the unspeakable eruption of his belated understanding that interracial male same-sex relations are ridden with volatile and self-destructive desires, that carnality can be in fact yet *more* obdurate in disrupting the ideal of cross-cultural friendship. Forster's recognition of the unpredictability of desire, his understanding that desire can arise from having the power to abuse, that it can rest upon the pleasure of giving pain, that homophilia can diverge from homosexuality—could not be openly manifested to explain the sudden change of relations between Aziz and Fielding after the trial, the odd yet nameless repulsion that impedes their friendship. Forster thus enables us to understand colonial relations not only as a phenomenon of male homoeroticism, as Sara Suleri has suggested, but also (even more radically) as one of violence, as founded very much on the eroticism of inequity and abusive power.

Finally, in trying to reconcile his overt liberal politics and desire for crosscultural understanding and in looking to the body as a liberatory life force, Forster seems to recognize two kinds of difficulty: one, that the bodily and the carnal are not just liberatory, that desire in the context of power and inequality can be violent and corruptive; and two, that there can be a contradiction between his agenda to speak the body and his liberal politics. Yet this radical realization is not something he chose to make public. As this chapter has shown, from 1911 through 1922 he struggled to overcome the obstacles that brought about his crisis, learning (as he wrote from and traveled in India) to combine his desire to speak the body with enacting political agency in his writing. But even though he was able to produce *Maurice* and other wartime writings, he found himself unable to speak the body in publishable fiction in the way he had envisaged. For now he understood how sexual desire was imbricated in power, politics, and the desire for dominance. But he could not make that part of his public persona. This darker belated knowledge of 1922 nevertheless silently undergirds the considerable achievement of *A Passage to India,* the last novel he completed, to which I now turn.

CHAPTER FOUR

At the Mouth of the Caves

A Passage to India and
the Language of Re-vision

IN 1922, the year that Forster wrote "The Life to Come" and resumed *A Passage to India*, he also wrote a short essay entitled "Pan."[1] Impelled by many of the concerns that underlie both the story and the novel, this essay offers a whimsical disquisition on the green leaf *pan*, or the Indian condiment (pronounced "paan"). Punning on the name of Forster's favorite Greek god, it recalls his important first story, "The Story of a Panic," in which English bourgeois complacency is violently disrupted by the emergence of Pan, the bringer of bodily truth.[2] Haunted by a similar notion of Pan, *A Passage to India* articulates Forster's sexual politics through a coded evocation of the suppressed body. Interrogating the intertwining of racial oppression and heterosexual desire, the novel crafts a new language as an agent of political intervention, seeking to disrupt English hegemonic codes of imperial, linguistic, and sexual oppression through the materialization of unspeakable bodily truth. As a paradigm for Forster's work in this novel, "Pan" can serve as a useful segue for reading *A Passage to India*: like pan, the potent work of art that is offered for the intake of friends and enemies, the novel enfolds multiple contents, purposes, and meanings, and is intended to produce bodily effects and material change in human relations.

The essay begins as a self-knowing narrative of colonial arrival and discovery —of a mysterious sylvan refuge that seems to foster a peculiar unknown crop. This mystery is grounded in earthiness, in a fertility of "warmth and manure" (319). Leading us on, refusing to name what it is that the Forster traveler-narrator has "come" upon (318), the writing is sensuous, sexually suggestive, exuding a desire to know that projects desire on what it observes: "Round each pillar a convulvus twines, aromatic and lush, with heart-shaped leaves that yearn towards the sun" (319). These pan leaves, grown in a delicately controlled darkness that evokes the beginning of "The Life to Come," suggest a desired art, as the narrator echoes Keats's address to the Grecian urn in overt tones of Hellenic homoeroticism: "Oh, and are those men? Naked and manure-coloured, can they be men? . . . What acolytes, serving what nameless deity?"

But then Forster the essayist ironizes his past epistolary self, the orientalizing traveler whose colonizing desire to name and know is rebuked by the effect the leaf induces on his tongue: "I think I know now; but to make sure, I stretch out my hand, I pluck a leaf and eat. My tongue is stabbed by a hot and angry orange in alliance with pepper. Exactly; I am in the presence of Pan" (319–20). Pan-ic, as Forster's first published story tells us, can bring painful truths and re-vision. As if a symptom of India and its effects on Forster's writing, the leaf refuses to surrender its name: leading the seeker to a cross-lingual pun on Pan the god, apparently its presiding deity; inducing violent bodily effects, which release that tongue into tongue-twisting play. "Pan; pan-supari; beetle, bittle, bettle, betl, betel: what an impression it made upon the early visitors to the East." Rolling off in tactile sounds various colonial and indigenous names for this startling leaf, Forster's wit soon makes clear that what he is after is not really "pan," or the "real India," but the history of naming, knowing, and treating pan, the history of European colonial discourse and language of power that he will attempt to counter. Tracing various European and other "visitors" who encountered and wrote about pan, he concludes with the British and their prohibitions: "Anglo-India will have no truck with Pan, and roundly condemns the 'natives filthy chewing betel nut,' although the natives would rather not be called natives, and what they chew is not the betel or filthy or even a nut. . . . [But] to consume the mixture would be un-British. What a pity!" (320).

Pan here becomes a signifier of the proscribed, racially other colonized body, proximity with which is forbidden across racial boundaries, and which is used by the British in India to constitute their identity through negation. To eat it would be "un-British." But having eaten of it, Forster strives through this essay entitled "Pan" to que(e)ry that Britishness, to feed another pan—his text—to his consumers and thus to educate his Anglo-Indian and English readers about their prejudices and history of misnaming and mistreatment. Enacting thus its agency, the essay offhandedly notes that "natives" may prefer to be called something else, that they too have been slandered like "pan." And, through the capitalized pun on "Pan," the essay carries another hidden connotation. What the British also proscribe is the spirit of "Pan," the bodily sexual truths that Pan represents. Like his Indian letters, encoded within Forster's public, anti-imperialist writing coexists a sexual politics that intimates that the two are linked, that racial oppression is systemically connected with the limitations imposed on the heterosexual as well as the homosexual body.

But the essay "Pan" goes on to do more, to explain what pan signifies in Indian culture, how it is a form of both art and social cement, a "bridge" to friendship across chasms of difference. Pan is productive of linguistic play, capable of enclosing several secret meanings and used for multiple purposes. In affluent Indian society, pan is a gendered art form, served by an "invisible hostess" on a "covered tray," prepared elaborately and individually from ingredients selected from silver boxes that are themselves intricate artifacts, remnants of a Bidari tradition almost erased by colonialism (323). This pan is produced by absent bodies that create material effects and is threatened by the incursions of colonial economies. It induces Forster the cultural translator to make cross-lingual puns—between a housewife's "pan" and "pin"-money, producing much laughter (321). And like a love letter, it can carry secret meanings: "There are many ways of folding the leaves; some are tucked in, *billet-doux* fashion" (321–22).

Like his own art, Forster continues, pan performs several overt and covert social functions. The "betel leaf," as he tentatively names it, has a softer side: "[I]t loses its violence after it has been gathered, and in a short time it is merely fragrant, pleasant, cooling" (320). If taken right, pan can function as a form of invitation, crossing lines of human division. "In its slight and harmless way it is a sacrament.... In a land so tormented over feeding arrangements, anything that can be swallowed without being food draws men into communion.... [I]t is a nucleus for hospitality, and much furtive intercourse takes place under its little shield" (311). Pan becomes an excuse for formal or informal receptions, light repasts, or banquets. Forster implies that the act of eating this folded leaf, laced with lime and areca nut, enables exchange despite difference, that it consolidates trust and goodwill because it is bodily, a synecdoche for the communal partaking of a shared substance. "Not food technically," it is a signifier for food. Like Forster's own leaves (pages of writing), pan has bodily and social effects that are political: though the leaf is green, the lime white, and the nut brown, it produces dark red mouths, associated frequently in colonial discourse with the bloody and violent Indian body. But Forster reverses the colonial stereotype: "Indians who take Pan night and day for years . . . do indeed get red permanently, and their teeth blacken. . . . Their looks are against them but their breath is sweet. They are the exact antithesis of Italians, and crowd for crowd I would rather be among them" (322). Finally, pan can be used to play tricks—"Comic pan, which contains salt, given to buffoons" becomes an edible pun, in comparison to which, "not even a [linguistic] pun is such fun"—or to take revenge: "Tragic Pan, which contains ground glass, . . . is given to enemies" (324).

Forster's seemingly lighthearted essay, named after this multipurpose pan, suggests that it too can function in similar ways, that it too may enfold secret serious meanings and have multiple political purposes. It critiques imperialism, deriding racial prejudice and exposing the dangers of colonial naming and labeling; it undermines the generalizing certainties of colonial language and epistemology and offers itself as a counterexample ("[T]here are so many ways of doing everything, all over India, that descriptions quickly shade into falsehood," warns Forster [321]); it plays with language to suggest its uncontrollability and polysemousness; and under cover of a racial egalitarianism, it draws attention to the centrality of the body and bodily functions, hinting at the sexual body, which is subject to similar oppression and silencing. In *A Passage to India* as well, Forster uses coded language, as dexterously folded as any pan, as an agent of political intervention. Like pan, the novel presents itself as a complex work of art, carefully crafted and productive of pleasure. Yet enfolded within it are efforts to speak the body, to bring the spirit of Pan into play, in order to articulate an otherwise unspeakable sexual politics, to explore how the body constitutes the boundaries between the speakable and unspeakable. Hence, the novel is fundamentally interested in language, particularly in Anglo-Indian colonial language: in the ways that language deploys power by naming, labeling, or categorizing. At the same time, it explores how Forster's language can rupture those hegemonic codes and build a new kind of language that may adumbrate both racial and sexual truths, avoiding the problems it tries to expose.

Forster began A *Passage to India* as an attempt to craft a literary agency that he understood in 1913 as the enabling of friendship across barriers of difference, to function, like pan, as social cement, as an invitation to human concourse. But this was a goal he would have to revise. As he resumed his novel, he wrote in an unpublished letter to Masood, "When I began the book, I thought of it as a little bridge of sympathy between East and West, but this conception has had to go, my sense of truth forbids anything so comfortable. I think that most Indians, like most English people, are shits, and I am not interested in whether they sympathize with one another or not" (September 27, 1922).[3] As we have seen, the creation of such a "bridge" of connection, like the doomed "bridge party," carries assumptions that Forster came to recognize as naive. As his letters from his second trip and unpublished short stories show, Forster's vision of interracial and sexual intimacy became more complicated, integrating his belated understanding that there is no prepolitical body or psyche, that history cannot be washed away, that resentment, rivalry, exploitation, and mistrust are necessary components of any interracial exchange charged with the contexts and histories of colonialism. Moreover, he also came to understand erotic desire as dependent on asymmetry, tyranny, and possession and came to realize that to promote friendship by assuming a common humanity is to ignore the complexities of internalized prejudices and the contradictory, (self-)destructive power struggles that inhere in such relationships.

Nevertheless, as a heavily revised text with new goals, constructed by the desire for his art to have political effect, *Passage* does achieve a different kind of agency. It deconstructs imperialist epistemology and representation—ways of knowing, seeing, describing—to examine the ways in which language can oppress. It seeks to expose and undo those effects in its own (earlier) language. It shows how the differences of power imbue and inflect every exchange, and what are the effects of colonization on both colonizer and colonized. This is underwritten by another politics, the egalitarian politics of sexuality that Forster developed after his reading of Carpenter and Whitman, the shift from the Platonic to the bodily. Hence, it also encodes a politics of the body, of homoeroticism and desire that must remain an invisible yet shaping force. The suppressed body, like the giant hollows of Forster's tales of the fantastic, will now be mapped on the terrain of Indian geography, the queering space that will resound with its echoes. As a giant force, this body, the site of the unspeakable—that is, truth itself—emerges repeatedly to rupture Anglo-Indian hegemony.

A *Passage to India* bears the marks of Forster's crisis and of his efforts to develop a literary, political agency and speak the prohibited body. It is shaped by the difficulties and changes that interrupted its composition.[4] But Forster turns revision and interruption into a subject and strategy of the novel—it becomes a novel about the difficulties of crafting an appropriate language, about describing and seeing in less harmful ways, about the inevitability of implication in power relations. It acts as a palimpsest, in which an earlier writing is overwritten by a later one. Ultimately, this act of revision constitutes its educational effort and its self-knowing agency. Like the essay "Pan," *Passage* calls upon earlier incursions of its central themes, revising and revisiting Forster's earlier writing, rewriting itself into something new.

The Problems of Language

Alerted by the post-structuralist attention to the "prison-house" of language as a dense, self-referential medium, Forster critics turned in the 1970s and 1980s from debating the failure or affirmation of liberal humanism or the social problems of colonialism in *A Passage to India* to noticing its concern with language.[5] Judith Herz, for instance, observes that language is at once the "subject," "medium," and "accomplishment" of the novel:[6] "[W]hile language in *A Passage to India* is challenged by its own demonstrated insufficiency, it also constitutes the means of that demonstration. Language is offered paradoxically as the text's ultimate achievement even if it is undermined in its unfolding by a structure of mutually excluding discourses" (70). Indeed, the novel is based on a self-contradiction: it announces the failures of language and the impossibility of communication yet itself purports to communicate; if it cannot build a bridge to friendship, then it seeks to convey reasons for that failure and build a bridge toward understanding.[7]

From a postcolonial perspective, however, readings that focus on language alone have critical problems, such as the occlusion of a political or historical context. If language fails, these readings assume, that is because failure is inherent in the nature of language. "Language comes to stand for everything that divides man: while memory and silence stand for what reconciles and unites," writes John Colmer.[8] "*A Passage to India* continually asserts . . . that language itself is powerless to convey the central experience to which the novel leads. . . . the language of cognition is avowedly insufficient as a means of incarnating mystical experience which exists outside time," states Michael Orange.[9] Alternatively, in assuming that Forster presents the impossibility of communication as due to the otherness of Indian language, critics end up subscribing to colonial stereotypes of Indian incomprehensibility. If Western language cannot capture India, they suggest, then either that language is inadequate for the great mysteries of the orient, or that orient itself is a muddle. Analyzing Forster's syntax, Molly Tinsley claims, "Sentences like this, *muddled and lumpy* as an Indian landscape, seem to have relinquished two conventions of Western form—climax and closure"; she concludes, "It is this India, of autonomous things, insoluble *muddle*, that strained and perhaps finally defeated the complex sentences of E. M. Forster the novelist" (my emphasis).[10] Thus, India is so "muddled" that Western form destroys itself in trying to represent it. Herz argues that the failure of language in *Passage* occurs because of an "underdrift, a mode of speech in which the words that constitute conversation are only tenuously connected to a deeper layer, [which] is a significant feature of Indian speech" (65). But this does not consider how those differences may be a result of colonial and racial politicization or how Forster's "achievement" may lie in his wrestling with the problems of colonizing language.[11] In his posthumously published short stories of same-sex interracial desire, "The Life to Come" and "The Other Boat," Forster shows how colonial miscommunication is imbued by the history and politics that produce mistrust on both sides: the subtexts are different for each; those subordinated hear what those in power do not.[12]

Postcolonial scholars, however, have tended not to attend to the novel's self-gesturing preoccupation with language. This has precluded a consideration of how its self-conscious attention to the problems of language may be an active political move. Benita Parry's influential reading places the novel ideologically on the cusp between (or overlapping both) colonial and postcolonial: "*A Passage to India* can be seen as at once inheriting and interrogating the discourses of the Raj" (28). She concludes, "[It] is the limit text of Raj discourse, existing on its edges, sharing aspects of its idiom while disputing the language of colonial authority . . . a text which disrupts its own conventional forms and dissects its own informing ideology." (30).[13] But even Parry identifies Forster's counter-discourse in the "icons of restfulness and spiritual silence" and the "language of deferred hope, imponderables and quietism," which, she suggests, provides the alternative to orientalist modes of seeing and describing India (29). One problem with this is that, as Sara Suleri has argued, Forster's rendition of India as the space of nothingness or oriental unknowability, even if it opposes the colonizing will to label and know, remains at best insufficient and at worst another form of exoticism.[14] To construct an alternative discourse through the vehicle of Indian mysticism or "authentic" religiosity, as Parry suggests, reifies it as ultimately other in contrast to the rationalism of Western epistemology. But Suleri reveals a different problem. If Forster is faulted for *not* describing India (or for describing it as indescribable), is colonial writing to be castigated as exoticizing both when it seeks to describe and when it seeks not to describe? Given that any act of representation is embedded in the networks of power, that to speak of another is in some sense to violate, that language inevitably makes its referents objects, prisoners of modes of representation,[15] what choice does that leave for any author, colonial or postcolonial?

By reading the self-consciousness of language in A *Passage to India* as inextricable from the novel's anticolonial and sexual politics, I propose that Forster was neither concerned with language as a universal phenomenon that fails before the mysteries of India nor a quietist liberal who failed to understand the intricacies of the political, material, and economic aspects of colonialism. Rather, I argue, Forster understood both the problems and politics of representation and sought to address them in his fiction. The language of Anglo-India, not language in general, becomes his subject because it *is* the problem, and re-vision through repetition of that language is one of his solutions in this colonial anticolonial novel.

We could well begin by charting this subject of language and writing in A *Passage to India* through its abundance of letters, few of which are actually reproduced in the text although they recur as telling figures of writing. Critics who attend to language in A *Passage to India* have focused on speech (or song) and silence, or on Forster's rhetoric. But none have noted the multiplicity of *letters* that are misread, misapprehended, mis-sent, unsent, unread, interrupted, or torn up, constituting a central motif for this novel, which started as a prodigious letter, an effort to communicate across distance. The novel opens with the famous description of Chandrapore, which is symbolic of the divisions of colonial India, and the question of whether "friendship" is possible across those divisions. But its frisson begins with the arrival of a letter that disrupts Aziz's mid-dinner recitation of poetry amidst his Indian friends, as a curt summons from his supervisor, Major Callendar, (mis)read by Aziz as a deliberate desire to "show his power."[16] Pulling Aziz back psychically and physically into the "net Great Britain had thrown over India," this summoning script interrupts both bodily and artistic pleasure, leading Aziz to an absent sender, a "snub" (14), and his first meeting with Mrs. Moore. It also leads him to write a double-edged response, testifying to his compliant presence, which he soon abandons ("tearing the protest up") as impossible to articulate without sounding either servile or sarcastic (15). Letters written in this India can both exert power on the part of the colonizer (violating privacy, friendship, pleasure, and autonomy; forcing bodies to enter into servile negotiations) and, on the part of the colonized, become unsent missives, tragic shreds, impotent containers of anger that embody the difficulty of voicing resistance.

But letters are also dangerously liable to be misread—on both sides of the colonial divide, even when written and read by those who try to cross those boundaries. To indulge Adela's misguided desire to see the "real India," Mr. Turton "issue[s] invitation cards to numerous Indian gentlemen" for the bridge party, as another unthinking colonial command that expects uncomplicated acquiescence yet reveals its own double inscription: selected upper-class Indians are invited to—but not *into*—the club forbidden to nonwhites in almost comically self-contradictory language (the collector "would be *at home* in the *garden* of the club") to be displayed as bodily specimens of local color (35). Yet this invitation, itself an act of violence, produces an intense flurry and discussion among its recipients, who misread it variously as a new strategy of exerting colonial power, an act of appeasement, an act of sincere kindness, and so on. The point that the novel makes repeatedly is that both the letter and its misreadings signify volumes, because they in turn reveal the conditions of oppression and the tendency to overread and distort every act of language in an atmosphere that warps every form of signification. To the disempowered, every word of power exceeds its intent.

In a parallel instance, Aziz misreads Fielding's letter of invitation (to a tea party that Fielding likewise sets up to "show" Adela a real Indian) first as an imperial threat, a container of palpable violence, promising punishment for not attending the bridge party—"it lay on his table like a high explosive, which at a touch may blow his flimsy bungalow to bits"—and then as "the civil deed that shows the good heart" (62–63).[17] (Indeed, Fielding's liberal invitation will act like an unintentional explosive in another sense, blowing Aziz's flimsy habitation to bits, even though it proceeds from good intentions.) Such misreadings indicate not ineptitude but the differential effects of colonization: Indians misread because to subjects of inscrutable power every act of signification carries enormous import; the English misread because of ignorance, prejudice, or sheer malice, since to those in power misreading accrues few costs. Language may be ineffectual in establishing trust or communication, but it is dangerously powerful and material—for good or ill. In this opening "Mosque" section, letters breed more letters, activating the sequence of the plot, which is structured in a scriptural chain of binding causality: like Adela's dreadful "mistake" later, whose chain of echoes resound and get magnified, Callendar's letter leads Aziz to meet Mrs. Moore, which leads her to tell Adela about her "romantic" adventure and inspires Adela's desire for a bridge party, the failure of which leads to Fielding's picnic, which in turn leads to Aziz's disastrous invitation to "visit" him in the caves. Throughout the novel, the material artifact of colonial writing constitutes its own agency and failure, its power and powerlessness.

In the middle "Caves" section, letters function as futile acts of communication, incapable of transporting some deeper bodily truth. Mrs. Moore emerges from the caves in a panic, haunted by their touch, to realize "that she didn't want to write to her children, didn't want to communicate with anyone, not even God" (166). Forster's language suggests a connection between the "writing pad" (165), on which she begins her letter, and the "vile naked thing" in the cave, which seems to have silenced her when it "settled on her mouth like a pad" (162), a "naked pad" that turns out to have been "a poor little baby" (163): as if somehow the bodily touch of the caves produces her aphasic terror. Aziz's letters are (mis)apprehended like his body, hauled into a colonial prison as "evidence" of his unspeakable sexual desires (187). Fielding's letter to Adela is similarly intercepted by colonial authority, as if undeliverable to her suffering body, because it asks her to consider Aziz's innocence (217–18). After his trial, ignorant of her death, Aziz wants to thank Mrs. Moore for saving him, but there is literally no body to receive his letter (282).[18] Even when a letter is written, as with Adela's letter of apology to Aziz, and delivered to its recipient, it is unable to repair the damage that her words have done.

After the trial, as misunderstandings between Fielding and Aziz grow, letters begin to proliferate, but only to exacerbate mutual mistrust, aggravating wounds already sustained. Unable to fathom Aziz's sexual suspicions but "conscious of something hostile," Fielding writes "an elaborate letter in the rather modern style," the scientism and abstract generalizations of which "hurt [Aziz's] delicacy" (312). Aziz replies "coldly" with formality and distance, as if his patent insincerity would convey his unhappiness. Fielding leaves India in silence, confirming Aziz's doubts, and writes "picture postcards" that communicate his increasing sense of the impossibility of communication, a "serious barrier" (314). In "Temple," the brief final section of the novel, we learn that Aziz refused to read past the opening of the letter that announced Fielding's marriage (presuming that he had married Adela, not Mrs. Moore's daughter), destroyed the rest "unopened" (328, 331), and made Mahmoud Ali write a letter for him. "Why have you not answered my letters?" asks Fielding when he sees Aziz, but he gets no answer (336).

But finally in this third section, the chain of letters takes a different turn. For the first time in the novel, we too are allowed to read these letters. Snooping at the guest house, Aziz reads Adela's and Ronny's letters to Fielding, repeating McBryde's violation of his own letters, looking for usable information in the continuing struggle of colonial power (344–45). These letters manifest the growing rapprochement between the English and reawaken Aziz's resentment: he envies the solidarity of the English (346). But they are finally scattered and doused (like all four bodies — Aziz, Fielding, Stella, and Ralph) in the monsoon rain, as Aziz's boat collides with Fielding's. Somehow this accidental destruction of letters (Adela's and Ronny's last words in the novel) seems to wash the survivors all clean of the Marabar, as Stella suggests, bringing a strange reconciliation (356). The last letter of the novel confirms this goodwill, as Aziz writes to thank Adela for her "bravery" (356). Yet Aziz writes it also for Fielding, inviting the latter's final approval and reconciliation. Like the photograph of Aziz's dead wife and the body of Adela, over both of which the two men bond earlier in the novel, this letter to Adela seals the friendship between the two men—

even though they know they will part. It becomes the medium they share, passed from hand to hand, smoothing the passage to mutual esteem. In this ending, letters are both destroyed and rewritten, to effect healing.

This extraordinary series of letters suggests the centrality and materiality of writing in this novel, which seeks to explore and rewrite the limits of both writing and language. Writing, as a material manifestation of language, is presented throughout as tied to the body, imbricated in the effects and contexts of power, carrying the material potential for both domination and resistance. Yet there is another point to be noted about these letters, a point that is perhaps so obvious as to be imperceptible: though originating from and ending with differently positioned subjects, these letters are all written in English. They test and explore language but, more specifically, the *English* language as a very particular medium of power, the language of *both* colonizer and colonized. Self-knowingly, this novel does not seek to speak in, or for, languages that exist beyond its province, though it marks their existence as bordering its edges. When Mrs. Turton patronizingly utters a few words of broken Urdu, assuming that the Indian ladies cannot speak English, and receives their reply in English ("Perhaps we speak your [language] a little" [42]), the text both mocks Mrs. Turton and makes visible its own boundaries: the limits of the English language and the difficulty of breaching gulfs between *types* of language. Yet it also suggests that other languages may be invented that avoid those problems, seeking "a new formula which neither East nor West could provide" (43).

A Passage to India, then, *is* a novel about language, although less about language per se than about Western forms of language that label, categorize, objectify, silence, and oppress—just as it is less about India than about Western modes of knowing, representing, and constructing India. Forster's even syntax is destroyed not by contact with non-Western cultures but rather through a recognition of Western practices of categorization, not because they are somehow inadequate to the great "mystery" of India but because they reveal their complicity in creating binarisms such as East/West in the first place. As an anticolonial colonial text, confronted with racial alterity and the intensely warping force of colonial signification amid unequal power relations, *A Passage to India* returns to writing, to its own language, not to reveal its incompatibility with some enigmatic other but to examine the dangers of its power to construct that other, showing how language in Anglo-India can cause injury, and struggling to find an alternative idiom. In this is created its dually colonial and postcolonial position and agency—in reenactment and reenvisioning, it builds critique precisely from its double location.

"Say, Say, Say . . . As If Anything Can Be Said!": The Language of Anglo-India

"Mosque," the first section of the novel, sets up both the problems of language in Anglo-India and alternatives that might redress those problems, presenting language as an agent of both oppression and resistance. Language can be itself material, with positive or negative bodily effects: it can "wound the ears and paralyze the minds" of Aziz's Indian friends (121); Fielding would "rather leave a thought behind [him] than a child" (128); when Adela is insulted in court by an anonymous voice, "her body resented being called ugly, and trembled" (243); Aziz "bleeds inwardly," being "cut to the heart" by Fielding's rebuke (304); echoes of suspicion spread like a "malignant tumor" in the social body (311) just as Adela's mistake spreads its irrevocable effects; and in an earlier version, Fielding believes that "talk . . . was a \living/ force in the world: it was absurd to contrast words and deed(s), because words *were* deeds" (*MPI*, 75).[19] Bourgeois Anglo-Indian language, however, is built on occlusion of the body, suppressing the bodily truths that exist on its margins. It is also constituted by a rigid grid of unspoken codes that determine, limit, and distort attempts to make alternative meanings.

A seemingly trivial scene sets the tone early in the novel. Legislating what can and cannot be said, the Anglo-Indian system of colonial codes is itself unspoken, because to make overt the logic upon which it rests would demystify it and open it to challenge. Ronny, the English subject who both inhabits and enforces these codes, tries to exert his superior knowledge of India to subdue the newcomers: Adela and his mother. But they question him, requiring him to explain. When he describes how he learned not to invite an Indian to smoke with him, because "they" took political advantage, Adela draws a different "lesson"— that Indians would not do so if the invitation to smoke with an Englishman were not so rare (30). Ronny responds with evasion: "[T]ime's limited and the flesh weak. I prefer to smoke at the club amongst my own sort," he says. (Whose flesh is weak, we might ask, and what kind of intimacy is so threatening?) But Adela persists. "Why not ask the Pleaders to the club?" she asks. "Not allowed," he replies. "He was pleasant and patient, and evidently understood why she did not understand. He implied that he had once been as she, though not for long" (28). But this too cannot be explained, for its power subsists upon the necessarily unsaid. Having silenced the questioning Adela Quested, Ronny avoids further confrontation by turning to summon his Indian servant. He does so, however, not by directly addressing the man but, in Forster's caustic terms, by calling "firmly to the moon," as if in an attempt to (re)establish his masculine colonial authority and prestige (28). Yet the moment is emblematic, for Ronny substitutes in that gesture one Indian body for another more remote and unearthly one (28).[20]

This moon is a body that functions as a synecdoche of what is suppressed and ignored by Anglo-India but palpably present to those responsive to it. Its silent power passes ineffably into Mrs. Moore's body and consciousness as a peaceful contrast to the language of the club and the self-affirming play performed within it. "Mrs. Moore, whom the club had stupefied, woke up outside" (28). Emerging from claustrophobic artifice, Mrs. Moore finds the moon, "whose radiance stained with primrose and purple . . . the surrounding sky" suddenly physically closer than in England, where "the moon had seemed dead and alien; here she was caught in the shawl of night together with earth and all the other stars" (28). This imagery can be accused of exoticism, but just as Forster's early letters seek in India an escape from English hegemony and his fantastic stories call upon giant bodily forces residing in the land, so too does Forster's language here suggest an unearthly yet bodily magic that opposes Anglo-Indian aridity, which unifies and encompasses earth and space, curative for all.[21] As I elaborate below, like the "exscribed body" of the landscape that remains ignored but present on the edges of colonial discourse, this startlingly proximate cosmic body appears as a tangible presence: "A sudden sense of unity, of kinship with the heavenly bodies, passed into the old woman and out, like water through a tank, leaving a strange freshness behind" (28). Like a wave of movement, this alternative address of the landscape, to which Ronny remains deaf, washes Mrs. Moore clean of Anglo-Indian staleness and confinement, connecting her momentarily through her *body* to this other physical and psychic space.

It is then that she recalls the mosque and her encounter with Aziz, as if reminded of a similar connection and release, or "que(e)rying" of Englishness in India. But this is immediately (mis)apprehended by Ronny, in a resurgence of Anglo-India's warping force field. "Ronny was ruffled.... What a mix-up! Why hadn't she indicated by the tone of her voice that she was talking about an Indian? Scratchy and dictatorial, he began to question her" (30). Was Aziz "well-disposed" to his masters? When Mrs. Moore, "ignorant of the force of the question," lets drop some of Aziz's complaints, Ronny pounces upon this as a calculated native move that has cleverly used his mother as a medium to transmit defiance (32). Continual suspicion and surveillance of the "native," as well as unspoken, racialized codes that include "tone of voice" to differentiate Indian from English, are operative at all times in Anglo-India, and Mrs. Moore is both rebuked and trapped when she fails to operate within them. These codes are imposed not only on the colonized but also on new English arrivals. Unable to hear any language outside of these binary categories of colonizer-colonized, Ronny is himself trapped as he tries to fit his mother's conversation with Aziz in that distorting grid of antagonistic relations.

But when made explicit, this ugliness is exposed to the shaming scrutiny of Adela's outsider's reasoning. What is the difference, she asks pertly, between Aziz asking an English person to take off her shoes in a mosque and the English requiring the removal of hats in a church? The prevailing asymmetry of power that disallows this equivalence is both invisible to her and wholly unspeakable for Ronny. "It's different, it's different; you don't understand" is his inarticulate response (30). Throughout the novel, this unspeakability of Anglo-Indian codes is signaled through abrupt changes of subject, named as the "thing" that cannot be said, just as Ronny "diverts" her attention to the Ganges or as the missionaries "change the conversation" when asked if all creatures go to heaven (38). But as Ronny's deflection of the question to the landscape suggests, the "difference" that answers Adela's question *is* the difference of place and of history.

This unspeakability forms the "underdrift," the constraining, warping force field that changes meanings between intention, execution, and reception, and that obstructs communication (80). It happens again when Ronny disrupts Fielding's tea party, a gathering that has hitherto run on bumbling goodwill. His unspoken annoyance is first directed at Fielding and his mother for leaving Adela alone with two Indian men—an unspoken Anglo-Indian code of gender and racial segregation that has been quietly broken. "If you can't see, you can't see," he says irritably to Fielding (83). It is important that all the main characters at Fielding's party, and in the novel—Aziz, Fielding, Adela, and Mrs. Moore—are boundary crossers who refuse to stay within their designated groups. Ronny ignores Aziz and Godbole and speaks only to Adela, an unspoken affront to which Godbole responds with quiet equanimity, as if he expected nothing else, and Aziz with a perverse desire to overlook it, because to acknowledge it would be too painful. "Ronny did not mean to be rude . . . but the only link he could be conscious of with an Indian was the official, and neither happened to be his subordinate" (81). Stuck in the net of Anglo-Indian codes, Ronny is unable to construct a mode of discourse or action outside it. Every encounter with a "native" is for him an occasion to test racial worth based on preconceived assumptions, so that Aziz's missing collar stud (in fact lent to Fielding) speaks to him of the "fundamental slackness" of the "race" (87), just as the car accident soon after proves that even the loyal Nawab Bahadur failed because he panicked as "no white man" would (104).

Aziz's effort to maintain the unprecedented intimacy he had just enjoyed can then only be articulated as "offensive friendliness," because Aziz also cannot invent an idiom out of this trap. "Come along and join us, Mr. Heaslop; sit down till your mother turns up," he invites Ronny, at once commanding and casual. "Aziz was provocative. Everything he said had an impertinent flavor or jarred. His wings were failing, but he refused to fall without a struggle. He did not mean to be impertinent to Mr. Heaslop, who had never done him harm but here was an Anglo-Indian who must become a man before comfort could be regained. He did not mean to be greasily confidential to Miss Quested, only to enlist her support; nor to be loud and jolly towards Professor Godbole. A strange quartette—he fluttering to the ground, she puzzled by the sudden ugliness, Ronny fumbling, the Brahman observing all three" (82). Aziz's painful efforts evoke a wounded creature caught in the net of Anglo-India, struggling to repudiate yet confirming the stereotypes that he knows it has inflicted on him, as he tries impossibly to engage with Ronny as a "man" and not as a colonial subject. His futile effort to wish away the pressure of this underdrift is rendered through the imagery of "failing wings," linking him with both the moth that intruded upon Mrs. Moore's kindness and the bird that Adela would later try to name, resistant animal bodies subjected to the ordering categories of Anglo-Indian codes. When Fielding tells Ronny that Aziz had been fine before Ronny's arrival, that he was not a "bounder" but just had his "nerves on edge," Ronny replies, "It's nothing I've said, . . . I never even spoke to him" (83). That *is* Forster's ironic point, for "nothing" has become "something," the omission that becomes commission, the not-saying that speaks louder than words. Godbole's silent refusal to speak then begins to look not like Eastern inscrutability but like an act of wisdom—though silence offers no escape from a system that will (mis)attribute meaning to that, too.

By contrast, we might consider a conversation between Aziz and Fielding that is threatened by the same underdrift. Watching Fielding dress, Aziz is disappointed to learn that there will be other guests at the party—the English ladies—"for he preferred to be alone with his new friend" (69). But Fielding has no idea of this and attempts to insert Aziz in the role of native informant: "You can talk to Miss Quested about the Peacock Throne if you like—she's artistic, they say." "Is she a Post Impressionist?" Aziz asks, to which Fielding replies, "Post Impressionism, indeed! Come along to tea. This world is getting too much for me altogether."

> Aziz was offended. The remark suggested that he, an obscure Indian, had no right to have heard of Post Impressionism—a privilege reserved for the Ruling Race. He said stiffly, "I do not consider Mrs. Moore my friend, I only met her accidentally in my mosque," and was adding "a single meeting is too short to make a friend," but before he could finish the sentence the stiffness vanished from it, because he felt Fielding's fundamental good will. (*PI*, 70)

Like Fielding's earlier remark to Aziz, "Please make yourself at home," this too is "unpremeditated," oblivious of how it would be heard, but "to Aziz it had a very definite meaning" (66). For a colonial subject to be invited to make himself "at home" in an Englishman's house was to receive an unreciprocatable privilege. Fielding's dismissal of postimpressionism bears no reflection on Aziz, but to Aziz, seeing himself through the colonizer's eyes, his ability to name the latest movements in European artistic circles is cultural and racial capital, a measure of his education and worthiness of good treatment.[22] He thinks this knowledge would elevate him in an Englishman's eyes, whereas Fielding can afford to scoff at it because for him it carries no such weight.

But unlike the silent tension with Ronny, here Aziz is able to "feel" a palpable goodwill—as he senses good "vibes," or reads the language of bodily expressions or gestures—that keeps him from rebuffing Fielding. Some alternative to spoken language works as antidote: Fielding's evident repudiation of Anglo-Indian codes of superiority.

> [Aziz's] own [goodwill] went out to it, and grappled beneath the shifting tides of emotion which can alone bear the voyager to an anchorage . . . [or] to the rocks. . . . In every remark he found a meaning, but not always the true meaning, and his life though vivid was largely a dream. Fielding, for instance, had not meant that Indians are obscure, but that Post Impressionism is; a gulf divided his remark from Mrs. Turton's "Why, they speak English," but to Aziz the two sounded alike. Fielding saw that something had gone wrong, and equally that it had come right, but he didn't fidget, being an optimist where personal relations were concerned, and their talk rattled on as before. (70)

Aziz is subject to mixed tides of emotions—the goodwill that can keep him "safe" but also the insecurity that can lead to the rocks—in this pioneering voyage to interracial concord. If Aziz finds a "meaning" in every remark, yet a meaning that is not always "true" or intended, it is because his antennae have been confused, his capacity to read bruised by the likes of Ronny and Mrs. Turton. Fielding, however, is too complacent, as the novel will show, a voyager who does not reckon with the rocks in his passage, optimistic that goodwill in personal relations alone would suffice.

This is not to say that British colonization is responsible for all that thwarts human relations in this India—for clearly, as in the distrust between Aziz's Hindu and Muslim visitors, differences of historical traditions, "mental conventions" (121), and power produce quarrels, tensions, intrigues. Rather, the novel suggests, colonialism has exacerbated these tensions and the charged atmosphere of distrust and distortion produced by living under constant prejudice. Aziz cannot understand how Fielding can be so "fearless," so free of the threat of "spies" (130–31), nor can Fielding, "born in freedom," understand the fears that cripple the Indians he befriends (194). The effort to find a new language constitutes itself in the unspoken, as in a crucial moment when, after the mutual disappointment of Fielding's visit, Aziz unexpectedly shows Fielding the photograph of his dead wife. In this rare moment of mutual understanding, a sudden glimpse of "flowers . . . between the stones of the desert" (125), Aziz knows that his inarticulate effort bespeaks the difficulty of traversing a desert that divides even those with goodwill: "It is beyond the power of most men. It is because you behave well while I behave badly that I show it you. . . . Mr. Fielding, no one can ever realize how much kindness we Indians need, we do not even realize it ourselves. But we know when it has been given. . . . Kindness, more kindness, and even after that more kindness" (126). Forster's text makes poignantly clear that Aziz does not behave "badly" or Fielding "well" because such behavior is inherent to Indians or Britons. Rather, each one's behavior is constituted by the tangled web of colonial relations in which they must struggle to find gaps of alternative possibility.

These unspoken codes also use strategies such as silencing or outlawing from language what they seek to exclude. To Mrs. Turton, for instance, a social gathering of Indians and Britons can have no name—she can only refer distastefully to the "Bridge Party," a neologism of her husband's, as "the thing," refusing to admit it into her language (38). Criticism (as of the play *Cousin Kate*) is banned, because independent thought or analysis is too threatening for this bourgeois Englishness (40). But the oppressiveness of this language acts upon Britons such as Adela as well, labeling and constricting her from the moment she arrives. Forster thus connects the ways in which language can be oppressive across several power axes. From the beginning, Adela is subject to the gossip, clannish disapproval, and surveillance of the Anglo-Indian women, who watch her every word and action, sensing that she, like Fielding, is not "pukka" (that is, literally solid, like the proverbial brick in the colonial wall) (27), that her tendency to question their codes, her desire for alternative bodily experiences that differ from those orchestrated for her by their society, mark her as other. Ronny testifies to this panopticon effect, even over "a silly little example: when Adela went out to the boundary of the club compound, and Fielding followed her, I saw Mrs. Callendar notice it. They notice everything" (50).

But Mrs. Callendar has rightly sensed something that threatens her. Disappointed by the bridge party, Adela looks beyond the parameters of Anglo-India to something opposing it, the bodily force of the Marabar Hills. As if they were an agent of some subterranean thing, the hills appear by some volition of their own, having actively "crept near, as was their custom at sunset," breaking through "a nick in the cactus hedge" that symbolically marks the arid prickliness of the club (46). Enabling Adela literally to turn her back to the Anglo-Indians and their narrowness, like the moon that speaks to Mrs. Moore, the hills invite her to look away, elsewhere, for an alternative to the club and the "gridiron of bungalows" that threaten to lock her in (23). Under their influence, she has her first conversation with Fielding and arranges to meet Indians at his alternative tea party. But these hills also awaken Adela to the blindness of the club that would entrap her if she agreed to marry Ronny. "Contemplating the hills," as if they spoke in another language to her, she realizes,

> How lovely they suddenly were! But she couldn't touch them. In front, like a shutter, fell a vision of her married life. She and Ronny would look into the club like this every evening. . . . [T]hey would see the Turtons and the Burtons . . . while the true India slid by unnoticed. Color would remain—the pageant of birds in the early morning, brown bodies, white turbans, idols whose flesh was scarlet or blue—and movement would remain as long as there were crowds in the bazaar and bathers in the banks. . . . But the force that lies behind color and movement would escape her even more effectively than it did now. She would see India always as a frieze. (48)

These hills, suggestive of an inviting bodily vitality, would become remote to her if she were caged by Anglo-India, unable to "touch" this other life, cast in sensory terms of color, contrasts, flesh, and movement. An earlier manuscript version intensifies this suggestion of India as abundant, prolific, sensuously and sexually inviting, an active bodily force: Adela notices that the English eat only familiar fruit such as "oranges and bananas when the trees and stalls were *loaded with strange growths* and *wooing with amazing smells*" (*MPI*, 58; my emphasis). It is for this purported Indian bodily abandon and difference that Anglo-India proscribes those nameless, uncategorizable food and fruits: "the menu lacked \equally/ imagination and courage" (*MPI*, 58). To consume such alterity might be dangerous for the maintenance of a constructed selfhood. Adela knows that if she were to ask about the "local fruits," she would be told it was not "pukka," and so she censors herself, silencing her desire; she is aware that "Ronny's reply would be 'I prefer to avoid enteric,'" for Indian fruit, a product of the earth like pan, would induce disagreeable bodily effects, evacuating him of his Englishness and control (*MPI*, 58). In the final version, Adela regards the "menu of Anglo-India," the "bottled" peas, the fleshless fish, "full of branching bones" (48), the sterile, tasteless "food of exiles, cooked by servants who did not understand it" (49), as emblematic of this Anglo-Indian denial of the bodily otherness of India. The image of the "shutter" evokes the sense of enclosure, silencing, and sightlessness that would be inflicted on Adela if she became a colonial wife, while India is presented as a force of the body, both outlawed by Anglo-India and resistant to it, enticing Adela to repudiate its threatening grip. Adela knows that if she were to marry Ronny and evinced curiosity about the fruits of these goblin markets, she would be "snubbed" as others before her had been "in the same good humored way until they kept to the accredited themes and began to snub others" (49).[23] Vowing to resist this co-optation, she knows that "she had come up against something that was both insidious and tough, and against which she needed allies" (49).

Yet the text makes clear that Adela still remains blind, unable to see the India she desires uninfected by the colonial discourse of exoticism that frames her vision. The details of color and movement, much like Forster's early observations in his letters ("brown bodies, white turbans," naked "bathers in tanks"), suggest that in her search for alterity she looks for what she has heard and read about, even though her response carries a longing for that forbidden physicality. As she thinks that she will only be able to see the "frieze"—aestheticized as a frozen but lifeless work of art—which she romanticizes as the "true India," she overlooks the real *Anglo*-India that surrounds her, unable to see that what she *is* seeing reflects the complex effects of the force of colonial encounter upon India and that she too is soon to be touched by it. Here is an example of how Forster revises his earlier writing, including it as a trace that is revised by his subsequent realizations. He recasts that early aestheticization of bodily movement that he recorded in his letters as a naive response to India's difference, but he also suggests how Adela is trapped, like him, in colonial ways of seeing and how she is herself the object of control of Anglo-Indian imperial power. For Adela as a sexualized and gendered subject is also subject to naming and categorization, subject to the same imprisoning heteronormative colonial system of language.

In an important moment in the novel, as Adela ponders the problems of being labeled Ronny's wife and of knowing India, she notices "a little green bird observing her, so brilliant and neat it might have hopped straight out of a shop" (*PI*, 90). (In an earlier manuscript version, the bird seems to have "come out of a cage" [*MPI*, 108].) Adela's mistaken response is to desire to possess that bird—by naming it, just as she seeks the "real" India she has read about in colonial writings. But the bird, and India through it, resist. Like Evelyn Beaumont in "Other Kingdom," the bird disappears into a tree, and the narrator comments, "But nothing in India is identifiable. The mere asking of a question causes it to disappear or to merge in something else" (91). Responding to Adela, Ronny also fails to capture this synecdoche of India; he recommends instead Mr. McBryde's "illustrated bird book" (91). That the naming and identification of this bird, another incarnation of a native body like Aziz, may only be done by consulting that policeman's tome of systematized colonial knowledge is telling: McBryde's categories of colonial knowledge and theories of racial science are precisely what he later uses to apprehend and judge Aziz through racial stereotyping. To resist naming, like the bird, is to resist the Anglo-Indian colonial system of appropriation and violation.[24]

This bird becomes an analogue and contrast to Adela Quested. It represents the Indian landscape's resistance to the colonizing systems that enact power and possession through naming, and is a counterexample to Adela, who succumbs to that colonial logic when she agrees to marry Ronny. Then she remembers the green bird: "She had meant to revert to her former condition of important and cultivated uncertainty, but it had passed out of her reach. . . . Unlike the green bird or the hairy animal, she was labeled now. She felt humiliated again, for she deprecated labels" (101). Her power, such as it was, had rested in her capacity to withhold her consent (and her body) from the "cage" of marriage, or labeled wifehood. Once she relinquishes the power of indeterminacy, she becomes subject to discursive imprisonment—as Ronny's fiancée—and to Anglo-Indian colonial social and legal power. An earlier version of *Passage* makes this point dramatically apparent. As Adela recalls "the bird whose name she would never know, . . . it seemed to her that she was \a bird, an unimportant one, shut up/ in a cage with two perches . . . labelled 'marriage' and 'not-marriage' and that she . . . hopped from perch to perch in order not to notice the cage" (*MPI*, 124). Indeed, the crisis of *A Passage to India* is precipitated by Adela's horror at this predicament. As she travels to the picnic, she announces to Mrs. Moore, "I won't be bottled up" (148) and "I will unbottle you in fact" (150). This horror of being labeled and "bottled" overcomes her as she climbs the mountain with Aziz, inducing her to let go of his hand and dash into the cave, where she confronts that oppressiveness of both colonization and marriage—for the two are linked. In revision, Forster may have decided to omit the obviousness of cage and marriage, because the cage that Adela fears is not simply marriage but the broader system of gendering, sexualizing, and racializing colonial power. This emblematic moment links the material and discursive as *systemic* modes of possession that mutually reinforce each other: the bird represents the territorial and discursive acquisition intrinsic to colonialism, racism, gender, and sexual subjecthood. The desire to name is akin to the desire to own and possess. It is, of course, ironic that her horror of being bottled up should lead Adela to turn upon Aziz, to make him subject to her identification via colonial and racial stereotyping, imprisoning him in the same colonial system that threatens her. Just as Adela is entrapped in a system that codes and then constrains her, so too does she seek to entrap the bird and Aziz: the former does not preclude her participation in the latter.

Hence, Forster is more concerned with the English characters who try to break the boundaries of this system than with those who try to reinforce it. The complexity of this novel lies in its insistence that it is precisely the Fieldings, Adelas, and Mrs. Moores whose efforts fail—not to endorse the Turtons and Burtons but rather to expose the powerful effects of the racial and sexual politics of Anglo-India, which disables the best intentions. Adela treats language as rational and transparent, as able to clear things up through straightforward sincerity, as if words simply meant what they appeared to say, as if there were no pain or subtext behind them. Fielding is similarly limited, unable to hear alternative realities or see the privileges that accrue to him in British India, as becomes clear in two important encounters he has with Hamidullah and Professor Godbole about guilt and responsibility right after Aziz's arrest. Horrified by Turton's "herd instinct" and McBryde's scientific racism, Fielding turns to Hamidullah as a friend of Aziz's. Surprised by the Muslim barrister's wary support of Aziz and obsequiousness toward him, Fielding reflects in uncomprehending racial generalization: "At the moment when he was throwing in his lot with Indians, he realized the profundity of the gulf that divided him from them. *They always do something disappointing.* Aziz had tried to run away from the police, . . . and now Hamidullah!—instead of raging and denouncing, he temporized. Are Indians cowards? No, but they are bad starters and occasionally jib. *Fear is everywhere; the British Raj rests on it; the respect and courtesy Fielding himself enjoyed were unconscious acts of propitiation*" (192; my emphasis). What Fielding fails to realize, and what Forster's voice steps in to explain, is that colonial subjectivity is formed (and de-formed) by colonial domination, as is the graciousness of Fielding. Fielding can be loyal to Aziz at comparatively little cost to himself; he cannot fathom the risks that Hamidullah has to run, nor can he understand that what he takes to be inherent Indian courtesy is tinged by the colonized man's desire to "propitiate" him as a representative of the privileged race.

Turning to Godbole's apparently impassive Hindu impartiality, Fielding demands an answer, *the* answer, via his Cartesian methodology, in which language refers to a stable truth (every signifier has a signified), seeking the one true culprit. "I ask you—did he do it or not? I know he didn't and from that I start. I mean to get at the true explanation in a couple of days. My last notion is that it's the guide," he states (196). But Godbole stalls and thwarts him. And Fielding, annoyed, misapprehends what he takes to be Hindu philosophy—a muddle, a collapsing of distinctions between good and evil—the other of the West. This is the mistake that Godbole corrects:

> "No not exactly please, according to our philosophy. Because nothing can be performed in isolation. All perform a good action, when one is performed, and when an evil action is performed all perform it. To illustrate . . . I am informed that an evil action was performed in the Marabar Hills. . . . My answer to that is this: that action was performed by Dr. Aziz." He stopped. "It was performed by the guide." He stopped again. "It was performed by you." Now he had an air of daring and of coyness. "It was performed by me. . . . And by my students. It was even performed by the lady herself. When evil occurs it expresses the whole of the universe." (197)

Fielding fails to understand him, as do many critics who read this as some authentic version of Indian philosophy. However, through Godbole, Forster critiques Western epistemology from within, questioning Fielding's very mode of inquiry. In a very literal sense, Godbole is right: in such a politically charged context, guilt cannot be isolated to a single doer. In British India, where all forces urge colonizing and colonized subjects to stay apart, all those who attempt to break those rules become responsible for ensuing catastrophe. Godbole *is* responsible because he delayed his prayers and missed the train, Fielding *is* responsible because he waited for Godbole, Aziz *is* responsible for extending the invitation, Adela *is* responsible for responding to it.

But in another sense, Fielding's either/or language is itself the culprit, for it seeks single agency and a linearity of causality that Godbole challenges through differential repetition. Instead of "did he do it," he asserts, the "action was performed": the agent has become invisible and passive (as Aziz becomes passive, like Adela and all those enmeshed in the colonial machinery of litigation, trial and error). And the event *has* become a performance, a spectacle for rehearsing colonial discourses of rape and power.[25] In its repetition (it was performed by X, Y, or Z), Godbole's scene of instruction implies that performers abound and that repetition can inform, enlarge, and defer the violating, punishing urgency to name and be done with it. Forster thus suggests the need for different kinds of questions, for it is through the deconstruction of this language that there may be hope for opening up space to construct something new.

Forster's Language of Re-vision

Forster's narrative adopts a variety of strategies to avoid the problems it critiques in colonial discourse; the strategies include the use of continuous negations that refuse to exoticize and the presence of double meanings that partner his public discourse with a secret language of homoeroticism. An example is Forster's continuous use of the term *friend*, which in his lexicon is also a signifier for *lover*. As his friend Masood would have told him, the name "Aziz" in Urdu and Persian poetry denotes both friend and lover, as well as the Beloved or God, the absent or veiled signified, the unavailable object of desire. Thus, the name "Aziz" syncopates the conventions of eroticism and religiosity in Urdu poetry with a suggestion of male homoerotic desire and embeds it centrally in Forster's narrative as a strategically double language. But Forster's key techniques are revision and repetition: his revisions of his earlier writing, as available to us from his manuscripts; and his deconstructive exposé of Anglo-Indian discourse through differential repetition. Though we cannot be certain exactly when each manuscript change was made, we know that Forster wrote the first eight chapters in 1913–14, so changes in those chapters stretch from

1913 to 1922, changes that can be read not only as evidence of Forster's artistic craftsmanship but also as telling a story of his politicized understanding of racial and sexual representation in the context of colonial history.

In the manuscript version, here is the first description of Aziz: "He lay in a <sort of> trance, <exquisite yet> \sensuous but/ healthy," inhaling tobacco from the hookah that "sanctified his body," uncaring about his friends' discussion (*MPI*, 7). In the final version, "he lay in a trance, sensuous but healthy," participating in a discussion about "whether or no it is possible to be friends with an Englishman"—a key question of the novel (*PI*, 6–7). The initial impression of indolent passivity is removed by deleting "sort of," as Aziz is described as taking restful pleasure in the inhalation of a smoke that fills his body, driving out influences of the workday. The earlier version aestheticizes Aziz as "exquisite," with a body "sanctified" by pleasure, whereas the revision presents him not as object but as the center of a subjectivity that both takes pleasure and engages in the political questions of the day.

After the Anglo-Indian ladies appropriate his carriage, "glanc[ing] at the Indian and turn[ing] instinctively away" (14), refusing to acknowledge his existence, Aziz prefers to walk away: "He was an athletic little man, daintily put together, but really very strong" (*PI*, 15). This is revised from "Aziz was a small but well developed man, with broad shoulders and strong arms. He had fenced in Germany, loved riding, and did dumb bells every morning. Indeed he made something of a cult of the body" (*MPI*, 19). Both versions counter the colonial stereotype of oriental effeteness and effeminacy by emphasizing Aziz's physical strength, despite his small stature. But the economic revision suggests more delicacy than massiveness and cuts the suggestion of threatening virility (given Adela's later accusation) or that Aziz might be only an unthinking body. It is important that the book opens with Indians in everyday conversation and not with the English as the primary subjects of this narrative. For the first time in English literature, Indians are presented not as caricatures but speaking in grammatical English and with nuanced perspectives, not in interaction with the English but as having an independent existence. It is also perhaps the first time that an English novel consciously addresses not only the English in England and the Anglo-Indians in India (like Kipling) but also English-speaking Indians. In revision, Forster deletes explanatory statements such as the following: "They always spoke in English together except in moments of excitement when they swirled into Urdu," which also cuts the stereotype of Eastern excitability and chaos (*MPI*, 7).

These manuscript revisions reveal the care that Forster took to avoid reinscribing colonial stereotypes. For Mahmoud Ali's sarcastic remark, "When we poor blacks take bribes, we perform what we are bribed to perform. . . . The English take and do nothing" (*PI*, 8), Forster first used *Indians*, then *niggers*, and finally *blacks* (*MPI*, 9). *Indians* would suggest political and national difference but not emphasize the bodily inscription of racial identity; the term *niggers* was possibly too embittered; so that finally Forster chooses *blacks*, which places racial above national politics. When Mrs. Moore finds a wasp in her room that, like Aziz, has found its way across barriers of separation, at first, the wasp is "large" (*MPI*, 42), but as with Aziz, the description is changed, this time to read "small" (*PI*, 34). "No Indian animal has any sense of civilization," the narrator reflects (*MPI*, 42). But *civilization* is changed to *interior*, as if to avoid suggesting that "civilization" belongs only to Europe and not India, and to oppose not East and West but interior spaces as human fabrications that exclude versus the exterior space of nature that includes all.

Another key technique is deconstructive repetition and resistant reading. When Ronny tells his mother how to behave in India, she rebukes him for his changed and ungenerous attitudes: "'You never used to judge people like this at home.' 'India isn't home,' [Ronny] retorted, rather rudely, but in order to silence her he had been using phrases and arguments that he had picked up from older officials, and he did not feel quite sure of himself. When he said 'of course there are exceptions' he was quoting Mr. Turton, while 'increasing the izzat' was Major Callendar's own. The phrases worked and were in current use at the club, but she was rather clever at detecting the first from the second hand, and might press him for definite examples" (*PI*, 33). This becomes a scene of double deconstruction.[26] First, Ronny's mother as skeptical audience undoes Ronny's adopted voice of masculine white colonial authority, which seeks to subordinate the native and silence the woman. She recognizes his language as unthinking repetition, as mimicry of his masters. In this telling example of what Homi Bhabha has called colonial mimicry—not simply the mimicry of the colonial subject repeating the master's discourse with a difference, but the colonizing voice as itself riddled and gaping—Forster shows how Ronny's Anglo-Indian language undoes itself by repetition, becoming aware of its impotence as Ronny hears himself repeating others who have repeated others, in a chain of echoes. As Forster repeats what Ronny repeats, his text undoes that colonial confidence, revealing how its systems of dominion are constructed, using repetition not to consolidate but to dismantle the voice of imperial power.

This dynamic between mother and son recurs after the bridge party, when Ronny defends himself in a speech that echoes Kipling and Conrad, evoking "the day's work" "surrounded by [native] lies and flattery," relegating English women to the separate sphere of "drawing-room" ignorance. Forster exposes this again through repetition: "We're not out here for the purpose of behaving pleasantly! . . . We're out here to do justice and keep the peace. . . . India isn't a drawing room. . . . You neither of you understand what work is, or you'd never talk such eyewash. I hate talking like this but one must occasionally. . . . We're not pleasant in India, and we don't intend to be pleasant. We've something more important to do" (51–52). Repeating himself as if needing justification, Ronny echoes the masculinist colonial ethos that justifies itself by privileging an unquestioned ethic of male "good work" over female frippery. Demonstrating how this imperialist logic is at once sexist and heteronormative, Forster positions Mrs. Moore as the focalizing consciousness that unmasks Ronny's colonial persona by reading his body as an alternate signifier of truth. "His words without his voice might have impressed her, but when she heard the self-satisfied lilt of them, when she saw the mouth moving so complacently and competently beneath the little red nose, she felt, quite illogically, that this was not the last word on India" (53). Unknowingly repeating the Indians' subversive name for Ronny, "Red-Nose" (7–8), Mrs. Moore decodes that nose, mouth, and voice, breaking the body into parts, identifying its lack of integrity, the disjunction of voice and word, body and language, truth and system—as does Forster's novel. But Forster makes clear that Mrs. Moore is not an alternative. Limited to the clichés of liberalism or the futile pieties of Christianity, she cannot provide a solution, for in British India these have become as inefficacious as her maternal injunction to goodwill (54). What provides far more powerful resistance in this novel is the suppressed body that speaks through the landscape of India.

A Medium That Pressed against the Flesh: The Unspeakable Body of British India

> As the flesh is de-realized, representation . . . is separated from it. . . . Neither wholly present, nor absent, the body is confined, ignored, exscribed from discourse, and yet remains at the edge of visibility, troubling the space from which it has been banished.
>
> —Francis Barker,
> *The Tremulous Private Body*[27]

The first chapter of *A Passage to India* begins, "*Except* for the Marabar Caves—and they are twenty miles off—the city of Chandrapore presents nothing *extraordinary*" (3; my emphasis). It ends with another exception, to the rule of the overarching sky: "*Only* in the south, where a group of fists and fingers are thrust up through the soil, is the endless expanse interrupted. These fists and fingers are the Marabar Hills, containing the *extraordinary* caves" (6; my emphasis). This brief descriptive chapter is thus framed by something extra—beyond the ordinary, something (as yet) indescribable that marks its edges, indicated as the exceptional and "extraordinary" but not further explained. The first and last to be named in this chapter, the Marabar Hills and Marabar Caves (this strange coupling of convexity and concavity) are constituted as an other but palpable bodily force, alien even to language, an agent of rupture and interruption, like emanations of a giant subterranean body extending its "fists and fingers," in a combined gesture of threat and invitation.

Contrasted with this are the divisions of British-Indian space: first the riverside Indian lodgings, both rich and poor; then the in-between border space of Eurasian habitation; and finally the physically elevated "civil station" where the Anglo-Indians retreat from the Indians they rule. The narrator presents these civic spaces through a precision of filmic detail and a series of negations: "the city of Chandrapore presents *nothing* extraordinary," "there are *no* bathing steps," "the Ganges happens *not* to be holy there," "Chandrapore was *never* large or beautiful, . . . *nor* was it ever democratic," "viewed [from the civil station] it is *no* city, but a forest sparsely scattered with huts," "as for the civil station itself, it provokes *no* emotion, it charms *not, neither* does it repel, it has *nothing* hideous in it, it shares *nothing* with the city *except* the overarching sky" (3–5; my emphasis). As many critics have noted, these negations debunk representations of the east as exotic, teeming, redolent of mystery and adventure. But this language of fixity and certitude will also be ironized and exposed in this novel, as it echoes the voice, in Forster's important early story "The Celestial Omnibus," of the Philistine father who denies the alternative reality his son alone sees: "There is *no* omnibus, *no* driver, *no* bridge, *no* mountain; you are a *truant, a gutter snipe, a liar*" (emphasis in original).[28]

The opening chapter thus tells a double story: the story of human division, and the story of language — of what can be described and ordered within the domain of ordinary language versus that which lies beyond. This Marabar topography coexists adjacent to the novel's language, bordering its edges, like the Ganges it describes. The original name of the Marabar was "the Barabar Hills" — as we know from Forster's letters from Bankipore, on which Chandrapore is based, where he stayed with Masood in 1912–13 — which translates as "the adjacent hills." Like the other side of the hedge, the other kingdom, and the road to the celestial omnibus in Forster's stories of the fantastic, the Marabar is an alternative space named by its proximate location, beside the city, on the edges of civic order, a manifestation of something ignored, invisible but present.

The implied power of these Marabar emanations is reflected in, and perhaps a response to, yet another force: the "overarching sky." Described in a poetic burst of language, this sky suggests a heterogeneity of "blending tints" as well as unbreachable distances. But it is also a homogenizing force, evoking a struggle for power between the "main tint blue" and the other colors that seek to "free" themselves from its dominating "dome" (5). Only in the infinite distance beyond the stars is there liberation from color difference and domination, a space that lies "beyond color, [at] last freed . . . from blue" (5). This sky is an active palpable force — as suggested by the strong verbs: it *"touches"* the land (a key word for this novel) and "settles everything"; "strong and enormous," it can choose to bring "benediction" or not.

Such a sky is not merely symbolic of colonial domination, for its power to connect suggests the dual power of language, which can connect and divide, unify, oppress, and resist. To this sky, the Marabar Hills and Marabar Caves respond, unlike the "prostrate earth," with their own bodily language, "thrusting" up "fists and fingers" to disturb its (tele)scopic expanse. Throughout this novel, the Indian landscape is described in active verbs, as a physical force that acts to resist colonization. As Mrs. Moore leaves India for the last time, she sees from her train the changing landscape that seems to seek her out, the moon that *"touched* the shrinking channels [of the Ganges] into threads of silver, then *veered* and *looked* into her window" (232), the "untouched places" and the "obscurer marvels that . . . sometimes *shone* through men's speech," "the bilingual rock of Girnar," and the palm trees, which like the waving fingers of the Marabar seem to mock her impulse to homogenize India: "[T]housands of coconut palms *appeared* . . . and *climbed* the hills to *wave* her farewell. 'So you thought an echo was India; you took the Marabar caves as final, they *laughed.* 'What have we in common with them . . . ?" (233; my emphasis). When Adela sees the Marabar Hills' "fists and fingers" beckoning, they *"cause"* her to remark that Aziz had forgotten his invitation to show her the caves. This is echoed back to Aziz and triggers the novel's crisis (138).

The unspeakable and silenced body of sexual and racial alterity will be mapped onto this Indian landscape, as embodied in the Marabar holes and hills. But it is not only the Marabar that speaks an alternative language of the body, resistant and other to Anglo-Indian language and its interconnected systems of power. From the first chapter, bodily agency is articulated by the cosmic powers of the land, by the river, sky, sun, moon, earth, air—the deities who watch over this land—as well as the creatures that proliferate: the animals, birds, insects, and even the microbes that bring disease. Like the radiance of the moon that speaks to Mrs. Moore outside the club, the hills that beckon to Adela through a gap in the hedge, the fruits that call to her silenced bodily desires, and even the wasp that intrudes upon Mrs. Moore, they represent a bodily alterity silenced by the imperialist discourse of Anglo-India, as well as the possibility of agency and resistance, as that which will rupture those codes, speaking in a language of repressed truth. Neither a pathetic fallacy nor a reiteration of the colonial trope of India's heat and dust, this land as body palpitates as a barely tangible but powerful presence that constitutes Forster's articulation of the forbidden body.

Throughout the novel, this "exscribed body," in Francis Barker's words, a body that is frequently figured as a disembodied touch or hand, returns to trouble the spaces from which it has been banished, a disturbing as well as inviting force that is both bodily in itself and also acts upon the bodies of humans. Each interracial (mis)encounter seems to release "something" palpable from the natural environment. When Aziz tries to "shake the dust of Anglo-India off his feet," to "escape from the net" (15) of "roads named after victorious generals and intersecting at right angles" (13) and walk out of the gridlike terrain in which he feels "caught," the narrator comments: "There is something hostile in that soil. It either yields, and the foot sinks into a depression, or else it is unexpectedly rigid and sharp, pressing stones or crystals against the tread" (15–16). "Something" suggests a force outside language, unsympathetic yet engaged in human concerns, so that both its yielding and its actively "pressing" into the flesh obstruct Aziz's body, causing him to become "exhausted" by these "little surprises" (16). Similarly, after Fielding's tea party, "everyone was cross or wretched. It was as if irritation exuded from the soil" (83), as the force of "something" outside language expresses its annoyance at the discordance produced by Ronny. When Fielding visits Aziz, and Aziz's Indian friends ply him with questions, uncomfortable with his presence, the surroundings bear upon them as an oppressive force: as they leave the house, "they [become] aware of a common burden, a vague threat which they called 'the bad weather coming.'" In the tropics, "the inarticulate world is closer at hand and readier to resume control as soon as men are tired" (123). Suppressed by the constructs of men, this farce exists on the edges of awareness and language, "closer at *hand*," at times threatening yet promising an alternative to those courageous enough to listen, like the world of Pan. "They felt that they could not do their work, or would not be paid enough for doing it. The space between them and their carriages, instead of being empty, was *clogged with a medium that pressed against their flesh*" (123; my emphasis). Inciting them to resist the colonial economic and civic order (their "work"), this nameless force acts upon their body parts, scalding their trousers, pricking their eyes, pouring sweat down their cheeks as if to instigate some other action and vision.

At the worst point of the crisis, as Adela's body lies prostrate in the McBrydes' bungalow and the Anglo-Indians drive "with studious calm" into the club, their drinks taste different, as if even the food of this land participates in the unease, and they look up to see "the palisade of the cactuses stabbing the purple throat of the sky" (200). Earlier, the cactus's prickliness has been associated with the club (which is enclosed by a prickly hedge), and the sky with both domination and the desire for connection. Now, mirroring the cactus thorns that lie embedded in Adela's flesh, this painful image suggests the cosmic impact of the violence that is spreading across Anglo-India, where that once blue sky, suggestive of sexual desire and union, is purple, impaled on the spears of racial hatred. It mirrors the ugly face of Anglo-India, visually dramatizing the spreading evil, as if calling on all who can see to intervene.

This bodily force, which seems to emanate from everywhere and nowhere, seems most concentrated around the Marabar Hills, opposed to both the narrow colonizing world of Anglo-India and to liberal English rationalism. Standing by the club, Adela can see but not "touch" their distant presence, because Anglo-India functions like a "shutter" (48). Fielding too is shuttered by a rationalist frame of mind that categorizes and limits, allowing him only to know that he has missed "something." Upon resigning from the club, he sees the Marabar Hills as "they leapt into beauty," an active and now gracious force, inviting him in a language he cannot comprehend. He can only make demands via specific questions ("What miscreant lurked in them . . . ? Who was the guide . . . ? What was the 'echo' . . . ?"), a mode of truth seeking for which Godbole has already rebuked him. "It was the last moment of the light, and as he gazed at the Marabar Hills they seemed to move graciously towards him like a queen, and their charm became the sky's. *At the moment they vanished they were everywhere*, the cool benediction of the night descended, the stars sparkled, *and the whole universe was a hill.* Lovely, exquisite moment, but passing the English man with averted face and on swift wings. He experienced nothing himself. . . . And he felt dubious and discontented suddenly, and wondered whether he was really and truly successful as a human being" (*PI*, 211–12; my emphasis). Like the epiphanic moment in "Other Kingdom" when Evelyn Beaumont does not just turn into a tree but transforms the universe into something that is also missed by the conventional narrator,[29] this moment of the hills' transformation into a Pan-universe is "nothing" to Fielding, as if even the benediction they might bestow passes him untouched. Yet it brings another ineffable truth—he wonders whether he is "truly" a successful human being, having "learnt to manage his life and make the best of it on advanced European lines, developed his personality, . . . controlled his passions." Now he considers whether perhaps "he ought to have been working at something else the whole time—*he didn't know at what, never would know, never could know*" (212; my emphasis). Like the cryptic ending of the novel, in which Aziz and Fielding's union is thwarted by the uprising force of another landscape, here too Fielding remains caught in a world that cannot acknowledge this other force.

Professor Godbole's mysterious song calling to the god Krishna to "Come!" can then be read as an other voice of this nameless force, producing inexplicable unease in all who hear it. It is first sung at Fielding's picnic after Ronny leaves, as if responding in some way to the disharmony. It is a song of inchoate longing, of carnal and spiritual passion, of a yearning from one's whole being, embodying both the erotics of disappointment and the prolonging of desire, as a god refuses to come. The environment responds, in a bodily way: man, beast, vegetable, and mineral. "It was the song of an unknown bird. Only the servants understood it. They began to whisper to one another. The man who was gathering water chestnut came naked out of the tank, his lips parted with delight, disclosing his scarlet tongue. . . . Ronny's steps had died away, and there was a moment of absolute silence. No ripple disturbed the water, no leaf stirred" (84–85). This "song of an unknown bird," like the bird that escapes Adela's identification and like the unidentified source of terror in the caves, is a synecdoche of the resistant landscape. It has a power that is sensed, not only by the hushed environment but also by humans of lower rank, enabling a secret speech among them. The naked man emerges, as if born anew from the water, touched by this earthly sound, his mouth open, like that of the caves, reddened by pan, as if visited by Pan. And Pan's presence, produced by this song, creates a kind of unspoken panic, a bodily unease that will linger in all its hearers. To the English visitors, the song is incomprehensibly disturbing, foreshadowing the befuddling effect of the caves: "[T]he [Western] ear, baffled repeatedly, soon lost any clue, and wandered in a maze of noises, none harsh or pleasant, none intelligible" (84).

The effects of this song echo through the novel, releasing suppressed bodily longings. After the party, Adela and Ronny quarrel and make up, and then crash suggestively into an unidentifiable animal. Aziz falls ill, and Adela and Mrs. Moore experience a bodily unease and disengagement with their surroundings. "Ever since Professor Godbole had sung his queer little song, they had lived inside cocoons, and the difference between them was that the elder lady accepted her own apathy, while the younger resented hers" (146). Indeed, the "queer little song" seems to have set in motion que(e)rying effects experienced as dis-ease. Mrs. Moore inclines toward death, feeling increasingly unwell as she goes to the caves, while Adela begins to question the sexual and colonial system in which she is becoming trapped. After the trial, when Adela loses her echo, the "buzzing sound in her ears" that she connects with being "unwell" that she has had since Fielding's party (265), she still cannot define it: "I was not ill—it is far too vague to mention: it is all mixed up with my private affairs. I enjoyed the singing . . . but just about then a sort of sadness began that I couldn't detect at the time . . . no, nothing as solid as sadness: living at half pressure expresses it best" (266; ellipses in original). Till the end she remains unable to explain or name it, except through negations ("I was not ill"), approximations ("far too vague to mention," "a sort of sadness"), self-contradictions ("no, nothing as solid as sadness"), circumlocutions ("private affairs"), or ellipses. Through it, she suggests a connection between her bodily unease, a physical effect of that song, and the subsequent chain of events. Yet she remains unaware that "private affairs" are infiltrated by the political, that her sadness or yearning is a product of the politicized miasma she breathes.

What is this other reality that this landscape represents? Forster's clues suggest that it is the colonized, racialized, and sexualized body, subject to the same oppressive system, and hence a form of resistance to it. Racial difference and racism are marked upon the body, inscribed on the skin. "They sneer at our skins," Aziz tells Fielding (126). After the trial, Aziz sarcastically imagines the Anglo-Indians saying, "Here is a native who has actually behaved like a gentleman; if it was not for his black face we would almost allow him to join our club" (279). Colonialism is described repeatedly as a disease that afflicts the body. The metaphor of English clothing, worn to "pass the Police" (69), like the imposition of the English language, functions as a blight, a "leprosy," that constrains and deforms the colonized body (39). After Fielding's tea party, when Aziz falls ill and Fielding genially asks whether he is really ill, Hamidullah replies, "He is ill and he is not ill. . . . And I suppose that most of us are in that same case," as if the ailment that assails them all is the colonial condition (119). As Aziz lies in bed, he thinks about "beautiful women" and sexual pleasure yet is "repelled by the pedantry and fuss with which Europe tabulates the facts of sex" (110), aware that Major Callendar regards his bodily needs as unspeakable and "disgusting" (109). Aziz's malaise is thus not only a symptom of his subjection to colonial power but also a conjoint response to the interlinked bodily forms of racial, colonial, and sexual oppression.

Hence, any physical contact, epitomized by the word *touch*, is always significant, especially across lines of difference. Throughout the novel, hands touch, or fail to touch, at key moments. Adela and Ronny become engaged when their hands touch after the accident in the Nawab's car, a patently sexual touch that is later noted as "animal contact at dusk" (168) but also consolidates their momentary connection amidst threatening racial difference (101). But such a touch can only be implicit between men. When Fielding arrives a moment too late to catch the Marabar train, he asks Aziz to give a hand, to help him jump on. "He jumped, he failed, missed his friend's hand, and fell back" (144). Such a failure is emblematic, for despite his efforts, Fielding will continually fail to help his friend. Climbing the Marabar Hills, Adela asks Aziz her "appalling, hideous" question about the number of wives he has. Breaking in every sense their brief rapport, Aziz "let go of her hand," seeking refuge in a cave to "recover his balance"—ironically to lose it (169). Just as Hamidullah repudiates her outstretched hand after the trial (269), when Adela returns from her illness, Mrs. Moore twice refuses her hand: "[Mrs. Moore's hand] withdrew, and [Adela] felt that just as others repelled her, so did she repel Mrs. Moore" (220). Soon after, Adela tries to take Mrs. Moore's hand again, and it is again "withdrawn" (223). Taking Ronny's hand instead, she "gasped as if she had risen to the surface of the water," for her echo becomes better (225). Ronny's touch reestablishes Adela's physical connection with him, but Mrs. Moore, Aziz, and Hamidullah reject Adela's touch as long as she remains an agent of colonial oppression. Until she repudiates the claims of Anglo-India, she cannot touch or connect with them. Indeed, the touch of her own hands is unwelcome to Adela's body. Before the trial, she tries to find comfort in God and the police: "Her deity returned a consoling reply, but the touch of her hands on her face started prickly heat, and she seemed to swallow and expectorate the same insipid clot of air that had weighed on her lungs all the night," as the antagonistic Indian landscape and air act upon her (234–35).

This suppressed body can also function as a site of resistance. Before Aziz's trial, the Anglo-Indians are beleaguered by "the queer reports coming in." "The Sweepers had just struck, and half the commodes of Chandrapore remained desolate in consequence . . . but why should the grotesque incident occur? A number of Mohammedan ladies had sworn to take no food until the prisoner was acquitted; their death would make little difference, indeed, being invisible, they seemed dead already, nevertheless it was disquieting" (238). These quietly noted instances are "disquieting" because they use the body to retaliate: the sweepers silently refuse to clean the "commodes," to reinforce the sameness of all human bodies, so that the oppressors are forced to confront both their dependence on the oppressed and the odorous physicality of their own excretions; the invisible Indian women threaten a ghostly but bodily death. The much noted punkah-wallah who materializes at the trial functions both as an articulation of homoerotic desire and as a reminder for Adela of alternative realities that throw her into disarray.[30] But the punkah-wallah is a creature of the landscape, as if he too were a messenger sent to disrupt the order of the colonial courtroom and of human categories and hierarchies: "When that strange race nears the dust and is condemned as *untouchable*, then nature remembers the physical perfection that she accomplished elsewhere, and *throws out* a god . . . to prove to society how little its categories impress her" (241; my emphasis). The active verb emphasizes the force of the land that produces this body, while the untouchability created by caste and racial prejudice seems the condition against which this force rebels, creating a body precisely desirable to touch. However, the primary locus for this nameless force—an articulation of the body, an emanation of the unconscious, the unspeakable, the repressed—is the Marabar Caves.

Flesh of the Sun's Flesh: The Extraordinary Caves

> A description of the notorious Marabar Caves seems appropriate since they are the center of the novel [as regards] action.
> —Forster, *The Hill of Devi*[31]

Forster began the description of the "notorious" caves in 1913–14 but gave up writing the novel at this point of intense difficulty. The caves episode, for which the greatest number of drafts and revisions remain, caused him the greatest trouble.³² Not only was Forster trying to rethink the symbolic and political implications of the drama that was to take place here, but also to link them to the description of the Marabar Caves, which is centrally concerned with the problems of language, representation, and the body that impel this novel. Hence, these almost overwritten descriptions ask to be read almost as poetry, impacted with layers of significance. They suggest an entity that is uncannily bodily, a site of an eroticism prior to human systems, and the epitome of unspeakability. To evoke the caves in language, the narrator's language calls attention to itself, to the problem of describing something that exists beyond its parameters. The Marabar conglomeration of caves and hills constitutes Forster's effort to articulate the unspeakable body of alterity, to construct an alternate language, and to show the limitations of the language he has to use.

The first chapter of "Caves" begins with a geological history that displaces the claims of both Hindu mythology and Western colonialism. "The Ganges, though flowing from the foot of Vishnu and through Siva's hair, is not an ancient stream. Geology, looking further than religion, knows of a time when neither the river nor the Himalayas . . . existed, and an ocean flowed over the holy places of Hindustan. The mountains rose, their debris silted up the ocean, the gods took their seats on them, . . . and the India we call immemorial came into being. But India is really far older" (135). Beginning again with negation, negating both the priority of the Ganges and of the Himalayas that Forster in his letters once took to be representative of India, the narrative voice distances itself from both Vedic myth-making and its own past self, the presumably European "we" that has dubbed all of India "immemorial." Revising and correcting itself, Forster's language now seeks to show something else.

This topography presents a scene of conflict and struggle, mapping an earlier drama of connection and disconnection, a commingled eros and rivalry of giant bodies that now lie dormant:

> In the days of the prehistoric ocean the southern part of the peninsula already existed, and the high places of Dravidia have been land since land began, and have seen on the one side the sinking of a continent that joined them to Africa, and on the other the upheaval of the Himalayas from the sea. They are older than anything in the world. No water has ever covered them, *and the sun who has watched them for countless aeons may still discern in their outlines*

forms that were his before our globe was torn from his bosom. If flesh of the sun's flesh is to be touched anywhere, it is here, among the incredible antiquity of the hills. (135–36; my emphasis)

Anthropomorphized as "the foot" of Vishnu and the "hair" of Siva, the contours of this land embody chthonic forces still engaged in titanic struggles. These invading Aryan "gods" now coexist with the aboriginal "high places of Dravidia," the Marabar Hills that were once connected to Pangaea (Pan's earth, the greater body of land that once combined all the earth's continents) but were then disconnected by the upstart Himalayas. This primeval land, "flesh of the sun's flesh," has been "torn from his bosom," as if it were a child or beloved, separated from the sun, which now burns upon its arid surface its disconsolate passion, an "outline" of a "form" that lies dormant but alive. Untouched by water, recipient of the sun's unearthly touch, this land, if touched by a human, may put one in touch with something prior to human existence or language, for it has some primeval desire that will burn through the layers of human artifice.

This uncanny force is not timeless or constant but is subject to history and seismic change: it is "sinking between the newer lands," threatened by an invading sea (136). The Marabar Hills rise out of its ancient body, a boundary site of struggle and survival, as emanations of a tormented, fragmented body parted violently from its life force: "[A]t the edge their outposts have been cut off and stand knee-deep, throat-deep, in the advancing soil" (136). Like the unspeakable, suppressed body of a threatening racial alterity or (homo)sexual desire, "there is something unspeakable in these outposts," "something" that lies beyond the narrator's language: "[T]hey are like nothing else in the world," he declares; "they bear no relation to anything dreamt or seen." So disturbingly uncanny—in the Freudian sense, as both familiar and known but repressed—they render meaningless even the efforts to name them "uncanny," because any such language brings with it the history and limitations of human epistemology. Even "pilgrims, who generally seek the extraordinary," stay away because here is "too much of it" (136).

Yet this narrative voice then moves on to state blandly, "The caves are readily described. A tunnel eight feet long, five feet high, three feet wide, leads to a circular chamber about twenty feet in diameter. This arrangement occurs again and again throughout the group of hills, and this is all, this is a Marabar

Cave" (136–37). This effort to diminish in rationalist language, to control by measuring in precise numerical dimensions, gives itself away, exposing the misguidedness that misses the mystery—just as, later, the machinery of colonial bureaucracy will try to control by numbering the caves "in sequence with white paint," to mark them with its whitening presence (221) and Fielding will "pace and measure" the caves to find the culprit he thinks they shelter (248). Even to say "this is all, this is a Marabar Cave" is to expose the self-contradiction, as if the Cave (though capitalized) is at once nothing, not very much, and also everything, "all." Hence, the narrator continues, the caves benumb the colonizing mind: "Having seen one such cave, having seen two, having seen three, four, fourteen, twenty-four, the visitor returns to Chandrapore uncertain whether he has had an interesting experience or a dull one or any experience at all. He finds it difficult to discuss the caves, or to keep them apart in his mind" (137).

If the narrator's language is baffled by these caves, the caves themselves seem to speak another language that is material, infusing the very air. "Nothing, nothing attaches to them," we are told, "and their reputation—for they have one—does not depend upon human speech. It is as if the surrounding plain or the passing birds have taken upon themselves to exclaim 'extraordinary,' and the word has taken root in the air, and been inhaled by mankind" (137). Echoing the word that begins and ends the first chapter, this disembodied pronouncement seems to emerge from nowhere and yet take over everywhere as a material presence, taking "root" in the air, shaping the language of humans, who "inhale" it. Indeed, these caves are represented as huge orifices that suggest not only the primal womb or anus, as some critics have suggested, but also giant mouths that speak, eat, and spew; that actively ingest and vomit out the human bodies that seek to enter them; and that speak their strange language to produce distorting echoes, reducing human language to nothing.

The cave beneath which Aziz's guests are camped is described as a "black hole," recalling the Black Hole of Calcutta, so inimical to English colonial history (156).[33] The term is repeated when Mrs. Moore and the rest "disappear" into the first cave: "The small black hole *gaped* where their varied forms had momentarily functioned. They were *sucked in* like water down a drain. Bland and bald rose the precipices. . . . And then the hole *belched* and humanity returned" (162; my emphasis). Active verbs identify this landscape as a doer of action. The precipices rise in a mocking commentary on these puny humans, and the sun "crashes" down on their backs (162). The caves are now described more specifically as mouths that "gape," "suck in," and "belch out" humans when done with them (162). Later they seem to hold secret dialogue with each other. The boulders speak ("I am alive") and "the small stones" echo in answer ("I am almost alive" [166]). Aziz loses Adela and calls to her in a panic, but the caves confuse him—"a Marabar cave can hear no sound but its own"—seeming to talk among themselves: "Caves got behind caves or confabulated in pairs, and some were at the entrance of a gully" (171).

These anatomically suggestive images—of mouth, anus, womb—also provide a clue. If their extraordinariness bewilders the conventions of human language and society, that is because what they represent—a suppressed primeval bodiliness—confuses conventional categories: at once speaking and echoing, sexually erotic and (re)productive, male and female, threatening and inviting. To Aziz, "Caves appeared in every direction—it seemed their original spawning place—and the orifices were always the same size" (170). They seem to give birth to each other, in some kind of asexual spontaneous regeneration, as if embodying the reproduction of echoes both within and without the cavities they enclose, yet they also act as "orifices," as entryways into some giant primeval body. And they speak of forbidden desire.

In one of the most remarkable passages of the novel, the narrator describes the darkness of the caves, in which a flame yearns to consummate union with its reflection:

> There is little to see, and no eye to see it, until the visitor arrives for his five minutes, and strikes a match. Immediately another flame rises in the depths of the rock and moves towards the surface like an imprisoned spirit: the walls of the circular chamber have been most marvelously polished. The two flames approach and strive to unite, but cannot, because one of them breathes air, the other stone. A mirror inlaid with lovely colors divides the lovers, delicate stars of pink and grey interpose. . . . Fists and fingers thrust above the advancing soil—here at last is their skin, finer than any covering acquired by animals, smoother than windless water, more voluptuous than love. The radiance increases, the flames touch one another, kiss, expire. The cave is dark again. (137–38)

Like the opening scene of "The Life to Come," which presents a perfection of homosexual interracial union in a darkness untarnished by an outsider's vision, the darkness of the cave spells a perfection and unity, unperceived and undistorted, that is broken by the advent of a seeing eye/I, the colonial visitor. Light, from the striking of a match (itself suggestive of violence), produces an "imprisoned spirit," yearning impossibly like Narcissus to touch his reflection—because, like the colonial visitor and Adela, it creates the conditions of its own separation. The tourist disrupts, because in order to see, he separates what exists united prior to language and sight. His instrument of sight is the instrument of desire—to know, to see, to have—which produces a projection of itself, a mirroring flame that it can never meet, just as Adela can never find the "real India," which is also a projection of herself.

Hence the cave is rendered as at once the site of a perfect but unspeakable eros, an impossible desire for alterity (for that alterity is a projection of oneself), and the site of separation, of desire that conflates erotic union with possession, incorporation, colonization. Forster's language evokes both interracial eroticism and enforced distance. The "pink and grey" stars that "interpose" to separate the flame "lovers" evoke the "pinko-grey" race of Europeans (as Fielding dubs them) who maintain racial distance and prejudice (65). The "mirror inlaid with lovely colors [that] divides the lovers" is the "skin" of this preternatural body, the boundary between body and world, and the site where they touch, but it is also the signifier of racial difference, because of which Aziz's white patients shrink from his brown hands. In contrast exists the perfect darkness of the Kawa Dol. Unseeable and indescribable, because no observer can be located within it, this is a symbol of the perfection untouched by human perception or language, like the caves that cannot be entered, "chambers never unsealed since the arrival of the gods" (138). "Nothing is inside them," for they are self-contained entities that human language cannot enter, allowing no viewpoint for an observer.

Throughout this description of the Marabar Hills and Marabar Caves, there is no mention of an echo, which seems to occur only when humans enter the caves. What is this echo, which has such lasting consequences for the characters? As in Forster's fantastic stories in *The Celestial Omnibus*, the caves are the site of an alternative reality that challenges human systems. Like the touch of Pan, or the branch of a tree from "Other Kingdom," the caves are a touchstone of truth: they induce material effects that express a suppressed other speech and bodily truth from those who touch them. (Interestingly, the caves' truth-inducing touch seems to affect primarily the women and Aziz—those more entrapped in the system—whereas Fielding experiences nothing.)

Forster's narrative sets up very carefully the different trains of thought that occupy each of the three main characters—Aziz, Mrs. Moore, and Adela—as they set out for the caves. For Aziz, the event is already loaded as a test of racial worth. Hoping that everyone has forgotten his rash invitation, Aziz re-extends it when he learns, through the distorting grapevine, that the ladies are offended by his apparent Indian forgetfulness (139). His effort to prove that Indians can be friends is thus instigated by the desire to counter Anglo-Indian stereotypes, by his need to show that Indians can be reliable, punctual, hospitable. Though distraught when Fielding misses the train, he realizes that Fielding's presence would keep him in "leading strings," that this is his chance to prove that Indians are not "incapable of responsibility" (145). By trying to disprove the categories imposed on him, Aziz falls into the trap that such a framework of expectations sets up: of being shaped by them and of attempting to negate them.

Mrs. Moore reflects on the train that she cares nothing for Adela's marriage plans: "She felt increasingly (vision or nightmare?) that though people are important, the relations between them are not, and that in particular too much fuss has been made over marriage; centuries of carnal embracement, yet man is no nearer to understanding man. And today she felt this with such force that it seemed itself a relationship, itself a person who was trying to take hold of her hand" (149). Later, the echo will appear "in some indescribable way to undermine her hold on life" (165). But she is already on the brink, unsure whether her new perspective is a "vision or nightmare," rejecting, for good or ill, human society. Just as later she is unable to distinguish between love, lust, and violence ("love in a church, love in a cave, as if there is the least difference" [224]), between acting on Aziz's behalf or not acting, here she rejects all categories, singling out the fact of the carnal alone and experiencing it as an aggressive physical force seeking to "take hold of her hand."

Adela is bored and apprehensive: her mind is filled with mundane plans and a lurking anxiety about "the Anglo-Indian life she had decided to endure" (149–50). "I won't be bottled up," she repeats (148, 150). Enacting the logic of what Peter Stallybrass and Allon White have termed "displaced abjection," whereby the disempowered seek further to disempower others who are more powerless, Adela turns upon the terrain of colonial land and bodies to restore her slipping control.[34] Desiring but unable to "take hold of such a country," promising to show the tourist sights to Mrs. Moore (150), and wishing that the Marabar cliffs would turn into a "Mohammedan object, such as a mosque" (156), Adela desires Aziz to function as their "Oriental guide" (159), so that she can possess the "real India." The caves as well as the Indian earth and sky thwart her, however, refusing her demands and silencing her by "quietly disappearing" so that "nothing was to be seen," while "the sky dominated as usual, . . . unhealthily near," like a Wordsworthian warning presence (155–56).

Both Mrs. Moore's and Adela's experiences in the Marabar Caves are triggered by a conversation broken by racial tension, from which the participants seek refuge in the caves. First, Adela breaks up Mrs. Moore and Aziz's unspoken harmony, demanding an account of India's Mughal empire and turning, to Aziz's discomfort, to a discussion of her "Anglo-Indian difficulty" (160). Mrs. Moore pointedly withdraws, but Adela announces that by marrying Ronny she is about to "become . . . an Anglo-Indian." Aziz politely protests against her "terrible remark" (160–61). But Adela persists: "I can't avoid the *label*. What I do hope to avoid is the mentality. Women like—" (161). Here she stops in midsentence, unable to criticize Mrs. Turton and Mrs. Callendar openly, having internalized the system. Naively, she asks Aziz for "advice," not understanding that by so doing she is destroying his fragile attempt to escape from that very system: "'I am told we all get rude after a year.' 'Then you are told a lie,' [Aziz] flashed, for she had spoken the truth and it touched him on the raw; it was an insult in these particular circumstances. . . . [H]er error broke up their conversation . . . which scattered like the petals of desert flower and left them in the middle of the hills. 'Come along,' he said, holding out a hand to each . . . [to go] sightseeing" (161–62). Adela's words place him in such discomfort that he can no longer sustain the conversation, making him retreat into his role of tourist guide and move them all into the caves. But the caves echo back to Adela and Mrs. Moore what they would rather not know, for the caves are a place to see (or mirror) themselves, the caves of their own psyches. Forster's language now explicitly connects the terrain of the Marabar with the terrain of their psyches and interrelations. Their harmony had been a rare "desert flower" but was now destroyed, amid the arid "hills" of interracial colonial relations. This rupture leads them to the first cave and to Mrs. Moore's experience of horror.

The structure of this interchange is repeated as Adela and Aziz continue without Mrs. Moore to caves located at a higher level of difficulty. While Aziz worries about providing breakfast, Adela continues to worry about her future. Again the landscape mirrors her psychic geography, throwing up an obstructive question. As she "toiled over a rock that resembled an inverted saucer," she is suddenly confronted by the question, "What about love?" "Somehow the question was suggested" by the marks upon the rock, as if she were struggling up a mountain of self-discovery, holding a conversation both with the landscape and with her self. These "nicks" remind her of the marks in the dust by the accident (when she became engaged to Ronny), recalling her desire for "animal contact" (168). Adela stops midway up this hill, for "the discovery [that she did not love Ronny] had come so suddenly that she felt like a mountaineer whose rope had broken," confronted by both her lack of sexual and emotional fulfillment and her fear of becoming co-opted into a multiply oppressive system (168).

To ward off these unwelcome truths that the Marabar has elicited, Adela turns to Aziz, trying to position him in a world she can grip by seeing him as a racialized and sexualized native informant: "What a handsome little Oriental he was.... She did not admire him with any personal warmth, for there was nothing of the vagrant in her blood" (169). In such a moment of focalization, the narrator renders Adela's perspective, her tendency to orientalize and segregate sexual desire through racial difference. Wondering about Aziz's sex life, as if somehow "on that eternal rock" he could provide an answer to her questions about her own, she asks him, "Have you one wife or more than one?" (169). This question again destabilizes Aziz. Adela expects that he can help her understand both India and herself, but like the flame that desires its reflection, she projects upon Aziz her desired (self-)construction. Nor can she see that this question is too close to the bone, a stereotype of Muslim male privilege that Aziz has tried to undo. "It challenged a new conviction of his community, and new convictions are more sensitive than old" (169). Breaking contact, both physical and emotional, Aziz lets go of her hand; thinking "Damn the English even at their best," he dashes, this time alone, into a cave of his own.

Mrs. Moore's and Adela's experiences following these respective conversations are rendered only through subsequent distortions and recollections. When each woman enters a cave, the narrator refuses to follow, remaining outside: in Mrs. Moore's case, he watches the group enter and then emerge from the outside;

in Adela's, he stays with Aziz. The narrative renders what "happened" through retrospective perspectives, echoed with increasing distortion by others. Mrs. Moore's experience seems to be triggered by the touch of human bodies in close proximity to her own, as if it were some boomerang effect of her earlier desire to erase differences, her refusal to acknowledge any "race consciousness," that erupts as if to prove to her her underlying fear of such equality (142). In retrospect, she recollects, "Crammed with villagers and servants, the circular chamber began to smell" (162). The physical proximity of bodies that are poor, smelly, and dark, that yet touch and crowd upon her own, seems to induce her visceral reaction of horror, as if in a resurgence of a racial consciousness that lies deeply embedded in a cave within herself. The echo sends back to her something within herself, reducing distinctions to nothing but also revealing her desire to maintain those distinctions. Like the match that projects its own image, Mrs. Moore projects herself, both physically and psychically: she strikes out and hits a baby and is not attacked, as she thinks, by "some vile naked thing"; looking for a "villain," she finds none there, realizing later that "nothing evil had been in the cave" (162–63). Indeed, her horror of the baby's touch and her subsequent inability to write to her children suggests a horror of bodily perpetuation. Like Adela later, "for an instant she went mad, hitting and gasping like a fanatic" (162). But unlike Adela, she emerges to find no one but herself responsible.

While obviously different, the separate cave experiences of Adela and Mrs. Moore have important similarities. For both, the cave brings out suppressed fears and anxieties that they already have. Both panic and project upon something in the caves unacknowledged fears they carry within themselves. Both register this resurgence of alterity as an attack upon their bodily sense of self, as a physical manifestation of something that they repudiate and fail to recognize as coming from within. But unlike our insight into Mrs. Moore, we are given no immediate access to Adela's psyche. The narrative breaks away from Adela after her question, staying with Aziz as if to vouch for his innocence, and becomes absorbed in the distortions magnified by the tensions of Chandrapore. Most modernist here, the narrative examines the epistemological and political drama of the processes of echo making and (mis)apprehension, insisting on the unavailability of any objective access to reality, playing off the contrasting multiple perspectives of each character as the only access to truth—where truth is something to be produced piecemeal and through negation: the culprit will only be declared as not Aziz, but not as what it was.

The narrator's first account of Adela's experience is ambiguous but symptomatic: "She had been touched by the sun, also hundreds of cactus spines had to be picked out of her flesh" (213). "Touched," like Mrs. Moore, by that primeval body from which the Marabar Hills were torn, Adela is both literally touched by the heat of the sun and idiomatically deranged by it. Later she will refuse to be touched, as if touch and the body induce their own horror: "I don't want your arm so don't touch me please," she tells Ronny and McBryde (219). Like Mrs. Moore, who imagines herself attacked but hits out at those around her, Adela pierces her own body with cactus spines when she "fling[s] herself about" (186).

In most explanations of "what happened in the caves" (the title of more than one essay on this novel), hallucination is attributed either to Adela's sexual fear or frustration or, as in David Lean's 1984 film, to the tropical heat and sexuality that are considered responsible for their deranging effects on the delicate sensibilities of civilized northerners. Other "causes" include, as in a highly speculative essay, a Jain guide and caretaker of the caves who tries to warn Adela off from her mistaken intrusion and desecration of the walls.[35] The problem with the hallucinatory type of explanation is that it disconnects sexual desire from the political systems that produce and regulate it, while the second type risks essentializing India, reinscribing stereotypes, or trapping itself in the very mode of identification and explanation that Forster worked to avoid. In the novel, identifying the caves as Jain or Buddhist is cast as a foolishly earnest colonialist mistake, an effort to render them irretrievably other (247–48). Forster's descriptions insist that these caves cannot be delimited to any system or religion—they stand outside human efforts to identify and name. Instead, the caves need to be read through Forster's mode of the fantastic, which he regarded as a serious form of art that could adumbrate otherwise unspeakable truths.

Just as there is an earlier manuscript version that suggests a real rape attempt (which, as Jenny Sharpe has shown, Forster rejected to avoid replaying the mutiny narratives of interracial rape) there is another version of what happens that Forster wrote and then rejected. In this rejected version, in the trial scene Adela recalls what happened: "[She] entered [the cave] and saw the reflection of a match in the polished walls, touched the beautiful veins \of granite /, <and> heard the echo.<Someone took her by the hand—not Mrs. Moore... How wonderful it was> \It was quite remarkable—a mental state she had never known before. And the cave was most impressive/—far more worth seeing than she had thought at the time" (*MPI*, 398). In this rejected version, Adela is a tourist whose desire for exotic pleasure is fulfilled by this Indian cave. Listing the things she can see (the flame's reflection), touch (the walls) and hear (the echo as requisite and unfrightening), it confirms her experience (as "someone [takes] her by the hand") as one of epistemological and sexual pleasure. Indeed, it would not be a stretch to read this description as suggesting orgasmic pleasure within the sexual cavities of a landscape originally cast in terms of "breasts" and "mounds" (*MPI*, 203). But the final version discards all this, making Adela the only human agent, whose hand no one takes (and Aziz drops) as she experiences only self-confrontation and horror.

In the final version, when Adela finally speaks, her language echoes her fear of Anglo-Indian "bottling": "I went into this detestable cave,... I remember scratching the wall with my finger-nail, to start the usual echo, and then as I was saying there was this shadow, or sort of shadow, down the entrance tunnel, *bottling* me up. It seems like an age, but I suppose the whole thing can't have lasted thirty seconds really. I hit at him with my glasses, he pulled me round the cave by the strap, it broke, I escaped, that's all. He never actually touched me once" (214; my emphasis). She struggles to render it mundane, to control it by making it seem ordinary, "as usual," but even the recollection of the Marabar begins to break down her language: the shadow becomes a "sort of shadow," vague, indistinct, indescribable. Though she tries to time the experience precisely, she cannot measure it or transfer it into language: it becomes a "thing." Most important is that what breaks is her link to a colonial instrument of vision, the tool of epistemic, scopic, and physical violence—the field glasses that she uses both to "see" and to "hit" her object, activities that are now demonstrated as coterminous. As Aziz would say later, her "pose of 'seeing India' which had seduced him... was only a form of ruling India; no sympathy lay behind it" (343). If the caves represent the touch that releases inner truth and the resistant suppressed body, what they damage in this encounter is Adela's ability to see and locate the romanticized India, so that the culmination of her experience is "the falling of the field glasses" into the cave (215), in a manner reminiscent of Kipling's Kim vomiting the contents of his tools of survey into the ravine. Yet whereas Kipling's text allows those tools to be relinquished, Forster's more knowing text suggests that they will be picked up again (ironically, by Aziz as the unknowing agent of his own indictment) and accrue meaning even when broken, for the colonial system will turn their very brokenness into evidence to convict Aziz, the colonial subject embroiled in its net.

Like Mrs. Moore, Adela identifies "something" that she confronts in the cave as "evil" (215), set off, like that resonant match, by her finger striking the polished wall. "She had struck the polished wall, for no reason," we are told repeatedly (215). The echo seems to originate as a response. Like a physical force that threatens to drown her psyche, "the sound had spouted after her when she escaped, and was going on still like a river that gradually floods the plain" (215). The caves then also echo back the signifying system of Anglo-India, epitomizing and magnifying its capacity to derange its subjects, through a distortion of every action and speech. As a resistant body, the caves play back to the colonizers the warping effect of their own system of mismeaning.

Adela's inexplicable echo is something that Mrs. Moore alone seems to understand. In the strangely hostile conversation that occurs between them, Mrs. Moore communicates an unspoken suggestion of Aziz's innocence to Adela (precisely by *not* naming him) (224), which, upon Adela's questioning, Mrs. Moore confirms (227). Mrs. Moore seems to know that Adela will not get rid of this echo as long as she stays a tool of the colonial system that circulates the rumors that have led to Aziz's misapprehension. The narrative validates this knowledge: Adela's echo diminishes when she doubts herself or considers Aziz's innocence; it returns when she rehearses her deposition with McBryde (236); and it disappears when she finally looks within herself to speak the truth and repudiate her charge (265). It thus appears to be a symbolic manifestation of her accusation, the sound of her guilt, only to be exorcised when she accepts responsibility and rejects the colonial system at the trial. Hence the trial scene — the crux, in every sense, of this novel — is what brings to a close the conflict between the invidious "machinery" of Anglo-Indian discourse (229) and the resistant forces of the land. This undoing is enabled through Forster's technique of differential repetition, by the echo that begins in the Marabar Caves and ends in the courtroom.

Re-playing Words: The Trial as a Scene of Repetition

The trial scene, clearly a trial not of Aziz but of Western justice, civilization, and knowledge, is also a trial of Forster's strategies of language as alternatives to what he critiques. As she goes to the stand, Adela prides herself on her "honesty" and desires to tell "the truth and nothing but the truth." But she knows she cannot tell the "whole" truth, because she cannot make public the thoughts that led her into the cave: "Her disaster in the cave was connected, though by a thread, with another part of her life, her engagement with Ronny. She had thought of love just before she went in, and had innocently asked Aziz what marriage was like, and she supposed that her question had roused evil in him. To recount this would have been incredibly painful, it was the one point she wanted to keep obscure" (252–53). Yet "something" seems to push Adela toward telling the truth she wants to suppress, something that seems to be linked with the renewed force of the Marabar. "But as soon as she rose to reply, and heard the sound of her own voice, she feared not even that [something coming out]. A *new and unknown sensation* protected her. . . . She didn't . . . remember in the ordinary way of memory, but she returned to the Marabar Hills, and spoke from them *across a sort of darkness* to Mr. McBryde. . . . Smoothly the voice in the distance proceeded, *leading along the paths of truth*, and the airs from the punkah behind her wafted her on" (253; my emphasis).

Somehow, as she hears her voice in this courtroom, as if by echo, something makes her lose her fear that the suppressed truth might emerge. This unspecifiable sensation and the "sort of darkness" that evoke truthfulness seem linked to the "airs from the punkah" (253) invisibly acting upon her (the punkah-wallah is another uncanny thing "thrown up" by the bodily force of the land), interrogating artificial hierarchies and reminding Adela of her body's desires (241). As McBryde leads her through her rehearsed deposition, "something" "causes" her to change it (254), just as, at the moment of breakdown, "something that she did not understand took hold of the girl and pulled her through," to withdraw her charge (256).

But if the unknown agent of these effects is the force of the Marabar Hills, the mechanism that releases this trapped truth is the echo of repetition. The scene of reenactment undoes, by echoing, the scene of the caves—it is the crucial moment in the trial during which repetition of her own words undoes Adela's accusation. As Adela revisits the cave scene, and we revisit it with her, she occupies a strange double position: "The fatal day recurred in every detail, *but now she was of it and not of it at the same time,* and this *double relation* gave it indescribable splendor" (253; my emphasis). In looking back, she is at once inside and outside her body: she sees herself go into the caves at the same time that she experiences herself going into the caves. Like Forster, looking back to his earlier visit to India, his earlier self, and writing, Adela has to test, revise, yet remember by occupying two positions at once. This double relation is what produces truth, which is rendered as a palimpsest, not as either one or the other.

Using the words Adela had submitted to McBryde's police record, McBryde now attempts to fix her meaning and "get" Aziz. But their reiteration, fanned by the punkah's breeze, produces a difference: "You went alone into one of the caves?" McBryde asks. As he guides her through this cave of memory, she is no longer alone in reentering those caves. "That is quite correct," she assents. "And the prisoner followed you"; McBryde's statement is no longer a question. Adela becomes silent, unable to acquiesce to this demand. "The court, the *place of question,* awaited her reply. But she could not give it until Aziz *entered the place of answer*" (254; my emphasis). The scene at the caves, where Adela awaited Aziz's answer to her question about his wives, is overlaid by the scene in the courtroom, as another space in which Adela awaits Aziz, as the answer to McBryde's question. "'The prisoner followed you, didn't he?' he repeated in the monotonous tones that they both used; they were employing agreed upon words throughout, so that this part of the proceedings held no surprises" (254).

As she tries to relive the moment at the caves in her memory and in the courtroom, she can have access to it only through a language that is empty, for which Aziz, the supposed signified, cannot be found. He cannot enter the "place of answer"—as if he were refusing to enter the cave of her linguistic space, the site of her desire. In the re-vision of double location, "her vision was of several caves. She saw herself in one, and she was also outside it, watching its entrance, for Aziz to pass in. She failed to locate him" (254). The shadow of her earlier memory fails to coalesce into something as definite or recognizable as Aziz. And like the unnamed animal that sprang from nowhere before she visited the caves, the palpable force of the landscape seems to touch her again: "It was the doubt that had often visited her, but solid and attractive, like the hills." It is at this point, as she tries to repeat herself, that her language fails. "I am not—" (she stops). "Speech was more difficult than vision. 'I am not quite sure'" she finally falters (254). Repetition undoes her language. She literally cannot re-call her words in both senses: she cannot withdraw them; and she cannot re-member and replay them.

The colonial machinery persists, battling this unexpected force. But like the echo, which began to "undermine" Mrs. Moore's "hold on life," this strange echo begins to undermine the hold of the courtroom and its language. "I didn't catch that answer," says the superintendent of police, looking "scared" yet giving away his urge to "catch," to apprehend both her words and their designated signified, Aziz (254). As he slams down his papers, displacing upon them the violence he wishes to enact elsewhere, McBryde, as the voice of colonial authority, tries to return her words to her, echoing them back to her, trying to fix them as the origin that she must not reject and, indeed, to impose on her his own meaning. But these words have already a disputed origin, for they were conscripted from Adela by his agenda, on his territory. "Now, Miss Quested, let us go on," he commands. "I will read you the words of the deposition which you signed two hours later in my bungalow" (255). This repetition brings resistance, as she repudiates those words of colonial distortion.

In an earlier manuscript version, Major Callendar advances toward her threateningly, in the full cloak of his medical authority, attempting to arrest both her body and her words, using his power of labeling to declare her mentally unsound. But here Adela cries revealingly, "Keep <him> \that man/ off me, <let me speak> \or he'll stop me speaking the/ the truth" (*MPI*, 400). These startling words suggest that in this cave of the courtroom, the real attacker is Callendar, confirming that the terror that assailed Adela in the Marabar Cave was of the colonial system that threatened to label and constrain her. Though the final version relinquishes the melodrama of such an utterance, preferring to convey this threat more implicitly, it also suggests that what threatens Adela is not so much sexuality as the system of colonial domination. Adela's illness, from which she now begins to recover, is the force of colonial suppression, against which she has been battling since she heard Godbole's song. Adela is thus at once resisting subject and the agent that participates in, and then withdraws from, that system of subordination.

While McBryde can only regard Adela as "mad," a "broken machine" (256) that has failed its task, even Fielding does not understand what has led

Adela to this point. He diagnoses her as about to "have a nervous breakdown," but this medical terminology is not validated by the text, nor can it represent what has enabled her to resist. Later, when Fielding and Adela converse, they leave it as an emanation from "worlds beyond which they could never touch" (293). Adela has learned, if nothing else, the mistake of trying to name what is beyond the limits of her language.

By the end of the trial scene, *A Passage to India* appears to have overcome much of what led to Forster's crisis of writing: it has found a way to bring the proscribed body into language, as that which borders the accepted codes of language, showing how this suppressed force of resistance can bring truth, erupting upon the violent hegemony of civic order. Touched by this return of the repressed, the deranging effects of the force of the Marabar, Anglo-Indian "civilized" language and control falls apart under its pressure. The novel also suggests self-referentially how repetition—structural, linguistic, figural—in Forster's own language can expose, undo, and deconstruct colonial discourse through revision. But as we know from the previous chapter, Forster faced new problems (consequent upon a more complex but unspeakable understanding of colonial same-sex erotics and of the asymmetries of power that can impel desire) that he remained unwilling to address in his published work. The effort of such writing, of a cautious double coding that must perforce not only not name homoeroticism but also not name the volatile dimensions of desire, was not to be repeated. After this novel, Forster's desire for the political agency of his writings would be channeled into the essay form—ironic, elliptical, often also double coded—rather than taking the form of imaginative fiction, while the desire to speak the body and its complicated desires, to address the recalcitrance of carnality in art, would become a private enterprise, restricted to the diaries and fictions that could not be published until after their writer's passing from his world.

CHAPTER FIVE

From a Full Stop to a Language
Rushdie's Bodily Idiom

> Outside the whale is the unceasing storm, the continual quarrel, the dialectic of history. Outside the whale there is genuine need for political fiction, for books that draw new and better maps of reality, and make new languages with which we can understand the world.
> —Rushdie, "Outside the Whale"[1]

TOWARD the end of A *Passage to India*, when Dr. Aziz is asked to contribute a poem to help build a "Hindu-Muslim entente," he wonders whether he might more appropriately write a prescription instead (296–97). But Forster suggests that a poem would work a better cure. Indeed, Aziz longs "to compose a new song which should be acclaimed by multitudes and even sung in the fields, . . . a song of the future [that] must transcend creed" (298), fueled by his experiences to forge a new nation of Indians united against colonialism. "Poetry must *touch* life," agrees Fielding, for literature must both be derived from life and, in turn, impinge upon it (308; my emphasis). Yet Aziz is unable to produce—because Forster is unable to imagine—a postcolonial language of agency. Aziz's poem is never written, because (unlike his grandfather, who "was also a poet, and fought against [the British] in the Mutiny" [308]) Aziz does not have the power to turn words into agents of political resistance or national reconstruction. "In what language shall it be written? And what shall it announce?" he wonders (298). Disabled by a heritage of anomie and lamentation, "the decay of Islam and the brevity of love" (298), Aziz cannot find a suitable idiom for postcolonial literary agency in Forster's novel.

But a grandson of another Dr. Aziz can: Saleem, the narrator of Salman Rushdie's *Midnight's Children*. Indeed, Rushdie's self-appointed task is to invent a new postcolonial language, a language that is neither dated nor effete, that is able to do what Aziz could not.[2] Early in the novel, Saleem describes himself as a fetus:

> By the time the rains came at the end of June, the foetus was fully formed inside her womb.... What had been (at the beginning) no bigger than a full stop had expanded into a comma, a word, a sentence, a paragraph, a chapter; now it was bursting into more complex developments, becoming, one might say, a book—perhaps an encyclopaedia—even a whole language ... which is to say that the lump in the middle of my mother grew so large, and became so heavy, that ... Amina found herself ... scarcely able to move beneath the weight of her leaden balloon.[3]

This striking passage both describes the gestation of a new language and functions as an example of that new language. It presents the genesis of a human body as the genesis of a text, of Saleem the narrator as both body and text, a creature produced by language, described in typographic or textual terms. This autobiography (or auto-embryo-graphy) also describes Rushdie's postcolonial narrative: his novel likewise aspires to begin from a "full stop" like Aziz's and grow into a history of family and nation that will help build a postcolonial future.

The passage disorders at least two kinds of hierarchies that its readers may take for granted. The first is the relation between the body and language, between material and discursive experience. Whereas Kipling could describe his book as his baby, moving from the seeming primacy of human reproduction to intellectual production, drawing on physical experience to render the discursive, Rushdie describes the unborn baby as already a book, "even a whole language," so that the text is not like a body, but rather, the body is like a text. He implies that language comes first, that this baby grows as a language grows, that the development of a new language can provide the terms to understand the growth of a fetus, that the production of language is somehow prior to and constitutes the production of the body.

Rushdie thus presents a central premise that undergirds his writing: that language, instead of being subsequent to, or a way to make sense of, physical experience in fact gives birth to our sense of reality; language constitutes—as it literally provides the terms for—our understanding of something as basic and apparently prelinguistic as embryonic selfhood, or the physical experience of our bodies. Rushdie emphasizes the power of language to shape material reality because that is the basic imperative that underlies his work. If nations are brought into existence as "imagined communities"[4] through a shared language, through collective willed acts of imagination, "a dream we all agreed to dream" (*MC*, 130), and if postcolonial citizens are "fathered by history," engendered by acts of language, by the written and told histories that produce them (*MC*, 137), so, Rushdie suggests, postcolonial writers of imaginative fictions can intervene in these processes of making communities, participating in how nations remember and (re-)create themselves. The self-conscious effort of Saleem's narrative, as well as of Rushdie's, is to transform the national body through his "pickled" history of alternative truths (*MC*, 549). If language has this politically and materially formative power, then Rushdie's self-conscious postcolonial goal is to take control of that language, to reinvent that language to begin anew, to reshape the world. This account of the fetus as comma is thus a self-reflective meditation on how he might produce such a "new language."

As this fetus grows from nothing into the potential for anything, from a "full stop" (a dot on the page) into "a whole language" (uncontainable in any frame), Rushdie's exuberant syntax enacts these "bursts of development" as his own sentence grows and bends under the weight of its accumulating catalog. At once describing the growth of narrator and narrative, the sentence suggests that, as an example of this language, it is slowly bringing Saleem into being—as a textual product. But because the adult Saleem is narrating his own gestation here, in some sense Saleem generates his own self—as fetus—in the telling. His language re-creates his past self, enabling him to re-create himself in—or on—his own terms. Writing thus has the capacity for self-creation and self-realization—

through the process of *re*-writing and gaining control of one's past—individual and collective. By the end of *Midnight's Children*, Saleem's body-as-text empties itself into the life story he has written, for as it slowly disintegrates from the sheer exhaustion of reliving his life as he writes his story, his book does not simply replace but becomes his (new) body, the physical and linguistic repository of a lived history.

But this passage also relies on a second inversion. This fetus begins from the finality of a period, or "full stop," and struggles past the obstacles of punctuation marks ("a comma") to increasingly unhampered units of textuality, "a word, a sentence, a paragraph, a chapter" and then into a language, a proliferating field of meanings. If we understand "language" in the Saussurean sense of *langue*, a set of discursive possibilities, then this fetus (like Rushdie's book) promises to grow into such a language.[5] This disordering of beginnings and ends, beginning from a full stop, from a fetus that looks like and grows from a comma, a pause, suggests that postcolonial beginnings may situate themselves upon colonial ends, setting process emblematically on its head. It sets up a fundamental dilemma that confronts postcolonial narrative—nationalist, historiographic, or fictive: how to begin again. Two-thirds of the way into the novel, when almost the entire older generation of Saleem's family—parents, grandparents, uncles, aunts—is destroyed in the 1965 India-Pakistan war, Padma weeps at these unexpected deaths, while readers might share her bewilderment: how can Saleem's story continue without most of its main characters? "A chapter ends when one's parents die," he tells her (and us), "but a new kind of chapter also begins" (414) (as he begins section 3 of his novel). This is Saleem's and Rushdie's challenge from the beginning: how to begin again, to build from the debris, and to hold his readers' interest after the end of the world they knew. For it is now that Saleem (and the new Indian nation) will have to grow up, become his own agent, and face his most harrowing challenges—both as an actor and as the narrator of his own story. When Saleem promises that there is much more to come, giving a quick preview of "exotic futures," Padma recovers. "Begin," she commands him. "Begin all over again" (415). And he does.

Rushdie's trope of Saleem as fetus suggests that to be a postcolonial narrator is to come to a full stop—to have to begin again, to construct a new language to formulate the conditions and possibilities of an unprecedented situation. It is an embryonic Rushdiean meditation on beginnings, a metanarrative of the beginning of his writing. It poses the beginning as, in some sense, the most difficult moment, as a full stop, a moment that commits itself to and thus limits what follows. At the same time, it also suggests that that period, that dot, is also an opening, as it can unfurl itself into something new, building exponentially upon itself. This, then, is Rushdie's project: to grow a "new [bodily] language" (as he puts it in the epigraph to this chapter), both to render and to reconstruct a new postcolonial world.

But what is this new language to do? What does it have at stake? Writing in 1970s Britain about India's first thirty-two years of independence, Rushdie strove in *Midnight's Children* to construct an idiom that has since come to define postcolonial literature. At the time, he was a fledgling writer, attempting both to address experiences yet uncharted in English and to construct a language that would not only tell the difference between "truth and untruth"—colonial or postcolonial—and "draw new and better maps of reality" (*IH*, 100) but would also help *make* new truths and thereby change the world. A central parable in *The Satanic Verses* makes this agenda explicit. Upon his arrival in London, Saladin Chamcha is subjected to brutal police racism and finds himself metamorphosing into a satanic goat with horns. But when he lands in a prison hospital, he discovers that other immigrant inmates have also turned into chimerical beasts. A woman has become "mostly water-buffalo," Nigerians on business have "grown sturdy tails," and holidaying Senegalese turned "slippery snakes." While Chamcha feels helpless, some of the mutant creatures have formed a resistance movement, as if they blame someone else. "The point is, . . . are you going to put up with it?" demands the manticore, a Bombay model turned "impossible" man-tiger with three rows of teeth. "But how do they do it?" asks Chamcha. "'They describe us,' the other whispered solemnly. *'That's all. They have the power of description, and we succumb to the pictures they construct'*" (167–68; my emphasis). Through this mode of magical realism, when reality has become so horrific, so deranging, so dislocating that conventional language cannot approximate it, Rushdie conveys the power of dominant racist discourse to have material bodily effects, to transform reality: human beings subject to colonial histories of denigration and abuse actually become freaks when they begin to see themselves as they are seen. But here is also where Rushdie suggests that postcolonial literature can have power and efficacy: it can appropriate that language to redescribe, invent new lenses for (re)vision, and reconvert the monsters into humans again. Just as Chamcha's devilish body will function as an enabling icon for underground black resistance, so too, Rushdie suggests, postcolonial writers, artists, and historians must "write back,"[6] demystifying and undoing "white" magic, drawing "new and better maps of reality," changing how the disempowered see themselves and are seen. To do this, they must have a "new language," both to re-"understand" the world and, as Rushdie asserts elsewhere, to "change" it (*IH*, 14). In his first major novels, I argue, this is Rushdie's primary goal.

Certainly, all literarily ambitious writers seek to wrench language out of conventionality, to defamiliarize, to produce languages that change the lenses by which we see reality—and ourselves and others. But for postcolonial writers such as Rushdie, writing for audiences in multiple geopolitical locations and consciously revisionist of colonial discourses, this effort carries a heightened political charge. Rushdie has openly cast his writing as doing political work.[7] "Description is itself a political act," he insists in his important essay "Imaginary Homelands" of 1982, "re-describing a world is the necessary first step towards changing it" (*IH*, 13–14). This "description" works in at least two important ways. One, as Rushdie frequently contends, is to (re)describe things as they are, as they are concretely, differentially experienced, to contest official versions of truth, to offer, like Richard Wright in the "war over the nature of reality," black realities to contest white ones (*IH*, 13). Imaginative fiction can counter the homogenizing generalizations of official discourses, perhaps because it offers the concreteness of particular experiences and requires an act of imaginative extension, of reaching beyond oneself, from readers as well. Rushdie's stance is both anticolonial and anti-*neo*colonial in telling contestatory truths about the past and present—whether in *The Satanic Verses*, in which he exposes the British racial discrimination that many white Britons deny; or in *Midnight's Children* and *Shame*, in which he combats state propaganda and censorship by offering alternative versions of the 1975 Indian Emergency and the Pakistan army's 1971 genocide in East Bengal. Foregrounding the unreliability of any single narration, insisting on the partiality of memory, selection, and story making, Rushdie casts suspicion on all claims to objective representations or singular histories, claiming for himself the only truth that totalizing singular claims to truth are more dangerous than those that make visible their limitations and their status as one of many. Thus, an intense awareness not only of the power but also of the responsibility of minority writers (who, as Gilles Deleuze and Félix Guattari have argued, must inevitably be political) suffuses Rushdie's prose: "If writers leave the business of making pictures of reality to politicians, it will be one of history's great and most abject abdications," he writes ("Outside the Whale," *IH*, 100).[8]

But a second mode of description is to describe things not only as they *are* or *were* but as they *might be* in the future and, by act of suggestion, to help make them so. In his 1991 introduction to *Imaginary Homelands*, Rushdie describes India as having "arrived at a full-blown crisis of descriptions," in which many Indians had begun to describe India in fundamentalist Hindu terms that ignored both its diverse history and its non-Hindu citizens (*IH*, 2). Given that communities are formed as acts of self-imagining, it matters how they imagine and describe themselves: as homogenous and exclusive, or as heterogeneous and inclusive. Imagining Englishness as inclusive of blackness, or Indianness as inclusive of Dalits, Muslims, Parsees, or Jews, can produce radically different societies. By offering these possibilities, literature can help forge better, rather than worse, imagined communities; it can infuse healthier self-descriptions into the body of a nation, evoking sympathetic identifications and cross-identifications across difference.[9] If the particularity and complexity of literary redescription can enable readers to imagine themselves and others as humans rather than monsters, as a community that includes a diversity of ethnicities, races, and classes, then that literary imagining can reproduce not only "pictures of reality" as it exists but also as it might be. In both kinds of description—in redescribing the past and present (historical verisimilitude), and in describing alternative future possibilities (creative novelty)—the postcolonial writer seeks to transform reality, to work toward communities that are more just. And for both kinds of description, to enable a new kind of imagining to happen, the writer must push and change language. This is not to claim, as postmodernists are often accused of doing, that language alone constitutes reality, but rather, to recognize that language works *with* material conditions, that it is one of the material forms of power, that it, together with brute force, constructs and affects political and social institutions. Rushdie's goal, like those of Kipling and Forster, is to identify the modes through which language enacts power, to understand its limitations and its liability for abuse.

Rushdie's writing is more boldly contestatory than Kipling's or Forster's, more explicitly impassioned about its own agency: stridently self-advertising, it asserts, declaims, insists, it calls on readers to reevaluate, to re-see the power of discursive legacies. It shows how colonial discourses have shaped postcolonial psyches, nations, and bodies, and it undertakes to recast that, to remake history, both past and future. Explicitly metanarratival, it meditates on the problems of both telling and making alternative truths, on the fictionality of histories, on the artist as historian, and on what writing can do. But like Kipling and Forster, Rushdie also uses the human body to address the complications of literary agency, though in quite different ways.

Whereas for Kipling and Forster, the human body and its relations seem prior to language, a truth that preexists and feeds the realm of the symbolic, Rushdie disorders that precedence of the body. Imbued with a more poststructuralist sense that language generates and shapes the apprehension of material reality, Rushdie keeps returning to the ways that language itself is prior. He seems most compelled by the ways that language may materialize into reality, and he attempts to devise rhetorical techniques that suggest the sheer corporeality of his language, to suggest how language *matters* by making it seem heavily, sensuously material—trying to make words *into* matter—by calling upon the human body to render that materiality. He literalizes metaphors and concretizes abstractions to make apprehension startlingly, pungently fresh; he revivifies dead metaphors and brings language to life but also re-creates it anew. He conflates different senses: smells can have colors and weights; feelings can be knitted into clothes and infuse bodies, thoughts, and actions; wifely anger can be smelt and felt as an "implacable perfume, a hard cloud of determination" (*MC*, 57). Such bodily effects, as we will see, are manifestations of unspoken words as bodily substances blocked from relief-bringing evacuation. While he recognizes the distance between words and things, between language and materiality, he also pursues their connectedness, attempting to collapse or reduce that distance, to merge or fuse the two. If language is other to the body, then his writing seeks to close that gap. Rushdie seeks both to suggest the corporeality of language and to produce this effect in his own language: he tries to make his language corporeal, to take on the flavor, tactility, liquidity, and volitionality of lived human bodies. In so doing, Rushdie proposes several ways in which language may relate to the body: how it produces and is produced by the body; how it resembles the body's vulnerability, power, and instrumentality; and what is most important, how, like the body, language is relational, interpenetrated by the world.

This chapter examines how Rushdie's recurrent concern with bodies, body parts, and bodily effluvia, is coincident with his efforts to construct a new idiom to render the agency of his postcolonial narratives, both to recast colonial legacies and to reimagine a postcolonial community or nation. Focusing on *Midnight's Children* and *Shame*, his foundational subcontinental novels of nation making, I look at the intensified bodiliness of their language to show how their primary effort is to make words matter, to infuse language with bodiliness, to emphasize the constitutive power of language, through three specific modes: bodily effluences as productive "matter out of place," in Mary Douglas's terms; unspoken words as a synesthetic force; and the dynastic webs of differential recurrence. This bodily idiom also enables Rushdie to structure his narrative as that which relates past and present as a familial relation, allowing him to reconcile the similarities as well as the differences, the connections as well as the disjunctions, between colonial and postcolonial literary and political history.

In chapter 6 I show how Rushdie's construction of this bodily idiom enables him to address the two key concerns of postcolonial literary agency mentioned above—describing things as they are, and as they might be—as ways of creating reality in and through his narratives. One is the issue of truth-telling (about the past): what factors condition what can and cannot be said; how censorship works in neocolonial contexts, and how a writer like Rushdie can evade state censorship. I consider how Rushdie indicts national mythmaking as a form of bodily violence, as a "rite of blood," and how he insists not inconsistently on both the partiality and the contingency of his own more salutary truth-telling as well as on the falsity of such nationalist histories. The second is the issue of truth-making (imagining a viable postcolonial future). Rushdie, I argue, adapts the dream as a fictive form of truth-telling, as another register of the bodily, through which he can articulate the otherwise impossible. This enables the peculiar dream-endings of his novels: they resist closure as a predetermining (or termination) of postcolonial narrative, and open up possibilities that may defy logic, in order to create terms that make such futures possible.

I focus on *Midnight's Children* and *Shame* (with some attention to later novels) because Rushdie first develops this new idiom and its complex of concerns in them and because both are central to Rushdie's efforts at postcolonial literary intervention and innovation. Of all of Rushdie's work, these two novels are also crucial, as is now apparent, for having fostered a renaissance in South Asian English writing, providing a new set of opportunities and possibilities for a generation through their invention of a new language, inciting writers as different as Arundhati Roy, Rohinton Mistry, and Shyam Selvadurai to reach beyond Rushdie and use his novelty to create their own.[10] Almost two decades after the fatwa, we can reread these novels without having to explain everything (which was necessary in the first wave of Rushdie scholarship) or address them in terms dictated by the notoriety of *The Satanic Verses*.

Rushdie's career has coincided with the explosive growth and institutionalization of postcolonial studies in the Anglo-American academy, and his critical reception has since grown into a virtual industry. Early scholars focused on *Midnight's Children* and *Shame* to examine Rushdie's literary sources and techniques; his uses and philosophies of language, hybridity, migrancy, history, and nationalism; his limitations regarding gender and class; his postmodern aesthetics versus postcolonial politics; his achievements in comparison to other writers; and the politics of his reception in the Western market.[11] They also produced controversies that continue in Rushdie scholarship: the degree to which his cosmopolitan location enables or compromises his work and politics; his use of the English language at the expense of writings in other Indian languages; his anticommunism or failure to produce a politics of subalternity.[12] The 1989 fatwa unleashed a now well-documented phenomenon of commentaries that explained, questioned, or reinforced binaries, as well as scholarship that emphasized (and exemplified) the importance of reading complexly his fiction as (politically and historically situated) fiction.[13] More recent scholarship on Rushdie has begun to address both the subsequent, less favorably reviewed novels and the phenomenon of his success and its imbrication in the politics of globalization.[14]

My approach to Rushdie's fiction both depends on this groundbreaking work and departs from it. Indebted to the scholarship that taught us to read Rushdie — his metafictive historiographic postmodern/postcolonial innovations, his emphasis on cultural hybridity, his complex politics of location—I ask new questions and advance new readings of the novels. Some of the early scholarship assumed an opposition between aesthetics and politics, between Rushdie's "literary devices" and linguistic choices and his "more narrowly 'political' purposes of commenting on Islam and on Indian, Pakistani, or British society and politics," an assumption that remains operative even in some recent approaches.[15] D. M. Fletcher, for instance, assumes in his introduction to *Reading Rushdie* a fundamental distinction between the political and the literary, or a certain prioritization between *kinds* of politics: as if a national or cultural critique were somehow different from, and superior to, strategic innovations of style or language; as if literary strategies were only a means for satiric or political "ends" (10); or as if choosing to revise Laurence Sterne, James Joyce, Günter Grass, or Gabriel Garcia Marquez as a South Asian British writer in a specific sociohistorico-cultural context were not in itself a political act. My work intervenes in this scholarship to show how Rushdie's literary techniques are themselves political and are seen by him as doing political work.

Scholars who have addressed issues of agency or the body in Rushdie's fiction include Josna Rege, who examines the problem of acting (as opposed to being a colonial subject) for characters in the Indo-English novel, and John Clement Ball, who charts the tension between negative critique and positive regenerative Menippean satire in Rushdie's novels.[16] But none connect the body and agency to pose the question of how *literature* can act or how the body is central to Rushdie's imagining of the capacities and limitations of his own language.[17] Mikhail Bakhtin's work on the grotesque body as a site of the carnivalesque, with its capacity for resistance and subversion of dominant hierarchies, has been understandably recognized by many scholars as relevant to Rushdie's work.[18] But Rushdie's fiction, while illuminated significantly by Bakhtin's writings, also departs significantly from them, when Rushdie makes the body a central trope for his language. I would like, nevertheless, to identify two or three broad principles elaborated by Bakhtin that help us understand Rushdie's work with the body.

For Bakhtin, a preeminent principle of the carnivalesque tradition is laughter, because it banishes fear and enables victory for the low against cosmic and human forces. "Carnival laughter ... is, first of all, a festive laughter [of the people], not an individual reaction.... Second, it is universal in scope; it is directed at all and everyone, including the carnival's participants. The entire world is seen in its droll aspect, in its gay relativity. Third, [it] is ambivalent: . . . it asserts and denies, buries and revives."[19] Unlike the satirist's negative laughter, which "places him above [and in opposition to] the object of his mockery," carnivalesque laughter is inclusive: "[H]e who is laughing also belongs to it" (12). Rushdie's is precisely not the sneering laughter of a V. S. Naipaul but the all-inclusive, self-ironizing Bakhtinian laughter that legitimizes what it represents and performs the cultural work of inculcating both familiarity and affection, making the forbidden proximate. His work has had unprecedented success (barring the catastrophe of *The Satanic Verses*) in different communities—from South Asian readers to metropolitan ones, across the divisions of gender, race, and age—perhaps precisely because, unlike earlier South Asian writers in English, he enables a laughter that produces a shared community across colonial and postcolonial divides even as it takes on courageously the task of laughing at, and demystifying, the power and authority of the metropolitan West as well as of the neocolonial state. Moreover, I contend, this spirit of self-ironizing, debunking, exposing laughter, as evidenced by his comically exaggerated, irreverent focus on conventionally unmentionable body parts and functions, acts as a countering principle to the self-consciously upper-class positionality of his narration; it speaks, in fact, for a popular ethos that is resistant to and indeed subversive of elitist class pretensions and power.

For Bakhtin, this healing, regenerative laughter is enabled by the grotesque human body, "the material bodily principle," because that laughter of the body, and what it represents, is what is repressed by high culture (19). This ultimately utopian, comic vision of the unidealized grotesque body emphasizes the grosser materiality of the lower bodily functions and exaggerates the areas of protrusion (noses, penises, breasts, bulges) and opening (mouth, nose, pores, genital and excretory orifices), in contrast with the later bourgeois or Renaissance "classic" canon (30), whose rules of decorum present the smooth, "finished, completed, strictly limited body" (29), closing off all the orifices and hiding all that "protrudes, bulges, sprouts or branches off (when a body transgresses its limits and a new one begins)" (320). The traditions of the grotesque body build egalitarianism and community by affirming the earthliness of the low, bringing the rarefied artificialities of the high literally "down to earth," turning "their subject into flesh" (20), by emphasizing the commonalities of the body. "The essential principle of grotesque realism is degradation, that is, the lowering of all that is high, spiritual, ideal, abstract; it is a transfer to the material level, to the sphere of earth and body in their indissoluble unity" (19–20).

> Degradation here means coming down to earth, the contact with earth as an element that swallows up and gives birth at the same time. To degrade is to bury, to sow, and to kill simultaneously, in order to bring forth something more and better. To degrade also means to concern oneself with the lower stratum of the body, the life of the belly and the reproductive organs; it therefore relates to acts of defecation and copulation, conception, pregnancy, and birth. Degradation digs a bodily grave for a new birth; it has not only a destructive negative aspect, but also a regenerating one. (21)

Thus, Bakhtin concludes, "debasement is the fundamental artistic principle of grotesque realism: all that is sacred and exalted is rethought on the level of the material bodily stratum or else combined and mixed with its images.... [T]he grotesque swing ... brings together heaven and earth. But the accent is placed not on the upward movement but on the descent" (370–71).

Bakhtin's insights about the grotesque body as an articulation of opposition to power structures through symbolic integration (rather than segregation) help explain why the body is central to Rushdie's representation of his language, its potential and constraints. *Midnight's Children* struggles to encompass the impoverished underclass and the privileged elite of the colonized nation with a promise of regeneration and renewal. "Nose and knees, knees and nose," Saleem switches places with Shiva, not once but twice, as each learns the positionality of other—the text spares neither.[20] The intellectualism of Saleem is brought low, made to experience the bodily horrors of war, poverty, torture, and mutilation before it can turn to the important task of national reconstruction. Even *The Satanic Verses*, when read within this carnal/carnivalesque tradition, emphasizes the bodiliness of the Prophet and his wives not to mock or vilify, as it has tragically been seen, but to imagine and revitalize them as human, to make them more immediate and not remote, to regenerate them as real and, indeed, to bring together "heaven and earth."

But there is another important way in which Bakhtin is useful to reading Rushdie's bodily language, namely, his understanding of the grotesque body as *relational*, as a site of the interpenetration of self and world. The grotesque body emphasizes protuberances and orifices because it is fundamentally a model of openness, not closure, of interaction with the world. Formally structured like this grotesque body, Rushdie's text also refuses to close, insisting on holes, gaps, for readers to fill in, to stretch out, extend beyond itself:

> The distinctive character of this body is its open unfinished nature, its interaction with the world. These traits are most fully and concretely revealed in the act of eating; the body transgresses here its own limits: it swallows, devours, rends the world apart; is enriched and grows at the world's expense. The encounter of man with the world, which takes place inside the open, biting, rending, chewing mouth, is one of the most ancient, and most important objects of human thought and imagery. Here man tastes the world, introduces it into his body, makes it part of himself.... Man's encounter with the world in the act of eating is joyful, triumphant; he triumphs over the world, devours it without being devoured himself. The limits between man and world are erased, to man's advantage. (281)

This model of interrelationality between self and world is central to Rushdie's conception of the body—for in his writing, the body is interpenetrated by the world, which enters it and acts upon it but is also taken in by it and is in turn acted upon by the body. Moreover, by conflating this corporeal body with his narrative, Rushdie suggests that his tale (as Saleem's body/book) is likewise such a bodily processual thing, growing, interacting, and also in a process of becoming. Thus Saleem's recurrent refrain that he has "swallowed the world" is a crucial paradigm for Rushdie's bodily narration, because it establishes its purposiveness and being as such a carnivalesque grotesque body, which has swallowed the world to conquer it, to incorporate all into itself, and will thus seek to change and to transform that world as a body inextricably linked to it. In a strange coincidence of phrase, Bakhtin continues,

> The grotesque body ... is a body in the act of becoming. It is never finished, never completed; it is continually built, created, and builds and creates another body. *Moreover, the body swallows the world and is itself swallowed by the world* ... This is why the essential role belongs to those parts of the grotesque body in which it outgrows its own self, transgressing its own body, in which it conceives a new, second body: the bowels and the phallus, ... the mouth [and] the anus. [In] all these convexities and orifices ... the confines between

bodies and between the body and the world are overcome: there is an interchange and an interorientation. (317; my emphasis)

For Rushdie, this body provides an important model of interrelationality: between bodies (of selves and others) and between the body and the world (self and physical environment, as well as structures of power, institutions, and so forth). Both kinds of interrelationality are integral to Rushdie's bodily writing: the fetus as comma, and eventually as a language, will take in and act upon the world; it will absorb parts of others and reshape others; and it will continue to grow, to become and shape something new.

And finally, as in Bakhtin's account of the carnivalesque tradition (283–85), truth in Rushdie's writing is also associated with the lower body, with excretion and dirt, as a synecdoche for that which is repressed, hidden, and outlawed, as the sexual, underclass, dirty, and undesirable, and which therefore stands for the truth. Poor women, doubly disempowered and perhaps therefore heavily associated with bodiliness, from Padma to Tai Bibi, are the purveyors and touchstones of often unwelcome truths: the pubescent girl who cleans toilets has a "frankness," an "honesty of latrine cleaners," a "tongue caked with excrement" (422). Tai Bibi, the "oldest prostitute in the world," tells Saleem the truth about his incestuous desire, a truth that is available to her through her preternatural body, its capacity to produce any smell on earth. Parvati, the girl from the slum, can alone tell Saleem his name and restore him to himself.

But there are also crucial differences between Rushdie's and Bakhtin's approaches to the body. For one, Rushdie deploys the body and its associations as a paradigm for his language, so that the truth-telling capacities of the body translate into the capacity of his language (as a bodily thing) to tell unwelcome truths or to have an impact upon the world. For another, the body in Rushdie's writing is not aggregate but individual—representative of individual agency, not (only) of collective resistance, because one of Rushdie's driving concerns is how an individual text can have effects beyond itself. And third, Rushdie's evocations of the human body are more multiplicitous (in the sense of being both multiple and duplicitous) than can be encompassed within even as capacious a model as Bakhtin's. What I find more apt, then, is to identify particular modes of Rushdie's bodily language and to draw upon different theoretical explanations for each to illuminate its multidimensionality and casting of literary agency.

Pointing Fingers: The Human Hand as an Emblem of Agency

It might seem unlikely, given Rushdie's confident, self-advertising style, that his writing could be assailed by concerns about agency. Yet the overemphatic excess and the continuous attempts to explain what he is doing and why suggest a need to demonstrate the importance and potential of postcolonial narration, description, and re-vision as a political aesthetic. In addition to the meta-moments, this concern is embedded centrally in his plots. All the (male) protagonists of Rushdie's novels are haunted by the desire to have political-historical-cultural impact. In *Midnight's Children*, Saleem's greatest concern from childhood is to *matter*, to have "meaning," to fulfil what he imagines is his special purpose. Longing to be the "bomb in Bombay," he insists upon the literal and metaphorical ways he has affected the nation (285), and driven by a sense of his destined importance, he longs to actualize that prophesied agency. Yet even this desire is fueled by his knowledge of others' expectations, which, if he were to fulfil, would make him an agent of *others'* desires, not his own. In a cruel paradox, young Saleem becomes an agent of the state, a "buddha" numbed out of conscience and memory. A failure as an autonomous agent of national history, made an instrument of others, he becomes finally a helpless subject of totalitarian power, literally castrated to ensure his silence and sterility, mutilated and tortured to betray the midnight's children whose potential he had once hoped to unite. Saleem thus embodies all three aspects of agency—autonomy (acting for oneself); instrumentality (acting for or being made to act by others); and subjection (being acted upon)—and the deceptive facility with which one kind may slide into another. Only when he starts to write his (and his nation's) history does he discover how he can fulfil the prophecies of his birth: through the *writing* that will transform how that nation comes to see and shape itself.

Omar Khayyam, the "peripheral hero" of *Shame*, is named after a famous poet but can neither write nor act for himself or for others. A toady who shifts loyalties from Isky to Raza, the country's rivalrous leaders, he reflects at the end on his life: "I watched from the wings, not knowing how to act."[21] But, as the novel shows, not acting is also a form of action—it affects historic outcomes. Omar, like Isky, is also a key player who affects the course of national history: when he refuses to act as Raza Hyder's instrument and chooses not to kill Sufiya Zinobia, his wife turned beast of shame, he allows her to wreak revenge, thereby triggering Raza's downfall and changing the course of national and familial history. In *The Satanic Verses*, it is no accident that both Saladin Chamcha and Gibreel Farishta, the main protagonists, are *actors*, at first very good at enacting the roles prescribed for them by others but then breaking out of those roles to act in other ways to effect change: Gibreel, imagining himself to be the archangel Gabriel, uses his voice to try to save London and his dream visions to reimagine Islamic history as communal survival; Chamcha, no longer allowing his ventriloquist's voice to be a tool for the entertainment industry's racism, enters the dreams of the black community and enables them to see themselves not as devils but as rebels against state oppression. In *Haroun and the Sea of Stories*, when his father loses his ability to tell stories and to act, Haroun steps in: he rescues the storytelling that then infuses the populace with the strength to repudiate evil politicians. The narrator-protagonist of *The Moor's Last Sigh* becomes the agent of gangsters; and the narrator of *The Ground Beneath Her Feet* is a photographer who records the story of the two rock stars in which he is peripheral, yet changes it by so doing.

But while these protagonists center on the ongoing complications of acting (or not acting) in a cultural-political process as writers, poets, artists, or historians, as shapers of truth and narrative, the ongoing metafictive preoccupation with literary agency in Rushdie's writing can be read most illuminatingly through the recurrent emblem of the hand in *Midnight's Children*. In her notable study *Dead Hands*, Katherine Rowe traces the literary and cultural history of the severed hand as a complex symbol that enables writers from Renaissance England to nineteenth-century America to address prevailing concerns about human agency.[22] She shows how these writers work through and intervene in cultural anxieties about legal, political, personal, or working-class agency through the trope of hands, because, she argues, Western culture has historically identified the body as the site of human action and responsibility, and the hand as the body part that concentrates the complexities of human agency. Deemed by Aristotle the "instrument of instruments," the hand functions as the primary trope of human action, intention, and control: the hand can serve oneself, as the primary tool for action or creation, and can be appropriated by others. Her work can help us read the proliferating images of the hand in *Midnight's Children* as a signifier of not only human but also *literary* agency, for Rushdie draws upon the heavy cultural symbolism of the hand in Western as well as in South Asian cultures.[23]

A quick look at idiomatic examples of the hand in English reveals these integral associations between hands and the capacity for human action and control. To "take matters into our own hands" is to take control; to "wash one's hands of X" is to absolve oneself of responsibility; to "lay one's hands on Y" is to claim ownership of it; "to have a hand in Z" (or a finger in the pie) is to be involved in the action; something "handy" is a good instrument. "A bird in the hand is worth two in the bush" associates the hand with possession but also threatens loss of control. For a woman to "give her hand in marriage" is to relinquish her autonomy, to submit her body and property to her husband.[24] The human hand serves as a primary synecdoche of selfhood, control, and action as expression of intention. In Urdu, Rushdie's other language, the hand carries similar associations: "hath pay hath dharay rakhna" (to drop one hand upon the other) is to enact passivity, to give up, to be unable to act—because hands in action represent the capacity to struggle or work; "mein ne hath bhi nahin lagaya" (one did not even touch something) is to say that one is not responsible for it, for the hand is the primary tool and extension of one's self. "Hathon ki lakeer" (lines of fate on the palm) suggests that hands are marked by destiny, that even when action is predestined and one is not responsible for it, that action is still inscribed upon and carried out by one's hands. Hands can be their own agents, refusing to work: "hath paon jawab dey jain" (one's hands and feet answer back, refusing to work), for one is unable to act when one's hands and feet are out of control. In Muslim lore, upon Judgment Day, one's hands will bear witness against one, for if one has used one's body to act wrongly, it will turn against one, refusing to serve human sin. Thus, in South Asian Muslim cultures as well, the human hand is a central bodily figure for human action, because intention is assumed to be enacted through the hand as instrument and signifier of autonomy.

In *Midnight's Children*, the first hand to which our attention is drawn is framed deliberately as an important subject of the novel. Jocularly reminding us of his Bollywood heritage, Saleem invokes film techniques as he focuses on Aadam Aziz's hand. "Close-up of my grandfather's hand: nails knuckles fingers all somehow bigger than you'd expect. . . . Thumb and forefinger pressed together, separated only by a thickness of paper. In short: my grandfather was holding a pamphlet. It had been inserted into his hand" (*MC*, 31). Larger than life, this strong, masculine doctor's hand is here not its own agent: it will act as the hand of another or of a text authored by someone else. This leaflet in his hand will change history. On behalf of Mahatma Gandhi, it declares a peaceful strike, calling for nationwide resistance to the British Rowlatt Act and to the continued colonial presence.[25] It will draw its reader, Dr. Aziz, out of his expensive hotel in Agra, literally into the battleground of history, the fateful Amritsar massacre, and into anticolonial struggle. The contiguity of his thick hand and the "thickness of paper" suggests that the two have become continuous: both inscribed by unknown invisible hands, both palpably material, both acting for others. The leaflet will act upon Dr. Aziz to make him a "hand" of Gandhi, inducing him to join the cause, while the doctor's hand will literally go to work tending to the bodies that fall victim to Colonel Dyer's zeal. Implicitly, Rushdie poses the question, what cultural work will his (hand)book do, similarly inserted into our readerly hands?

This focus on Dr. Aziz's hand is juxtaposed with that on two other hands that elaborate this initial question of human and textual agency. The first, mirroring Dr. Aziz's hand, is the powerful hand of the hotel guard who kicks the leaflet-bearing urchin out: "[C]haprassi-hand demands a close up too, because it is pressing thumb to forefinger, the two separated only by the thickness of urchin-ear. Ejection of juvenile disseminator of gutter tracts; but still my grandfather retained the message" (*MC*, 31). This hotel-guarding hand does not act for itself, for as the servant "hand" of its employers, it enacts brute power and censorship, for it prevents the anti-British leaflets from reaching the hotel's rich clients. But this "hand," this agent as employee, fails in part, for Dr. Aziz has got the "message," the call to join the battle on the street. The chapter closes with a yet more significant hand, Saleem's, the writer-historian-artist. For if any body part most intensely figures the artist's work, creativity, and agency, it is his hand. Saleem's hand, unlike these others, will engage in battles of his own, to enact an effective political and literary autonomy. But it is also vulnerable and, like his grandfather's, comparable to the materiality of texts. "My own hand, I must confess, has begun to wobble; not entirely because of its theme, but because I have noticed a thin crack, like a hair, appearing in my wrist, beneath the skin," he adds (*MC*, 36). This hand embodies the writer's intentionality and agency, his potential to produce national solidarity and (post)colonial resistance, while avoiding becoming an agent of others. In an optimistic moment, Saleem describes himself as "the hands holding the puppet strings," for he both records and *makes* what happens in his narrative (72). But this hand (and body) can become detached from his consciousness, it can become an agent of others' —for good or ill. Like the paper to which it is akin, it is already vulnerable, cracking and tearing under the pressures of telling (and living) this story. And it can be censored or broken. By the end, the puppeteer has become the puppet: "I must jerk towards the crisis like a puppet with broken strings," he remarks (509). Broken strings, however, suggest that even this damaged puppet can act —partially—by itself.

The figure of this materially textual hand recurs throughout *Midnight's Children* as an index (literally) of the novel's preoccupation with human and literary agency. At times, it signifies political power, intention, and control. The departing British masters "washed their hands of India," as if they relinquished control to rid themselves of a pollutant (108). Paternal authority is manifested as a giant "thick-fingered, heavy jointed" hand that slaps ten-year-old Saleem for his blasphemous claims, shattering both a glass table and his innocence, introducing him to a "green, glass-cloudy world filled with cutting edges" (194–95). The image is repeated in the Widow's green-skinned "hand" tipped with black fingernails: Saleem's dream-memory of torture and bodily castration. Agent of the termination of his productivity, this hand tortures and exterminates the midnight's children and grows eventually into the national "Hand" of totalitarian power (249–50). But this hand as symbol of agency remains slippery, as the term the "Widow's Hand" also refers to Indira Gandhi's officiating minion, the woman who serves as her tool (or agent) at the Widow's Hostel (521). By analogy, the writer's hand and the text it writes continually pose this question: what kind of hands are they?

Severed or detached hands litter *Midnight's Children*. Not apparently subject to anyone's will, they suggest either the power of an invisible agent or the ineffectuality of hands broken from the center of control, unable to act. Bombay is "an outstretched, grasping hand" (105, 107) that seems to contest the ownership of "British [Company] hands" (106). Strange substances in the shape of human hands appear at moments of crisis, as cautionary directives or accusatory fingers. When Ahmed Sinai and his Muslim partners are blackmailed and their godowns subjected to arson attack by the Ravana gang in Delhi, the rising cloud of burning fumes takes shape as a pointing finger, prefiguring the religious-ethnic violence of Partition, and a hand dropped by a vulture slaps Sinai. In the 1965 and 1971 wars, pointing fingers of mosques suggest the impotence or complicity of religion when inhuman acts are committed in their shadows.

As a recurrent image for the writer's hand and his text, the detached hand accumulates significance. It also suggests the denied autonomy of the underclass —the poor, unemployed, or disenfranchised, or the resurgence of the laboring repressed body. In the crisis when Aadam Aziz's family learns that Amina's first husband is impotent and Major Zulfikar chases after Nadir Khan, the Major crashes into the underground poet's friends (the street artists), impoverished old men who play the bystanders' game of spitting betel juice. "A low hard jet of red fluid caught him squarely in the crotch. A stain like a hand clutched at the groin of his battledress; squeezed; arrested his progress. Major Zulfy stopped in almighty wrath. . . . [A] second player, assuming the mad soldier would keep on running, had unleashed a second jet. A second red hand clasped the first and completed Major Zulfy's day" (68). Effeminizingly menstrual, yet reminiscent of Forster's Pan-like ethos, these bodiless red hands (shaking hands in collective action across the soldier's crotch), bodily liquids of the underclasses, have real effects: they prevent the fugitive poet from being caught; thwart the "progress" of a state official; and render impotent his ambitious martial gait. Representing the solidarity of these apparently idle street artists, this red hand suggests also the power of such popular (bodily) art.

Perhaps the most telling hand appears when child-Saleem watches his mother secretly reunite with her banished ex-husband. In a ghetto restaurant, unable to fulfill their now adulterous desire, Nadir Khan and Amina Sinai enact a peculiar ritual. Not allowed to touch in public, they do the "dance of hands," the strangely erotic enactment of unfulfilled longing, approximating physical contact by touching what the other has touched. While suggesting the helplessness of a desire only intensified by proximity, these dancing hands also enact a resistance to dominant social norms and sexual regulation, because they achieve a limited reconnaissance despite the constraints imposed on them. But this game gathers more significance when understood as a replay of resistant tactics learned from Bombay films. Amina's brother the film producer Hanif has just invented the "indirect kiss" (actors not allowed to kiss on screen would sensuously kiss an apple and pass it to the "beloved" to kiss), a tactic devised to elude the censorship of the Indian film industry (168). "So it was that life imitated bad art," comments Saleem (260). Indeed, Hanif's art, bad or not, has achieved what Saleem (and Rushdie) aspire to do: to act upon life, to transform it for the better, not only by representing what it sees as the truth but also by creating possibilities that infuse the imaginations of its audience, transforming those lives, as life imitates that art. The invisible hand, the effective agent that induces this extraordinary erotic performance and act of resistance is that of the artist, Amina's dead brother, Hanif.

This recurrent hand motif, which otherwise makes little sense in *Midnight's Children*, is thus a register of the novel's central concern about literary agency. An emblem of action and intention, it is associated with artistic creativity and the political resistance of the suppressed. Human and literary agency, these hands suggest, is enacted upon and through the body. But this agency is slippery: an individual can be in control, able to help or oppress others, and at other times be made to act for others or be rendered impotent. Rushdie creatively, indeed brilliantly, draws upon cultural histories of the hand to articulate his concerns about literary agency. But the hand is still not sufficient for Rushdie's purposes, possibly because the metaphor implicitly retains a Western, Cartesian mode of dividing the body and mind. What he needs—and devises—is a language that casts the body as more multidimensional, with more complicated connections between the body, language, and the world, to suggest the materiality of language, its relationality, and its uses in the world.

Why Do I Choose to Wallow in Excrement? The Bodiliness of Rushdie's Language

Rushdie scholars have generally not paid attention to the almost obsessive preoccupation with bodies, body parts, and bodily effluvia in his work or connected it with his self-referentiality or political work. While many have noted the significance of such evident tropes in *Midnight's Children* as Saleem's disintegrating body, ravaged by history like the nation,[26] or blushing in *Shame* as a metaphor for the psychosomatic effects of cultural shame and violence,[27] there has been no extended examination of the many ways Rushdie deploys the human body to represent his language or, indeed, to change how we understand language itself. In both *Midnight's Children* and *Shame*, Rushdie's imagination dwells intensely on bodies in many forms: bodies as they are acted upon (dismembered, diseased, tortured, rendered ridiculous); human bodies as they are experienced (being born, blushing, suffering, dying, rotting, in pain, in situations of naked humiliation or absurdity); bodies as they are seen, inspected, and fragmented, but also bodies engaged in lived processes (excreting, bleeding, sweating, urinating, crying, smelling); bodies in their relation to other bodies (breast-feeding, parenting, enacting violence); familial bodies as generating both similarity and difference; and (though not very often), bodies desiring. Animal bodies are dismembered or die grotesquely, often representing relations between humans and prefiguring the fates of human bodies.[28] Much of this recalls satiric traditions from Swift to Kafka, intensifying the grotesque inhumanity of what is described or the horror and disgust that lie beyond literal representation.[29] But Rushdie is primarily interested in the body as a paradigm for the central issue of how language acts in, and is acted upon by, the world. His language turns most intensely to the body when it seeks to represent language. He presents language as either a part of the body, a flow of bodily substances, given out or taken in, productive and produced; or linguistic entities as analogs for the body as an organic whole, so that a text (a book or a story) can be a sentient body, a relational thing, a whole with permeable boundaries, interacting and intersecting with the world.

Midnight's Children opens with Saleem explaining why, to tell the story of his life, he must first tell the stories of his family and nation. This meta-moment also introduces the multiple connections the novel makes between storytelling and the human body:

> And there are so many stories to tell, too many, such an excess of intertwined lives events miracles places rumours, so dense a commingling of the improbable and the mundane! I have been a swallower of lives; and to know me, just the one of me, you'll have to swallow the lot as well. Consumed multitudes are jostling and shoving inside me; and guided only by the memory of a large white bedsheet with a roughly circular hole some seven inches in diameter . . . , which is my open-sesame, I must commence the business of remaking my life from the point at which it really began, some thirty-two years before anything as obvious, as *present*, as my clock-ridden, crime-stained birth.

(The sheet incidentally, is stained too, with three drops of old faded redness. As the Quran tells us: *Recite, in the name of the Lord thy Creator, who created Man from clots of blood.*) (MC, 4)

The passage begins with a metaphor that equates the physical act of ingestion with the consumption of history. Even as an individual, Saleem is a composite of others, because he has grown out of all the members of his literal and metaphorical family, which includes every relative, every acquaintance, every bystander, colonized and colonizing, everyone whose life intersected with any of the lives that intersect with his. He renders this relation in bodily terms: as a "swallower" of the lives he seems to have fed upon and incorporated. And as a storyteller, he has swallowed *histories* of those lives, stories that merge into, feed, and impact his, and that in turn will merge into, feed, and impact his readers, who will "swallow the lot as well." That is why his life story must begin years before his actual birth. At the end of the novel, Saleem repeats this central point: "Who what am I? My answer: I am the sum total of everything that went before me, of all I have been seen done, of everything done-to-me. I am everyone everything whose being-in-the-world affected was affected by mine. I am anything that happens after I've gone which would not have happened if I had not come. Nor am I particularly exceptional in this matter: each 'I,' every one of the now-six-hundred-million-plus of us, contains a similar multitude. I repeat for the last time: to understand me, you'll have to swallow a world" (MC, 457–58).

This complicated trope of swallowing (as reading, passing on stories of the past, and as becoming who one is, or forming a relational identity) seems to apply to both the tellers and the listeners of a story. As Bakhtin helps us see, it suggests interaction between what is inside and outside the body: if swallowing suggests both engulfment and credibility, if we are what we eat and what we believe, then Saleem (and we) consume or take over what we swallow and are in turn made by it. This Rushdiean fiction of the constitutive power of stories, then, also carries a warning: to read carefully, skeptically, *not* to swallow everything we are told—because it will change who we are. Language, both oral and written, is bodily, and the body is at once singular and relational, autonomous and interpenetrated by the world, acting and acted upon. And Saleem's act of telling his life story is at once constitutive and constituted, for though it purports to describe how he was made, the process of retelling is also one of "remaking" his life.

Rushdie's trope of storytelling slides into another, then another, as if only a succession of trope upon trope can suggest the proliferating connections between language, body, and world that Rushdie needs to inaugurate his narration. Rushdie/Saleem shifts almost without warning from this metaphor of eating to one of birthing, from digestion to gestation, from one orifice to another. Having swallowed, he will give (re)birth to what he has taken in: "Consumed multitudes" "jostle and shove" inside him like unborn children competing for precedence, to emerge onto the white sheets of his page. To describe the birth of the midnight's children, Saleem repeats this image: "I . . . feel the children of midnight queuing up in my head, pushing and jostling like Koli fishwives," as if they are about to emerge from his body via the ink from his pen (123). Conflating literal and literary birthing, Rushdie also combines male and female reproduction in this composite image.

Yet here he slides from metaphor to metonymy, for the "bedsheet" that was stained by birthing fluids (as the writer's sheets are stained by writing) is also the perforated sheet of family history. This is a hol(e)y sheet that we will hear much about, for it is both a relic of grandparental romance and the barrier that prevents wholeness of vision (itself a metaphor for the partiality of knowing and telling). But this sheet is metonymic of Saleem's storytelling, for it is associated with (and instrumental to) the beginning of his story, a representative of his family's origins. It becomes Saleem's mnemonic "talisman" and "open-sesame" to that formative past. By alluding to the fabulous opening enabled by a magic word that led to a wealth of treasures, Rushdie suggests that just as Ali Baba climbed through a cave—an orifice that here suggests both mouth and womb—so too will the writer enter through a perforated sheet into the cave of the past, using his words as magic to open this hole of memory and retrieve a forbidden history. The telling and recovering of stories are thus strenuous bodily acts in many ways, with material consequences.

This enabling originary sheet is literally stained with family history: with three talismanic drops of blood from Aadam Aziz and Naseem Ghani's wedding night. As the publicly displayed writing of two grandparental bodies, these drops encode a heavy social script, signifying both sexual consummation and chastity: his masculinity and her virginity. This bodily writing clearly suggests the literal act of creation (of children and family) and hence of the beginning of Saleem's narrative. But this moment is important for Saleem's narration also because these three drops of blood allude to the opening words that produced the Quran, which began with the Revelatory injunction to Muhammad: "Recite, in the name of your Lord who created—created Man from clots of blood" (Quran, 96:1).[30] In Islamic lore, the prophet Muhammad, while meditating in his cave, was hailed by these words by the angel Gibreel, which initiated the divine Revelation, and hence the Islamic faith.[31] In this gnomic account of human origin, words are somehow linked with bodily origins, inciting us to ask, what does recitation (one kind of beginning) have to do with creation from clots of blood (another kind of beginning)? Why must one recall the other? Whose clot of blood (God's or man's own) created man, and from what (gendered) bodily part did this blood come?[32] Rushdie's text does not answer these questions, but it highlights two points—that the act of divine creation was bodily, and that the genesis of a sacred text needed to recall the genesis of the human body from blood—as if the two were integrally linked. For this Quranic text, about to be revealed, will also *re*-create man, as the followers of a new faith: Islam.

Like the Ramay painting discussed in the introduction to this book, Rushdie also recalls the power of these inaugural Quranic words, because they changed humans and human history. They remind man of how he was created, and as material agents, these words work to remake those who read or hear them. By linking the drops of blood that inaugurate his novel and the clots of blood from which the human form was created, invoking this originary textual-historical-religious moment, Rushdie suggests that *Midnight's Children*, as a secular text of communal, familial, and individual history, may also form, and is formed of, clots (and drops) of blood. And, he daringly suggests, this secular text will create man and text anew, in a secular mode, to have similarly powerful effects. Later, Saleem invokes this formative phrase again, as if this image of creational clots of blood haunts his imagination as a paradigm for his narrative. When ten-year-old Saleem discovers his telepathic abilities and tells his parents about what he thinks is another revelation of divine voices, the narrator Saleem recalls that originary moment of prophetic injunction: "Gabriel or Jibreel told Muhammad: 'Recite!' And then began The Recitation, known in Arabic as Al-Quran" (193). Violently rebuked for his claims, young Saleem then begins his telepathic communication with the midnight's children, imagining that he too has heard voices directing him to recite, to carry their message to others. Like the Prophet,

Saleem becomes a messenger, an agent of communication between these magical children, enabling a new imagined community to form, representing new possibilities that can transform the nation. In writing his book, the adult Saleem will do the same. Saleem's memory of the phrase "Recite in the name of the Lord thy Creator, who created Man from clots of blood" (193), at this occasion of beginning, is significant because it suggests that recitation, or language, is what makes possible the re-creation of the human. This is what gives Saleem the grandiose meaning of his life, his "reason for being born": only by this transmission of language can he actualize his agency, or bring about change in the world. In trying to identify Rushdie's multiple cultural legacies for *Midnight's Children*, scholars looking to his Indian heritage have focused on Hindu mythologies but not paid sufficient attention to how deeply Islamic sources also undergird his work.

This opening passage therefore establishes some of the key connections that *Midnight's Children* will develop—between language, the human body, and the world—that suggest how writing is made by and can remake its world. This passage refuses to fix upon a single way to understand the bodiliness of language, insisting, through its figural shifts, on the sheer multiplicity of those connections. With the metaphors of eating, swallowing, and giving birth, Rushdie suggests how the self, as body, is both productive and a composite of others, how it is relational, and how that absorption of others is discursive.[33] The production of language, he suggests, is a physical act and at the same time has physical effects: it can open forbidden caves to retrieve stolen treasures. The perforated sheet, marked by bodies, suggests how bodies carry meaning and function as signifiers that are differently coded in different social contexts. And it prefigures how Rushdie's sheets will be marked by bodily writing, a writing of blood and ink that will be equally formative. But it also suggests that the postcolonial writer must begin by invoking the past and making something new of it, through a language of blood and family relations. Finally, the emphasis on recitation and retelling suggests how language is both taken in and acts upon bodies, how it enacts power.[34] This passage is a metanarratival overture, clustering many of the ways that Rushdie will link the body with language in this novel, to show and to enact how words do—and are—matter.

Throughout *Midnight's Children* and *Shame*, Rushdie's writing emphasizes its own materiality. The act of storytelling can be physically violent, having literal effects on other bodies: it can render its audience a helpless hostage, as Saleem's story has Padma "by the throat" (MC, 38), or pierce with its "knife-tang of pickle fumes" (MC, 251). Ahmed Sinai's vituperative abuse emerges as a bodily discharge, "oaths that he spews from his lips like an animal . . . of the gutter" (MC, 340); Rumi Shakil's curses make the "air boil," as if his words have an intense kinetic energy (Shame, 4), just as Isky's curses ricochet upon him literally as a bullet (Shame, 262). Language is regularly presented as performative, enacting what is said in the act of saying. The very act of articulation can make a thought or dream or fear materialize into being: prophecies, dreams, lies, and curses come true, so that language literally shapes reality. The act of saying or imagining something seems to make it happen, because by articulating it, one has made it possible, brought it from nonexistence into existence. Picture Singh tells Saleem not to lie about sexual impotence to avoid marrying Parvati, because it might tempt the gods (MC, 481), but Saleem's lie comes true, for he is "ectomized" by the Widow (MC, 521). Naming shapes the future of a child (or wife), as the meaning of the name is lived out by the person: Shaheed, true to his name, becomes a martyr to war. Even Ahmed Sinai's boastful invention of a family curse comes true, burdening his family for the rest of their lives. Repeatedly, the power of suggestion takes physical form, as if once something is formulated in language, it makes that thing first possible and then real. Writing is a bodily activity, as Saleem's body empties itself into his book. Censorship is rendered as a brutal act of bodily excision or damage—from Saleem's "ectomies" in *Midnight's Children* to the poet's body hanged and tortured in a Pakistani jail (Shame, 22). Omar Khayyam's brother Babur the poet's dead body, riddled with bullet holes, is returned to his mothers together with his diary, the equally "brutalized volumes" with missing pages that mirror his body (Shame, 138, 143).

Even the "characters" of Rushdie's novels are literalized metaphors, rather than individuated creatures of interiority.[35] Saleem is a textual body that is filled with stories, a product of language that in turn produces language for other bodies to consume. While most novelists use their characters to make arguments, Rushdie's characters are in addition embodiments of abstractions, as if they were a thought made material, a theme or topic given body to move about the world, to work out how a linguistic construct (such as a text) acts in the world. The real protagonists of *Shame*, Sufiya Zinobia and Omar Khayyam, are, respectively, embodiments of shame and shamelessness. In *The Satanic Verses*,

Gibreel Farishta and Saladin Chamcha embody different types of cultural hybridity. Rushdie's novels can then be read as simultaneously telling stories of "characters" and turning ideas into embodied characters.

While these techniques intensify the effect in Rushdie's novels of the materiality and constitutive power of language, there are three specific modes running through his work that carry even greater significance: language as a bodily product or force, such that the body is a vessel into or from which language is poured; the material force of unspoken words, represented as bodily manifestations; and the representation of narrative structure as a genealogical web, using the physiology of generation to examine the links between postcolonial narrative and its literary and political colonial past.

Matter Out of Place: The Body as a Vessel and the Fluidities of Language

Midnight's Children recurrently casts the human body as a vessel, a container of bodily fluids (and semifluid matter) that are conflated with language and emanate from, are imbibed by, or circulate through the body, making the body a linguistic thing, composed of, overrun with, awash in, and constituted by this linguistic as bodily matter. These bodily fluids (milk, sweat, spit, urine, blood, snot, semen, or amniotic fluid) serve different functions (nurturing, circulating, connecting, battling, fertilizing, destabilizing) as they embody different ways of interacting with the world. They emerge from different orifices or gashes in the body's boundaries, to tell their respective tales: the mouth (the site of speech and of nourishment); reproductive and excretory openings (sites of bodily production and self-perpetuation); but also pores, eyes, or wounds.

Female bodies actively produce stories and language as bodily substances. Durga, the washerwoman with "inexhaustibly colossal breasts," feeds Aadam, Saleem's son, saving him from the mysterious illness of the Emergency as if her milk had the power to disinfect and to counter political exigency. But her milk is also the substance of her stories: "[S]he was as full of gossip and tittle-tattle as she was of milk: every day a dozen new stories gushed from her lips" (532). Repudiating her stories, she tells Saleem as she offers him her breast, is equivalent to repudiating life itself, for to lose interest in her stories is to welcome death (533). And Durga's body has a power of political resistance. Embodying the power of the underclasses and of a dangerous femininity, she "thrashed the life out of shirts and saris, . . . which ended up flat, buttonless and beaten to death," a "succubus" who combats the power of the privileged (532).

Similarly, Padma "leaks" into Saleem's body, "quietly dripping in, with her down-to-earthery" (38–39). In contrast with his impotence, or incapacity to leak into her, *she* fertilizes and changes his narrative with her demands and interruptions. The "leaking" of bodies into each other is not only a metaphor—people "leak into each other, like flavors when you cook"—but also a literalization of the metaphor of influence, of the inflow of words, gestures, sayings, actions. Amina's body becomes such a literalization, a vehicle for the transmission of language, composed of language itself. When she faces a murderous crowd, "her womb bursting with its invisible untold secret," her amniotic fluid literally enfolds a fetus (as yet her secret), a physical body (85). But Amina's body is also, by implication, a container of language, of unspoken words, a secret coincident with the body in formation, the narrator and narrative of Saleem. When that secret is released (its "annunciation saved a life"), this pregnant act of language has powerful material effects (86).

Bodies in *Midnight's Children* are thus not only receptacles of linguistic matter that flows in or out of them but also aggressive agents that change the world into which they exude their material secretions. Saleem continually tells us that though only thirty-one, he is "falling apart," cracking "all over like an old jug" (37). By the end, we understand that his growing, changing, disintegrating body is a literalization of a metaphor: he is a container of history, which has been poured into him, and a receptacle that has been drained both "above" (his parents have had his nasal passages emptied and disabled him from communicating with the midnight's children) and "below" (the Widow's agents have removed his sperm sacs so that he can neither produce children nor perpetuate the promise of midnight).[36] But Saleem also grows as a product of stories as linguistic matter, as a flow of language that he actively absorbs and incorporates as liquid food through his umbilical cord. The stories that he tells or exudes are the "inheritance" he absorbed as a fetus: "acquiring Mahatma Gandhi . . . , ingesting thumb-and-forefinger, swallowing . . . [Aadam Aziz's confusion of identity] . . . , drinking Mercurochrome, . . . gulping down Dyer, . . . feed[ing] on a hum, . . . getting heavier by the second, fattening up on washing chests, . . . plumping out . . . swallowing [Zulfikar's dream]" (124–25).

As this voracious fetus grows bigger, battening upon a history that he absorbs as a constitutive fluid through his lifeline, making his germinating body a composite of all that came before, Rushdie's sentence also grows bigger, as if it were itself that lifeline and that germinating body, passing on all that went before and that made and will make what will come after.[37] Like the fetus as comma, this fetal body is a product of language, a conglomerate of historical events turned stories, a linguistic thing that grows out of the fluids it absorbs, an embryonic textual beginning that will grow into a greater story as it feeds upon the histories that nourish it. After he is born, Saleem's infant body grows preternaturally, drinking milk so vigorously that he depletes a series of ayahs, or wet nurses. What he takes in so aggressively is the milk of the past, stories and secrets of his neighborhood that he "swallows" (152). This intake of discursive matter as breast milk makes him who he is, both nurturing and monstrously blowing him up. Saleem's infant body then (re)produces this intake in many varieties of bodily matter, recycling what it absorbs. "Waste matter was evacuated copiously from the appropriate orifices; from my nose there flowed a shining cascade of goo" (145). This infant and (eventually) adult extruded matter—ranging from urine and excrement to spit, snot, and blood—is not wasted but productive, linked with the aggressive act of writing, of acting upon the world.

"Why do I choose to wallow in excrement?" asks Saleem in an emblematic moment, as if he had literally dipped himself, and his pen, in fresh ordure (56). Why indeed does Rushdie's writing reek of the unseemly, the impure, the undesirable, the bodily matter that bourgeois disgust would rather efface from consciousness? Saleem asks this question when he presents his grandfather seated on a toilet, suffering from constipation, until the shock of being addressed by the concealed fugitive poet Nadir Khan evacuates Dr. Aziz's bowels (56). This unexpected materialization of the repressed, of a poet escaping annihilation, suggests that this bodily extrusion is somehow a salutary artistic effect. Excrement is representative of the lower, suppressed, underground body, of bourgeois disgust and shame, of the censorship of what is deemed undesirable.[38] It also represents the secrets of sexuality and desire, of Mumtaz and Nadir's underground love, of fertility, regeneration, and, indeed, of the resistant politics of the marginalized and suppressed. "But Love has pitched his mansion in / The place of excrement," Yeats's Crazy Jane reminds the bishop.[39] Excrement can thus serve as a signifier of the resistant politics of the body, representative of those subjected to various forms of social or political oppression.

Therefore, Padma is the "Dung goddess" to whom Saleem sings an ironic but self-correcting paean—for Padma his illiterate servant (and mistress and reader), named after her, indeed fertilizes his storytelling (30). She becomes so invaluable that his narrative comes to a halt when she disappears (197–231), for her earthiness and working-class sensibility, in an important gender reversal, inseminates his story (38).[40] In South Asia, cattle dung is an organic fertilizer, regenerative of crops and life, representative of a harmonious environmental and human coexistence. It is a source of warmth or fuel (it literally strengthens human dwellings) and a form of native art (it is used for ornamentation). Village women insulate and decorate their houses with pats of cow dung, "thin chapati-like cakes" that literalize the nutritive value of their shapes (30).[41] Human and animal excrement in *Midnight's Children* thus suggests a salutary politics of the resilient body, the resistant survival strategies of the underclasses, and is associated from the beginning with a bodily and useful form of art.

Padma's exasperation with Saleem's "writing-shiting" thus works as a bilingual joke (21). Commemorating Urdu-Hindi habits of double-rhyming words in a meaning-enhancing pair, it associates his writing with a shit that is not disgusting but regenerative, recycled to be socially useful. Unlike Swift, whose excremental satiric vision serves to anathematize and debunk, Rushdie's use of excrement reinforces the power of bodily politics as poetics. And unlike Naipaul, whose horror of public defecation notoriously provided an occasion for denouncing Indian hygiene and social myopia, Rushdie regards the same phenomenon as an act of making community and art.[42] Toward the end of *Midnight's Children*, Saleem watches a man on the street squat and excrete. Noticing him watching, the man companionably invites him to compete in a "longest turd" competition (545). The exhausted Saleem declines; besides, he says, his own tale is already too long.

Rushdie also revises the conventional valorization of other forms of bodily matter, such as Saleem's "shining cascades of goo," though each bodily effluence carries different meanings in his writing. Tai the boatman, proud of Aadam Aziz's large nose, teasingly suggests an obvious connection between snot and sperm: "That's a nose to start a family on, my princeling. . . . There are dynasties waiting inside, . . . like snot" (8). Ironically, Saleem's overdetermined nose—at once a phallic, epistemological, and literary instrument—is not inherited from Aadam Aziz, his putative grandfather. Nor will the reproductive capacities of his snot-as-sperm fulfil Tai's promise. But Saleem's snot is magically productive in another way, for it serves to interconnect the midnight's children, to produce a larger imagined community instead of a genealogical one, and to offer the revolutionary promise of a magical, self-transformative postcolonial nation. Nasal congestion blocks his olfactory capacities in Saleem's childhood years, but the accident in the washing-chest produces a strange benefit from his disability. Trying to suppress a sneeze, young Saleem triggers a "feverish inhalation": "[N]asal liquids are being sucked relentlessly up up up, nose-goo glowing upwards, against gravity, against nature. Sinuses are subjected to unbearable pressure, . . . until . . . something bursts. Snot rockets . . . into dark new channels. Mucus, rising higher. . . . Waste fluid, reaching as far . . . as the frontiers of the brain. . . . [T]here is a shock. Some-thing electrical has been moistened. Pain. And then noise, deafening" (*MC*, 191).

The surge of this bodily "mucus" and palpable contact with yet untouched cerebral areas, despite internal and external resistance, produces Saleem's miraculous telepathy and activates his unique midnight's child's gift of communication. These bodily effluvia initiate the flow of a magical language; they are a connective force that opens blocked channels both within and outside of Saleem. Yet another powerful image for Rushdie's own writing, this nose-goo connects the dissimilar, promotes communication and understanding, and promises a national unity and cooperation that is not based on bloodlines or ethnic affiliations. It *makes* words matter, literally making a new world through language. That Saleem's "pulverized body" is drained from "above and below" is unsurprising, then, for the capacity of his bodily language to have such powerful effects is what threatens the powers that be (550). But after both his mutilations, Saleem's body fights back. Drained of snot, his nose takes over as an organ of truth; it learns to smell, to uncover what would remain hidden. And drained of sperm, Saleem uses another pen: he begins to write, to fulfil that promise of midnight through words.

In *Midnight's Children, every* emanation of the body is associated with powerful linguistic as material effects. The spittoon, an otherwise puzzling motif, is another emblem of Saleem's body, a "receptacle of juices" (535), a container targeted by a variety of expectorators, from competing street bystanders who spew dark red *pan* (betel juice) to the intellectual and social elite gathered around the Rani of Cooch Nahin (the Queen of Nothing) (46). This strange pre-Partition pastime of hitting the spittoon is "an art form of the masses," a forceful form of bodily self-expression, an ejection of self-into-community, but also a playful act of forming community, of making what is inside the body project itself upon the world (535). It is yet another act of bodily language, of writing with the liquids of the body. It is also practiced by Nadir Khan and Mumtaz from their conjugal bed, as an art form that replaces sexual activity and enacts a bodily practice that crosses lines of class and gender (63).

Of all these bodily substances, however, blood is the one that tells the most harrowing tales, spilling secrets contained within the body. When Saleem's parents discover that he is not their biological child, the betrayer is literally his blood: it matches that of neither of his parents. In retrospect, the thirty-one year old Saleem reflects,

> O eternal opposition of inside and outside! Because a human being, inside himself, is anything but a whole, anything but homogenous; all kinds of everywhichthing are jumbled up inside him, and he is one person one minute and another the next. The body, on the other hand, is homogenous as anything. Indivisible, a one-piece suit, a sacred temple, if you will. It is important to preserve this wholeness. But the loss of my finger . . . has undone all that. . . . Uncork the body, and God knows what you permit to come tumbling out. Suddenly you are other than you were; and the world becomes such that parents can cease to be parents, and love turns to hate. And these, mark you, are only the effects on private life. The consequences for the sphere of public action, as will be shown, are—were—will be no less profound. (283)

Whereas Kim's body exposed him as the child of his father and of his race, revealing his identity by the writing on his chest and the whiteness of his skin, Saleem's body dissipates given social identities, as it reveals only that he is *not* the child of his parents. Indeed, it suggests that he and his body are products of multiplicity, of many inflows, that he is connected to and produced by unknown histories and genealogies, or a network of *multiple* nonbiological parents. At first, Saleem contrasts the self and the body: as if the individual were composite, permeable, interpenetrated by a variety of influences, and the body a self-contained unit, bounded by physical contours. But this opposition breaks down once that body is "uncorked" and turns out to be as heterogeneous as the world that infiltrates it. It too is overrun by prior histories; it is *subject* to history, as it is also productive of new histories; it is imbricated in the world. In turn, it can have "profound effects" upon that world, throwing certainties into disarray, telling unexpected, unwanted truths.

While *Midnight's Children* retains an optimism about the material agency of writing (Saleem may disintegrate but his writing will continue to have efficacy, to operate within the imagined community of its readers), *Shame* intensifies the sense of the body oppressed by language. But here, too, language is a semifluid bodily effluence, an agent usually of oppression. Here the body bursts with rage and shame when subjected to gossip and surveillance, the languages of power. The writing body in this novel is only a visiting body—it has had to remove itself to survive. Both human and literary agency in *Shame* are the province of those who are themselves fluid, who move across national and ethnic boundaries of identity. Hence, Omar Khayyam is unable to write "great things" or to effect change through writing, for, unlike the poet after whom he is named, his story is "poorer, ... it was marinated in bile" (36), as if it grew out of and was cooked in a bitter bodily substance. "Gossip is like water. It probes surfaces for their weak places, until it finds the breakthrough point," the narrator comments. This destructive force of language can act so violently upon the surfaces of bodies that they burst. The malicious "stories" of a community obsessed with sexual surveillance "got inside" Omar Khayyam's blockaded body, "they got under his skin and into his blood and worked their way, like little splinters, to his heart" (46). This gossip induces shame as a physiological effect, a grotesquely powerful bodily liquid that flows in and out of bodies, a "thin yellow fluid" of vomit (52) and a "sweet fizzy tooth-rotting drink" that emerges as a "pissing stream" of urine (131). This shame is produced by talk, by cultural regulations imposed through the circulation of language that enters and acts upon human bodies like a noxious bodily substance.

Hypersensitive Sufiya Zinobia, the eponymous central character of *Shame*, becomes a "janitor of the unseen," absorbing this fluid emanation from other bodies into her body until she explodes. Omar Khayyam, her purportedly shameless antithesis, is "possessed by a demon which made him shake ... , whose fingers reached outwards from his stomach to clutch, without warning, various interior parts of himself, ... so that he suffered from moments of near-strangulation and spent long unproductive hours on the pot" until he throws it up (51). These psychosomatic effects of shame (gagging, vomit, constipation) suggest a disorder of the bodily systems of speech, evacuation, and digestion.

They are induced by talk, by the slanderous, accusatory stories that the shamed ingest, which act upon their bodies like food poisoning.

However, even in the noxious atmosphere of *Shame*, talk can also function as sustenance and resistance, connecting and forming a community of women. A two-way "nourishing" umbilical "cord" (literally a telephone wire) carries "messages of support first one way, then the other" between Rani and Bilquis until it is finally severed by their warring husbands (209) — just as the migrant narrator's book (Rushdie's *Shame*) can sustain its readers and is itself sustained by discursive inflows from the land to which he cannot quite bid farewell. This power of language to cement community remains double-edged in *Shame*, but its political and material power is rendered repeatedly as an infiltration of bodies that are linguistically, discursively constituted. The megalomaniac Iskandar Harappa's self-promoting posters "stain . . . minds" across the country, as if their omnipresent "stamp" across every wall flows into the bodies that cannot help but see them (193). He spatters abuse at his subordinates that is coextensive with the dark red betel juice that accompanies it, so that the effect of animal slaughter ("it looked as if turkeys and goats had been struggling wildly in their death-throes, . . . with the blood spewing from the red smiles on their throats") literalizes through physical replication what he has done through language (248).

In her important study *Purity and Danger*, Mary Douglas argues that in most cultures the human body functions as a natural symbol for the larger body politic. Anxieties about the boundaries of the social body are mapped onto actual bodies in the form of cultural practices, rituals, taboos, and fears of pollution.[43] (The specific forms that this takes in each culture depends on the particular anxieties of each culture at different times.) This suggests a rather different understanding of the relation between microcosm and macrocosm than the European Renaissance trope of the body politic, in which the human body represents the hierarchized social body at large (as, for instance, in Menenius's fable of the belly: *Coriolanus*, act 1, scene 1, lines 97–147). Instead of the literal body serving as vehicle to describe the social body as tenor, with the human body being used as a figure, a template for the social system, in Douglas's account, anxieties about the social body are *actually* enacted upon and have concrete physical effects on real bodies. Physical matter — menstrual blood, excrement, sweat, snot, and other forms of effluvia — that emanates from the human body symbolizes an intensified site of power and danger to the social body because it is boundary material: it exudes from bodily boundaries, disturbing the holiness of the whole, the hypothetical smooth, contained body. Therefore, it is legislated as impure, rendering bodies impure if they exude it, because it symbolizes a threat to the social body.

Moreover, the viscosity of matter such as snot (and clots), Douglas suggests, is disturbing because it is liminal; it challenges the stability of the difference between liquid and solid, two recognizable forms of matter. It is regarded as repulsive because it unsettles our primal sense of bodily discreteness, of separation from the world. "The viscous is a state half-way between solid and liquid. . . . It is unstable, but does not flow. . . . Long columns falling off my fingers suggest my own substance flowing into the pool of stickiness" (39). Learning about this in-between matter teaches us about the "interrelation between self and other things" (39). Matter that breaks the boundaries of the body (flowing out of it) and the boundaries humans create between liquidity and solidity becomes an intense focus of control, because it is held to have extraordinary power, the power to dissipate the self-defined boundaries of the community. To maintain their own boundaries, communities (especially beleaguered minority ones) impose pollution controls on what they define as "dirt," which Douglas describes relativistically as "matter out of place" (36). What is defined as dirt thus depends on a system of ordering both internal and external lines of social division.

Rushdie's focus on and valorization of the human body as a site of flowing, boundary-breaking matter can then be understood as an attempt to rupture that body politic and its implicit cultural and national norms and taboos, as an effort to reverse the logic that Douglas describes. His repeated insistence on impurity—from the swallowing of *haram* flesh for a truthful, unbled storytelling (as I discuss in the introduction to the present volume) or the noisome odors of suppressed cultural secrets that Saleem noses out, to his denunciation of the "purity" of Pakistan, the Land of the Pure—is thus an ethical commitment to cultural hybridity, heterogeneity, and multiplicity, as a celebration and not a rejection of difference. This is ultimately not dissimilar from Bakhtin's claims about the egalitarian force of the carnivalesque grotesque body that confounds the dominance of repressive high culture. But through the convergence of language with this bodiliness, through this metalinguistic discourse of bodily effluvia, Rushdie positions his own language as such dirt, as "matter out of place," as bodily refuse that is in fact vital for the healthy survival and coexistence of the body and the body politic. This is the work, or the literary agency, of his writing: it will act as such dirt, disordering social and political boundaries and hierarchies within and without the imagined communities he deals with, thereby enacting salutary social change. It aspires to a radical political act of reordering or rearranging hierarchies both external and internal to the social body.

Synesthesia, or the Force of Unspoken Words

Drawing upon magical realist techniques, Rushdie conflates different sensory modes to produce synesthetic effects. Often this is a way to make the intangible tangible, representing the force of feelings, felt and manifested as a physical experience. But what it also reveals is the power of unspoken words, greater because they are repressed. This power of repressed language is manifested as a bodily force with bodily effects that have intensified and metamorphosed precisely *because* of being repressed. "The smell of silence, like a rotting goose-egg, fills my nostrils; overpowering everything else, it possesses the earth.... While Nadir Khan hid in half-lit underworld, his hostess hid too, behind a deafening wall of soundlessness" (58). When Saleem's grandmother protests her husband's granting asylum to a political poet and fugitive by using the power of angry silence, Saleem is able to "smell" and hear her unspoken feelings in his imagined visit to a past before his birth. This synesthetic imagery suggests both the bodily apprehension of the artist and the materiality of the unspoken, which swamps other bodies as well. This silence has a smell that speaks louder than words, that oppresses and takes control, like a "rotting goose-egg," or potential in atrophy (58). Soon, this accumulated bodily force of unspoken words begins to blow up the (non)speaker: food shortages "thickened her rage like heat under a sauce. Hairs began to grow out of the moles in her face. Mumtaz noticed with concern that her mother was swelling, month by month. The unspoken words inside her were blowing her up.... Mumtaz had the impression that her mother's skin was becoming dangerously stretched" (64). Naseem swells as if pregnant with the unsaid that grotesquely erupts through the pores of her body as hair. Later, her daughter Alia's "undimmed jealousy" and hatred also propel "thick dark hairs of resentment" to "sprout . . . through her skin" (367). This bodily force, a dammed river of "three years of words," will later "pour of out of her (but her body, stretched by the exigencies of storing them, did not diminish)" (66).

Four generations later, the infant Aadam Sinai, Naseem's great-grandson, exerts a similar willed silence that withholds expression as if it were a bodily substance. Reversing metaphors, his mother, Parvati, comments, "Sickness is a grief of the body. . . . It must be shaken off in tears and groans" (504–5). She administers magical drugs, but Aadam resists. "The child's cheeks began to bulge, as though his mouth were full of food; the long suppressed sounds of his babyhood flooded up behind his lips . . . as he tried to swallow back the torrential vomit of pent-up sound" (505).

This bodily power of unspoken words is not limited to resistant silence. Aadam Aziz's mother's unspeakable shame at having to emerge from purdah manifests itself in bodily "rashes," "blotchy bits," boils, and headaches (14–15). Unspoken bodily feelings—intransigence, guilt, or fear—are transmitted by Mary Pereira's and the Reverend Mother's hands through their culinary art (pickles or curries) to those they feed (164), just as Aunt Alia's vengeful envy turns into a bodily malignance that is transmitted from her hands to the bodies she clothes. By sending Amina "an unending stream of children's clothes, into whose seams she had sewn her old maid's bile, . . . the baby-things of bitterness, . . . the rompers of resentment, . . . [and] white shorts starched with the starch of jealousy," she "binds" Saleem and his sister in "webs of revenge" (183). Histories of dispossession and vindictiveness are thus conveyed to the bodies of children who in turn act out familial legacies and infectious feelings of whose origins they remain ignorant. Rushdie's tongue-twisting alliteration calls attention to the way this transmission is bodily—a surrogate for the unspeakable and a measure of the power of the unsaid.

This synesthetic tangibility of the unspoken combines different bodily senses to suggest the intensified power of repressed words. "Secrets go bad inside you," Amina warns the child Saleem, as if his unreleased words, like anal retention, will decay within him (189). Thoughts and dreams "leak" from one body to another, through the "osmotic tissues of history," to produce material effects (MC, 501). Body temperatures rise in a summer of political turmoil as "the air [is] filled with the stickiness of aroused desires" (MC, 199). As an adolescent, Saleem's incestuous desire for his sister produces a verbal-as-physical disorder, periodic explosions of the putrefying unspeakable matter held within. In addition to blushing "furiously," "he also developed a penchant for lapsing into broody silences, which he interrupted by bursting out suddenly with a meaningless word: 'No!' or 'But!' . . . 'Wham!' Nonsense words amidst clouded silences: as if Saleem was conducting some inner dialogue of such intensity that fragments of it, or its pain, boiled up from time to time past the surface of his lips" (*MC*, 396). The internal conflicts of guilt, desire, and self-disgust within Saleem produce a bodily disorder as linguistic fragmentation, an aphasic turmoil that "boils" up to the "surface" in the form of verbal eruptions, clots of bodily effusions that break out to add to the miasma of unspoken feelings surrounding him.

This broken language is figured as not just *representative* but as *part* of an internally diseased body that cannot contain the volcanic forces seething within it. Because of this intensified sensory sensitivity, Saleem can smell the unspoken feelings of others around him, "secret aromas of the world," "the smell-trails of dispossession and fanaticism," love and hate (368). As the subliminal intensity of familial discord rises to a crisis, the images become more intense, increasingly solid in their materiality. Aunt Alia's hatred of Saleem's parents grows into "a tangible visible thing, it sat on her living room rug like a great gecko, reeking of vomit" (394–95). What was once barely suppressible inside the body, emergent in insidious ways through the transmissions of touch (cooking and sewing), becomes independent, a body of its own, a regurgitation of what has been taken in, now in a new form, poised to attack. This transmissible palpability of the unspoken develops into "an art-form: the impregnation of food with emotions" (395). All these familial bodies have become related in another sense: they recycle unspoken emotions through their art, passing them from one body to another, reshaping them into new forms. Alia's malevolence transmits itself to Saleem, producing his linguistic and bodily disorder. In turn, through his writing, he will pass on these preserved pickled feelings to others in the family of his readership. But each body changes what passes through it and is hence a site of intermittent agency, both transmitting and transforming what it passes on.

In *Shame*, we first hear of the pervasiveness of shame as something that has been lived with long enough to become "part of the furniture. In 'Defence,' you can find shame in every house, burning in an ashtray, hanging framed upon a wall, covering a bed" (*Shame*, 22–23). This is the palpable shame of the unspoken—of that which, like a cigarette, has been snuffed out, as ordinary as material household objects yet also used to cover something up. The city of Karachi is an "obese harridan," a bloated syphilitic body that has grown out of control, upon which "gaudily painted beach houses of the rich" have "erupted, like boils." This body has beckoned the impoverished and gullible: "The streets were full of the darkened faces of young men who had been drawn to the painted lady . . . , only to find that her price was too high to pay; something puritan and violent sat on their foreheads and it was frightening to walk amongst their disillusions" (126–27). This desperate collection of unspoken feelings, this "something" that has materialized on these disillusioned foreheads, seems to mirror the city's excrescent boils; it "sits," like an animal or a monstrous growth, a bulbous tumor threatening to explode, to turn upon the very social body that produced it. It is a bodily expression and extension of unspoken feelings of exploitation, disempowerment, and rage that have been withheld and reached a breaking point. Indeed, already this "thing" has broken free, extended beyond "foreheads" to occupy public space, as "disillusions" that jostle and threaten the rich.

These two paradigms of the materiality of language—the body as an open vessel of linguistic (semi)fluid substances, and the unspoken as synesthetic and bodily—serve to emphasize the interrelationality of Rushdie's language, its vulnerability, and its potentially subversive political power. But in addition to suggesting the materiality of language, Rushdie sets up another central bodily paradigm for the very *structure* of his narrative: the genealogical web of familial inheritance. This biological model for narratival repetition allows Rushdie to construct a narrative that can incorporate both similarity and difference and thus offer the possibility of autonomy despite the determining hold of the past.

The Dynastic Webs of Recurrence

Rushdie frequently uses a "web" metaphor oddly mixed with one of the "family tree" to evoke a sense of genealogy that structures historical and familial events as well as his own narrative. When he marries Parvati, pregnant with Shiva's child, Saleem remarks forebodingly, "[O]nce again destiny, inevitability, the antithesis of choice, had come to rule my life, once again a child was to be born to a father who was not his father, although by a terrible irony the child would be a true grandchild of his father's parents; *trapped in the web of these interweaving genealogies*, it may even have occurred to me to wonder what was beginning, what was ending, and whether another secret countdown was in process, and what would be born with my child" (MC, 495; my emphasis). When his infant son falls dangerously ill, Saleem comments, "Once, in a blue room overlooking the sea, beneath the pointing finger of the fisherman, I fought typhoid and was rescued by snake-poison: now, *trapped in the dynastic webs of recurrence* by my recognition of his sonship, our Aadam Sinai was also obliged to spend his early months battling the invisible snakes of disease" (MC, 504; my emphasis). The "web of interweaving genealogies" and "the dynastic webs of recurrence" both spell a trap: history, rendered as biology, seems to disable the possibility of postcolonial agency. These "webs" of familial histories represent the palpable stranglehold of the past on the present and future, constraints that produce a reproductive repetition over time. Just as families are bound to repeat themselves, so too, Rushdie suggests, is (national) history patterned like familial legacies, also bound to repeat itself. In both cases, these "genealogies" are not produced by relations of blood, for just as Saleem is not the biological son of his parents, Aadam is not the biological son of Saleem, though he is the biological grandchild of Saleem's adoptive parents.[44] How, then, can Aadam be "trapped" by these complicated genealogies that are not his own, by the same "webs" that entrap his not-father Saleem, by the genealogy of not-genealogy?

This entrapment of genealogy is in fact an entrapment by a *constructed* genealogy, the material inheritance of constructed familial relations. Both parent-child relations, though not biological, are real, constructed by custom, habit, and social contract. Both produce real, material legacies that do not merely resemble but *are* the legacies of families. Both Aadam's and Saleem's genealogies are constructed not by biology but by history, by the *imagining* of biological relations, in which the power of naming, custom, and acceptance equals, or even outweighs, that of biology. Rushdie's point is that inheritance, even when it is not biological, is materially powerful and real. Even families that are biologically based require social and discursive validation to be made real: family is as much a social as a biological construct.

In *Midnight's Children*, the power of biology gives way to that of discursive and social practice. Even apparently primal biological relations reveal that their linchpin is social *belief*. Reality is constructed from belief, made from language. Families are families not because they are biologically related but because (as in marriage and adoption) they are constructed and solidified over time and thus carry material links, repetitions, and connections that are as real and lasting as biological inheritance, if not more so. When Saleem is discovered to be not the Sinais' biological son, it does not matter, because after eleven years a family has formed from sheer habit, memory, and experience; knowledge of biology cannot undo that formation. His "parents" could not think of him as other than their son: "I remained their son because they could not imagine me out of that role" (360). Hence, they do not try to find Shiva, for they are unwilling to "accept into their bosom an urchin [from] the gutter" (361). After Mary Pereira's confession that she switched babies in the hospital, the Reverend Mother's performative act of language, coupled with her culturally endowed matriarchal power, overrides biological fact to "legitimize" Saleem. Angered by Ahmed Sinai's abuse, she orders her daughter Amina to leave her husband and take "*both* her children"; upon this pronouncement, Saleem is readopted by the family he thought was his (340). Later, as an adolescent, Saleem tries to seduce Jamila, claiming that they are not biological siblings, but that power of lived history resurfaces to overwhelm them with the reek of incest:

> [S]he listened to him explaining that there was no sin, he had worked it all out, and after all, they were not truly brother and sister; the blood in his veins was not the blood in hers; in the breeze of that insane night he attempted to undo all the knots which not even Mary Pereira's confession had succeeded in untying; but even as he spoke he could hear his words sounding hollow, and realized that although what he was saying was the literal truth, there were other truths which had become more important because they had been sanctified by time; and although there was no need for shame or horror, he saw both emotions on her forehead, he smelt them on her skin, and, what was worse, he could feel and smell them in and upon himself. (387–89)

"Truths" of history have superceded biology; indeed, they have become real enough to take bodily form: Saleem can "see" and "smell" the horror they produce on both his body and that of Jamila. The imagining of reality makes it real, and the effort to dismiss that reality can only fail.

Both *Midnight's Children* and *Shame* center on the idea of nation as such an extended family, constructed but real. *Midnight's Children* presents us with two alternative models of family: the biological networks of the Sinai-Aziz clan and their saga of inheritance and recurrence, which extends five generations, from Aadam Aziz's father to Saleem's adopted son (including nonbiological members who also bestow their traits, such as Tai the Boatman); and the mythically constructed family of the midnight's children, born of a concept—Time— a national family affiliated by its shared moment of "birth" on the cusp of historic transformation, imagined in biological terms as "fathered by history" (137). Both kinds of families are ultimately "imagined," though real. And both are mutually interdependent: the biological family is constructed by acts of language and will, and the national family requires the model of the biological family upon which to base itself. *Shame* opens with the overarching family tree that connects—by blood or marriage—the Hyder, Harappa, and Shakil clans. This inescapable family to which all—enemies and friends—belong becomes the central trope for a nation created on the monotheistic affinities of one religion, combining both the genealogical and the socially constructed familial models of *Midnight's Children*.

Thus, paradoxically, while insisting on the reality and materiality of imagined and constructed relations, Rushdie draws on the primariness of bodily relations as a template for the materiality of language. Indeed, in both *Shame* and *Midnight's Children*, the "traps" of genealogical inheritance not only affect individual characters but also are integral to the very fabric of history and narrative. The "web of . . . interweaving genealogies" and the "dynastic web of recurrence" offer a model for history, for the repetition of events over time. To be born *not* the son of your supposed father, to inherit the same childhood diseases, or to be intersected by coincidental similarities instead of inherited ones seems to have become a condition of the time, which is inherited by subsequent time. The process of time or "history" is presented as a force that operates as a relational network, patterned like a biological family tree, with recurrences and repetitions that occur like family traits and with a logic as inexorable in its will to replicate and entrap as the coding of genes and chromosomes. History seems to have a material texture, a tissue of familial repetitions, that seems to be biological, growing, connecting, yet mutating into new forms. Saleem's narrative in turn is also structured by this biological tendency to repeat, as if the bodily relation of handing on traits from parent to child also shapes the sequentiality of narrative, producing a recurrence of traits, events, and figures in the text as well.

But while the webs of multiple genealogies offer a deterministic model for the contingencies of history, they also suggest how biological inheritance leaves room for partial differentiation, self-determination, and agency. The model of the genealogical web allows for the concurrence of similarity and difference, for simultaneous connection to and disconnection from the formative power of the past. For just as repeated traits reveal individual differences in families (Amina's nose is like but slightly different from her father's), historical and narratival repetition, in different times and places, produces crucial differences. Just as every member on a family tree is related to all the others, resembling but different from any other, so too is every event in Saleem's (and India's) history related, produced, or influenced by another: connected but also independent. Rushdie thus recasts the biological model of the family tree. By conflating two metaphors—the family tree and the spider's web—"the web of interweaving genealogies" collapses the vertical unidirectionality of the former into the multi-directionality of the latter. This model of the familial web substitutes unidirectional predetermining lines of descent with multidirectional connections that are nonlinear and nonconcentric, that have neither center nor periphery but are criss-crossing, interweaving, without hierarchy: over time it can grow in any direction, changing, surviving in accordance with the vagaries of chance.[45] By transposing the web on the family tree, Rushdie suggests that the effect of these multiple genealogies (and multiple histories) is not hierarchical but multidirectional, whereby children are produced by (and can themselves produce) multiple parents by exerting active choice. It suggests multiple lines of generation: each "point" of intersection is not only created by the lines in the network but also able to produce a proliferating set of lines and possibilities.

This model of the genealogical web of familial history allows for greater agency. Instead of being "trapped" by these genealogies, Saleem and writers like Rushdie can "choose their own parents," as they rework the paradigms provided by several different models. So too can nations and peoples, depending on what stories they tell themselves about themselves, and about others, and what parents they choose to adopt. Clearly, the postcolonial writer's and nation's relation to the past is crucial in forging postcolonial agency. Unknown, the past is dangerous and prone to repetition. This trope of genealogy allows Rushdie to pose a key question: whether the mistakes of the past are bound to be repeated or whether repetition can be conscious, that is, whether it can open up difference.

Working out how to balance both remembering and forgetting painful colonial history is one of the central problems of postcolonial literature (and peoples). In his important essay "The Muse of History," Derek Walcott has argued that the exclusive remembrance of past grievances can be self-destructive, for it can lead postcolonial nations and writers to dwell only upon histories of victimization, to ignore the complicities of colonizer and colonized, slave master and slave seller, to trap themselves in a futile dialectic of recrimination that precludes the creation of viable futures. Urging forgiveness of both kinds of ancestors, Walcott prefers instead to look at the bitter fruit of a "second Eden," to celebrate the novelty and potential of a hybrid Caribbean culture. But certain kinds of selective forgetting, as political theorists such as Benedict Anderson remind us, can also be pernicious, if they involve self-exculpation from past culpability. When Euro-Americans, for example, forget that their (postcolonial) nation is founded upon immigration and the extermination of native peoples or when Pakistanis forget the genocide that their army carried out in Bangladesh, then communal self-imagining is based on an evasion of collective responsibility. Some forgetting is necessary, Anderson reminds us, for people to carry on and build community, though that may be possible only after some process of collective working through has occurred, such as that of the Peace Council in postapartheid South Africa.

For Rushdie as well, national and communal histories must be remembered because they are formative; indeed, Rushdie casts them as familial histories, understanding unsentimentally that families and their legacies can be as abusive and damaging as generative or supportive. But this is not a remembrance that is based on the staking of a self-righteous victimhood. Rather, it is a remembrance that is necessary for the *regaining* of agency, because only by knowing their complicated history can individuals and communities avoid repetition of past tragedy and work toward greater control of the future. Therefore, histories must be revisited precisely in order to enact, through repetition, difference. Hence Rushdie suggests, through his narrative, that the agency of narrative lies in its ability to enact through repetition the capacity to make a difference, to build different possibilities for the future. And Rushdie's narrative too can enact difference, by differentially returning to and repeating that which engendered it.

We have seen how, as he begins his narrative, Saleem invokes the perforated sheet as a talisman for his own beginnings. Telling the story of his grandparents' romance, conducted through this sheet, he makes a parenthetical leap forward in time to his own childhood:

> (... And now I am cast as a ghost. I am nine years old and the whole family, my father, my mother, the Brass Monkey and myself, are staying at my grandparents' house in Agra, and the grandchildren—myself among them—are staging the customary New Year's play: and I have been cast as a ghost. Accordingly—and surreptitiously... I am ransacking the house for a spectral disguise. My grandfather is out and about his rounds. I am in his room. And here on top of this cupboard is an old trunk.... And here, inside it, is the answer to my prayers. Not just a sheet, but one with a hole already cut in it!... the sheet's appearance in our show was nothing less than a sensation. My grandfather took one look at it and rose roaring to his feet. He strode up on stage and unghosted me right in front of everyone. My grandmother's lips were so tightly pursed that they seemed to disappear.... I fled..., not knowing what had happened... swearing over and over that I would never again open a forbidden trunk, and feeling vaguely resentful that it had not been locked in the first place. But I knew, from their rage, that the sheet was somehow very important indeed.) (*MC*, 29–30)

In this parable of the exposure of familial secrets, it is worth noting that as the child-transgressor is "unghosted" and exposed, so too does the authority-figure betray himself, the grandfather who plays the self-exposing Claudius to Saleem's *Mouse-trap*. What Saleem hoped to enact was his own play, but unbeknownst to him, the only materials available to him are drenched in past histories. To enact his own play, he has to learn those histories, to understand their burdens. Without that knowledge, his first effort at *acting*—in any way—leads to disaster. Rushdie's narrative too, the author suggests, must replay past narratives, histories, and literary and political legacies that engendered it, to learn what has been hidden but formative in its own making, to take control of and remake that material into its own, to reshape the sheet of the past knowingly to gain control over the future.

Through this image of the hole of origins, this child's epistemological stance toward familial and national history is imagined as a transgressive reentry into the womb, as if in order to make his own beginning he has to return, through repetition, to create difference, his own point of departure. Like the inversion of movement from a full stop to a language, this child inverts the process of time, and of birth, by attempting to reenter a forbidden history. The desire to be a ghost would ordinarily bespeak a desire to enter the future from the past, to be dead in order to return. But this child-ghost becomes a "ghost" from the future who attempts to enter literally (and figuratively) the hole through which he may gain access to the past, to invert the act of birth (giving birth to himself anew), to poke his head through this overdetermined hole, to find and remake the source of his story. But in replaying this history, Saleem also changes it— he wears the sheet for a different purpose. Analogously, Rushdie's narrative suggests its need to construct its beginning by rewriting other occasions of beginning: it must learn and repeat—with a difference—the structure of grandparental (hi)stories. Only by so doing, Rushdie suggests, will he (and postcolonial peoples) make his (and their) own story anew.

Rushdie embeds this structure of familial repetition in the structure of his narrative in two ways. First, his narrative shows how repetitions occur with a difference; and second, it repeats past history in the retelling to regain control of it. His narrative repeats itself in the way that it shows history repeats itself as families repeat themselves. Answering the key question of *The Satanic Verses*, "How does newness come into the world? How is it born?" Rushdie uses the metaphor of the genealogical web to formulate the terms for the production of a postcolonial novelty that can remain linked to what engendered it. This web of family history and repetition suggests a model for the coexistence of similarity and difference, of remnants of the past *and* the germ for the future. It serves as a model for history that reconciles recurrence with alteration.

Rushdie's narratives are themselves built around such structures of repetition. In *Shame*, Sufiya frequently repeats her mother's history. "She was on all fours and stripped as naked as her mother had been by the legendary firewind of her youth—no, more so, because there was nothing clinging to her shoulders, no dupatta of modesty and shame" (279–80). In her escape from home, Shame is here as naked as her mother (Bilquis) once was in her own departure from her home, replicating the female nakedness that suggests the removal of cultural structures of shelter, protection, and restriction. But Shame repeats her mother's history with a difference—instead of becoming a victim to be sheltered by others, she embodies independence and freedom (however dubious), and she rejects that restrictive signifier that signifies womanly modesty, the veil, or *dupatta*, of honor. On another occasion, she mimics her mother's horror of the wind and a migrant's desire for "fixity," but instead of obsessively fixing furniture to one place, Shame as obsessively moves it around (70, 73). The close repetition of familial inheritance emphasizes not the reproduction of identity but the production of difference.

This kind of repetition is practiced by Rushdie's own rhetoric as well. Near the end of *Midnight's Children,* when Saleem's son Aadam is born, the narrative returns to an almost exact repetition of its own beginning:

> He was born in Old Delhi ... once upon a time. No, that won't do, there's no getting away from the date: Aadam Sinai arrived at a night shadowed slum on June 25th, 1975. And the time? The time matters too. ... On the stroke of midnight, as a matter of fact. Clock-hands joined palms. Oh, spell it out, spell it out: at the precise instant of India's arrival at Emergency, he emerged. There were gasps; and across the country, silences and fears. And owing to the occult tyrannies of that benighted hour, he was mysteriously handcuffed to history, his destinies indissolubly chained to those of his country. ... [A]s my time neared its end, his began. (*MC,* 500)

Such self-conscious repetition overtly invites comparison.

> I was born in the city of Bombay ... once upon a time. No, that won't do, there's no getting away from the date: I was born in Dr. Narlikar's Nursing Home on August 15th, 1947. And the time? The time matters too. ... On the stroke of midnight, as a matter of fact. Clock-hands joined hands in respectful greeting as I came. Oh, spell it out, spell it out: at the precise instant of India's arrival at independence, I tumbled forth into the world. There were gasps. And outside the window, fireworks and crowds. ... [I]n the benighted moment, ... thanks to the occult tyrannies of those blandly saluting clocks, I had been mysteriously handcuffed to history, my destinies indissolubly chained to those of my country. For the next three decades there was to be no escape. (*MC,* 3)

Rushdie's narrative presents itself as not merely a story *about* a family, not only a parable of history as an uncannily familial (and familiar) process, but also as itself embodying in its narrative structure what it means to be familial and historical. At the same time as it emphasizes repetition, the narrative rhetorically undoes that repetition. The exact repetition of syntax—of words, phrases, and order of sentences—shows how in that very similarity lies difference, how, almost like recurrent dreams, repetition opens up new possibilities, endless holes in sheets of the past, places to begin, and begin again.

Saleem and his son are both born at midnight, both simultaneously occupy public and private spaces, both embody individual and nation, both are "handcuffed to history." Yet the similarity of the two passages also points to the differences—of place, time, class, and historical location. The son begins where the father ends; he is born in a ghetto while his father was born in a hospital; clock hands join palms in both cases, but only upper-class Saleem is accorded a "respectful" greeting; and the Emergency of 1975 (curtailing civil liberties and imposing totalitarian rule) is the dark inversion of the optimistic Independence of 1947, for Aadam represents a new generation born of this exigent time: "I understood once again that Aadam was a member of a second generation of magical children who would grow up far tougher than the first, not looking for their fate in prophecy or the stars, but forging it in the implacable furnaces of their wills" (534). To forge one's own fate "in the furnace of [one's] will" alludes to another famous aspiration: to forge the conscience of one's race in the smithy of one's soul. Rushdie's writing enacts another form of (literary) repetition as it echoes the ending—which was also a beginning—of James Joyce's A *Portrait of the Artist as a Young Man*: "I go to encounter for the millionth time the reality of experience and to forge in the smithy of my soul the uncreated conscience of my race."[46] Aadam becomes an emblem of a new artist-as-a-young-man, different from Saleem and from Stephen Daedalus, who can craft a new destiny, who may not be as "trapped" in webs of history as his father feared, and who represents both individual and nation, a second Adam, promising the construction of another time. Whereas Stephen Daedalus aspires, as an artist, to construct an amalgamation of individual and aggregate, a postcolonized "race" from the "smithy of his soul," the Aadam that Saleem envisions will shift Stephen's terms from "soul" to "will," from being to intention, from experience to transformation. In revising such a moment of high modernism, Rushdie also suggests how postcolonial writing may both repeat and revise its own genealogies.

In the Sundarbans: The Phantasmagoric Body of the Dream Forest

"In the Sundarbans," the twenty-fifth chapter of *Midnight's Children*, describes how Saleem, as the "buddha," leads his three Pakistani soldier companions away from participating in the genocide in Bangladesh into a strange sojourn in the "Sundarbans," the phantasmagoric dream forest that exists apparently out of time and space, where they are sucked in, punished, educated, and then ejected back into history and the world. This is a pivotal episode in which Saleem recovers his lost memory and conscience, where he tells his story for the first time, when he first defects, refusing to be the mindless agent of a terrorist state, when he seemingly retreats from action and yet becomes a teller of truth, forcing others to confront their inner selves as well. Readers often find this chapter bizarre, baffling, or even irrelevant—perhaps because it is written in so intense an idiom of the lyrical, macabre, and allegorical that it does not seem to fit within the rest of the novel,[47] or perhaps because it comes so late, four-fifths of the way through a five-hundred-page novel, that it is too exhausting to cope with. This episode deserves a closer look because it exemplifies most compactly how Rushdie uses all the three types of bodily language outlined above to enact an ethical and literary agency.

The episode draws upon a rich conglomerate of literary paradigms as points of departure, setting up a literary historical colonial-postcolonial relation of conjoint similarity and difference. Just as Saleem and the three boy-soldiers must recall their pasts (that is, their childhoods and parentages) to build their own selfhood and autonomy, so too, by recalling a variety of literary forebears, must Rushdie's narrative, at this pivotal moment, both mark and grow away from its own. It recalls popular Victorian boys' adventure stories, such as Kipling's *Kim* (in which an adolescent protagonist becomes an instrument of state power because of his powers of cultural translation) and *Soldiers Three* (in which three boy-soldiers and their sagelike mentor "discover" India). And as in Conrad's *Heart of Darkness*, the narrator and his companions follow an uncharted river in a frail boat, at the mercy of an "invisible force" that draws them deeper into the mysterious jungle, "directing their footsteps, drawing them deeper into a darker heart of madness, . . . south south south" to confront the unspeakable horror of their own histories and actions (*MC*, 428). But these "boys" will not prove their manhood upon a colonial terrain, nor will they make advances in self-knowledge en route to self-improvement: the jungle is instead both an alien force and an extension of themselves, a psychic landscape that teaches them "lessons" that only one will carry any further. Nor will the narrator find a Kurtz upon whom to displace his colonial savagery, for these adventurers will confront their own *post*colonial savagery and madness.

This episode also serves, as in classical epic journeys, as the paradigmatic descent into the underworld, the visit to hell. However, in this Rushdiean hell of memory, no sage will be available to tell the hero how to continue, nor will a mother be present to instruct Aeneas; for the only wisdom that Saleem will be able to find is in himself, in reunion with his past self, which alone will enable him to carry on. Perhaps the most pointed literary allusion is to Coleridge's *The Rime of the Ancient Mariner*. Their travails begin when Ayooba shoots and kills an old man chasing after Saleem for his presumed sexual encounter with the man's wife or daughter. Ayooba's arm is paralyzed as the peasant's translucent ghost leaks "a colorless fluid" upon it: Ayooba must bear his sin of violence upon his body, just as the Mariner has to wear the albatross on his neck (435). Like the Mariner, Saleem as narrator must expiate a collective guilt through the act of repeated narration, though the unforgivable act is committed not against a creature of nature but against helpless human beings. Saleem and his cohort have been engaged in the brutal slaughter of their own, of innocent civilians, of East Pakistani citizens slaughtered for their ethnic differences by fellow-Muslims of the West Pakistani army. And this crime is compounded by another: the effort to erase it from memory. This aged man then also represents "Father Time," a "peasant with a scythe," for they have also killed Time, or history, because their grotesque actions have been excised from national records (429).

This episode is thus centrally concerned with the recovery and trauma of an event that remains unspeakable in Pakistani history, unacknowledged even by subsequent governments, unknown to most (remaining) citizens. "But how convenient this amnesia is, how much it excuses!" exclaims Saleem as he begins narrating this section (426). When Sheikh Mujib-ur-Rehman, the Bengali candidate from the more populous region of East Pakistan, won the national election of 1970, his opponent from West Pakistan, Zulfikar Ali Bhutto, would not accept defeat or the rule of democracy: Bhutto's crony, Yahya Khan, the army's commander-in-chief and then-president, sent in the army to intimidate the Bengalis into withdrawal.[48] But what is not well known in Pakistan even now is the army's genocidal campaign of slaughter and rape of Bengalis, the calculated torture and extermination of intellectuals and political leaders, and the violent destruction of villages suspected of harboring the Mukti Bahini, the Bengali resistance fighters. In the ensuing civil war, as over ten million Bengali refugees fled into India, India joined in, resulting in 1971 in the splitting of the two former wings of Pakistan into what are now Bangladesh and Pakistan.[49] Public discourse in Pakistan is still silent about the atrocities committed by its army, for which many Bengalis still abhor all Pakistanis and for which Pakistani citizens in some sense bear collective responsibility.

Thus, the cultural *work* of Saleem's (and Rushdie's) narrative is to remind the (Pakistani) nation of this unspeakable event, to reinsert it into collective memory and imagined selfhood, to confront national and individual complicity. Linda Hutcheon has claimed that postcolonial narrative exercises (and exorcises) colonial trauma, that in the act of telling and listening lies a cure, through the process of bearing witness and working through the trauma.[50] That is the case for those who were *targets* of oppression. But as Ashis Nandy has argued in the case of those who *participated* in the ethnic violence of 1947, even those who are complicit in or beneficiaries from the perpetration of such acts must undergo the process of telling and retelling, not necessarily to atone (for atonement may be impossible) but to confront their individual or collective responsibility. For until that confrontation, there can be no psychic recovery, no collective healing, and no end to the cycle of violence and retribution. The unspoken remains a gash, a festering wound in the national psyche, engendering further sanguinary outbreaks.[51] In attempting to undo the silence and complacency that has congealed over this history, Rushdie's narrative addresses not one or the other but at least three kinds of audiences: the nation knowingly or unknowingly complicit in these atrocities; the nation whose subjection has been forgotten; and all those bystanders from East to West who intervened or failed to intervene.[52]

Bitterly ironic, Saleem's narrative attempts to recover the unspeakable, to tell the truth about the atrocities that were committed and about the excision of their memory from journalistic and historical records—for the two are coterminous acts of violation:

> And while we drove through city streets, Shaheed . . . saw things that weren't-couldn't-have been true: soldiers entering women's hostels without knocking;

women, dragged into the street, were also entered, and again nobody troubled to knock. And newspaper offices, burning with the dirty yellowblack smoke of cheap gutter newsprint, and the offices of trade unions, smashed to the ground, and roadside ditches filling up with people who were not merely asleep—bare chests were seen, and the hollow pimples of bullet-holes. Ayooba Shaheed Farooq watched in silence through moving windows as our boys, our soldiers-for-Allah, our worth-ten-babus jawans held Pakistan together by turning flame-throwers machine-guns hand-grenades on the city slums. . . . [T]he buddha had closed his eyes. ("Don't fill my head with all this history, . . . I am what I am and that's all there is.") (426)[53]

The unindividuated "Ayooba Shaheed Farooq" must break their collective silence and individually confront their ignorance as well as their participation as "dogs of war" (427), just as the "buddha" must open his eyes to this history, for he is *not* what he would like to think he is. He must confront, and unmake what he has helped create.

It is from this horror that the boy-soldier Saleem (or "not-Saleem," as the narrator Saleem calls him) seeks escape in the Sundarbans, there to confront the greater horror of himself. The white albatross he carries consists of the blank pages of history, whitewashed clean of this record of atrocity. The jungle he enters is therefore a figurative one at several levels: it is the jungle of collective silence, "so thick, that history has hardly ever found the way in" (429). But it is also a jungle that is eerily bodily, as if it were a materialization of the unspoken. Given Rushdie's insistence on the bodiliness of the unspoken, his rendition through synesthesia of the bodily effects of unspoken words both on the speaker and on others, this phantasmagoric account of the Sundarbans also suggests such a magnification of the bodiliness of the nationally unspoken. Saleem's account of his sojourn in the jungle of the Sundarbans (which may translate as "beautiful silence" or "beautifully closed"—in Bengali, *sundar* means "beautiful"; in Urdu, *bund* is "closed"; in English, *ban* is "the forbidden") is also an account of what happens when the unspoken weighs upon us, upon our individual and national bodies. It is an intensified example of the kind of bodily language discussed above, in which the unspoken produces bodily growths, emanations, or convulsions of speech as a bodily substance. Later, Saleem is able to tell this tale only after he has come to terms with this magnitude of the unspoken, through the painful process of confronting his own culpability and instrumentality.

This jungle is bodily in other ways as well. Saleem and his companions' encounter with this jungle seems to occur in at least three or four distinct phases. The first is engulfment, as if the jungle were some large gargantuan mouth that had literally swallowed them into some preternatural giant body. (But there is no escape from history inside the body of this whale—they cannot wait out the storm that awaits them here.) We first learn its name as they flee from the burning streets of Dacca: the "impossible endless huge green wall" that covers the horizon is "The Sundarbans: it swallows them up" (429). This image of a large mouth is soon repeated: "The jungle closed behind them like a tomb, and after hours of increasingly weary but also frenzied rowing through incomprehensibly labyrinthine salt-water channels overtowered by cathedral-arching trees, Ayooba Shaheed Farooq were hopelessly lost.... The buddha remained silent, but in his silence they read their fate, and now that he was convinced that the jungle had swallowed them the way a toad gulps down a mosquito, ... Ayooba Baloch ... broke down utterly and wept like a monsoon" (432). This sense of a large inimical body that has ingested them is reinforced as the jungle begins to grow in the rain, "gaining size, power, force," producing body parts that seem uncannily animal or human: "huge stilt-roots of vast ancient mangrove trees could be seen *snaking* about thirstily in the dusk, *sucking* in the rain and becoming thicker than elephant trunks"; "leaves in the heights of the great nipa *palms* began to spread like immense green cupped *hands*, swelling in the nocturnal downpour" (432–33; my emphasis). These arboreal body parts —outstretched hands that also pun on the word *palms*—are uncannily familiar because they recall the body parts that we have already seen most emphasized as Saleem's primary bodily tools for writing and knowing the truth: his hands, mouth, and elephantine nose. This jungle then also prefigures, or functions as a projection of, Saleem's writing body, of what he can do and become. It is a gargantuan body as an agent of education, frightening for its potential.

Therefore, this jungle seems at once an active naturalistic body and something manufactured, an artifact of the human imagination. The towering "cathedral-arching trees" and the closing in of a "tomb" suggest highly crafted architectural spaces that may enable either opening or final rest, while the "incomprehensibly labyrinthine channels" connote textual difficulties, through which these adventurers must negotiate. It is a place of death and rebirth, a tomb and womb from which finally, seven magical months later, in an immense "tidal wave" of amniotic fluid, they will be thrust out, "ejected unceremoniously," "borne" or (re)born again into the world (440). But first, in this overdetermined magical space, inside this (their) body, confronting the grotesquely unspeakable as a giant bodily emanation, they must individuate, in a process that begins with infantilization. The "huge figure" of "Ayooba-the-tank" breaks down to weep, "blubbering like a baby," crying "without stopping for three entire hours or days or weeks, until the rain began, . . . and the Sundarbans began to grow in the rain" (432). Like Alice in Wonderland, who almost drowned in a pool of her own tears, Ayooba seems to produce the tearful rain that deluges them, as if they grow literally smaller, shrinking as the projected jungle of their terrified imaginations grows bigger, threatening to drown them in their sorrow. But unlike Alice, they have no magical antidote to grow big again. This large body that has engulfed them is also an extension of their own. Ayooba's bodily effluences seem to have triggered the growth of this large surrounding body in which they are all caught. Perhaps it is their own bodies—selves—that they must explore, for this body is also the site of truth, of autonomy and responsibility.

In this initial phase of engulfment, this body that sucks them in also sucks in their juices, as if to learn the truth of who they are, to learn literally of what substance they are made. They must merge their bodies with its body, mixing bodily matter; they must learn their interrelationality with others and with their world, in and through their bodies. Like Saleem's metaphor of storytelling, which entails both swallowing the world and being swallowed by it, the jungle swallows them, tastes and feeds upon them, as they feed upon it. Just as they have bombarded others, so too are they bombarded by "nipa palms," deadly hands that drop upon them fruits "larger than any coconuts on earth," falling from "dizzying heights" to "explode like bombs" (433). When their boat capsizes, they are forced to crawl ashore, to make direct contact with the jungle, which covers them in "three-inch-long leeches" that glut upon their sleeping bodies and explode, "being too greedy to stop sucking when they were full" (433). Then the jungle literally sucks in their bodily juices to test their inner substance: "Blood trickled down legs and on to the forest floor; *the jungle sucked it in, and knew what they were like*" (433; my emphasis). Suggesting a mechanism for gaining a conjoint sexual, carnal, and cerebral "knowledge," this jungle seems now to be a giant mode of (self-)evaluation, identifying each before it will assign appropriate punishment.

After this taste test, the jungle intensifies its mimicry of the interior of their bodies (and psyches), for the nipa fruits smash on the jungle floor to "exude a liquid the color of blood, a red milk which was immediately covered in a million insects" (433). Before, the jungle's creatures were colorless, transparent because of the "absence of direct sunlight"; now they seem to fill up as the bloody incarnations of these soldiers' bodies and actions, as externalized forms of what they are and have done. As the jungle drinks in their blood and turns red, mimicking the blood they have shed and the blood they bear in their veins, in turn, the four soldiers also eat and drink in the jungle, ingesting its "insanity" as a bodily substance that merges into and changes their bodies. "Rainwater poured off leaves all around them, and they turned their mouths up to the roof of the jungle and drank; but perhaps because the water came to them by way of sundri leaves [which had given their name to the jungle] and mangrove branches and nipa fronds, it acquired on its journey something of the insanity of the jungle, so that as they drank they fell deeper and deeper into the thralldom of that livid green world" (434). Infected by the "miasma" of this raindrink, this product of their tearful bodies, they prepare their first meal, "a combination of nipa-fruits and mashed earthworms, which inflicted on them a diarrhoea so violent that they forced themselves to examine their excrement in case their intestines had fallen out in the mess" (434). Physical contact with rainwater from leaves seems to conduct (or return) the insanity of the jungle (or of their tears) into their bodies, which convulse violently, turning their insides emblematically out. Horrific and nightmarish though this "dream-jungle" is, it is at once also intensely bodily, like their own bodies, suggesting that it is a projection of their psyches and that that projection is horribly, inescapably real and material. This dream forest nurtures them as they drink the "red milk of nipa fruits," struggling for survival and shelter within its strange environment. But after this mutual recognition, the jungle also punishes them, for now each must confront his own ghosts alone—the ghosts of their victims. It closes in upon them "like a vice, so that [Saleem] felt unable to breathe," for the grip of these punitive memories is as tangible as strangulation (435).

With this punishment comes reeducation in individual responsibility. Infants no more, each of these now-individuated soldiers is visited by visions of his past, by parents whose constraints and sacrifices he finally understands and for whom he learns empathy. Ayooba "understood his mother for the first time, and stopped sucking his thumb." He grows up when he relinquishes his egocentric memory of her as someone who loved him and gave him sweets, in favor of a vision of "a white wraith-like monkey with the face of his mother," remembering instead how "she liked to sit among the boxes of her dowry, as though she, too, were simply some sort of thing, simply one of the gifts her father gave to her husband" (435). Shaheed moves toward "a new adulthood" and "sense of responsibility" when he relinquishes the zombie state of "just-following-orders" (as he had done in the army) and recalls his father as a monkey—a model of mindless imitation—who had instructed him to live up to his name: to die a holy martyr (436). Here, in "the heart of the Sundarbans," Shaheed comes to understand that individual responsibility and moral worth entail *not* following orders blindly, not becoming a tool of another's design, an instrument in an unjust war.

But the culmination of this process occurs when the buddha, or "not-Saleem," is bitten by "a blind, translucent serpent" (436). In one of Rushdie's greatest ironies, Saleem became the buddha when he became a citizen of Pakistan, brained into submission and "purity" when he forgot his impure past, that is, his extensive family and links with Hindu polytheistic India (403). To become a citizen of Pakistan, self-named "the Land of the Pure" (368), Rushdie suggests, Saleem, like his parents, had to forget his past (371) and had to "conform" and "acquiesce" to the homogenizing authority of an absolutist religion and state (369): "I am stripped of past present memory time shame and love. . . . I bow my head yes I acquiesce yes in the necessity of the blow" (409). That amnesia, that unrelenting purge of "purity," led to the carnage that Saleem enabled, to the abuse of his skills, for he lost the capacity for empathy, for making connections, for responsibility and autonomy. Now, in the heart of this darkness of interiority turned bodily, this anti-Eden, Saleem is bitten by a serpent that brings him knowledge of good and evil, recovering his memory and relinquishing self-absolution to become a moral agent whose responsibility begins with an acknowledgment of his past. Stricken by the snake poison of memory, Saleem's body struggles against itself, poison against poison, as this snake poison reactivates the physical antidote that saved him in infancy and is still present in his body:

> I was rejoined to the past, jolted into unity by snake-poison, and it began to pour out through the buddha's lips. As his eyes returned to normal, his words flowed so freely that they seemed to be an aspect of the monsoon. The child-soldiers listened, spellbound, to the stories issuing from his mouth, beginning with a birth at midnight, and continuing unstoppably, because he was reclaiming everything, all of it, all lost histories, all the myriad complex processes that go to make a man. Open-mouthed, unable to tear themselves away, the child-soldiers drank his life like leaf-tainted water. . . . You see, Padma: I have told this story before. (436–37)

This is the crux of this episode, and indeed of the novel, for here Saleem finally remembers and begins to tell his story, thus beginning to enact change. This story will affect both the teller and his first listeners—as it will, later, upon retelling, affect Padma and, in turn, Rushdie's amnesiac readers. Saleem's recovery of the past is hence the recovery of himself, as the act of telling is the act of regaining control and enacting change.

This recovery is initiated by the physical penetration of Saleem's body by an agent of this jungle, by a serpent whose venom enters and circulates in his body. This jungle-poison, this antidotal (or anecdotal) bodily fluid pours out as his stories, issuing from his lips as fluid bodily matter, as (in Rushdie's new idiom) a salutary material force. For this moment discloses another dimension of this jungle: it is a jungle of dreams, of psychic projections; it is inherently a discursive jungle, material because, Rushdie repeatedly suggests, discursivity is as deeply and integrally material as is the human body. Indeed, Rushdie's language here finally confirms these links between Saleem's storytelling and the corporeal matter of this phantasmal jungle, for his stories are the "monsoon" rains, the tears, the blood, the painfully excreted intestinal diarrhea, the antivenom that enables life and survival, the unspoken that is finally released. And like that "life-tainted [rain]water" of the jungle, this liquid storytelling is swallowed by the "open-mouthed" child-soldiers because it is necessary for their survival. They take it into their bodies so that it can enact reeducation, guilt confrontation, inculcation of responsibility, repentance, and adulthood. (The only thing Saleem cannot recall is his name—perhaps because that is an identity given to him by others.) Only after this first storytelling does it become clear how akin the nature of the jungle and of Saleem's linguistic powers are. After hearing Saleem's narrative, the "child-soldiers" undergo (again) a process of guilt, recrimination, and punishment, as they hear the voices of their victims.

Finally, literally and figuratively, the jungle of tears rises and grows above them, forcing them to search for "higher ground," so that they enter the last stage of their sojourn and learn about their dreams (437). In this last phase, the four soldiers have one more lesson to learn: the responsible use of dreams. As adults, "having survived the onset of memory and responsibility and the greater pain of renewed accusation," they come upon an idyllic space that combines the sexual fantasies of both Hindu and Muslim cultural traditions. In a glade filled with songbirds, they find a temple of Kali, with a "towering statue" of the Hindu "black dancing goddess," covered in erotic sculpted figures, and they meet "four young girls of a beauty beyond speech," recalling the promised "houris" of Quranic (male) heaven (438–39). Night after night this miraculous quartet "of their most contented dreams" brings the four men to a "united peak" of sexual fulfillment, until one day they discover that "they were becoming transparent, that it was possible to see through their bodies, not clearly as yet, but cloudily. . . . [T]hey understood that this was the last and worst of the jungle's tricks, that by giving them their heart's desire it was fooling them into using up their dreams, so that as their dream-life seeped out of them they became as hollow and translucent as glass" (439). They have united with their past, but they have yet to make responsible use of it. Dreams (as I discuss in the next chapter) are intensely material because they enable the future; only by imagining new possibilities can a new future be brought into being by those who seek to exercise an autonomous and salutary agency. As adults, these four have yet to enact their dreams responsibly; once they leave the Sundarbans, only Saleem will remember his lessons, only he will survive, and only he, by writing, will attempt to inject the nation with his antidotal serpentine poison, his stories as dreams that will enable alternative futures. Here, the boy-soldiers have fallen into self-indulgent dreams, the immediate gratification of selfish desire. These women are not real; they are figments of the young men's imaginations, fantasies made real. Upon waking, they find four sets of ashes, as of the burnt bodies of four ancient satis, four monuments to masculine self-glorification.

Thus, the jungle shows them that dreams have material content, that dreaming and imagining are part of their bodies, so that by "using up their dreams" wrongly they use up parts of their bodies; they begin to lose their materiality, their agency, their capacity to act in the world. The last "trick" of the jungle is to make them transparent, to lose the substantiality of their bodies, to make them live out their dreams through this stagnant fantasy instead of enacting their dreams in real life. As they become transparent, they realize that dreams are what give them reality and body. This dream forest itself is material because their dreams are material. But they lose that materiality if they allow fantasies of a lost past or an irresponsible future to use up their dreams. Instead, they have to return and use those dreams with agency—as Saleem will do.

The bodiliness of Rushdie's new language thus provides an idiom for enabling the agency of postcolonial language and narration. Moreover, as the next chapter shows, it also suggests powerful possibilities for the narrative form of the dream, which is itself material, which bears truth, and which, despite the constraints of history, allows for the imagining and making of postcolonial futures.

CHAPTER SIX

When Truth Is What It Is Told to Be

Rushdie's Storytelling, Dreams, and Endings

> [P]olitics and literature, like sport and politics, do mix, are inextricably mixed, and the mixture has consequences.... It seems to me imperative that literature enter such arguments, because what is being disputed is nothing less than what is the case, what is truth and untruth. If writers leave the business of making pictures of the world to politicians, it will be one of history's great and most abject abdications.
>
> —Rushdie, "Outside the Whale"[1]

IN 1947, shocked by the partition of time as well as of country, when Indian standard time is set half an hour ahead of Pakistan's, Mr. Butt, Saleem's father's friend, exclaims, "If they can change the time just like that, what's real any more? I ask you? What's true?" (MC, 90). His question resonates in this text as it voices the trauma of loss, of finding truth, language, and system unfixed from their comforting gold standard and of encountering the dizzying instabilities of post-Independence reality. Saleem responds with a little disquisition on truth:

> I reply across the years to S. P. Butt... "What's real and what's true aren't necessarily the same." *True*, for me, was from my earliest days something hidden inside the stories Mary Pereira told me: Mary my ayah who was both more and less than a mother; Mary who knew everything about all of us. *True* was something concealed just over the horizon towards which the fisherman's finger pointed in the picture on the wall, while the young Raleigh listened to his tales. Now, writing this in my Anglepoised pool of light, I measure truth against those early things: Is this how Mary would have told it? I ask. Is this what the fisherman would have said? (*MC*, 90)

Saleem thus proceeds to define not what is "real" but what is "true." The term *real* drops out of his reply, suggesting that "truth" is accessible only by ellipses, as "something," or "something hidden." What is "true" is rendered instead by Saleem as a deeply subjective knowledge, as founded in his childhood experience of engaging with two kinds of texts: the orally told stories of Mary, his ayah; and the painting of the fisherman's pointing finger that hung in his bedroom, itself a visual representation of instructive storytelling.[2] In both, what is "true" is cast as something that lies beyond linguistic definition, "something hidden," oblique, elusive, that cannot be captured in a moral but is hidden in a tale or is pointed to by a finger that leads the eye beyond the frame, so that the observer in the painting (no less than the paradigmatic colonizer, Sir Walter Raleigh) must look beyond that frame, into what cannot be contained within the work of art. Truth is thus what escapes the colonizing gaze. And in both cases, what is "true" is signified by parental figures in scenes of familial instruction, whose indirect but foundational criteria of "truth" engender and shape the writing of the adult Saleem as well. This centrality yet elusiveness of truth underwrites both *Midnight's Children* and *Shame*.

We have seen how Rushdie establishes the agency of his narratives by constructing a new language that purports to be material and bodily by nature and by its effects. He thus suggests how his writing can act: how, as a bodily emanation, it can affect its environment, breaking the boundaries between self and world; how unspoken words have material physiological effects; and how narrating the past can enable control of that past and of the future. Rushdie applies this capacity of his narration to the issue of truth telling and truth making as ways of creating reality in and through his fiction. Rushdie knows, perhaps better than either Kipling or Forster, that truth is not only something that may (or may not) be told, to which language may *refer*, but also something that can be made, that language actually *constructs*. As we have seen, and as the epigraph above indicates, if the goal of Rushdie's postcolonial cultural work is to describe (or redescribe) things both as they *are* or *were* and as they *might be*, then the effort of his new materially powerful language is both to *tell* the truth to the best degree possible and to *make* it, making a better future a material possibility.

Rushdie addresses the issue of truth-telling in the construction of community through storytelling, or the building of nations through narration, as a form of bodily violence, or a "rite of blood," and contrasts this with his own postcolonial fictive truth-telling. The centrality of dreams in Rushdie's narratives is a mode of truth-telling, another register of the body that addresses these problems of knowing, telling and making truths. Rushdie constructs dream-endings in all his major novels as a form of resistance to closure, opening up fresh possibilities to create terms to make such postcolonial futures a material truth.

Rites of Blood: National as Familial Storytelling, Purity, and Truth

When Saleem reemerges from the Sundarbans, he is still wearing his soldier's badge and uniform, clothing that identifies him as a Pakistani secret agent. But he soon replaces these clothes with those of a dead notary, "an arbiter of what was true and what was not" (MC, 449). From now on, he will become his own agent, refusing to be the instrument of a brutal state, taking on this preferred garb of an independent teller and verifier of truth, bound to no nation. Saleem then writes the narrative of *Midnight's Children* as an act of telling such forgotten but important truths, to be passed on to his son, Aadam, who is representative of the next generation. Saleem knows, as does Rushdie, that his "truths" likewise are partial and unreliable and that, as the fisherman's pointing finger warns, they cannot be easily accessed. His goal is to make that partiality clear, undermining all claims to absolute or only truth. But not until *Shame* does Rushdie offer a full-fledged paradigm of national storytelling as bodily, comparing and contrasting his own storytelling and truth-claims with those of the official narratives that he contests.

Perhaps because the process of communal self-formation and censorship is most acutely seen and felt by an outsider, this paradigm is presented through the experience of a migrant, far more disempowered than the narrator of *Shame*, the orphaned Bilquis, who migrates from India to Pakistan as a young bride to find herself trapped in the "joint-family system" of her husband's maternal grandmother: "Lost in the forest of new relatives, wandering in the blood-jungle of the matriarchal home, Bilquis consulted the family Quran in search of these family trees, and found them there, in their traditional place, monkey-puzzle groves of genealogy inscribed in the back of the holy book" (*Shame*, 77). Unlike the webs of genealogy of *Midnight's Children*, which open up possibilities for revision, and unlike the Sundarbans, which offer self-knowledge, this "blood-jungle" of a new family tree promises only confusion and violence. In this family as allegory for nation, how is the newcomer to negotiate its networks or enter its "groves" or be inscribed into the religiosities of its book?[3] "Trapped in a language which contained a quite specific name for each conceivable relative, so that the bewildered newcomer was unable to hide behind such generic appellations as 'uncle,' 'cousin,' 'aunt,' but was continually caught out in all her insulting ignorance, Bilquis' tongue was silenced by the in-law mob. She virtually never spoke except when alone with Rani or Raza; and thus acquired the triple reputation of sweet-innocent-child, doormat, and fool" (78). In this "empire of Bariamma," ruled over by the family matriarch, the immigrant is silenced, arriving as a new citizen to a nation already constituted as a claustrophobic clan and forced to learn their language, on their terms. These terms of belonging, of conditional inclusion and exclusion, transcribed sanctimoniously in a holy book, clearly carry the power of a religion. For she is always a "mohajir," as she is abusively labeled later (89), confirming her as representative of the millions of dispossessed Muslim migrants who sought refuge from India in the newly formed Pakistan and whose descendants are still considered outsiders.[4]

This paradigm of discursive disempowerment and incorporation into a dominant discourse is repeated when Bilquis finally tells her story. Her language and history are taken from her as her story is homogenized into the family's repertoire of self-making fictions. For this is a family—and nation—that is built from such storytelling:

> As the officially designated poor-thing, Bilquis was also obliged to sit each evening at Bariamma's feet while the blind old lady recounted the family tales. . . . The telling of tales proved the family's ability to survive them, to retain, in spite of everything, its grip on its honor and unswerving moral code. "To be of the family," Bariamma told Bilquis, "you must know our things, and tell us yours." So Bilquis was forced, one evening, (Raza was present but made no attempt to protect her), to recount the end of Mahmoud the Woman and her nudity in the Delhi streets. "Never mind," Bariamma pronounced approvingly, when Bilquis was shaking with the shame of her revelations, "at least you managed to keep your dupatta on." (78–79)
>
> After that Bilquis heard her story being retold, wherever one or two of the family were gathered, . . . because stories, such stories, were the glue that held the clan together, binding the generations in webs of whispered secrets. Her story altered at first, in the retellings, but finally it settled down, and after that nobody, neither teller nor listener, would tolerate any deviation from the hallowed sacred text. (78–79)

Sympathetic to the modes of coercion and gossip endemic to such familial networks, this model of storytelling also functions as an allegory for the construction of a postcolonial nation such as Pakistan. Like *Midnight's Children*, *Shame* is structured on the idea of the nation as an imagined but *real* family, here a claustrophobic and murderous clan, foundering on the sanguinary rivalry between Raza Hyder and Iskander Harappa (modelled on Zia ul-Haq and Zulfikar Ali Bhutto).[5] But more so than in the earlier novel, here families (and nations) are built not only on (imagined) bloodlines but also on the repetition of stories about themselves, circulated through "webs of whispered secrets." Indeed, the act of communal storytelling (a discursive relation) seems to bind more ineluctably than any blood relation, as relating becomes an act of materially connecting units of narrative as well as bodies and psyches. Rushdie's language of bodily narration here becomes an extended metaphor for the familial (re)production of community and nation.

Bariamma ("Big-mother"), the matriarch and arch-storyteller, the arbiter and producer of these fictions, functions as an ominous figure for this power of (self-)generation: through the telling and exchange of the stories over which she presides, she forms and strengthens familial bonds. She generates this family/ nation not only by producing children (and arranging their marriages and orchestrating their lives) but also by (re)producing, circulating, and controlling the stories that make them into a family. An example of Rushdie's misogynistic projection of totalitarian power onto older female figures,[6] she can also be read as the generative power of storytelling, as the formative matrix from which community is born.[7] This is how, Rushdie suggests, nations, like families, are made to belong, and individuals within them defined, bound together by the "glue" of their purportedly collective past, by stories that are retold until they become hygienically transformed into the acceptable versions upon which the group depends. This is how nations, especially new ones, tell their histories, by creating a community that must believe in one safe, hermetically preserved version, in the totalizing fictions that then become "sacred." Nations are founded and maintained by the censored recasting of their histories, by, as Benedict Anderson has put it, selective remembering and forgetting.[8] In both novels, Rushdie represents Pakistan as founded on an act of self-excision: to cut themselves off from India after Partition, he suggests, Pakistanis had to separate themselves from their families and history, so that their very being is founded on forgetting and self-censorship.[9]

This parable of national self-invention suggests how this kind of storytelling, while constructive, is also pernicious. First, it leaves little choice or control to the newcomer it draws into its fold. Blind old Bariamma's Homeric tale telling is all-absorbing: it both compels its listeners to listen and engulfs them, divesting the story and the newcomer of their foreign, undesirable elements. "Forced" to hear their stories and then to tell her own, Bilquis can only be fully incorporated into this new family when she engages in an almost conjugal exchange of narratival "fluids" that merge her with this new body. This is not an equal exchange, because Bilquis the migrant loses her story (and history) to the dominant narrative of this family-nation. In the retelling, she is dispossessed of it as it is distorted by the family to fit their agenda and desires: after "it settled down, nobody, neither teller nor listener, would tolerate any deviation from the hallowed, sacred text."[10] Ironically, a story of the censorship of Bilquis' father's political tolerance (his movie theater in India was bombed because he showed films that did not favor either Hindus or Muslims), it is itself censored by her new family/nation. The scandal of her orphanhood and nakedness is covered up, as she is reclothed, in every sense, in garments of others' making.

The bodiliness of this narrative process indicates the power of stories as material building blocks of communal cohesiveness. But Rushdie's bodily discourse also conveys the injuriousness of this national narration to the notion of truth. Bariamma's selective storytelling, which repeats with a stultifying sameness (not, as we have seen Rushdie validate, with a novelty-producing difference), damages the stories in the retelling even as it preserves them as (family) history. "Bariamma's mildly droning recital of the catalogue of family horrors had the effect of somehow *defusing* them, making them safe, embalming them in the *mummifying fluid* of her own incontrovertible respectability" (79; my emphasis). The process of mummification involves the removal of blood and vital organs so that a dead body can be refilled with preservatives. In this novel of deadly motherhood, in which wombs produce strangled fetuses and pregnancies kill, this pun on "mummifying fluid" suggests an amniotic liquid that preserves these stories by killing them. What is lost, or cut out, consists of the vital bodily organs of truth. Through selective retelling, Bariamma's partial censorship works better than wholesale suppression. Dropping out unwanted bits and wrapping the rest in the authoritative language of respectability, she asserts the family's capacity to control and outlive untoward aspects of its past. Her conventionality and tradition provide an "embalming" quality, as she preserves the version the family wants and numbs the original of its threat. By sheer force of repetition, the stories acquire the glaze of safety, till they have also lost their sharp edges, their capacity for self-questioning, their potentially unsettling force.

The bodily language that describes this pernicious (re)making of history is reinforced by vivid images of blood. Upon the reduction and congealment of her tale, "Bilquìs knew that she had become a member of the family: in the sanctification of her tale lay initiation, kinship, blood. '*The recounting of histories*,' [her husband] Raza told [her], '*is for us a rite of blood*'" (*Shame*, 79; my emphasis). At one level, where blood is the formative substance of kinship, to relate stories in this way is to become related, to become a family, for that circulation is a material vital thing, like the currency of the bloodstream. Nations that tell themselves such stories form a selective blood-kinship. At another level, this bloodiness embodies violence. The "rite of blood" suggests the ritual bloodshed that marks the entry to a new stage of life or marks initiation into a community—as in the rites of adolescence, marriage, or fertility. (Such a "rite" recalls the bloodbath of the 1947 Partition of British India into modern

India and Pakistan, the grotesque violence produced by such logics of communal belonging, and the ethnic "purification" that followed that national formation.) But here, it also seems that to enter into family and history, stories themselves must undergo this ritual: they must be cut, marked, and branded, their blood spilled. Entry into familial or national kinship becomes a conditional rite of sanguinary initiation that excises and transforms the body of the story, entailing a ruthless loss of truth. Such a "rite" is cast as both necessary and injurious: to literal bodies, to stories, and to the nation that is thus formed. To engage in it, then, is also to *(w)rite* of blood, because these (re)written or "recounted" histories both describe and enact a violent bloodiness.

That this episode allegorizes national as familial histories soon becomes clear, for this is the story of the Pakistani nation/family and its president, Zia: "But neither Raza nor Bilquis could have known that their story had scarcely begun, that it would be the juiciest and goriest of all the juicygory sagas, and that, in time to come, it would always begin with the following sentence . . . : 'It was the day on which the only son of the future President Raza Hyder was going to be incarnated.' 'Yes, yes,' the audience would cheer, 'tell us that one, that's the best'" (79–80). The family of this nation thrives on the retelling of this story, on a bloodthirsty consumption of its "juicygor[iness]." Unlike Saleem's delight in swallowing both the *halal* and the *haram*, the blood with the "body of the tale" (as discussed in the introduction to the present volume), this national bloodthirstiness requires that its stories be strictly halal, that though they may be about blood, they should be clean, purified of their inconvenient elements. In this final version, Bilquis' first meeting with Raza is understood by this audience in terms of the national desire for patriarchal self-perpetuation, as a prologue, important only because it produced the "President's son," eliminating the concerns and specificities of Bilquis' individual or gendered experience.

This parable of national storytelling as both bodily and familial, a simultaneously constructive and destructive process, identifies the problems inherent in the official discourse that Rushdie seeks to counter. It suggests how storytelling can function as the "glue" of community formation but also how pernicious that glue can be as it mistreats those it includes or excludes, or as it alters truth, stabilizing authorized versions through sheer repetition. But it also highlights the problems that accrue to Rushdie's own storytelling, self-reflectively posing analogous questions for the counterdiscourse to which Rushdie aspires: as an alternative effort to form different kinds of communities, to tell untold truths, to what extent does it, too, suffer from the very problems that it censures? To what extent does it also gloss over what it finds unsuitable to tell? The anxiety of agency that impels Rushdie's work induces not only the need to establish the material effectivity (both potential efficacy and harmfulness) of storytelling but also the need to address the same problems in his writing that he identifies in the official narratives he contests. If he too alters and omits, then how is his storytelling different from what he critiques? How does it violate those whose stories he tells or incorporates into his own? What makes his versions of truth more salutary or reliable than those of others? How might his *recounting* of history also be a rite of blood?

Rushdie faces a significantly different problem from Kipling or Forster. Instead of covertly trying to expose censorship without appearing to do so, like Kipling, or protesting it while implicating himself, like Forster, Rushdie (at least before 1989) could be only too overt about the censorships and abuses of neocolonial regimes. Yet while cognizant of the urgency as well as the luxury of voicing such outrage, throughout these foundational narratives Rushdie is always aware that what he critiques can apply to his own storytelling. In exposing the abuses of nationalist rhetoric, Rushdie sets up comparisons to his own storytelling, to work through both the similarities and the differences between modes of telling, remembering, and forgetting. Throughout *Midnight's Children* and *Shame*, directly and indirectly Rushdie dwells on the problems of censorship and truth telling in both the official, nationalist narratives he critiques as well as in his own. But his writing also seems riven by a major self-contradiction: on the one hand, Rushdie tries to expose official elisions of truth, self-righteously distinguishing his narrative politics and historiography from those he challenges; on the other hand, he points out similarities, that is, the inevitability of omission, bias, alteration, and relativity, in the narratives he tells. To combat the falsehoods and propaganda circulated by neocolonial powermongers and nationalist ideologues and to redress damage to the very concept of truth,[11] Rushdie upholds the ethical duty of the postcolonial writer to contest those falsehoods, to teach readers and postcolonial citizens to question and challenge those who hoodwink them, and he seems to believe in the existence of some truth to which writers are responsible. At the same time, he seems to undermine the possibility of truth altogether if he, as a defender of truth, can only posit the notion of truth as a fallacious or inaccessible ideal.

As a result, to a casual reader, Rushdie can seem both confused and confusing. If he regards truth as relative, as ultimately a matter of perspective, as if anyone's version were equal to any other (as many of my undergraduates conclude), then how can he also insist on the reality of falsehood and abuse, on the necessity of distinguishing between truth and untruth? Is it not inconsistent, we may ask, to regard truth as constructed and inaccessible and at the same time to insist on contesting untruth, on retaining some fundamental, inalienable difference between truth and falsehood? If Rushdie himself points out the similarities between his narratives and those he denounces, what makes his "truth" or vision more compelling, or less "true," or less culpable, than any other? How can he have it both ways?

At the point, for instance, when Saleem describes the censorship and destruction of the midnight's children, his narration becomes divided against itself, torn into voices that urge, censure, and self-censor, that destroy the sanity of his syntax as they destroy the integrity of selfhood: "But the horror of it, I can't won't mustn't won't can't no!—Stop this; begin.—No!—Yes. About the dream, then? I might be able to tell it as a dream" (*MC*, 503). Saleem's contestatory account bears the marks of damage and omission, revealing its own fragmentation. In denouncing the state's destruction of truth, why does Rushdie cast doubt on Saleem's construction of truths? Similarly, when describing the sycophantic and mendacious journalism that celebrated a rigged election—and the end of democracy—in Pakistan, Saleem comments, "The newspapers . . . announced a crushing victory for the President's Muslim League . . . proving to me that I have been only the humblest of jugglers-with-facts; and that *in a country where the truth is what it is instructed to be, reality quite literally ceases to exist,* so that everything becomes possible except what we are told is the case" (*MC*, 389; my emphasis). Distinguishing his own "humble" "juggl[ing] with facts" from the blatant censorship and lies of a country where "truth is what it is instructed to be," Saleem's comment opens up the question of the extent to which what he or Rushdie tells is true.

Frequently, Rushdie pauses in midnarration to comment more openly on how he also distorts, selects, or omits the truth. In *Shame*, after cataloguing disingenuously all that he cannot say (including a series of examples of state censorship), the narrator confesses, "And now I must stop saying what I am not writing about, because there's nothing so special about that; *every story one chooses to tell is a kind of censorship; it prevents the telling of other tales*" (Shame, 72–3; my emphasis). Such comments blur the difference between his own writing and nationalist lying or censorship. However, by pointing out these similarities, Rushdie can move on to accentuate the differences. In an important moment in *Midnight's Children*, Saleem explains to Padma what makes his own narration not "objective" but also not false: "'I told you the truth,' I say yet again, 'Memory's truth, because memory has its own special kind. It selects, eliminates, alters, exaggerates, minimizes, glorifies, and vilifies also; but in the end creates its own reality, its heterogeneous but usually coherent version of events; and no sane human being ever trusts someone else's version more than his own'" (MC, 253). As *Midnight's Children* makes clear, Rushdie wishes to perpetuate no illusions about the historical accuracy or "objectivity" of his narrative, as he continually emphasizes the inventiveness and partiality of representation and the fictiveness of the writing of history or telling stories. At one point, Saleem realizes that he had made Gandhi die at the wrong point in an earlier chapter, but he refuses to change that detail—for it represents precisely how history is constructed, as well as how fallible memory and record making are—in his text Gandhi will continue to die at the wrong time (198).[12] His point is, as numerous theorists and historians have argued, that writing is necessarily situated in its own historicity, its ideology, its partiality—and the effort to encapsulate the whole "objectively" is an idealistic impossibility. The "truth" of Rushdie's tale is to reveal these contingencies of truth making and to inculcate in his readers a healthy suspicion of claims to truth that present truth otherwise. Something is not "true" just because we remember it that way; rather, it provides a truth about the conditions of memory and of living through a particular history.

Likewise, in *Shame*, Rushdie interpolates, in his own voice, "As for me: I, too, like all migrants, am a fantasist. I build imaginary countries and try to impose them on the ones that exist. I too face the problem of history: what to retain, what to dump, how to hold on to what memory insists on relinquishing, how to deal with change" (Shame, 91–92). Recognizing the inevitability of its own omissions and acts of erasure, Rushdie's narrative seeks to highlight those occasions of loss. There is no claim for the singularity of his version. Instead, totality can be suggested only by multiplicity, not by unity or the seamlessness of a single version. "I am forced to reflect that world in fragments of broken mirrors. . . . I must reconcile myself to the missing bits," he explains (*Shame*, 71). To acknowledge the fragmentation of knowledge is to be more truthful than to claim the only truth.

Thus it is not inconsistent for Rushdie to insist *both* on the relativity of the truths he seeks to tell and on the absolute difference between falsehood and truth. Rather, resolving this apparent contradiction is a self-conscious goal of Rushdie's narratives. As a postmodern writer, Rushdie is aware that truths are constructed, partial, subject to the vagaries of language and the conditions of power and knowledge — but at the same time, as a postcolonial writer, he is also politically committed to the need to identify and expose falsehood, to maintain a belief in truth instead of succumbing to the relativism of accommodating all claims to truth as equal. As discussed in the introduction to the present volume, even for postmodern thinkers, there is no question of the *existence* of truth or reality beyond human language or knowledge — only the need to emphasize the considerable difficulties of ascertaining truth. Thus, it is not inconsistent to insist on the constructed nature of truth, to emphasize the problems of knowing, while also insisting on the importance of approximating and understanding those difficulties and of identifying the deliberate distortions of narratives produced for political or ulterior motives. Total relativity, in Rushdie's book, may be more dangerous or, indeed, a dark twin of an uncomplicated or zealous belief in single, objective truth.

In both *Shame* and *Midnight's Children*, Rushdie offers a compelling argument for distinguishing between the truth-claims of nationalist narratives and those of his own. The problem with the truth-claims of official state narratives is that they claim to be the only truth and authority, threatening and disallowing other versions and self-servingly falsifying what they know to be true. Rushdie, in contrast, distinguishes between the narrative techniques of his storytelling and those he opposes by manifestly foregrounding his self-knowledge of partiality and provisionality, revealing how truth is made. By so doing, he suggests that there is a crucial difference between the kinds of truths he makes up and the falsehoods he indicts. He does not claim to have access to a single or correct version. But he does contend that deliberate mendacity created to mislead for political purposes is different from the inevitable distortions created by language or epistemology or emotional memory. Some versions are of a different order of falsity than others; rather than claiming to tell an objective and only truth, he demonstrates the importance of understanding one's own history and position, as a way to understand the contingency and approximate nature of the version of truth one has. The only truth that he can tell is the truth that all truth is provisional, inculcating in his readers a healthy suspicion of whatever they are told. This constitutes the agency of Rushdie's writing.

Providing a plurality of versions, as many postcolonial writers do, is another strategy for approximating truth rather than insisting on one correct version. As a writer of fiction, Rushdie can expose the falsity or exploitativeness of various claims to truth, not by substituting an alternative "true" version of his own but by offering a more self-knowing, openly fabricated version that points to the limitations of any singular claim to truth. (Hence Saleem's version explains his history as formative of his way of seeing and thus also foregrounds his biases as part of the story he tells.) There is thus a critical difference between the mode of storytelling that Rushdie indicts and the one he deploys: Rushdie's is self-knowing of its partiality and self-exposingly open about its processes of making. In a brilliant exemplum of this in *Midnight's Children*, Saleem as a little boy cuts up newspapers to construct his message, an anonymous "lethal missive" that incarnates selfish motives to disclose a neighbor's adulterous liaison to her husband. In so doing, he shows how "history" can be "rearranged" or "cut up" to suit one's own purposes. Here Rushdie literally bares the device of his own "recounting of history," making his reader piece together his message in the process of its construction. To write, "COMMANDER SABARMATI, WHY DOES YOUR WIFE GO TO COLABA CAUSEWAY ON SUNDAY MORNING?" Saleem proceeds thus:

> From GOAN LIBERATION COMMITTEE LAUNCHES SATYAGRAHA CAMPAIGN I extracted the letters "COM"; SPEAKER OF E-PAK ASSEMBLY DECLARED MANIAC gave me my second syllable, "MAN." . . . [I]nto my second word now, I excised "SAB" from RIOTS, MASS ARRESTS IN RED-RUN KERALA: SABOTEURS RUN AMOK . . . but I refused to be tied exclusively to politics, and turned to advertising for the "DOES YOUR" in DOES YOUR CHEWING GUM LOSE ITS FLAVOUR? . . . "ABA" was hard to find, turning up at last in a cinema advertisement: ALI-BABA, SEVENTEENTH SUPERCOLOSSAL WEEK. . . . Events in East Pakistan provided me with

my finale. FURNITURE HURLING SLAYS DEPUTY E-PAK SPEAKER: MOURNING PERIOD DECLARED gave me "MOURNING," from which, deftly and deliberately, I excised the letter "U." (MC, 311–12; capitalized in original)

Demonstrating the art of reconstruction from fragmentation, Rushdie turns excision into a form of communication. Saleem, while creating his message, creates a palimpsest that is revealed in this text, producing an effect of two simultaneous texts at once: the poisonous little message that he constructs; and an image of his time derived from the political news, social news, and advertisements that he cuts up. Yet even as Saleem reshapes, arbitrarily juxtaposes, and disperses the newspaper text (which itself cuts up, reshapes, juxtaposes, and disperses the cultural, social, commercial bits of history that it reports), Rushdie's text highlights the cultural collage that makes up contemporary postcolonial history.

This palimpsest effect of reading two divergent texts at once—the newspaper snippets and Saleem's personal narrative—functions as a paradigm for the construction of Rushdie's own narrative. Saleem's text co-opts another text for his purposes yet exposes both his own text and that which it excises, just as Rushdie's text does. But by the very act of self-exposure, his text proffers itself as different: for instead of concealment, it seeks to reveal its own acts of censorship. Here, then, is a text that differentiates itself from what it mirrors. Instead of excluding and erasing its prior text (as the narratives of Pakistan's nationalist historiography do),[13] Rushdie's text allows its prior texts to seep through, mirroring and then distinguishing itself from the palimpsest that obscures—as the one that reveals. In this replication with a difference, then, lies the difference—in Rushdie's recognition of a complicity that by re-presenting itself differentiates itself.

Moreover, as we have seen, to emphasize their centrality to the agency of his narratives, Rushdie presents both truth and censorship as intensely bodily matters, as registers of materiality and sentience. His writing continually presents truth as material and bodily, as that which is considered impure and therefore prohibited from official discourses. Like Kipling, Rushdie also represents the censorship of stories or texts, or the destruction of truth, as a graphic act of physical violence, as bodily amputation or injury. When Saleem describes

Indira Gandhi's 1975 "Emergency" as a calculated attempt to root out and destroy the midnight's children, Rushdie renders through the phantasmagoria of magical realism the horrors of such historical events as the suspension of democracy and civil liberties, the forced sterilizations of the poor under a ruthless birth control program, the razing of shantytowns, and the persecution of rural migrants in big cities as a destruction of the hope and possibilities created by India's Independence. Officially these abuses remain off the record: the event was divided into "the white part—public, visible, documented, a matter for historians" and the "black part . . . secret, macabre, untold" (MC, 501). This act of national silencing is presented as the bodily excision of the midnight's children's powers of production and transformation, of hope, possibility, and imagination: "Ectomy . . . : a cutting out. To which medical science adds a number of prefixes: appendectomy, tonsillectomy, tubectomy. . . . Saleem would like to add one further item . . . to this catalogue of excisions . . . : Sperectomy: the draining out of hope" (521). Censorship, the cutting short of discourse, becomes an excision of the body (indeed, of the body's productive possibilities), and the destruction of historical truth a destruction of the nation and of its future viability. "Test- and hysterectomized, the children of midnight were denied the possibility of reproducing themselves" (MC, 523).

These renderings of damage to truth—something linguistic—as physical serves at least two purposes. One is that the telling and making of truth can then be understood as acts of power that make a material difference, as material shaping forces on human lives and societies. Another is to suggest the sentience of bodily loss and pain as inherent to the loss of truth. But there is yet a third, more compelling reason why Rushdie needs this bodily discourse to imagine or represent truth. Truth, in his writing, begins to emerge as dirt, in Mary Douglas's sense of "matter out of place." It becomes that impurity which has been excised and excluded from "proper" discourse by various forms of power, undesirable to those who seek control. Rushdie's postcolonial counterhistories, he suggests, then must constitute that wholesome dirt, in every sense, in that effort to rectify, to tell things differently and more wholly. In *Midnight's Children*, Saleem constructs a complex paradigm of storytelling as eating and as feeding his audience *haram* (not *halal*) meat. To tell the whole uncensored truth is to "press on to the unspeakable part," to consume the entire, impure, unbled "body of the tale"

(*MC*, 64). His famous metaphor, "pickling," involves "inevitable distortions" through the addition of "spice-and-vinegar," of "impurities," and of "the occasional speck of dirt," for the "art" of truth telling involves dirt (*MC*, 549). For Rushdie, truth *is* impurity, understood as inherently impure, hence salutary. Thus, he suggests that as a writer his agency lies in contesting the official narratives that disallow dirt, or the impurity of truth.

Midnight's Children therefore consistently celebrates impurity, for purity implies absolutism, exclusion, cleansing, excision, and indeed censorship. Rushdie makes much, for instance, of the newly coined name "Pakistan," which translates as both "the pure land" and "the Land of the Pure." In the war of 1965, Saleem is bereft not only of memory but also of family, of history, of knowledge of truth, of all feeling, and of his name. In other words, he "became a citizen of Pakistan. . . . [E]mptied of history, the buddha learned the arts of submission, and did only what was required of him" (*MC*, 419). A postcolonial Kim for this period of his life, amnesiac Saleem becomes a spy for a totalitarian state, rewritten upon by being first "wiped clean as a slate" (418), "clean as a wooden writing chest" (410). It is on this occasion that the narrator Saleem disowns himself, alienated from the self he became, and speaks of himself in the third person. To be a citizen of Pakistan, Rushdie suggests, is to exist in a state of religious purity that is akin to self-excision to destroy the link with the polytheistic cultural heritage of Hindu India, to be constituted upon the denial of the past. Such self-censorship both symbolizes and replicates the traumatic event of Partition and the very formation of Pakistan. For Pakistan to cut itself off from the body of India, to make itself "pure," is to found itself on such an act of violation — and violence. Such self-enabling notions of national "purity" are dangerous precisely for the genocidal violence they authorize, exemplified in the massacres that accompanied the Partition of 1947 and in the rhetoric of "ethnic cleansing" that have impelled crises such as those in Bosnia and Rwanda.[14]

Upon their migration to Pakistan, Saleem's parents attempt such "purity": "Saleem's parents said, 'We must all become new people;' in the land of the pure, purity became our ideal. But Saleem was forever tainted with Bombayness, his head was full of all sorts of religions apart from Allah's (like India's first Muslims, the mercantile Moplas of Malabar, I had lived in a country whose population of deities rivaled the numbers of its people . . .); and his body was to show a marked preference for the impure. . . . [B]ut in the end, purity found me out, and even I, Saleem, was cleansed of my misdeeds" (*MC*, 371). Disliking this purity, Saleem's preternatural nose discovers that his "new fellow citizens exuded the flat boiled odours of acquiescence," as distinct from the "highly-spiced conformity of Bombay" (369); in "the Land of the Pure," he says, he "sought the company of whores" (394). By contrast, his sister Jamila becomes tainted with purity. As her newly discovered singer's voice takes her to sudden heights of national popularity, she becomes the "Voice" and the "Daughter" of the nation, singing soldiers to their deaths in the name of faith. The president of Pakistan informs her, "Jamila daughter, . . . your voice will be a sword of purity; it will be a weapon with which to cleanse men's souls" (*MC*, 376), exemplifying the violence inherent in the co-optation of art for the nation—a use to which Saleem refuses to lend himself. Such stardom diminishes the artist as well, committing her to the "exaggerations and simplifications of self," to the "blind and blinding devoutness and the right-or-wrong-nationalism" that is the terrible side effect of such purity (375). Saleem's sudden outbreak of incestuous love for his "sister" can then be read as his "impure" desire to incorporate into a larger wholeness of impurity that which seeks to separate itself as pure, to muddy the purity that needs to recognize itself as cognate with impurity, to uphold the impure, and to break down the boundaries that demarcate transgression.

This Rushdiean celebration of the impure in (trans)national and migrant culture is also the provocative, serious objective of *The Satanic Verses*, a text that examines the potential for the survival of cultures that eclectically reconstruct themselves and assimilate, versus those that insist on the absolutism of a monolithic unchanging purity of origin. Its ideal is suggested by Zeeny Vakil, the iconoclast—like Rushdie—who writes a book that creates a "predictable stink" because it attacks the "confining myth of authenticity . . . for was not the entire (Indian) national culture based on the principle of borrowing whatever clothes seemed to fit, Aryan, Mughal, British . . . ?" (52). No nation or culture is "pure," Rushdie insists: its vaunted "purity" is always predicated on the forgetting and cleansing of hybridity. Truth is hence a matter of impurity: always relative but still necessary to distinguish from falsehood, and yet elusive, existing beyond the frames of narrative. To this end, to suggest the truths and possibilities that lie beyond the grasp of ordinary language or logic, Rushdie constructs the structure of dreams.

"Tell It as a Dream": Truth and the (Im)possibility of Dreams

Around the middle of *Midnight's Children,* Saleem's narration is interrupted by a dream that makes little sense at the time:

> No colours except green and black the walls are green the sky is black (there is no roof) the stars are green the Widow is green but her hair is black as black. . . . Between the walls the children green the walls are green the Widow's arm comes snaking down the snake is green the children scream the fingernails are black they scratch the Widow's arm is hunting see the children run and scream the Widow's hand curls round them green and black. Now one by one the children mmff are stifled quiet. . . . [T]he Widow laughs her tongue is green but see her teeth are black. . . . [T]he Widow's hand comes onebyone the children scream and mmff and little balls and hand and scream and mmff and splashing stains of black. (249–50)

Only when the dream is repeated, almost word for word, two hundred and fifty pages later do we understand it as an account of the 1975 Emergency imposed by Indira Gandhi, prime minister of India (503). This dream of the Widow becomes a necessary mode of representation for a truth so horrific that no straightforward "realism" could suffice, requiring instead techniques of fantasy, repetition, broken allusion, and inversion. The rooflessness inverts the possibility of openness to suggest the unending control of her totalitarian reach; the obsessive repetition of two colors replicates the reduced two-dimensionality and unreality of the hallucinatory reality that she creates; the unpunctuated, childlike syntax indicates the unrelieved strain and infantilism enforced upon those captive in such an environment. Indeed, the terror of this universe is accentuated by its associations with a child's world: the intonations of song, the jarring internal off-rhymes (the snake is green—the children scream; fingernails are black—they scratch), the fragmentary echoes of nursery rhymes (see the children run, as in "Three Blind Mice"), the fear of being eaten by a gargantuan mouth turned into a fairy-tale terror of bodies squished into balls of black ink; and a child's phonetic language (mmff) to represent such silencing.

How are we to read such dreams, and indeed Rushdie's narratives, which often mirror the structure of these dreams? What does the haunting prevalence of dreams as a form in Rushdie's novels suggest about his narration? With the exception of Gayatri Spivak, who interprets the schizophrenic nature of Gibreel's dreams in *The Satanic Verses* as an index of the migrant postcolonial experience, few scholars have addressed the singularity of dreams in Rushdie's work, least of all as a form related to his narration.[15] Dreams are central to *The Satanic Verses*, but it is in the novels preceding that work that Rushdie sets up the crucial role of dreams for his narratives. In the example from *Midnight's Children* above, Saleem's dream-story is "hallucinatory" not because he is hallucinating but because postcolonial reality itself has become such that it seems hallucinatory, unreal, an inversion of itself. As a mirror for Rushdie's mode of narration, the structure of dreams in his fiction suggests both possibilities of invention and alternative forms of representation for postcolonial truths. The dream recurs in Rushdie's narratives as an emblem of an art form and as a mode of truth and of reconstruction of reality. It occupies a space both within and beyond the frame of the narrative, a mode that Rushdie's narrative may mimic, creating an alternative that, in its very ambiguity, enables the possibilities of postcolonial narration. Thus, the dream offers itself as a deeply ambiguous structure, as a discursive mode that suggests alternatives even to the conventions of fiction.

Moreover, dreams in Rushdie's fiction are imagined as bodily in many ways. They are, on the one hand, intensely bodily and visceral in the ways that they are described or experienced, with powerful bodily sensations of smell, touch, pain, or brutality. On the other hand, they seem to have powerful bodily effects (at times they can literally kill others); they are productive of reality, as they have the power to make or "unmake" others. Most important is that they suggest the constitutive material power of dreams, in that what is dreamed becomes bodily reality. This may seem counterintuitive, for in modern Western cultures, dreams have come to be understood as connected to the (dreamer's) realm of the mental or spiritual, not the physical. But thinkers from Freud on have contested that assumption, linking dreams with emotions, sexuality, desire, anxiety, and fear—that is, dreams are symptomatic of the somatic in some way, making inextricable the psychic and the physical. Neurologically, after all, they are connected to the body: scientific researchers can identify when we are dreaming, when they monitor our brain waves. Philosophers such as Merleau-Ponty and Mark Johnson have begun to radically contest the assumed separation of mind and body, to argue, from different angles, for the embodied mind.[16] And for political reasons, magical realists and writers such as Rushdie also dismantle that Western mind-body division (often encoded as a hierarchy of reason versus emotion, irrationality, physicality, and so forth), reasserting and validating bodily ways of knowing, as articulated through the radically other, alogical language of dreams.

In Rushdie's work, dreams have a material presence in their effects as well, a shaping power to create and transform reality. New nations are dreamed into being by the collective will of a people, "in a dream we all agreed to dream" (MC, 130); "dark dreams of discontent" or "flowers of the imagination" lead processions of language marchers to the collective violence of the language riots of Maharashtra (MC, 199); Saleem's dream of Kashmir creates both Pakistan's and India's dream (and desire) for the same, leading to the war of 1965. In *Shame*, Omar Khayyam's dreams have such "an unpalatable reality" that he tries not to sleep, preferring the "more acceptable illusions of his everyday, waking life" (16). The "truth" of Omar's dreams is not a source of comfort, but his preference for waking illusions highlights the greater "reality of dreams" over the lesser illusions of the everyday. In the hallucinatory reality of his death cell, Iskander Hyder imagines himself in a dream dreamed by someone else:

> If it is a dream, and sometimes in the fever of his days he thinks it is, then (he also knows) the dreamer is someone else. He is inside the dream, or he would not be able to touch dream-insects; dream-water would not burn him[;] ... someone is dreaming him. God, then? No, not God. He struggles to remember Raza Hyder's face.
>
>   ... The General of whom this cell is one small aspect, who is general, omnipresent, omnivorous: it is a cell inside his head.... *From darkness into light, from nothingness into somethingness. I made him, I was his father, he is my seed.* ... An inversion: the parent become child. *He is turning me into his son.*
>
>   His son. Who emerged dead from the womb with a noose about his neck. *That noose seals my fate.* ... *Yes: I am being unmade.* (*Shame*, 253–54; italics in original)

To dream seems to father reality as one's child. In this "monologue of a hanged man," Isky tries to assert his consciousness even as he imagines it as constituted by another's dream, imprisoned in the cell that replicates the brain cell of his mortal adversary, in a dream of himself that dreams him into "unmaking."

Rendered in bodily terms, dreams seem to have the power to make *and* unmake, to create *and* to violate. Isky imagines himself as another's child, being made by another's dream, just as Saleem reminds Padma that in Hindu theology "Brahma dreamed, is dreaming the universe," or our reality (*MC*, 253).

This one-sided model of coercive power, of a consciousness constituted by another's dreams, is revised in a powerful paradigm in *The Satanic Verses* to one of a peculiar reciprocity of coproduction that makes the dreamer indistinguishable from the dreamed. When the actor Gibreel Farishta dreams his revisionary dream of himself as Gibreel the angel of Revelation, he dreams of himself dreamed by Mahound, so that Mahound's coercive dream of Gibreel is impossible without Gibreel simultaneously dreaming of Mahound: "[A]nd now Gibreel, who has been hovering-above-looking-down, feels a confusion, *who am I*, in these moments it begins to seem that the archangel is actually *inside the Prophet*, I am the dragging in the gut, I am the angel being extruded from the sleeper's navel, I emerge, Gibreel Farishta, while my other self, Mahound, lies *listening*, entranced, I am bound to him, navel to navel, by a shining cord of light, not possible to say which of us is dreaming the other. We flow in both directions along the umbilical cord."[17] In this strange dynamic that conflates the language of organic production with that of discursive creation, the dreamers are connected, each to each, by an umbilical cord of light: each constitutes the other's dream, born of the other *and* creating the other from his own imaginative desire. Dreams are thus fiercely material, bodily, in their power to create. They are also coercive: in their co-dreamed encounter about the satanic verses, Gibreel Farishta dreams of himself as the Angel Gibreel, dreamed by Mahound's will into giving the counterrevelation that dismisses the satanic verses (111–12). In his dream, Mahound forces Gibreel to dream of what Mahound wants, attributing it to Gibreel, and then making his own dream a reality. The reproductive image of navels connected by a golden cord of light also insists on the *mutuality* of this coproduction. It is repeated in Gibreel's waking life and Rushdie's narrative (which becomes increasingly indistinguishable from Gibreel's dreams) when Gibreel's presence is similarly needed to complete the stories of Rosa Diamond. Just before her death, Gibreel finds that she "needed him to complete the last revelation. As with the businessman of his dreams [Mahound], he felt helpless, ignorant. . . . [S]he seemed to know, however, how to draw the images from him. Linking the two of them, navel to navel, he saw a shining cord" (SV, 154). If this bodily, connective mutuality, this relation of storyteller and listener, represents a dynamic of coproduction, so does the relation of dreamers who dream each other into being, where one dreamer coerces the other into what he dreams to be his own subjection. In such a model of the constitutive power of dreams, the relation between subjecthood and objecthood is collapsed: the dreamer is also the dreamed; each needs the other to dream him into being. Gibreel's capacity for receptivity enables the production of stories—from Mahound as well as Rosa Diamond. And indeed for the entire text, the dream is both the cause and the result, the producer and the product, of the narrative.[18]

In *Midnight's Children* and *Shame*, dreams also provide a form of magical foreknowledge that is validated by the text itself. Saleem's grandmother, for example, dreams her daughters' dreams to discover their secrets and desires (45, 60). These dreams, like those of Saleem's insane Aunt Sonia, are "true" in that they form a mode of access to hidden knowledge and can therefore be used as instruments of control. Such control by means of dreams also suggests an allegory of a narrator's power of storytelling, for Saleem too is able to dream his grandfather's dream of himself as "a crumbling old man" with a "gigantic shadow," a hole in the center of his body (224). This kind of psychic knowledge of his grandfather's secret self-image grants Saleem the power to narrate, to invade and know family secrets as decisively as his grandmother does.

At other times, dreams are "true" in that no matter how fantastic they may seem, they anticipate future events or serve as prophecies that are fulfilled by the narrative. Just before his death, Raza is visited in a dream by Sindbad Mengal, the man he had vindictively murdered and dismembered, who warns him of his own impending death (*Shame*, 301–2). That Raza's subsequent death almost exactly replicates Mengal's death suggests the nature of dreams both as a form of magical, truthful revelation and as a re-vision of something past. Saleem's companion, Shaheed, has recurring dreams of his imminent death by way of a "bright pomegranate" (*MC*, 421), which is fulfilled by his being blasted by a grenade that he sees as "a pomegranate, . . . like a light-bulb" in his head, the very "grenade of his dreams" (450). The dream thus becomes such a figurative pomegranate, with verbal and semantic play on *pomegranate/grenade*, as a container bursting with seed, spilling not fertility but destruction, an explosive image of light that sheds fatal foreknowledge.

This constitutive and truth-bearing power of dreams suggests that these dreams have a predictive or causal relation to the future, that they constitute the plot of narrative and of history. Saleem's uncanny dream of his classmate's death, for instance, transmutes foreknowledge into agency. He wakes to hear that Jimmy had indeed died of a heart attack: "Is it possible to kill a human being by dreaming his death? My mother always said so; and, in that case, Jimmy Kapadia was my first murder victim" (298). To dream an event seems to inscribe it on the parchment of the future.

Shame more explicitly presents the dreamer as a figure for the writer. Omar Khayyam, named after the famous poet, has continuous dreams that carry multiple meanings, giving him access to truths about past and future. Sara Suleri has read him as a "surrogate" for the ineffectual Rushdiean narrator (*Rhetoric*, 188), but as we have seen, Omar is not ineffectual: he "affects" the course of history despite his "position on the periphery" (*Shame*, 116); he refuses to follow Raza's orders to kill Sufiya, allowing her to wreak vengeance across the nation (258); and he lets slip secret information that irrevocably changes the relationships of the "central figures" of "history" (116). Moreover, such readings do not account for the power of Omar's dreams, which grant him an inexplicable omniscience, a strange mode of relating past and future, and even the capacity to dream—and determine—the end of the narrative.

Soon after he meets Sufiya Zinobia, Omar has "vivid dreams of the past," of his teacher and chosen "father," Eduardo Rodrigues. He later realizes that the dreams were

> prescient warnings against the dangers of falling in love with under-age females and then following them to the ends of the earth, where they inevitably cast you aside, the blast of their rejection picking you up and hurling you into the great starry nothingness beyond gravity and sense. He recalled the end of the dream, in which Eduardo, his white garments now blackened and tattered and singed, seemed to be flying away from him, floating above a bursting cloud of fire, with one hand raised above his head, as if in farewell.... [A] father is a warning; but he is also a lure, a precedent impossible to resist, and so by the time that Omar Khayyam deciphered his dreams it was already far too late to take their advice, because he had already fallen for his destiny, Sufiya Zinobia Hyder, a twelve-year-old girl with a three-year-old mind, the daughter of the man who had killed his brother. (153)

These dreams combine repetition of the past (Omar's teenage impregnation of the underage Farah, whom Rodrigues subsequently married) with a synoptic knowledge of the future. In fact, this dream becomes a moment that forms a narratival centerfold in the novel, as it unfolds the mirroring of past and future. It prefigures the rest of the narrative, in which Sufiya (or Shame) is the "underage female" for love of whom Omar goes to his death, and it presents Omar's future as a repetition of the fate of Eduardo. It is also a miniature replica of the ending of the novel, almost as if this dream in the middle of the narrative determines its end. After Omar Khayyam's death at the hands of Shame, the narrator concludes, "And then the explosion comes, a shock-wave that demolishes the house, and after it the fireball of her burning, rolling outwards to the horizon like the sea, and last of all the cloud, which rises and spreads and hangs over the nothingness of the scene, until I can no longer see what is no longer there; the silent cloud, in the shape of a giant, grey and headless man, a figure of dreams, a phantom with one arm lifted in a gesture of farewell" (317). Someone else (or is it still Omar Khayyam?), the narrating "I," now witnesses what Omar (fore)saw in his dreams. The omniscient power of Omar Khayyam's dream foreshadows and merges with that of the narrator-dreamer who narrates (or dreams) the end and suddenly intrudes as a hitherto unintroduced "I" who can "no longer see." It is as if, in death, Omar Khayyam the dreamer passes the baton of dreams to the narrator who dreams the end of the narrative that Omar dreamed into being. In an exemplification of its structure, the dream-cloud over which Eduardo presided in the first dream has become what constitutes him. He is now the silent cloud itself, as if the dream is what gives shape to the figure. That first dream of Omar Khayyam seems to create what it dreams, as it shapes the narrative and its conclusion.

At the end of the novel, Omar Khayyam's uncanny dreams again blur the boundaries between foreknowledge and predetermination. Upon his last return to Nishapur, Omar is plunged into a delirious fever that engenders a series of hallucinatory dreams. ("Nishapur" can be translated as both "the place of dreams, or land of illusion" and, by extension, "a drugged state.") The inescapable "mother-country" that gave birth to him thus also produces his dreams, and to it he must return to dream his own death. "The fever was a fire that made you cold. It burned away the barriers between consciousness and sleep, so that Omar Khayyam never knew whether things were really happening or not. . . .

In his delirium, . . . in the burning clutches of the sickness and the foetid atmosphere of the house, only endings seemed possible. He could feel things caving in within him. . . . 'This motor,' he said aloud somewhere in that halted time, 'will not run any more'" (*Shame*, 302). The phantasmagoria of this dream state seems to infect the narrative as well, burning away the boundaries between sickness and knowledge, dream and reality, dream-within-narrative and narrative-as-dream. This dream extends into visions that become forms of knowledge that are validated by the narrative that seems to exist beyond the dream yet, by its correspondence with the dream, begins to merge with the dream. Omar's dreaming knowledge of "endings" is ratified when he wakes, or dreams he wakes, beside his three mothers, to have them confirm his knowledge of his own imminent death. His deliriously uttered words, "this motor . . . will not run any more," they tell him, are an exact replication of his great-grandfather's dying words, which thus indicated his great-grandfather's foreknowledge of his own death. Thus, Omar's unknowing dreaming repetition of a familial tradition becomes a touchstone of truthful prophecy. The words also register Omar's uncanny knowledge of a family secret: that his great-grandfather's death, occasioned by a wife's adultery and brother's revenge, occurred with these very words (307). As the dream blurs into Rushdie's narrative, logical distinctions fall away, as the text seems to embrace irreconcilable possibilities that characterize dreams and validate them as true.

Omar is now presented as simultaneously, alogically, occupying the position both of a character within the novel and of the omniscient narrator, as one who acts both in ignorance *and* in omniscience, occupying a position both within *and* without the narrative. His dreams seem a "sickness" that foretell not only his own death and the death of his narrative but also knowledge of events after his death, pointing, like the fisherman's finger, to truths beyond the frame of his narrative: "During recessions in the fever he remembered dreaming things that he could not have known were true, visions of the future, of what would happen after the end" (306). How does Omar know, in his dream, that Raza has been dismembered, "neatly sliced" by Omar's mothers' contraption of knives, an event of which we are informed in the framing narrative that supposedly occurs in the "real" world outside of Omar's dream? Is the narrative also part of his dream? Is the narrative, indeed, itself his dream? If he has dreams within dreams in his dream, then what separates the narrative we read from his dream? As the narrative of *Shame* winds to a close, it seems to swerve almost defiantly into the open, turning compulsively to the structure of dreams as if to rescue itself from the finitude of ending, bursting into a proliferation of questions and possibilities suggested by the multivalent, open structure of the dream.

Like Saleem, Omar Khayyam dreams of the future, of a narrative that continues beyond his death. "Great powers shifting their ground, deciding the army had become unstable. And at last Arjumand and Harappa set free, reborn into power, the Virgin Ironpants and her only love taking charge. The fall of God, and in his place the myth of Martyr Iskander. And after that arrests, retribution, trials, hangings, blood, a new cycle of shamelessness and shame" (306). Omar Khayyam's penultimate dream sequence thus combines knowledge of both past and future, both of which seem to be suddenly opened up to him.[19] His dreams blur the boundaries between prophecy and agency, foreknowledge and causality, dream and narration, imagination and truth. What Omar dreams becomes his story, as if he dreams it into being.

In *Midnight's Children*, Saleem has a dream that parallels the power of Omar Khayyam's, and that, in its deliberate dismissal of knowledge in the face of death, offers some important clues for reading the strange dream-endings of Rushdie's novels. After his return to India from the 1971 war in Bangladesh, Saleem finds shelter in the house of his uncle Mustapha, from whom he learns of the deaths of his parents and of the disappearance of Jamila, his sister, who "had been driven a little crazy by the news" of Saleem's alleged death in Bengal: "[S]he, purest of the pure, . . . turned rebel when she heard about my death. . . . Two days after her tirade against the perpetrators of the war, my sister had disappeared off the face of the earth. Uncle Mustapha tried to speak gently: 'Very bad things are happening over there, [Pakistan] Saleem; people are disappearing all the time; we must fear the worst'" (*MC*, 469).

Saleem responds to such knowledge by dreaming another ending for his sister:

> No! No no no! Padma: he was wrong! Jamila did not disappear into the clutches of the State: because that same night, I dreamed that she, in the shadows of darkness and the secrecy of a simple veil, . . . fled by air from the capital city; and there she is arriving in Karachi, unquestioned unarrested free, she is taking a taxi into the depths of the city, and now there is a high wall

with bolted doors and hatch through which, once, long ago, I received bread, the leavened bread of my sister's weakness, she is asking to be let in, nuns are opening doors as she cries sanctuary, yes, there she is, safely inside, doors being bolted behind her, exchanging one kind of invisibility for another, . . . yes, she is there, safe, not vanished, not in the grip of police who kick beat starve, but at rest, not in an unmarked grave by the side of the Indus, but alive, baking bread, singing sweetly to the secret nuns; I know, I know, I know. How do I know? A brother knows; that's all. (MC, 469–70)

Where once Saleem's dream of the Emergency provided an alternative mode of describing the unspeakable, the otherwise unimaginable, here the dream becomes a much more ambiguous mode that teeters between denial, self-deception, knowing, repudiating, and coping. This powerful account of Saleem's dream opens up not only the simple question of what happened to Jamila (for the narrative neither corroborates nor repudiates this dream) but also the problem of how we are to read such dreams and their presentation and, by extension, Rushdie's narrative, which is in part built upon such dreams.

Given the magical validity and truth value ascribed to dreams in *Midnight's Children* and the telepathic powers of Saleem the midnight's child, we have been prepared to believe that Saleem's dream of his sister is "true": it must be a reflection of reality, a valorized form of access to a knowledge denied to others. Like Saleem's dream of the death of Jimmy Kapadia or Shaheed's dream of the pomegranate or Naseem Aziz's dreams of her daughter's dreams, this dream too appears to be a form of knowledge before which we must suspend our disbelief. The cinematic reporting of Jamila's actions even as they seem to happen, as Saleem seems to witness them, merging the present of his observation with the immediacy of her escape, suggests almost a psychic form of sight.

At the same time, however, the novel also carries an alternative strain within which dreams are discredited, rendered synonymous with fantasy, unreality, even folly. Earlier, for instance, befuddled by drink and failure, Saleem's father, Ahmed Sinai, had succumbed to the "dream-world of disturbing unreality" (240), thereby becoming unable to fulfill his "daydream (of) . . . reshaping the Quran" (155), and then had fallen victim to the "dream" of land reclamation of Bombay's beaches (156) that led to financial disaster. The tawdry "Pioneer Café" where Amina Sinai secretly visits her former husband is described as "the repository of dreams," the resort of actors whose dreams had failed.

Saleem's Uncle Hanif, the self-proclaimed "high-priest of reality," wants to write film scripts about poverty, exploitation, and agrarian economies that will "wake up" the nation that, he claims, "had been dreaming for five thousand years" (292). Such instances code dreams negatively as irresponsibly opposed to "reality," as leading to failure. In fact, when Saleem has this dream of Jamila, he too has another "dream": "of saving the nation" (470–71). Thus, Saleem's own dreams at this point are set up as absurd, misplaced, and hopeless.

Saleem's dream of Jamila could hence be read as willful self-deception, as a self-knowing refusal to know what it knows, the overinsistent stridency of which betrays its own knowledge of its futility against the likelihood of unspeakable reality. Why else, even as he describes the dream, does Saleem paint the alternative scenario of police brutality and murder and contrast it with the saccharine quality of his vision of Jamila "singing sweetly to the nuns"? Why else does his syntax repeat the structure of overemphatic negation, of "not . . . not . . . not," and his final "I know, I know, I know" that is undermined by its consonance with the opening "no no no"? And if Saleem recognizes the hopelessness of his dream, then are all dreams to be read as offering such Nietzschean fictions, willing belief despite knowledge of their fictionality?

However, the dreams that are stigmatized as fallacious and harmful in Rushdie's narratives are self-aggrandizing projects for the future, to be distinguished, therefore, from the dream visions that are indices of a validated knowledge: dreams that people dream as *narratives* (instead of projects) come "true" and have a meaning that may be "deciphered." Against the undermining of dreams suggested by Saleem's comment that the generation of his son, Aadam, will be more powerful and effective because Aadam "does not . . . surrender to dreams" (507) stands the validation of dreams in the episode of the Sundarbans, the therapeutic "dream-forest." Like the umbilical cord of light in Gibreel's dreams, here too dreams give materiality, color, and substance to bodies—for through the loss of those dreams they become unreal. This dream of Jamila, then, can also be such a dream, more real than waking reality.

Saleem's dream of Jamila offers at least two mutually incompatible endings to the story of his sister, neither of which can be given priority over the other. Indeed, the nature of such dream visions seems to be the creation of narratival undecidability, to offer irreconcilable endings that must coexist in a narrative tension that refuses closure or limitation to a single possibility. While the dream insists on its own validity, it frames itself in its own negation, producing both possibilities as simultaneous. Jamila lives on in Saleem's narrative, reappearing ghoulishly to prevent the consummation of his relationship with Parvati. (Parvati, the third most powerful of the midnight's children, the only true magician in the magician's colony, is also Saleem's midnight's child "sister" and so appropriately merges with Jamila, Saleem's other "sister.") Saleem interprets Jamila's ghostly recrudescence as a materialization of his guilt for his adolescent incestuous desire for her:

> [A]s I kissed [Parvati] in the dark of that illicit moonlight I had seen her face changing, becoming the face of a forbidden love; the ghostly features of Jamila Singer replaced those of the witch-girl; Jamila who was (I know it!) safely hidden in a Karachi nunnery was suddenly also here, except that she had undergone a dark transformation. She had begun to rot, the dreadful pustules and cankers of forbidden love were spreading across her face. . . . [T]he rancid flowers of incest blossomed on my sister's phantasmal features, and I couldn't do it, couldn't kiss touch look upon that intolerable spectral face. (MC, 473)

This ghastly palimpsest of memories in which one woman's disfigured features are superimposed on another's can, however, also be read as a manifestation of Saleem's knowledge of Jamila's death. What he sees psychically are the features, not of guilt, but of a decaying, perhaps mutilated corpse, a vision that extends and materializes from the negation of his earlier dream as Jamila's features appear increasingly blotched in each successive vision. The next time he sees "(his) distant vanished sister . . . no, not my sister . . . the putrid, vilely disfigured face of Jamila Singer" (479).[20] Again, Saleem's recurrent dream both ensures Jamila's life—as it perpetuates her being in this way in the narrative—and suggests her death, physically concretized in the image of a corpse, decaying like memory. The vision negates that earlier dream, yet in substituting its own dreamlike vision, it again validates the power of dreams. Denial is accompanied by affirmation, and knowledge of death by an uncanny, impossible perpetuation.

Dreams clearly offer an alternative form of truth telling and knowledge of reality in Rushdie's narratives. But the structure of dreams that Rushdie constructs does still more. Dreams offer not only a measure of truth telling, and a form of externally validated prophecy, but also the alogical possibility (neither logical nor illogical but outside of structures of logic) of simultaneously maintaining both truth telling and doubt, of a fundamental structure of undecidability that seems to be necessary, he suggests, as a strategy of openness for the conclusion of postcolonial narrative. By collapsing logical restrictions into fantasy, prediction, and simultaneous possibility and impossibility, Rushdie makes possible an ending that disallows definitive meaning or closure and suggests the manifold future possibilities in the face of disaster. In addition, he suggests implicitly, such a structure impels the continuity of postcolonial nations, of the stories they tell themselves to perpetuate themselves. Saleem's dream of Jamila, and its structure of undecidability that resists narratival closure, becomes, like Omar Khayyam's ongoing dreams, a mode of reading the narrative of each dreamer-narrator, particularly of their endings. Both *Midnight's Children* and *Shame* end as dream visions, and these dreams set up by the narrative—Saleem's of Jamila and Omar Khayyam's of his own death—provide a language to make sense of the endings of each novel. For this understanding of dreams—as at once material, true, and alogical, bodily with bodily effects and felt as bodily sensations—is what provides Rushdie with a novel form of postcolonial literary agency: to open up the endings of his narratives, to defy the limitations of closure, to suggest ways of imagining and hence *making* unending possibilities for a postcolonial future.

The Empty Jar and the Problem of Ending

Two pages before the end of *Midnight's Children*, Saleem interrupts his narrative yet again, apparently to consult his readers on how to construct a suitable ending. Offering four alternatives, Saleem openly addresses the problem of ending, as if talking about the problem might provide an ending in itself:

> One empty jar ... how to end? Happily, with Mary in her teak rocking chair and a son who has begun to speak? Amid recipes, and thirty jars with chapter-headings for names? In melancholy, drowning in memories of Jamila and Parvati ... ? Or with the magic children ... but then, should I be glad that some escaped, or end in the tragedy of the disintegrating effects of drainage? ...
> Or with questions: now that I can, I swear, see the cracks on the backs of my hands, ... why do I not bleed? Am I already so emptied, desiccated, pickled?

> Or dreams: because last night the ghost of Reverend Mother appeared to me, staring down through the hole in a perforated cloud, waiting for my death. . . .
> No, that won't do, I shall write the future as I have written the past, to set it down with the absolute certainty of a prophet. But the future cannot be preserved in a jar; one jar must remain empty. . . . What cannot be pickled because it has not yet taken place, is that I shall reach my birthday, thirty-one today, and no doubt a marriage will take place. (MC, 550)

These penultimate metanarratival reflections set up several questions: How can a story this varied and gargantuan—not of an individual but of a nation, of all those swallowed lives—be rounded off? How can history ever end? What are the implications of setting up the "ending" as a problem? How exactly is it a problem? And why, having rejected the option of "dreams" as a form for ending, does the novel end as a dream vision of its narrator's death?

Saleem's ellipsis in "One empty jar . . . how to end?" places the problem of closure at the center of the sentence, as the central problem, a gap, as if unable to end with a period, opening up the sentence as a question. One option is to end "happily," in accordance with the plot of comedy, which, as Northrop Frye describes, ends with the overcoming of obstacles, the reconciliation of generations and the passing of power from parents to children.[21] Finally, after all the wars, losses, and deaths, Saleem is reunited with Mary Pereira, the closest he has to family. Aadam, his son (and the heir to this story), will both perpetuate and embody the perpetuation of Saleem's story. But evidently this option is not satisfying, perhaps because it does not account for much in the past. Another formal option is the tragic, ending "in melancholy" and mourning. But there are still things to celebrate, such as the escape of some of the midnight's children. Each option that Saleem suggests seems inadequate, for each spawns further possibilities, new openings, willing the story to continue, to burst into a further proliferation of plot.

Dissatisfied with conventional plots, Saleem turns to more "questions." Asking why his dying body does not "bleed," he looks back to the syncopation of body and story, of language and the "juicy" materiality of bodily fluids that generated his narrative but now seem to be as "mummified" as Bariamma's stories in *Shame*. Is this what happens to all stories as they congeal, and is Saleem's lament for his bloodless body also Rushdie's lament for the inevitable rigidification of his once-proliferating narration now headed for termination? Such an inability to bleed suggests the encroaching death of the story as well as of the storyteller, for both have reached an unwanted stasis, an inability to live, flow, and change.

On his shelf stand thirty pickled jars of Saleem's "special blends" (548), with each jar representing each of the thirty chapters of *Midnight's Children* (and each year of his life), which preserve Saleem's history for his "amnesiac nation" of readers (549). Yet now he announces that in this thirtieth final chapter, when the thirtieth pickle jar is not yet closed, there stands a thirty-first jar that "must remain empty" as the narrative of thirty chapters winds to a close, because the future will continue beyond his narrative. As this last chapter, or thirtieth jar, approaches fullness, the thirty-first jar must represent the openness of further possibility. Is it too literal minded, then, to ask which one is the last jar—the one that is almost full or the one standing empty? If the thirtieth jar/chapter contains the thirty-first within it even before it ends, then where, if at all, and how, is the narrative to end? At what point is the last jar to be full, the last chapter to end, if it contains the emptiness of the next one within it?

This splitting of jars, trivial though it may seem, reiterates the problem of ending that becomes the pressing concern of the concluding pages of the narrative.[22] Saleem's guise of ineffectuality and vacillation belies Rushdie's very serious wrestling with the problem of endings, a problem that he engages with in all his narratives, and one that carries implications extending beyond his narratives. The problem of ending Saleem's story reflects the problem of ending his and his nation's history. If Saleem's story is also the story of his nation and the story of postcolonial narration, then how can or *should* it be concluded? Is this where the generic energies of the novel and of historiography diverge? Given the teleological presuppositions of novelistic closure, would not a too rounded closure to Saleem's story preempt (indeed, foreclose) the future of the histories it also tells? Given Rushdie's troubling over the problems of beginnings, and his theorizing its multiple causality and directionality in terms of the familial network of the family tree, the problem of ending becomes the counterproblem that raises questions about the perpetuation of postcolonial history or narrative and the artificiality of human design in presuming to shape its ends. What kind of agency can a postcolonial novel have if it cannot imagine a future or leave it open?

There is a difference, as Barbara Hernstein Smith points out, between "ceasing" and "concluding," between merely stopping and providing closure: "We tend to speak of conclusions when a sequence of events has a relatively high degree of structure, when . . . we can perceive these events as related to one another by some principle of organization or design that implies the existence of a definite termination point. . . . The sense of stable conclusiveness, finality, or 'clinch' which we experience at that point is what is referred to here as *closure*."[23] Thus, closure is "gratifying" because it releases often deliberately built up tension, making the end yet more satisfying, and because it casts meaning retrospectively upon the whole that is past, enabling a rereading of what one has read. Closure "announces and justifies the absence of a further development; it reinforces the feeling of finality, completion, and composure . . . ; it gives ultimate unity and coherence to the reader's experience . . . by providing a point from which all the preceding elements may be viewed comprehensively and their relations grasped as part of a significant design" (Smith, 36). Indeed, Frank Kermode argues that all narratives are sustained by a tension between their desire to reach the end (which is what impels narrative) and the opposite desire to defer that end (which is what sustains narrative).[24] Man's position "in the middest" (164), Kermode writes, between birth and death and between the beginning and ending of the world occasions the need for "end-determined fictions" (6), for the apocalyptic desire for meaning, so that "the paradigms of apocalypse continue to lie under our ways of making sense of the world" (28). This desire shapes not only literature but also the stories that we tell ourselves in discourses as varied as religion, science, and history. Contrary to this may seem the desire to "postpone the end" (36), to delay it by means of a complicated plot, but that very delay *enhances* the end, creating, as in the structure of peripeteia, by the rectification of falsified expectations, a greater sense of "reality" (18). In fact, Peter Brooks's quite self-consciously erotic, even phallic, model of narrative propulsion places the resistance to closure in the service of a *heightened* closure, which privileges closure as the desired end, as the consummation of narrative.[25] All these accounts of the narrative desire for ending, and of the resistance to the ending, share a sense of the preeminence that narratives confer upon their ending, even when the narratives appear to defer or subvert those endings.

However, Rushdie's resistance to closure is concerned not with the dynamics of delay to heighten the end but with actual deferral and dispersion, in a form of narrative that recognizes the inevitability of ending but attempts to undermine both its finality and its importance. His narratives celebrate multiple possibilities; they attempt to generate a proliferation of constructive openings for postcolonial narration and imagined futures. If, as Kermode suggests, endings provide the final meaning for all that precede them, then Rushdie's preference for beginnings and his aversion to endings signify an aversion to that closure of meaning, a horror that the family tree will converge to a point instead of opening to a widening network. Moreover, Rushdie's narratives resist closure because, they suggest, postcolonial narration cannot afford to wait till the end; it cannot postpone or abdicate in faith of a future its responsibility to its present. Therefore, it must resist the tradition of locating meaning and knowledge in a point of termination and favors instead a feisty continual struggle with meaning that loops together present, past, and future. Yet the genre of the novel, as of any text, necessitates ending, and Rushdie's narrative is cognizant of the need to stop, though questioning the need to close.[26]

As a consequence, Rushdie's narratives self-consciously foreground their trouble over endings, either (as in *Midnight's Children*) by signaling that trouble and talking obsessively about it or (as in *Shame* and *The Satanic Verses*) by contriving an ending so absurd, arbitrary, and dissatisfying to narratival expectations that it calls attention to its own artifice and conventionality. They foreground their resistance to closure by exploring the effects of such resistance on narration itself. They ask their reader to become interested in what happens to a narrative that is aware of the necessities of ending, that is then marked by its foreknowledge of an encroaching end, and that reshapes itself to resist the ending, not to delay but to withstand the totalizing, even colonizing force of closure. This is thus also a good example of how the formal and political dimensions of Rushdie's writing dovetail. Drawing an analogy between the imperialism of nations and of locating meaning of the whole in the end, Frank Kermode connects "the mythology of Empire and of Apocalypse" (6–10) (in Kermode's case, the empire of Revelation and the Roman Empire, the "End" from which Virgil gave meaning to the epic of Aeneas) to suggest that a hermeneutic imperialism coincides with imperialisms of power, privileging closure as the mode by which meanings are also enclosed and controlled. Rushdie's horror of closure, of the foreclosure of meaning, is thus consonant with his postcolonial politics, finding its aesthetic correspondence in a resistance to ending, to colonizing a text by claiming to know it fully or by circumscribing its potential to signify. Rushdie is thus interested in the *dis*-closure of how a narrative inscribes its anticipation of its end into its ending pages, how it articulates and is shaped by its reluctance or refusal to end.

In *Midnight's Children*, syncopating the imminent death of the narrator with that of the narrative, the narrative becomes clogged by such moments of ominous anticipation and foreboding:

> Scraps of memory: this is not how a climax should be written. A climax should surge towards its Himalayan peak; but I am left with broken shreds, and must jerk towards crisis like a puppet with broken strings. This is not what I had planned; but perhaps the story you finish is never the one you begin. . . . if I began again, would I, too, end in a different place? Well then, I must content myself with shreds and scraps: as I wrote centuries ago, the trick is to fill in the gaps, guided by the few clues one is given. Most of what matters in our lives takes place in our absence. (MC, 509)

Saleem has begun to see himself as increasingly absent from his own narrative, removed from the centrality that he once occupied. This dissatisfaction becomes the subject of the narrative that is now propelled by its own sense of its poignancy, its regret at its own inadequacy. The text is continually marked by such signs of its ending and by Saleem's laments over his approaching end, the most chilling sign of which is his sudden uninterest in new stories, the surest sign, as Durga tells him, of death (532–33).

Yet at the same time, this waning desire for new stories is coupled with Saleem's refusal to end the stories that accompany his, to give them closure. In pursuit of Mary Pereira (the mother he thought lost), he leaves Picture Singh (his surrogate father) and that story dangling. "I do not know the end of the story of Picture Singh; he refused to accompany me on my quest, and I saw in his eyes that . . . his victory was in fact a defeat; but whether he is still in Bombay . . . or back with his washerwoman; whether he is still alive or not, I am unable to say" (544). Picture Singh's story seems to continue by itself, as if by relinquishing it, by allowing it to diverge from his, Saleem is offering it the possibility of continuity unavailable to himself. This deliberately frustrating incompletion becomes a form of overt resistance to closure: Picture Singh is left in the middle of a street, turning away to an unknown destination, continuing his story in a parallel universe that cannot dovetail with Saleem's.

Thus Saleem, as both narrator and subject of his narrative, seems caught between two contradictory drives: to know and acknowledge the ineluctability of approaching death (of both narrative and narrator); and to create possibilities of continuity beyond it. On the one hand, Saleem expresses his foreknowledge of the end, his almost psychic certainty of imminent annihilation acquired through his telepathic communion with clocks and their meaning—and indeed, his desire to welcome or preempt the end that is coming. In this he exemplifies the repetition-compulsion that Peter Brooks describes in relation to the death drive: in the repetition of a nonpleasurable experience, one chooses the inevitable to exert mastery over it (*Reading*, 98). Before the bomb destroys his entire family (and his memory and history) in 1965, Saleem knows that "time is counting down to an end, not a birth" (*MC*, 391), and he drives around in the streets, "looking for death" (*MC*, 407). In another instance, just before the Emergency of 1975 destroys his new family of magicians, he awaits the end, for he alone can hear "the inexorable sound of the future stealing upon [them]" (*MC*, 496).

On the other hand, however, at each of these moments, he also articulates the possibility of continuity, of circumventing these deaths. This can take the form of inserting into his narrative his foreknowledge of the continuity of his narrative beyond his own death. At Aadam's birth, he writes that "as my time of connection [to history] neared its end, his began" (500): Aadam, an infant possibility, will continue Saleem's link to his nation and grow perhaps into another language. Alternatively, the very fact of continuing his narrative after talking about ending confounds the ending: "But now time is counting down to an end, not a birth; there is, too, a weariness to be mentioned, a general fatigue so profound that the end when it comes, will be the only solution, because human beings, like nations and fictional characters, can simply run out of steam, and then there is nothing else for it but to finish with them" (391). This seems to convey an irrevocable finality with the deaths of family and of narrative, but this moment of ending occurs in the very center of the novel: despite its "fatigue," Saleem's narrative continues beyond each ending to new chapters and new beginnings (414). For all the foreboding that accompanies such moments of climactic disaster in the novel (which often occur at midnight, that numinous, transitional moment), moments that Saleem calls endings, each is accompanied by continuity, by a phoenix-like renewal of narrative. So when we finally arrive at the end of the novel—and at Saleem's midnight death, which echoes syntactically (in its two-page single sentence) the pseudo-ending of Saleem's family—and repeats the same language of fatigue and inevitability, the narrative has taught us as readers to suspect such an ending and to read it for its concurrent signs of continuity.

After the "ectomies" of the Emergency, Saleem laments the end of the midnight's children: "O insidious nostalgia for times of greater possibility, before history, like a street behind the General Post Office in Delhi, narrowed down to this final full point!" (519). This is the end of the powers of the children, who "were are shall be the gods you never had" (522), and the termination of the possibilities promised by the proliferating powers of the children and of his narrative. "History," once imagined as an infinite network of possibility, has become narrowed to a "final full point," the period that terminates narration. But in its very defiance of temporality and syntax (the children "shall" be gods), the sentence suggests its links to a future. In this unexpected metaphor, the "street behind the General Post Office in Delhi," narrow blind alley that it may seem, is adjacent to the post office—the place from where the letter is transmitted, the nexus of national and international communication and of the circulation of writing. The end that seems a halt is adjunct to the point of dissemination; continuity emanates from even this "point" of termination. This tension between these two oppositional directions for the narrative—simultaneously accepting what is posited as an external force of death, *and* suggesting modes of continuity—constitutes the resistance to closure in *Midnight's Children*, for the tension is maintained unresolved.

Midnight's Children then ends with a two-page sentence—separated from the rest of the text as the future may be separate from the present, or the imagined from the lived—that is presented in the form of a dream vision, Saleem's dream of his own death. This last dream reflects Saleem's powers of knowledge that extends, like Omar Khayyam's, to events beyond his death: Saleem dreams of his death as a repetition of his grandmother's death by bombing, surrounded by a smoke cloud that shaped itself into an image of her framed in a hole in a cloud (408). Like Omar Khayyam's dreams, it syncopates the past and the future: the past reappears in the guise of Saleem's grandmother's death and the motif of the hole in the sheet; while the future is adumbrated in a synopsis of what will occur later. That last option of the dream, then, seems to be the one he finally chooses, for it includes all the options that he has tabulated into its inclusive, alogical structure. Clearly, the form of the dream is what provides a solution of some sort to this problem of endings.

In fact, most of Rushdie's important novels end with dreams, presenting and then addressing the problem of ending in different forms. The narrative of *Shame*, as we have seen, turns self-consciously to metaphors of explosion and apocalypse, articulated through dreams dreamed by both Omar and the narrator. The doubling of the headless Omar with both Isky and Rodriguez in the figure of the cloud and the repetition of Omar's prophetic dream emphasize the structure of excess, of doubling and repetition that characterizes this ending. Such a structure of excess, in which violent deaths are repeated and multiplied and no single event seems adequate, suggests that the very excess calls attention to its inadequacy, to its inability to provide satisfactory closure, and indeed itself deliberately demonstrates the absurdity of such an imposition of closure. Moreover, the structure of dreams seems to provide the strangely dual possibility of both fragmentation and excessive closure: for while the fragmentation suggests the scattering of meaning, the repeated endings also represent the huge (and hugely inefficacious) attempts to end.

The repeated valedictory figure of the dream, the "phantom with one arm lifted in a gesture of farewell," suggests a figure for this narratival resistance to closure. The repeated farewells—of Omar, of Rodrigues, and of Rushdie himself—signify the failure of each to work: the repetition of the valedictory gesture emphasizes its inefficacy, inviting further repetition in a cycle that expresses both the desire to bid farewell and the need to undermine that farewell. Thus, an inverted double of the phenomenon of incompletion is that of excess. The repeated endings, the overdramatic explosions that subvert the possibilities and desire for closure by giving it *too* much closure are another form of calling attention to the artifices of ending, as if ending were a compulsion forced upon this narrative that refutes death by seeking it. In the very excess—the repetition, the melodrama, the self-conscious overdoing of attempts to close that only underline their own failure—lies another form of resistance to closure. Many critics have expressed, for different reasons, their disappointment with *Shame*'s ending.[27] Yet that disappointment may be precisely evoked and shared by the narrative itself, as symptomatic of the limitations of providing closure. The final moments, frequently seen as apocalyptic, are a mimicry of apocalypse: in ending thus, the novel defrauds its reader of an ending, rendering itself as *anti*-apocalyptic by refusing to congeal or solidify into any form of revelation or meaning.

The Satanic Verses provides two endings: one that teaches the skeptical Mirza Saeed to die by "opening," and one that self-consciously mimics the endings of conventional plots. In his final dream vision (dreamed via Gibreel), which ends the penultimate chapter, "The Parting of the Arabian Sea," Mirza Saeed "opens" to the faith that he has resisted—after he realizes that he was the only one present to fail to see the miraculous opening of the sea promised by the prophet Ayesha: the opening that led his wife and other faithful pilgrims to their deaths and/or salvation.

> "Open," she was crying. "Open wide!" Tentacles of light were flowing from her navel and he chopped at them, chopped, using the side of his hand. "Open," she screamed. . . . They were under water, lost in the roaring of the sea, but he could hear her clearly, . . . that voice like a bell. "Open," she said. He closed.
>
> He was a fortress with clanging gates.—He was drowning.—She was drowning too. . . . Then something within him refused that, made a different choice, and at the instant that his heart broke, he opened.
>
> His body split apart from his adam's apple to his groin, so that she could reach deep within him, and now she was open, they all were, and at that moment of their opening the waters parted, and they walked to Mecca across the bed of the Arabian Sea. (SV, 507)

Mirza's dream offers a mode of connection that promises a paradoxical survival in the choice of death and also a choice between two kinds of death—termination versus migration, perhaps to another story. In this dream, which is also his moment of death and the end of his story, Mirza repeats the end of the pilgrimage for those who followed Ayesha to the sea. Like Gibreel's dream, connecting navel to navel, this dream offers a similar connection: Mirza is connected to Ayesha by the "light flowing from her navel," paradoxically, by the right choice between two kinds of death—by opening or by closing. At first he refuses to cooperate, trying to cut the bodily-light connection between them, to "chop," an endeavor that spells death for both prophet and unbeliever, both writer and reader. Whereas Mirza's attempt to "chop" such an ending suggests termination, a refusal to connect or to continue, Ayesha's urgently repeated injunction to "open" rings clearly, insistently, as the ambiguous but paradoxical way to survival—through faith. In this scenario, to close means that both drown; to open is the more difficult and painful choice, itself a dream and the result of a dream, the dream of Mecca.[28] The anti-absolutist stand of the novel is thus itself not absolutist, for it finally opens itself to the possibility that faith—though not in its institutionalized forms—may be redemptive and psychically restorative.

This crucial injunction to "open" is then also made to the dream-narrative. That opening, however reluctant or belated, enables the best form of death—it prescribes the narrative that ends most miraculously and paradoxically by remaining open. To open in the end, suggests this powerful ending, is more difficult (indeed, seemingly impossible) but is preferable to remaining closed. The novel enacts its own opening by offering multiple endings. It "concludes" with another ending that, like that of *Shame*, calls attention to its overdone efforts to close. As Salahuddin Chamcha walks off into the sunset with Zeeny Vakil, the genre of a happy ending that Saleem had once regretfully dismissed ("Love does not conquer all, except in the Bombay talkies" [*MC*, 530]) suddenly reappears, calling overtly into question its ability to close off, of all narratives, *The Satanic Verses*.[29] As in *Shame*, the conventionality of the plots of two powerful cultural traditions—the romantic comedy and the Bombay film industry—is invoked in constructing, over and over again, the ending of this postmodern postcolonial novel. But in the sheer excess of conventional endings syncopated into one chapter—the death and reconciliation of the father and son, the death of Gibreel (who is removed as an obstacle for his alter ego Chamcha), and the romantic reunion of estranged lovers who walk off to (an ironically punctured) future bliss—the story closes almost too many times, each waiting on the next gesture of ending.

Haroun and the Sea of Stories itself narrativizes the battle against the end—of stories and of storytelling. Written in the aftermath of the fatwa, *Haroun* lends itself to an easy allegorization of Rushdie's confrontation with the forces of silencing: when his wife leaves and his son Haroun questions the efficacy of his stories, Rashid Khalifa ("the Shah of Blah" or the "Ocean of Notions") loses his magical gift of story.[30] This meta-story about stories written, like *Alice in*

Wonderland, for adults as well as children, makes its central theme the generation, perpetuation, and efficacy of stories. Rashid's son Haroun's attempt to retrieve Rashid's lost power lands both father and son on "the Earth's second Moon," Kahani (67) (*kahani* means "story" in Urdu): for that loss of story and the search for it is what creates their story. To arrive in Kahani, however, is to be embroiled in the great struggle against the dreaded Khattam-Shud, "the Cultmaster of Bezaban," the terrible power of Silence who controls and inhabits the dark side of the moon known as "the Land of Chup."[31] As Haroun discovers, Khattam-Shud "is the Arch-Enemy of all Stories, even of Language itself. He is the Prince of Silence and the Foe of Speech" (79). The two sides of this moon Kahani, divided uncompromisingly into two equal and opposite halves, are now at war: the land of Bolo [talk or speech], the capital of which is Gup City [city of conversation, gossip, talk], is under attack by the Land of Chup [silence], which lives in "Perpetual Darkness."

In the psychic and narratival geography of this moon Kahani is located the mythical Sea of Stories:

> So Iff the Water Genie told Haroun about the Ocean of the Streams of Story, and even though he was full of a sense of hopelessness and failure the magic of the Ocean began to have an effect on Haroun. He looked into the water and saw that it was made up of a thousand thousand thousand and one currents, each one a different colour, weaving in and out of one another like a liquid tapestry of breathtaking complexity; and Iff explained that these were the Streams of Story . . . and as all the stories that had ever been told and many that were still in the process of being invented could be found here, the Ocean of the Streams of Story was in fact the biggest library in the Universe. And because the stories held here were in fluid form, they retained their ability to change, to become new versions of themselves, to join up with other stories and so become yet other stories; so that unlike a library of books, the Ocean . . . was much more than a storeroom of yarns. It was not dead but alive. (*Haroun,* 71–72)

As in *Midnight's Children,* stories are here also associated with bodily liquidity and fluidity, indeed, with the waters of generation and life. Various creatures live in their enabling medium, and when these waters are poisoned, the creatures start to die. In this marvelous vision of story as an endless colorful and revivifying force, a power of life, lies the subject of the story: Story as infinitude—exemplifying the infinitude of the family tree-as-web, represented in intermeshing mixed metaphors of a liquid, a text, a fabric(ation), and life. This story constitutes a text that is not an inert object, not only textile (a "yarn") but also a thing that is "alive," perpetually changing and adjusting, both ephemeral and perpetual, alive because transformed by and transformative of temporal reality. This liquid power of stories is intensely bodily, for these waters emerge from a hole, another womblike source, the "Wellspring, or Source, of Stories" (167). This plethora of stories and their power of adaptation, re-vision, reconstruction, and amalgamation of past stories, suggests Rushdie, are what sustains humanity through change, through migration, through loss, past the many "posts" of colonialism—in an allegory that extends beyond the story of *The Satanic Verses*. And this life-liquid is threatened by Khattam-Shud, who seeks to poison and destroy that ocean and to plug forever its ultimate source. "The world is for Controlling," he tells the bemused Haroun, "and inside every story . . . there lies a world, a story-world, that I cannot Rule at all" (161). This struggle, of course, is also the struggle epitomized by the so-called Rushdie affair: between the attempts to curtail, to terminate the rereadings both of older stories and of *The Satanic Verses*, versus the attempt that *The Satanic Verses* makes to reimagine the stories that nurture postcolonial and postmigrant sensibilities that are themselves vitalized as products of such changes.

Yet in Rushdie's allegory, the moon Kahani is not split by any easy binarism of good and bad. In fact, the absolutism and binarism of *both* Gup and Chup, of Perpetual Darkness and of Perpetual Light, are what threaten Kahani's Ocean of Stories, just as, Rushdie suggests, all stories and the powers of storytelling and renewal are threatened by such binarisms.[32] The "good" city of Gup controls the "world" and its rotation, and that controls the rotation of the moon to maintain "Eternal Daylight," depriving Chup of light. If this is the difference between "East" and "West," then surely, Rushdie suggests, these binarisms of good and evil are too simplistic if the "good" is that which has the power to deprive "evil" of light. (This is also an allegory—written long before September 11, 2001—of the continuing exploitation of the "third world" by the neo-imperialist "first world," which is then surprised by the rise of violent fundamentalist communities against it.) That Haroun succeeds in retrieving his father's lost gift and in breaking the stasis of the dark and light sides of the moon, setting off a revolution that makes both share *both* darkness and light, can thus be read as the optimistic hope of *Haroun*.

Haroun's battle against the fearsome Khattam-Shud is, therefore, a story of resistance to closure, here cast as resistance to silence. The struggle within Kahani (Story) can be read as the energizing tension that Peter Brooks identifies as key to all narratives: the attempt to end against the desire to continue. Khattam-Shud is not merely the greatest personification of censorship but the final censorship of all forms, the termination of story: "Khattam-Shud" is the formulaic sign of conclusion; like "Amen," it signifies the end of the story and marks the point of terminus. In Middle Eastern conventions of storytelling, as, for instance, in *The Thousand and One Nights*, its large bold type forewarns the reader, announcing "The End," as if preparing for the release in imminent closure. What Haroun struggles against (as does the book named after him) is that fate of termination, of conclusion. Closure signifies the end of life, as of stories, not only of the individual but also of a collective, of a family, and of a people. Each successive generation must perpetuate the story, *their* story, opening into multiple versions that coexist as mutually validating truths.

Thus, although Haroun's story ends seemingly with the most satisfactory form of closure, the conventional, artificial "happy ending" that the Walrus obligingly manufactures for him, it is an ending that can come only in the "middle of the story" (201). (Haroun's mother returns, as does his father's gift of storytelling; Haroun returns to his "sad city" to find it rejoicing at having remembered its name, which is "Kahani"—as if Haroun's trip to the moon Kahani was a dream voyage and exploration of his own home.) But as the Walrus has warned him, it can only "cheer things up for a while" (202). As if fully conversant with the difficulties of endings and the knowledge of unknown futures, young Haroun replies, "That'll do" (202).

Yet *Haroun* also depends on another structure that maintains its resistance to closure. At the same time that it purports to end "happily," it also leaves itself open structurally in a strange infinite loop that, like a snake's tail, coils around itself and leaves an end dangling. When Haroun returns to earth with his father, he finds that his trip was a dream: the story of his visit to Kahani has become a tale within a tale, for it is framed by the tale of Haroun's trip to the "Valley of K," where his father had been hired to tell stories to further the election campaigns of corrupt politicians and where his earlier "gift of the gab" had been blocked by silence. Yet as *Haroun* returns to this frame tale, the frame intertwines itself into the story it is supposed to enfold: the "story" that Rashid Khalifa now tells the awaiting populace of K *is* the story of *Haroun and the Sea of Stories*, which begins in an exact replication of the beginning of *Haroun*: "There was once, in the country of Alifbay, a sad city, the saddest of cities, a city so ruinously sad that it had forgotten its name" (*Haroun*, 15, 206). Thus, the story within the story of *Haroun* is the story of Haroun, linking itself most dizzyingly to its frame tale, so that frame and content become coterminous. Such an ending validates Haroun's dream, for Haroun has dreamt the same dream as his father, that of retrieving his story, and his father's story is the story of that retrieval of story. And this dream is materially efficacious in two ways: first, it mirrors the political conditions that surround Haroun's father and his listeners, so that, in the retelling of that dream-story of Khattam-Shud, Haroun's father creates in his listeners a recognition of and aversion to the tyrannical realities of the politicians who ordered his story; and second, the telling of this dream (which is the story of the overthrow of the totalitarian power of Silence) is able to subvert the very power Rashid has been hired to buffer, and it results in the "bad" politicians being hissed out of power. It suggests, then, that even the story authorized by the powers-that-be can, because of its openness and multidimensionality, become the story of the people, the voice of the populace that those powers were trying to suppress.

This repetition of the beginning at the end is not simply a formulaic strategy of avoiding closure by returning to the beginning, for instead of creating a circle, it weaves an infinite loop into the structure of the tale, creating a *mise en abyme* in which each repetition of the story of *Haroun* brings the reader to the point where the story must be repeated again, from another point, at the same time that it also forks off to end alternatively with the return of Haroun's mother. In such a model of infinite looping, the story is told forever within the story, in a form of narratival repetition that performs an infinite regression—to no end. Even with the end of Khattam-Shud, there is no end to this story, as it retells itself in the hope of mirroring and defeating other versions of Khattam-Shud, self-perpetuating its struggle against the forces of tyranny. As in all Rushdie's major novels, this ending is necessarily cast in the mode of a dream, for only through the particular structure of the dream can Rushdie open up his narratives to such resistance to closure, to shape the future.

This then is how Rushdie finally ends *Midnight's Children*, as Saleem's dream of the future:

> [I]t will be Independence Day and the many-headed multitudes will be in the streets . . . and yes, I will be separated from Padma, . . . until she drowns in the crowd and I will be alone in the vastness of numbers, the numbers marching one two three, I am being buffeted right and left while rip tear crunch reaches its climax, and my body is screaming . . . they are all here, my grandfather Adam and his wife Naseem . . . they throng around me pushing shoving crushing . . . there is Jamila who has left her nunnery to be present on this last night . . . there is countdown to midnight and I see that I shall never reach Kashmir . . . because now I see . . . the terrifying figure of a war-hero . . . who has found out how I cheated him of his birthright, . . . the crowd . . . is now wholly composed of familiar faces, . . . I see a mythological apparition approaching, the Black Angel, except that as it nears me its face is green its eyes are black, . . . I am the bomb in Bombay, watch me explode . . . and at last somewhere the striking of a clock, twelve chimes, release. (MC, 550–52)

In this penultimate sentence that syntactically refuses to end, Saleem syncopates in the structure of the dream all the previous options that he had rejected: he ends "happily," in a ghostly family reunion, at which all the dead characters reappear, as if to preside over his demise and welcome him into their midst; but also he ends "in melancholy," as he is separated from Padma and lost in a crowd that promises his death. This dream also opens up "questions" about his supposed death: does Saleem die by autonomous disintegration; or "buffeted" by the crowd of numbers that terrorized him in nightmares; or by the vengeance of Shiva, his double who finds him at last; or by the proclamation of the "Black Angel" of death, Azrael, who merges into the Widow; or by the power of his earlier dreams of the Widow and of the crowd; or as the "bomb in Bombay," exploding into a thousand and one pieces; or by some combination of all these pressures of family and history and narrative?

Saleem's presentation of his death as a dream does not merely serve to avert the classic problem of autobiography, in which the gap between the narrating and the narrated self narrows to a convergence as the story ends, but the gap cannot be closed, as the death of the narrator cannot logically be told by himself. Rushdie's choice of the dream vision for his ending also resonates with the structure of dreams that he constructs in his narratives and is crucial to addressing the problem of endings. First, the truth-validity of the dream allows him to disrupt the temporality that dictates the impossibility of describing, and thus narratively living beyond, the narrator's own death. Second, its all-inclusive, alogical form (neither logical nor illogical but beyond binary logic) allows him to include the other options for ending—the repetitions, inclusion of past and future—that precluded each other. Most important is that it allows him to end without giving in to the necessities of closure, to present the end as both ending only too conclusively and as not ending at all, and thus open up the possibility of effecting political change by suggesting many possible futures that may be realized through such a narrative.

In the multiple forms of death that Saleem seems to undergo is present the same (im)possibility generated by the dream that we see in the other narratives. To die so many times, in so many ways, suggests the problems of overkill: nothing, on the one hand, could be more certain than Saleem's death; yet on the other hand, if every form of death must be repeated, then all must be thrown into doubt. In announcing the "fission of Saleem," Saleem pronounces his own death: "I am the bomb in Bombay—watch me explode" (552). This can be read as Saleem's final performative utterance, the dream that enunciates its own enactment. In turning disaster into triumph, Saleem seems to turn death into a willed act of self-destruction. However, the declaration can also be read as one that defeats death in another explosive dissemination of meaning. It becomes a self-celebration of his verbal and acoustic play, a volitional performance of the self that is both a part of Bombay—that cosmopolitan urban collective—and apart from it, the postcolonial individual separating himself from the collective by the force of his words, which will explode with the power of his verbal facility and storytelling: the bomb that may represent but that cannot be enclosed by Bombay.

Such fission, such fragmentation of the self, is celebratory of the narrative's nucleic energies and the possibilities of signification it releases. Moreover, such an ending maintains the dream's alogical (im)possibility of ending and not-ending, death and not-death, the coexistence of oppositions. "Yes, they will trample me underfoot, the numbers marching one two three, . . . reducing me to specks of voiceless dust, just as, in all good time, they will trample my son who is not my son, and his son who will not be his . . . until the thousand and first generation, until a thousand and one midnights have bestowed their terrible gifts and a thousand and one children have died, because it is the privilege and the curse of midnight's children to be both masters and victims of their times, . . . and to be unable to live or die in peace" (MC, 552). Even when the two-page sentence ends, another begins. The novel ends not with Saleem's death but, like Omar's validated dreams of the future, with what-will-happen-next. Saleem does not die but knows that he *will* die at midnight on his birthday, having completed not thirty but thirty-one years (indeed, thirty-one years and one day), keeping open his own end. At no point in Rushdie's narratives is a number rounded off—signifying, again, in this preference for the structure of "a thousand and one" (like the thousand and one stories of *The Thousand and One Nights*) the trope of incompleteness and infinitude, of perpetual addition and openness that Rushdie attributes to the cultural traditions of Islam. And in enabling this strange balance of possibility and impossibility lies the relevance of dreams to Rushdie's narrative endings: for as he tells us himself, only such a structure—of death and perpetuation, of ending and not-ending, of dreaming in the face of certainty of the end—can embody the impossible contradictions of the postcolonial condition that must continue even as it ends: "[F]or it is the privilege and the curse of midnight's children to be both masters and victims of their times." Only such a dream structure can encompass such simultaneity of possibility and impossibility: the midnight's children are destroyed but also hold out promise; it is the worst of times and the best of times; the future holds both hope and despair; it is to end and not to end. Thus, Rushdie suggests, postcolonial narrative cannot end, even as it ends. As in Samuel Beckett's repeated refrain, postcolonial narrative must go on, even when it cannot, for its privilege and curse is to be both a subject and an agent, a dream of simultaneous possibility and impossibility, an ending and a continuation.[33]

EPILOGUE

The Body as the Basis for Literary Agency
South Asia, Africa, and the Caribbean

THIS PROJECT originally began as an investigation of the self-referentiality of colonial and postcolonial writing. When I undertook graduate study, it was a literary commonplace that postmodern writing was self-referential, self-aware, and self-ironic — usually in positively valorized ways — as was the kind of cosmopolitan postcolonial writing exemplified by Rushdie. But as I discovered that self-referentiality and self-awareness in earlier writers such as Kipling and Forster and began to notice a concurrent and concerted preoccupation with the human body, I came to read the two features as symptomatic of a profound concern for the agency of writing itself, inscribed into the very form and rhetoric of their writing. Through intensive, detailed readings of the work of three writers, I have tried to show how literary agency is a central concern for colonial and postcolonial writers with very different agendas, from different time periods and different locations, and how inseparable it is from imaginings of the body. The body makes possible the articulation of this concern about the power and susceptibility, the autonomy and subjection of writing in a variety of writings that emerge from fraught political contexts. At the same time, I have also tried to show how this collocation of concerns with literary agency, body, and text is not obvious, not easily visible, and not simple to chart. Indeed, its very subtlety, complexity, and variability are some of the challenges that this book attempts to navigate.

For Kipling, the body of the English child breast-fed on Indian women's milk functions as the basis of an imagined linguistic and cultural hybridity that enables at once imperial power and right of rule, as well as an insider's knowledge and imperial critique. But the centrality of this body also allows this ambivalent colonial writer to articulate his anxieties about the censorship of his writing and the damage that imperial interests could wreak upon artistic and cultural truth telling or meaning making. Forster calls upon the body not so much as metaphor or trope but as the fundamental condition for artistic truth. This enables him finally to produce an ethics of writing, to craft a mode that couples a critique of empire with a critique of heteronormativity and that speaks at once (for) the racialized, colonized, gendered, and sexually suppressed body. And Rushdie devises a new language of bodiliness to emphasize the material, cultural work of postcolonial fictions, their capacity to function salutarily as outlawed "dirt" that crosses a variety of boundaries, to tell truth or remake communities through dreams.

But is this linking of the body with literary agency in Kipling, Forster, and Rushdie typical or exceptional? How useful is it for reading other colonial and postcolonial writers? And why these three writers? Let me begin by answering the last question first, by way of declaring my own "geopolitical baggage."[1] After the decolonization and Partition of British India in 1947, both my parents migrated with their families to West Pakistan from northern India (my mother from Gorakhpur and my father from Jaipur). I was born and raised in Karachi, at once rooted and the child of migrants who never quite belonged, and was educated in English schools whose mission it was to perpetuate a strong British colonial legacy. Like the writers I study in this book, I too was both fostered by and torn between frequently conflicting cultural allegiances and embattled histories produced by British imperialism. At graduate school in the United States, Rushdie's *Shame* was the first novel I ever read that mentioned Karachi. In 1989, his work had a freshness and novelty, a galvanizing excitement for a reader who had grown up on canonical British literature as well as on the landscapes and timescapes he described: I was seven in 1971 when the Pakistani army attacked its own people in Bengal, and in the ensuing India-Pakistan war, a bomb destroyed the house next to ours; I was fifteen in 1979 when, under martial law,

Bhutto was hanged by a secret jury and the nation went into another state of trauma. Rushdie led me to Kipling and Forster; for all three writers were engaged not simply with South Asia but with the dilemmas of intercultural legacies, multiple allegiances, unfixed locations, and the efficacy of writing in difficult times. And they also understood, in all their different positionalities, the vulnerability of human bodies. I chose these writers finally not only because they were connected with each other, or because they were linked with South Asia, but also because they were among the most self-conscious about their writing and its political role and because their cultural affiliations extended beyond South Asia, to reflect more broadly on how migrancy, travel, and shifting homes consequent to painful colonial and postcolonial histories produce an intense anxiety of literary agency. (The contexts and sources of Kipling's work include Britain, India, North America, and South Africa; Forster's include Egypt and Italy as well as India and Britain, and Rushdie's cosmopolitan connections include India, Pakistan, Britain, and North and South America.)

Yet they are not, by any means, the only writers who incorporate into their writing this concern about literary agency via the human body. Indeed, I would argue that they are simultaneously exemplary and exceptional: exemplary in that they allow us to identify concerns that are also key to many other outstanding colonial and postcolonial writers; exceptional in that, unlike others who may highlight these questions on occasional or critical moments, they sustain such questions throughout their work. But for each writer, the *way* in which the body serves as a register of literary agency is distinctive and unpredictable, not to be reductively mapped on another writer, hence it requires the kind of attentive close reading that I have attempted in this book. Through some key examples in other writers, here I want to suggest how the arguments of this book may extend to others, with what kinds of differences, and to gesture toward what may be new angles for viewing their work.

Perhaps the most classic postcolonial novel *par exemple*, included on most postcolonial syllabi, is Chinua Achebe's *Things Fall Apart*.[2] Notable in that it describes a precolonial Ibo culture and an individual and familial dynamic in all their variegated complexity prior to the arrival of British traders, missionaries, and army in Nigeria, the narrative requires its readers—non-African and African—to understand and respect it on its own terms. It concludes with the appalling image of a dead body "dangling" from a tree, the body of Okonkwo the once heroic protagonist, who has desecrated his community by committing the execrable act of suicide, arguably to forestall the (in)justice and further humiliations about to be wreaked upon him and his tribe by the newly established district commissioner (207). Representative of the death of a culture as well of its martial ethos, this body, whether read as an icon of disgraced defeat or as a symbol of partial victory, of defiance, resistance, or acquiescence, certainly encapsulates the final act of agency by a man who at least chooses the mode of his own death. The last paragraph moves in a strange shift, however, to the thoughts of the English district commissioner (at once colonial administrator, writer, and ethnographer), who altogether fails to understand the significances of Okonkwo's act but imagines mentioning it in "a reasonable paragraph" in his projected book, "*The Pacification of the Primitive Tribes of the Lower Niger*" (209). That the title of this book should constitute the last words of Achebe's novel is ironic on multiple levels, for in a neat reversal, Achebe's novel relegates to a mere paragraph the putative colonial text that relegates to a dismissive paragraph the entire story of Okonkwo we have just read; indeed, Achebe's counterdiscursive novel ironically enacts the postcolonial agency of rewriting those arrogant colonial discourses, complicating and retelling those silenced stories, of seeking to restore the dead of a culture killed by the incursions of the white man and then doubly killed by being rendered silent. Thus, we understand retrospectively that what animates Achebe's entire novel is that final image of Okonkwo's dead body: it finally speaks through the novel; it functions symbolically and literally as the impetus for his narrative and its work; and it provides the novel's purpose, which is to reassign dignity and meaning to that Ibo past and to restore to its postcolonial descendants a fuller, deeper understanding of their past as they begin to build a new future. Thus Achebe draws upon the body *as text* to speak self-referentially of the aspirations of his work: to replace the text (colonial discourses of power) that replaced the text of that body and its multiple meanings, and open up those meanings to be read. Achebe's novel thus returns to that body as its raison d'être, its point of origin even as it cites the body and seeks to replace it as a descendant text that will speak and contest the powers that Okonkwo could not.

In Caribbean literature, emergent from histories of the Atlantic slave trade and slavery, the wounded body, as Jahan Ramazani has notably shown, is a central multivalent trope.[3] In Derek Walcott's epic poem *Omeros*, the speaking wound may represent the Caribbean postcolonial condition of historic and continuing injury, or the infliction of colonial language, as "dumb mouth," the inarticulate condition of pain to which others may only be voyeurs (Ramazani, 66). But in the work of Caribbean poets, fiction writers, and essayists, the body is also central to the self-representation of art or writing and to the agency of its cultural work. Walcott's well-known early poem "A Far Cry from Africa" (1956) concludes with the dilemma of the poet's tormented allegiances to the multiracial blood and cultures that have accumulated in his body:

> I who am poisoned with the blood of both,
> Where shall I turn, divided to the vein?
> The drunken officer of British rule, how choose
> Between this Africa and the English tongue I love?[4]

The poet's choice of the English language (and its literary legacies) is an inherently bodily choice; the division within him down "to the vein" is not only symbolic of dual or multiple cultural allegiances but also is literally embedded in the poet's body. The self-conscious challenge for this postcolonial poet, then, will be to voice both sides of his ancestry, to attempt not to erase, if not to reconcile, both. The agency of his poetic work is thereby fundamentally linked to a body that is irrevocably created of slave, "slave seller and slave buyer" "in the filth-ridden gut of the slave ship" though he seeks in his writing to recognize, and even celebrate, the survival and creation of a new hybrid identity.[5]

Likewise, in a somewhat different vein, the Guyanese poet Grace Nichols writes of her non-choice of language, since, like all Afro-Caribbean peoples, after the Middle Passage, she does not have access to an originary, ancestral language:

> I have crossed an ocean
> I have lost my tongue
> From the root of the old one
> a new one has sprung[.][6]

More so than Walcott, Nichols here manifestly puns on "tongue" as language but also as literally the *organ* of language, the body part that has been amputated to silence the enslaved and colonized. But, she suggests, that body part has renewed itself, regenerated, to grow something "new." Formally, the poem reiterates that sense of bodily dismemberment and loss through the missing feet of the second and fourth lines, but it also suggests growth and continuity through the enjambment that connects the third and fourth lines. Moreover, Nichols also puns on *root* to suggest the literal bodily site or stub from where the old tongue was cut, as well as figuratively the root of her old, perhaps ancestral African language. Hence, she suggests, Caribbean poets, writers, and cultures have produced a new language that bears the marks of violation and loss but also combines partially re-membered African words, syntax, and rhythms with English words to make what Edward Kamau Brathwaite has called a new "nation language."[7] Again, for Nichols, as for Rushdie and others, the body is the site of pain and violation but also of a new agency of revival, for it represents the power of her own writing as the agent that will produce another voice and create a distinct language to address the history and experiences of the Caribbean.

Likewise, in his important essay "The Limbo Gateway," the Guyanese novelist Wilson Harris unravels the multiple significations of the legendary term *limbo* in relation to Caribbean art: "The limbo dancer moves under a bar which is gradually lowered until a mere slit of space, it seems, remains through which with spread-eagled limbs he passes like a spider. *Limbo* was born, it is said, on the slave ships of the Middle Passage. There was so little space that the slaves contorted themselves into human spiders."[8] Punning on *limbo* as a state of in-betweenness (the Middle Passage between Africa and the New World) and on the loss of the phantom *limb* that continues to hurt, the art of limbo becomes symbolic of loss and pain, as well as of a new art of adjustment, adaptation, and survival. Thus, in Wilson's argument, the bodily art of the limbo dance represents more broadly the creativity and culture of the Caribbean; it refers to his own work as a writer as well as to others', as enacting and exemplifying survival and rebirth, "the renascence of a new corpus of sensibility" (380); and, as in the work of the writers studied here, the power of this art too is founded upon the body and its concurrent ability to experience violation as well as to craft (itself) anew.

Yet, as I emphasize in the introduction, the work of every writer is distinctive and singular, and attempting to map a single blueprint or confluence of concerns too easily or programmatically from one to another would be a mistake. J. M. Coetzee's work, for instance, may seem at first glance to be highly concerned with both writing and bodies, but its complexity and strangeness also thwarts any easy mapping or predictable reading along the lines of any pattern. In fact, it provides a good case in point of how a text may both fulfill and resist the schemes we as critics attempt to impose. In his 1986 novel *Foe*, Coetzee's remarkable revision of *Robinson Crusoe*,[9] the paradigmatic colonial text, Foe is the writer as enemy (Defoe? De Foe) (or the enemy of truth?), who presumably later unscrupulously appropriates and alters the story he gets from his unacknowledged source, Susan Barton, an Englishwoman who was also shipwrecked on Cruso's island and who, after Cruso's death, has returned to England with Friday, a former slave, possibly from Africa.[10] Perhaps one question the text poses is what is the agency of the female storyteller whose story will be misapprehended, transformed, and silenced by the male storyteller who erases her from her own story? Another is, what is the agency of the storyteller (Foe) who takes her story, or the agency of the one (Coetzee) who attempts to restore it? But the one whose story, silence, and silencing become overtly the subject of this heavily layered narrative is Friday, whose tongue has literally been cut out (by slavers, we are told) and around whose stub Susan and Foe weave their speculations and narratival desires. However one reads this bizarre novel—as a white South African writer's attempt to give voice to those silenced and victimized by brutal colonial histories or as a self-knowing documentation of the failure to listen or restore—the victimized body of Friday remains the silent center of the novel. It may be written upon, as others impose narratives on it, but it is not the site of agency or of the production of writing itself. When Susan finally struggles to teach Friday to write, he can write only the same letter *o* over and over again, perhaps to symbolize the cipher that his language and subjectivity remains to others (152). By contrast, Foe begins to write Susan's story after she has sex with him, "straddling" him as a visitation of the "Muse" (139), so that the story he produces is in fact "fathered" by her (140), a joint production of both their bodies. If in Friday's case the wounded body could be read as the site of the failure of literary agency, in Foe's and Susan's the sexual body is the source of it.

In *Waiting for the Barbarians*, Coetzee's horrific semi-allegorical account of torture and complicity in an outpost of an unspecified "Empire," the body is the site of unspeakable truth.[11] The magistrate-narrator, who can at best testify to what he cannot actually witness, can only attempt to gather evidence from bodies after they have been mutilated. The body he obsesses over, in a dubious conflation of sexual with epistemological desire, is that of the nameless barbarian "girl" whom he rescues after the torturers of empire are done with her: "[U]ntil the marks on this girl's body are deciphered and understood I cannot let go of her," he remarks (31). If the magistrate's attempts to read this body are modes of penetration, possession, and sexual desire, they are also to be understood, Coetzee suggests, as ethical attempts to heal and restore, for the magistrate undertakes assiduously to wash her, to massage her nightly, to repair her impossibly injured body and finally return it to the home from which it was wrenched. This desire to restore and repair may be perhaps the hope of literary agency of Coetzee's writing, self-mirrored and embedded into its narrative. Yet the magistrate remains unable to write or intervene—at the end, after he suffers the grotesque attentions of the true barbarians, his own government's officials, he attempts to record the history he has lived, but cannot. There can be no simple reading of what such a novel suggests about its own agency, whether it delineates the magistrate's failures in contrast to its own efforts to intervene and to record the horrors of history, or whether it presents itself as sharing in the magistrate's desire but limited capacity to bear witness, to mourn its own ultimate ineffectuality.[12] To what extent Coetzee's work understands its own literary agency in terms of the body is unclear, however. While Coetzee certainly casts the body as a central site of pain and violation, marked and read by others who hold power over it, and his work is highly self-reflexive and occupied with questions of its own agency, the relationship between that body and literary agency remains slippery and indefinable, for the body is not used for self-reference to address the power of writing.

I would like to conclude with two diasporic postcolonial women writers whose work does exemplify the arguments of this book, yet also reveals some useful differences. Both Sara Suleri (with Pakistani-Welsh origins, now settled in the United States) and Michelle Cliff (Jamaican-American) figure the human body in novel ways to articulate the agency of their postcolonial writing, but they also call attention to the body in markedly feminist, differently gendered terms. Like Rushdie in *Midnight's Children*, Sara Suleri recounts the intertwined histories of self, family, and nation in her memoir *Meatless Days*.[13] But unlike him, she suggests that a postcolonial feminist agency of writing is crafted both by writing of "private" or domestic and familial matters that intertwine with "public" political events and by breaking away from her father's (and perhaps Rushdie's) masculinist understanding of nation and history. Inventing an idiom of her own that valorizes the everyday experiences of women as constituting an equally important "national" history, Suleri also seeks to tell alternative truths of nation and subjectivity. She too draws upon the body, though differently, to render her language and her writing as a form of bodily agency. Her sister Ifat's brutal death, for instance, is the consequence, she implies, of the traumas that Ifat's soldier-husband suffered while fighting for the Pakistani army in Bangladesh. That national horror is thus inseparable from, implicated in, and not merely allegorical of this private one. This is how she describes the effects of Ifat's murder, sensationalized in the news: "[I]t was as though I did not have the idea of a sister any more, for Ifat had become the news. Her name was everywhere, a public domain, blotting out her face and its finesse into the terrible texture of newsprint" (125). The letters of Ifat's name in the newspapers seem now to materially replace her face, as they literally imprint themselves so heavily upon her remembered features as to replace her bodily with the material textuality of newsprint, and her body's palpability gives way to the reality of gossip. The sensationalist language of "the news" physically takes over Ifat and her memory, redefining and reconstituting her in ways that wrench her yet again from her remembered self. As in Forster's and Rushdie's work, the power of words can work ill material effects, as here its very materiality blots out the memory (and body) of a beloved sister.

But Suleri's own language, Suleri suggests, can enact a bodily labor to enable Ifat's release and rebirth. In figurations that combine childbirth with midwifery, Suleri describes her effort to retrieve her sister from such painful publicity, from victimization by a deranged national politics into the steadfast resistance of familial re-membering:

> Now it is sweet relief to me to know that I need not labor to describe what happened in my mind when Ifat died. . . . I could not conceive her body then, nor tolerate the tales of that body's death, the angle of its face, the bruise upon its neck. . . . Then commenced keen labor. I was imitating all of them, I knew, my mother's laborious production of her five, my sisters' of their seven . . . , so it was their sweat that wet my head, their pushing motion that allowed me to extract in stifled screams, Ifat from her tales. We picked up our idea of her as though it were an infant, slippery in our hands with birthing fluids, a notion

most deserving of warm water. Let us wash the word murder from her limbs, we said, let us transcribe her into some more seemly idiom. And so with painful labor we placed Ifat's body in a different discourse, words as private and precise as water when water wishes to perform both in and out of light. (147–48)

Combining metaphors of birth and death, Suleri's meta-language here suggests how it, as language, sought to give painful (re)birth to Ifat even as it relinquished her to death, how it selected and cleansed her of journalese and gossip, in the idiom of Muslim funeral rites, to rewrap her decorously in an alternate discourse. (In Islamic custom, dead bodies are washed clean with water and wrapped in plain white sheets before burial, without coffins, directly in the earth.) Suleri's "labor" (as if emulating her mother's and sisters' acts of giving birth, as well of washing a dead body) is the work of rewriting Ifat, of reproducing her and delivering her through an act of intellectual childbirth. Yet it is also a metaphorical reenactment of Islamic funereal rites that cleanses her of gossip and (re)covers her in a more appropriate language before releasing her brutalized body into the grave—both literal and metaphorical—of memory. Unlike Kipling, who uses the metaphor of childbirth to represent his production of stories, Suleri complicates it, combining birth with death rites. Moreover, she suggests that she too is born of those collective female birthing fluids—her mother and sisters in giving birth to their children have also "wet her head"—so that *her* language of rebirthing Ifat (which emerges, like Athena, from her head) is also a bodily and communal production. Like Rushdie's, Suleri's language itself becomes heavy with metaphor, as it accumulates trope upon bodily trope.[14]

Thus for Suleri too, her writing is a powerful bodily experience, a matter of "stifled screams," as painful and harrowing as childbirth, as final, intimate, and valedictory as the cleansing ablutions performed on a corpse. Indeed, Ifat's body itself seems to be a textual thing, transformed by and written on by news. But Suleri's writing, she suggests, is also a form of political and feminist agency, once she realizes that her chronicle of family works as a counterhistory to her nationalist father's understanding of Pakistan and its politics. Earlier, inducted into the service of journalism by her father (who regarded history exclusively as the doings of the male "leaders" of Pakistan), she transcribed his handwriting, "wearing out" her fingerprints (and identity) under "the impact of [his newspaper's] ink" (122). At that youthful stage, Suleri suggests, she was complicit in her father's (and others') masculinist version of national history (122). Only after the deaths of her mother and sister does she realize that history was also hers to write:

> It was only then that I became historical, a creature gravely ready to admit that significance did not sit upon someone else's table. . . . I listened to the chattering of my ghosts . . . *"You were the state, and yet you did not know!"* Oh my mind's fool, I thought, astonished: it has taken you the deaths of a dear mother and a dear sister, the loss of three dear children, before you could contemplate such a dangerous simplicity? . . . Now comes the time when you must make yourself historical.
> An impossible task, however, to explain to Pip [her father] who needed badly to retain his version as the only form of history. (127; my emphasis)

This "history" is in fact her genre-crossing memoir *Meatless Days*, and this self-reflective metanarratival moment of epiphany marks the beginning of its writing, when she understands that "history" is not merely an account of public male figures but (what is more important and "dangerous" to traditional historiography) an account of the imbrication of private and public in female and male lives. Literary agency for Suleri as well, then, is constituted upon an understanding of the bodiliness of language, upon a sense of its vulnerability as well as its power—for language can be subjected to another's agenda or can erase and destroy or, more enablingly, can give rebirth to what is lost.

Like Kipling, Forster, and Rushdie, Sara Suleri uses the subjectivity and materiality of the human body as a central metaphor to articulate the moment of arrival at literary agency. By contrast, however, reading her work enables us to see how even male writers such as Rushdie who draw upon the human body in novel ways are constrained by their experiential or gendered apprehension of it. Both Kipling and Rushdie, though they seek to draw upon breast-feeding or childbirth metaphors for linguistic production, approach them as observed from the outside, not as experienced by female bodies. Women writers such as Suleri also call upon such bodily experiences to articulate their concerns with literary or political agency, but they do so in their own ways. This is not to say that women, who have been traditionally associated with the body (whereas men have been associated with the intellect), articulate the body in some uniquely different "feminine" ways, because women as well as men in different cultural locations and times are differently gendered, and all apprehend bodies in terms of their own specific sociohistorical cultural matrices. Hence, I am not suggesting in any essentialist way, as do the French feminist theories of *écriture feminine*, that women write uniquely from the body.[15] On the contrary, men do too, as we have seen; Kipling, Forster, Rushdie, Walcott, and Coetzee, for example, also apprehend the male body as central to writing, in terms of pain, torture, sexuality, desire, aging, and so on, and their experiences of the body too are fundamental to how they understand the relation between body and writing. However, women writers in different cultural and temporal locations may call upon or emphasize *different* bodily experiences than do most men.

Rushdie, for instance, despite his encyclopedic inclusiveness of bodily processes (see chapter 5), does not mention menstruation, least of all as a mode of bodily or linguistic flow. By contrast, Michelle Cliff ends her semi-autobiographical first novel, *Abeng*, with the trope of menstruation to suggest the climactic bodily flow of writing that will bring agency for the young protagonist, as a force of bloody cleansing, remembering, and healing.[16] At the end of *Abeng*, Clare, its light-skinned, middle-class Jamaican protagonist, is banished from her parents' and grandparents' homes because of a huge gender transgression: she has accidentally killed her grandmother's bull on a bold escapade with a borrowed gun with her dark-skinned peasant friend, Zoe. In 1950s still-colonized Jamaica, only boys (such as her male cousins) are allowed to use guns and go into the jungle, and for Clare to take the gun without permission and then to kill the bull is doubly unacceptable. Intended to teach her her proper place (in terms of gender, race, and class) in this rigidly hierarchized society invested in borrowed colonial values, her punishment is to be sent away from her family to live with Miss Beatrice, a racist old woman from an old white Jamaican family. But this also allows her to meet Miss Winifred, Miss Beatrice's "mad" old sister (160), who tells Clare not to "let them cross [her] up," unlike herself, who lost her "coon baby" to the system that punished her for having sex with a black male servant (162).

Thus, Clare's punishment unwittingly teaches her the very unseemly histories of imperialist injustice and racial and gender oppression that her multiracial family would rather suppress, and this triggers in her a resistance to the very values it is designed to inculcate. The occasion of crafting her own agency, of developing an alternative or resistance to the restrictions imposed on her from every direction, is marked by three concomitant events: Clare's dream, the onset of her first period, and her act of writing in her diary:

> That night Clare dreamed that she and Zoe were fist-fighting by the river in St. Elizabeth. That she picked up a stone and hit Zoe underneath the eye and a trickle of blood ran down her friend's face. . . . And she went over to Zoe and told her she was sorry—making a compress of moss drenched in water to soothe the cut. . . .
>
> When she awoke the power of the dream was still with her. But soon the dream was covered by her consciousness and a sharp pain in her vagina. . . . She touched herself . . . and found blood. . . .
>
> Then she returned to the house. . . . The sun was just rising. . . . Her diary was in her lap, and she was writing about what she had just woken to. (165)

In this final passage, laden with meanings that have accumulated over the course of the novel, Cliff's writing revises and rectifies first the fabrications of colonial fiction: unlike the famous episode in Jean Rhys's *Wide Sargasso Sea* in which Tia, the poor black girl, wounds Antoinette, the rich white Creole one, with a stone,[17] here, more symbolically true to colonial history, the Creole wounds her poor black friend and playmate. In her mad escapade, Clare has unwittingly wounded Zoe, and her dream attests to her knowledge of this, as well as to her desire to make reparation, to heal the damages inflicted by her own and her ancestors' bloody history.

But the dream "compress" "drenched in water" that she uses to perform this act of healing and friendship, in answer to her conscience and in contravention of her family's dictates, seems connected to the "icy-cold water" and "folded linen handkerchief" she uses in reality to stem her own body's menstrual flow, as if the two were somehow consonant. Repairing the wounds that she and her class have historically inflicted on those of the island's racial underclass seems consonant with the act of stemming her own bodily flow of blood. Painful but "sweet," menstruation—this long-awaited bodily experience—is complex and heavy with associations: it is something that her friend Zoe had first told her about; a "culmination" of the processes of her physical and intellectual growth; a "milestone"; and a "friend" linked with the diary of Anne Frank, who also wrote of it in secret "as though it was something that she had achieved" (106). It is thus associated with Clare's growing independence as she questions her family's racism; with her covert political self-education as she learns to connect various racial and imperialist crimes in history, from the extermination of indigenous Caribs to that of Jews in the Holocaust; and with the beginning of her writing, at once introspective (turning inward) and critically scrutinizing of her world (outward) (66–80).

Now Clare has moved from reading to writing, from reception to action. This involves a turning inward, toward some kind of bodily truth, as she ignores the old lady and her cautionary past and focuses instead on the mysterious flows of her body, as if that has led to this flow outward into writing and action. The triple connection between the compress Clare uses to stem Zoe's wound, the handkerchief she applies to her own bodily flow (as her body writes on it), and the sheets on which *she* writes suggest that the acts of healing, reparation, coming of age, and turning to (bodily) writing as a form of critical action are also connected—for Clare. The final words "writing about what she had woken to" suggest that she has not only awakened from (or into) her dream of seeking rectification for the past, even if it involves further transgression, but also that she has woken to awareness of her self, of her body, of her growth, and of her new knowledge of her society and history. Clare's bodily flow of blood seems concurrent with, causative of, and certainly symbolic of the flow of her writing, which, like Michelle Cliff's novel, *Abeng* (titled after an instrument of slave insurrection),[18] might seek, as its own act of agency, to repair and retell histories of injustice and oppression. Indeed, if menstruation literally represents Clare's ability to reproduce, it also signifies, Cliff suggests, her bodily capacity to produce not babies but books, writing that will have material effects in the world. The novel concludes, "She was not ready to understand her dream. She had no idea that everyone we dream about we are" (166). It leaves us with the suggestion that Clare's dream, both written about and imagined, is an agent of becoming, that, like Rushdie's dreams, it has the material power to shape the postcolonial future.

This is not to imply, of course, that women writers use exclusively different or exclusively female bodily experiences to address the agency of their writing. Grace Nichols, as we have seen above, uses the same image of the cut-off tongue that Coetzee does in *Foe*, though both may allude to the classical legend of the tongueless Philomela, who defied her rapist by identifying him through her needlework. As another example, the Indo-Trinidadian Canadian writer Shani

Mootoo uses the image of a diasporic female artist in Vancouver creating a new art and medium by molding a "mixture of mendhi and plaster" with her hands, at once to imprint her bodily identity ("fingerprints") on it; to recover a lost ancestral Indian tradition (mendhi); to hybridize and modernize the old medium by combining it with plaster; and to "excavate" aspects of her identity through sheer tactile pleasure (66–67).[19] Self-referentially emblematic of Mootoo's own diasporic writing and its agency, this new artwork calls upon the same bodily image of the hand that Rushdie does to posit what else it can do: commemorate ancestral tradition as well as come to terms with new diasporic conditions; and combat prejudice, educate, and devise new modes of living and creating such that her "finger and hand imprints in the mendhi practically squealed with ecstasy" (67). Thus, like Sushila, the artist in her story, Mootoo can "take a turn that skirted needing to be pinned down as Hindu, or as 'Indian,' or as Trinidadian (in themselves difficult identities to pin down) in favor of attempting to write a story of her own, using her own tools" (66–67).

The turn to the human body for the purposes of addressing literary agency is thus not confined to male or Anglo-Indian writers. What is striking to me is that *both* male and female writers in different times and places, and in different ways, locate the body as central to their imagining of their work's agency. Understanding how three colonial and postcolonial writers such as Kipling, Forster, and Rushdie cast the issue of literary agency through the human body can help us to understand why this is a central concern for other postcolonial writers, to see why they too draw upon the body to address literary agency, and to appreciate how they adapt this fundamental preoccupation and linkage to their particular concerns. It can help us read other colonial and postcolonial texts even as we remain alert to the specific conditions of each writer's ways of thinking about agency or assumptions about the body; we can appreciate how other writers come to different conclusions as they turn to different kinds or aspects of human bodies. Finally, it is not because these three writers are unique but because their work is so intriguingly, persistently haunted by this specific linking of literary agency and the body that they are the subjects of this study—for it is predominantly, and exemplarily, in their work that we find this ongoing, ardent effort to make (their) words matter.

NOTES

Introduction

1. Salman Rushdie, 1995 interview with David Shef, in *Conversations with Salman Rushdie*, ed. Michael Reder (Jackson: University Press of Mississippi, 2000), 197.

2. Marcella Nesom Sirhandi, *Contemporary Painting in Pakistan* (Lahore, Pakistan: Ferozesons, 1992), 81.

3. Calligraphy is integral to Islamic art, such as the margin commentary in Mughal miniatures and manuscripts and the Quranic inscriptions that sanctify and ornament the architecture of tombs and mosques. Twentieth-century Western artists such as Paul Klee were fascinated by the shapes and contours of Arabic lettering and incorporated the calligraphy as nonrepresentational abstractions in their art. Some Pakistani painters, including Anwar Jelal Shemza, were in turn influenced by Klee (Sirhandi, *Contemporary Painting in Pakistan*, 80). Others, such as Sadequain, use anthropomorphic calligraphy for powerful social commentary. Ramay (1930–2006) was a pioneer in the development of modern Islamic calligraphic art.

4. Islam forbids visual representation either because it may daringly approximate divine creation or because it may lead to idolatry: reverence for God (by definition infinite and unimaginable) or for the Prophet may degenerate into worship of a material object or literalized representation.

5. Haneef (also spelled Hanif) Ramay was an artist and intellectual who not only pioneered modern Islamic calligraphic painting in the 1950s but also founded a literary magazine, *Nusrat*, in Lahore in the 1960s. See Afzal Mira's commemoration of Ramay's life at http://drafzalmirza.blogspot.com/2006/01/haneef-ramay.html. In the 1960s and 1970s, Ramay switched careers from art and literature to politics. As a left-leaning, socialist poet-intellectual, critical of both feudalism and dictatorship, he became involved with Bhutto's People's Party but was soon disillusioned and imprisoned in the 1970s. He was a minister and governor of the Punjab from 1972 through 1976 and a Speaker of the Punjab Assembly from 1993 through 1996. One cannot help wondering, however, whether art and politics were not deeply connected for him and, indeed, whether the political concerns of his art, the desire for material effectivity, led him to a more overtly interventionist role in national politics. He published, in addition to several writings in Urdu, a mythical novel in English entitled *Again* (Xlibris Corporation, 2000) about the "death and rebirth of humanity."

6. Salman Rushdie, *Midnight's Children* (New York: Viking Penguin, 1981), 64. Hereafter cited as *MC*.

7. As in the Jewish custom of keeping kosher, Islam directs its followers to consume only the halal flesh of animals, which means that they have been purified after a prayer is read over them and the blood has been fully drained from their bodies. The prayer

asks divine forgiveness for the killing of one of God's creatures, an action permitted only for sustenance. Contrary to frequent misconception (for example, V. S. Naipaul in *Area of Darkness* [New York: Vintage, 1981], 135), this custom does not entail the cruel and prolonged bleeding of animals to death. The carcass is drained after death.

8. Salman Rushdie, *Shame* (New York: Aventura, 1983), 79.

9. Salman Rushdie, *The Moor's Last Sigh* (New York: Pantheon, 1995), 53. Hereafter cited as *Moor*.

10. I use the term *colonial* to signify writers such as Kipling and Conrad who are primarily affiliated or identified with the colonial metropolis or ruling peoples; whose sympathies lie, by and large, with imperial or European power; and whose work depends on such imperial contexts. I use the term *postcolonial* to refer to writers such as Rushdie, Chinua Achebe, and Derek Walcott, whose work emerges from and is usually contestory of the experience or aftermath of British imperialism. The term *postcolonial* has a well-known (self-)problematized status, which I will not rehearse here; for excellent brief accounts, see Ania Loomba, *Colonialism/Postcolonialism* (New York: Routledge, 1998), 1–19; and Jahan Ramazani, *The Hybrid Muse: Postcolonial Poetry in English* (Chicago: University of Chicago Press, 2001), 1–20. Recognizing the temporal and ideological duality (and ambiguity) that Loomba identifies (of both coming "after" and being opposed to colonialism), like Ramazani, I include in "postcolonial" the period of decolonization prior to Independence (Ramazani, 186n12) that would allow us to include pre-Independence writings such as Mahatma Gandhi's. Writers such as Forster, however, occupy an interestingly peculiar in-between position of being both colonial (British, not fully able to understand the condition of being colonized) and anticolonial (opposed to imperialism and its attendant racial ideologies).

11. Trinh Minh-ha, *When the Moon Waxes Red: Representation, Gender and Cultural Politics* (New York: Routledge, 1991), 75; Salman Rushdie, *Imaginary Homelands* (New York: Viking Penguin, 1991), 15. Many, but not all, colonial and postcolonial writers exhibit these conflicting loyalties; others, such as Rider Haggard and Shashi Deshpande, do not.

12. William Jewett, *Fatal Autonomy: Romantic Drama and the Rhetoric of Agency* (Ithaca, NY: Cornell University Press, 1997), xi.

13. We might recall here Stanley Fish's important shift from asking what a text *means* to what it *does*, because, he argues, what they do *is* what they mean (Fish, "Literature in the Reader: Affective Stylistics," in *Reader-Response Criticism: From Formalism to Post-Structuralism*, ed. Jane Tompkins [Baltimore, MD: John Hopkins University Press, 1980], 70–100).

14. Perry Anderson, *Arguments within English Marxism* (London: Verso, 1980), 18.

15. Norman S. Care and Charles Landesman, eds., introduction to *Readings in the Theory of Action* (Bloomington: Indiana University Press, 1968), vi.

16. A. I. Melden, "Action," in Care and Landesman, *Readings*, 27.

17. Anthony Giddens, *Central Problems in Social Theory: Action, Structure and Contradiction in Social Analysis* (Berkeley: University of California Press, 1979), 55.

18. C. B. Macpherson, *The Political Theory of Possessive Individualism: Hobbes to Locke* (Oxford: Oxford University Press, 1962), 78.

19. John Locke, *The Second Treatise of Civil Government* (1690), ed. C. B. Macpherson (Indianapolis: Hackett Publishing, 1980), section 27, p. 19.

20. As Foucault notes, though scientists had studied the physiological workings of the human body, social scientists had not considered how "the body is also directly involved in a political field," because "power relations have an immediate hold upon it; they invest it, mark it, train it, torture it, force it to carry out tasks, to perform ceremonies, to emit signs" (Michel Foucault, *Discipline and Punish: The Birth of the Prison*, trans. Alan Sheridan [New York: Vintage, 1977], 25).

21. Mikhail Bakhtin, *Rabelais and His World*, trans. Helene Iswolsky (Bloomington: Indiana University Press), 1984.

22. Elaine Scarry, *The Body in Pain* (New York: Oxford University Press, 1985).

23. Bruce Robbins, "The Butler Did It: On Agency in the Novel," *Representations* 6 (Spring 1984): 90.

24. Jerome McGann, *Towards a Literature of Knowledge* (Chicago: University of Chicago Press, 1989), ix.

25. Chris Tiffin and Alan Lawson, *De-Scribing Empire: Post-Colonialism and Textuality* (London: Routledge, 1994), 3.

26. Bill Ashcroft, Gareth Griffiths, and Helen Tiffin, *The Empire Writes Back: Theory and Practice in Postcolonial Literatures* (London: Routledge, 1989), 8.

27. Srinivas Aravamudan, *Tropicopolitans: Colonialism and Agency* (Durham, NC: Duke University Press, 1999), 4–5; Ketu Katrak, *Politics of the Female Body: Postcolonial Women Writers of the Third World* (New Brunswick, NJ: Rutgers University Press, 2006).

28. Homi Bhabha, *The Location of Culture* (New York: Routledge, 1994); Sara Suleri, *The Rhetoric of English India* (Chicago: University of Chicago Press, 1992); Edward Said, *Orientalism* (New York: Vintage, 1979); Abdul R. JanMohamed, *Manichean Aesthetics: The Politics of Literature in Colonial Africa* (Amherst: University of Massachusetts Press, 1983).

29. See, for example, Suleri, *Rhetoric of English India*, 174.

30. Gaurav Desai, *Subject to Colonialism: African Self-Fashioning and the Colonial Library* (Durham, NC: Duke University Press, 2001), 17. See also Rocío Davis and Sue-Im Lee's recent introduction, urging a similar attention to aesthetics in literary critical approaches, in *Literary Gestures: The Aesthetic in Asian American Writing* (Philadelphia: Temple University Press, 2006).

31. Derek Attridge, *The Singularity of Literature* (New York: Routledge, 2004), 13.

32. Margery Sabin, *Dissenters and Mavericks: Writings about India in English, 1765–2000* (New York: Oxford University Press, 2002), 4–5.

33. Giddens, *Central Problems*, 52.

34. Louis Montrose, "Professing the Renaissance: The Poetics and Politics of Culture," in *The New Historicism*, ed. H. Aram Veeser (New York: Routledge, 1989), 30.

35. Bart Moore-Gilbert, ed., introduction to *Writing India, 1757–1990: The Literature of British India* (Manchester, UK: Manchester University Press, 1996), 13. See also Deepika Bahri's recent argument for reading the aesthetics as well as politics of cosmopolitan postcolonial writers (Bahri, *Native Intelligence: Aesthetics, Politics and Postcolonial Literature* [Minneapolis: University of Minnesota Press, 2003]).

36. I include here the term *difference* in both senses of the word, borrowing from Barbara Johnson: difference *from* others (what makes a text unique or individual), and difference *within* itself (a text as non-unified and self-contradictory), such that the very idea of (a text's) wholeness or identity is subverted. See Johnson, *The Critical Difference: Essays in Contemporary Rhetoric of Reading* (Baltimore, MD: Johns Hopkins University Press, 1980), 4–5.

37. Paul Smith, *Discerning the Subject* (Minneapolis: University of Minnesota Press, 1988), xxxv.

38. Jane Austen, *Mansfield Park* (1814), ed. Tony Tanner (London: Penguin, 1985), 168; my emphasis.

39. Edward Said, *Culture and Imperialism* (New York: Knopf, 1993), 80–97.

40. Hanif Kureishi, *The Buddha of Suburbia* (New York: Penguin, 1990), 146–47.

41. Paul Smith, *Discerning the Subject*, xxviii, xxvii, 164n2.

42. Anthony Giddens, *Central Problems*, 69–70, 56. Giddens's more recent work continues this argument in the context of modernity: "The self is not a passive entity, determined by external influences; in forging their self-identities, no matter how local their specific contexts of action, individuals contribute to and directly promote social influences that are global in their consequences and implications" (Giddens, *Modernity and Self-Identity: Self and Society in the Late Modern Age* [Stanford, CA: Stanford University Press, 1991], 2). See also Pierre Bourdieu, *In Other Words: Essays Towards a Reflexive Sociology* (Stanford, CA: Stanford University Press, 1990), on "habitus" as a structure that functions as a matrix, enabling and constraining but not disallowing human agency (62–63).

43. Meili Steele, *Theorizing Textual Subjects: Agency and Oppression* (Cambridge: Cambridge University Press, 1997), 10.

44. Louis Montrose, "The Elizabethan Subject and the Spenserian Text," in *Literary Theory/Renaissance Texts*, ed. Patricia Parker and David Quint, 333 (Baltimore, MD: John Hopkins University Press, 1986).

45. Anderson, *Arguments within English Marxism*, 3. Anderson distinguishes between three kinds of human agency: "private goals," or everyday actions, such as choosing who to marry, where to live, and so forth, free choices that, he argues, we all exercise to varying degrees but that are nevertheless still "inscribed within existing social relations" and do not change the status quo; "collective or individual projects" that are "not aimed to transform social relations . . . to create new societies or master old ones"; and "a conscious programmme aimed at creating or remodeling whole social structures," such as the American and French Revolutions (19–20). Thus, he holds the possibility of agency as a goal.

46. Simon Gikandi, *Maps of Englishness: Writing Identity in the Culture of Colonialism* (New York: Columbia University Press, 1996), 38. The work of the subaltern studies collective, of postcolonial feminists, and (more recently) of Gikandi, Srinivas Aravamudan, and Gaurav Desai are examples of this trend.

47. For one thing, as Giddens points out, the assumption of action theory that agency must be bound to intention is flawed—Giddens redefines agency as "logically prior to subject/object differentiation" (*Central Problems*, 92). For another, as the philosophers Michel Callon and John Law have proposed, the tendency to think of

agency in terms of intention is problematic because "there *are* non-human agents." What we take to be human agents are the confluence of a variety of objects, effects, and structural relations that work together to produce agency—in a single body. Michel Callon and John Law, "Agency and the Hybrid Collectif," *South Atlantic Quarterly* 94, no. 2 (Spring 1995): 483.

48. Jane Tompkins, *Sensational Designs: The Cultural Work of American Fiction, 1790–1860* (Oxford: Oxford University Press, 1985), xv.

49. Montrose, "Elizabethan Subject," 306, 332.

50. Kenneth Burke, *Language as Symbolic Action: Essays on Life, Literature, and Method* (Berkeley: University of California Press, 1966), 44–45.

51. Percy Bysshe Shelley, "A Defence of Poetry," in *Shelley's Poetry and Prose*, ed. Donald Reiman and Sharon Powers (New York: Norton, 1977), 508.

52. Wolfgang Iser, "The Play of the Text," in *Languages of the Unsayable: The Play of Negativity in Literature and Literary Theory*, ed. Sanford Budick and Wolfgang Iser (Stanford, CA: Stanford University Press, 1987), 326, 327.

53. McGann, *Towards a Literature*, vii.

54. Rudyard Kipling, "Literature" (1906), in *A Book of Words: Selections from Speeches and Letters Delivered between 1906 and 1927* (New York: Doubleday, 1928), 3–4.

55. Kipling begins this speech by modestly disclaiming the honor he has been given as a writer and complimenting his audience by admitting the "gulf that separates even the least of those who do things worthy to be written about from even the best of those who have written things worthy of being talked about" (3). See also his 1891 story "A Conference of the Powers," in which a famous writer is envious of the experiences of four younger Englishmen, who have done more in India than many men at home several times their age (in Kipling, *Mine Own People* [New York: Lovell, Coryell and Co., 1891], 197–216).

56. An important exception is the new field of life-writing studies, in which maintaining a belief in truth and distinctions between fact and fiction remains an ethical imperative. In his excellent essay, Paul Lauritzen argues that "the problem with any defense . . . that sacrifices the importance of referentiality is that it leads to a kind of corrosive skepticism. Menchu's defenders properly point out that we cannot know the whole truth or truth with a capital T. But it does not follow from this epistemic humility that there is no truth to be had, and to suggest otherwise is morally dangerous" (Lauritzen, "Arguing with Life Stories: The Case of Rigoberta Menchu," in *The Ethics of Life-Writing*, ed. Paul John Eakin [Ithaca, NY: Cornell University Press, 2004], 31). This is precisely my point about fiction as well, for fiction also refers and degrees of truthfulness matter.

57. Donald Thomas, *A Long Time Burning: The History of Literary Censorship in England* (London: Routledge, 1969), 296.

58. This could begin with Plato's famous dismissal of poetry from the Republic for its falsity, its twice displaced representation (as art) of representations (our reality) of ideal forms (Plato, *The Republic*, trans. Francis Cornford [New York: Oxford University Press, 1941]). It reappears in the challenge posed by the "hard sciences," which concludes that literature cannot convey verifiable or testable truths that correspond to the external world. And ultimately, it was such a category mistake that led to *The Satanic*

Verses being burned and its author placed under (illicit) death sentence, because fiction was misread as literal, as presuming to supplant received "knowledge" with blasphemous untruths (that the Prophet's wives were prostitutes; that the Quran, as the pure word of God, was tampered with by human intervention; and so forth).

59. Literature, according to Sir Philip Sidney, conveys a different and superior kind of truth than either philosophy or history does, because unlike the abstraction of one and the specificity of the other, literature both concretizes experience and is general enough to apply more broadly (Sidney, "An Apology for Poetry," in *The Norton Anthology of Theory and Criticism*, ed. Vincent B. Leitch et al., 323–62 [New York: Norton, 2001]).

60. Tzvetan Todorov, "Fictions and Truths," in *Critical Reconstructions: The Relationship of Fiction and Life*, ed. Robert M. Polhemus and Roger B. Henkle, 33 (Stanford, CA: Stanford University Press, 1994).

61. Hanif Kureishi's work, for instance, has occasioned such controversies, as he depicts Islamic fundamentalism in the film *My Son the Fanatic* or sexual experimentation among racial minorities in *The Buddha of Suburbia*.

62. Graham Dunstan Martin, *Language, Truth and Poetry: Notes Towards a Philosophy of Literature* (Edinburgh: Edinburgh University Press, 1975), 90–92.

63. Friedrich Nietzsche, *The Portable Nietzsche*, ed. and trans. Walter Kaufman (New York: Viking Penguin, 1954), 46–47; Michel Foucault, "Truth and Power," in *Power/Knowledge: Selected Interviews and Other Writings, 1972–1977*, ed. Colin Gordon (New York: Pantheon, 1980), 131.

64. Michael Riffaterre, *Fictional Truth* (Baltimore, MD: Johns Hopkins University Press, 1990), xiv.

65. Here, Foucault merely considers truth as that which is produced by dominant discourses, rather than the kinds of resistant or oppositional truth that are unwelcome to those who have greater power than others do.

66. Christopher Norris, *Reclaiming Truth: Contribution to a Critique of Cultural Relativism* (Durham, NC: Duke University Press, 1996), 78–79.

67. Peter Brooks, *Body Work: Objects of Desire in Modern Narrative* (Cambridge, MA: Harvard University Press, 1993), xii–xiii.

68. Elaine Scarry, introduction to *Literature and the Body*, ed. Scarry (Baltimore, MD: Johns Hopkins University Press, 1988), xxi.

69. Jewett, *Fatal Autonomy*, xiii.

70. Judith Butler, *Gender Trouble: Feminism and the Subversion of Identity* (New York: Routledge, 1990), 130.

71. See, for instance, Mark Johnson, *The Body in the Mind: The Bodily Basis of Meaning, Imagination, and Reason* (Chicago: University of Chicago Press, 1990); and George Lakoff, *Philosophy in the Flesh: The Embodied Mind and Its Challenge to Western Thought* (New York: Harper Collins, 1999).

72. Brooks, *Body Work*, xii.

73. Scarry, *Body in Pain*, 4.

74. Francis Barker, *The Tremulous Private Body: Essays on Subjection* (London: Methuen, 1984), 12–13.

Chapter One: Children of an Other Language

1. Kipling, "My First Book," in *Rudyard Kipling: Something of Myself and Other Autobiographical Writings*, ed. Thomas Pinney (Cambridge: Cambridge University Press, 1990), 177; hereafter cited as *Something of Myself*. Originally published in *The Idler*. This "first book" refers to Kipling's collection of poems, *Departmental Ditties* (Lahore, 1886), though, as Pinney notes, Kipling's juvenilia had been published earlier in informal collections that included pieces by his family (171).

2. This was only the case with white men and Indian women—the converse was too taboo to make it into print. See, for example, the sudden tragic deaths of Ameera and her child in Kipling, "Without Benefit of Clergy," in *Life's Handicap* (1891), ed. P. N. Furbank (New York: Penguin, 1987), and the ironical story "Kidnapped," in which a mésalliance between a woman of mixed race and a promising young English lieutenant is stopped by his solicitous peers, in Kipling, *Plain Tales from the Hills*, ed. Andrew Rutherford (Oxford: Oxford University Press, 1987). See also Teresa Hubel on Kipling's representations of the relation between Britain and India as a dubious and impermanent marriage (Hubel, "'The Bride of His Country': Love, Marriage, and the Imperialist Paradox in the Indian Fiction of Sara Jeannette Duncan and Rudyard Kipling," *Ariel* 22, no. 4 [1987]: 3–19).

3. In troping literary parenthood, Lawrence Sterne's *Tristram Shandy* typically conflates the engendering of the text and of the writer as a process of childbirth. Similarly, writing in 1818, Keats renders his poetic work as (re)productive labor, "glean'd" from his "teeming brain" ("When I Have Fears"). Recent critics have extended this trope, from Harold Bloom's theory of poems propagating poems in a poet's patricidal anxiety of influence, to Wayne Koestenbaum's model of male literary collaboration as a "metaphoric sexual intercourse" that leads to a homoerotically produced child-text. See Bloom, *The Anxiety of Influence: A Theory of Poetry* (New York: Oxford University Press, 1973); and Koestenbaum, *Double Talk: The Erotics of Male Literary Collaboration* (New York: Routledge, 1989).

4. In describing himself as a "child" author and a child of empire, Kipling enlists biographical truth: he began writing at a very early age and upon his early success was considered a precocious "boy genius" (John Carrington, *Rudyard Kipling: His Life and Work* [London: Macmillan, 1955, 68, 71). In fact, many readers, such as Henry James in his introduction to Kipling's *Mine Own People*, wondered whether Kipling's "freshness" would last (ix). In colonial discourse, both colonizer and colonized could be represented as a child, with very different implications: for the former, childhood became a mode of self-exoneration via a rhetoric of magic, innocence, and adventure; for the latter, child status signified the need for paternalistic control.

5. Zohreh Sullivan, *Narratives of Empire: The Fictions of Rudyard Kipling* (Cambridge: Cambridge University Press, 1993), 6. Kipling was born and raised in Lahore but, as was customary for many Indian-born English children, was sent to England at the age of six to live with foster-parents. He returned to his parents at age seventeen, when he began working as a journalist for the *Civil and Military Gazette*.

6. The term *Anglo-Indian* in colonial times referred to British colonizers living in India, though it is now used for people of European and Indian descent, who were then called "Eurasians." In this discussion, I maintain Kipling's usage to avoid confusion.

7. S. P. Mohanty notably examines Kipling's constructions of race, hegemony, and children in "Kipling's Children and the Colour Line," *Race and Class* 31 (1989): 21–40. See also the brief consideration of Kipling's childhood to read ambivalence in *Kim* in Radha Achar, "The Child in Kipling's Fiction: An Analysis," *Literary Criterion* 22, no. 4 (1987): 46–53.

8. Edmund Wilson, "The Kipling That Nobody Read," first published in *Atlantic Monthly*, 1941, reprinted in *Kipling's Mind and Art*, ed. Andrew Rutherford (Stanford, CA: Stanford University Press, 1964), 17–69. Wilson's influential reading cast Kipling as "fundamentally submissive to authority" (28) and conflated his life and work into the "thesis, antithesis, synthesis" model: having a "sensitive understanding of India" (32); becoming patriotic and imperialistic in his middle period after his sojourn in America; and finally, embittered by war and the death of his son, elliptical, ironic. and detached in his late period.

9. George Orwell, "Rudyard Kipling," in Rutherford, *Kipling's Mind and Art*.

10. Benita Parry, *Delusions and Discoveries: Studies on India in the British Imagination, 1880–1930* (Berkeley: University of California Press, 1972), 214; Alan Sandison, "Kipling: The Artist and the Empire," in Rutherford, *Kipling's Mind and Art*.

11. Sullivan, for instance, describes Kipling's discourse as "dynamic, slippery and sometimes oppositional" and notes that "while mimicking the varied voices of its uneasy and half-denied ideology, . . . [it] questions official structures and raises the possibility of repressed and alternative rereadings of official imperial mythology" (*Narratives of Empire*, 10).

12. See also Hai, "On Truth and Lie in a Colonial Sense: Kipling's Tales of Tale-Telling," *English Literary History* 64, no. 2 (Summer 1997): 599–625, in which I elaborate on Kipling's use of fiction as a "lie" or disguise to tell colonial truths and I read his early piece "The Biggest Liar in Asia" as an example of the anxiety of literary agency.

13. All the stories I refer to are from *Plain Tales*, unless otherwise stated. Published as a collection in 1888, *Plain Tales of the Hills* catapulted the twenty-two-year-old Kipling to sudden fame in India and abroad. Thirty-two of the forty tales in the collection had appeared earlier in the *Civil and Military Gazette* and the *Pioneer* earlier (Carrington, *Rudyard Kipling*, 129, 134–37).

14. In fact, Kipling's facility in "Hindustani" was a nostalgic fantasy. See Rushdie's cutting remarks on Kipling's knowledge of the vernacular, which was limited to imperatives (Rushdie, *Imaginary Homelands*, 77).

15. Kipling, *Wee Willie Winkie* (1889), ed. Hugh Haughton (London: Penguin, 1988).

16. See, for example, the stories "Miss Youghal's Sais," "The Bronckhorst Divorce Case," and "To Be Filed" in Kipling, *Plain Tales*.

17. Kipling, "The Son of His Father," in Kipling, *Land and Sea Tales for Scouts and Guides*, vol. 35 (New York: Charles Scribner's and Sons, 1923), 218.

18. Later, Rushdie also uses this image. In *Midnight's Children*, Durga, the large-breasted washerwoman who feeds Saleem's son, supplies both milk and stories (532). In

Haroun and the Sea of Stories, Haroun's father's endless supply of stories is likened to the child's supply of milk (17–18).

19. Frantz Fanon, *Black Skin, White Masks,* trans. Charles Lam Markmann (New York: Grove Press, 1967), 38.

20. I use the male pronoun here advisedly, for these colonial children and their imperial enterprise are nearly always gendered as masculine. See also Kipling's story "A Conference of the Powers," in which a young Anglo-Indian subaltern's account of his exploits has to be translated from this hybrid language for the "home-staying Englishman," a famous writer who envies these young boys for both their experiences in colonial warfare and their artless facility in storytelling (Kipling, *Mine Own People,* 201). In fact, this native-born's mixed language includes only a sprinkling of Indian words (and these are inaccurate): "Good chap, but too *zubberdusty,* and went *bokhar* four days out of seven. He's gone out too," says the "Infant" mystifyingly (italics in original). "The other subaltern . . . was overbearing in his demeanor. He suffered much from the fever of the country, and is now dead," translates the narrator (204). Idiomatically and semantically, the soldiers' (and Kipling's) language mistakes the Urdu, for "*zubberdusty*" is a noun, not an adjective, denoting force, and "went *bokhar*" would more appropriately be translated as "got fever."

21. See Sara Suleri's account of the "economy of the borrowed breast" in her discussion of Anglo-Indian women's writing (*Rhetoric of English India,* 81). See also Gayatri Spivak's translation and discussion of Mahasweta Devi's story "Breast-Giver," in which the milk-mother dies of breast cancer after suckling over fifty children of an affluent household (Spivak, *In Other Worlds: Essays in Cultural Politics* [New York: Routledge, 1988], 222–68). Whereas both critics focus on the women concerned, here I explore the Anglo-Indian child's imagined access to language via this dual mothering and discuss the ensuing knowledge of the sacrifice on which this biculturalism depends.

22. Homi Bhabha, "Signs Taken for Wonders: Questions of Ambivalence and Authority under a Tree outside Delhi, May 1817" (1985), in Bhabha, *Location of Culture,* 114.

23. Robert Young, *Colonial Desire: Hybridity in Theory, Culture and Race* (New York: Routledge, 1995), 6.

24. Kipling may well have been familiar with the notion, which was then current in northern India, that children who had been breast-fed by the same foster-mother or "wet-nurse" were to be regarded as siblings. Relations between them included incest prohibitions—suggesting that such a maternal relation was considered bodily enough to create "real" lifelong physiological links between children.

25. Thomas Macaulay's program for instituting English in India to create a small buffer zone of natives who could mediate between the British and the rest of India is well known: "I feel . . . that it is impossible for us, with our limited means, to attempt to educate the body of the people. We must at present do our best to form a class who may be interpreters between us and the millions whom we govern; a class of persons, Indian in blood and colour, but English in taste, in opinions, in morals, and in intellect" (Macaulay, "Minute on Indian Education" [1835], in Macaulay, *Selected Writings,* ed. John Clive and Thomas Pinney [Chicago: University of Chicago Press, 1972], 245). But for Anglo-Indians such as Kipling, these *babu* figures were not welcome; hybridity was an asset only for Anglo-Indian children, not for educated Indians.

26. Gauri Viswanathan, "The Beginnings of English Literary Study in British India," *Oxford Literary Review* 9 (1987): 2–26.

27. Both are collected in Rudyard Kipling, *The Man Who Would Be King, and Other Stories*, ed. Louis Cornell (Oxford: Oxford University Press, 1987). These are, of course, the more well known Indian stories that come to mind as examples of Kipling's ambiguous questioning of empire. In *Plain Tales* as well, many stories are ironically cynical about the damage done by empire, if not on an aggregate scale, then on an individual one; these include "In the Pride of His Youth" (a youthful colonialist loses his child, then his wife, because of hard work and low pay) and "The Madness of Private Ortheris" (which describes the derangement and near desertion of a soldier in India). Most suggestive are the stories (such as "To Be Filed") that show how empire imposes damage by (self-)censorship yet assert their power to resist by exposing it in the writing of the stories.

28. These deaths are, of course, partly understood as another sacrifice for the white man's burden, the inevitable cost of empire. In fact, the 1899 poem of that title, "White Man's Burden" (in Kipling, *War Stories and Poems*, ed. Andrew Rutherford [London: Oxford University Press, 1987]), includes the following lines:

> The ports ye shall not enter,
> The roads ye shall not tread,
> Go make them with your living,
> And mark them with your dead!"
>
> (29–32)

29. See, for example, Harriet Tytler's account of unexpected deaths of children (including her own) and adults from disease, accident, or hardship in Anglo-India (77, 82–88). Especially notable is her story of a colonial regiment being perversely sent to the "gates of death" (Dacca) by Lord Dalhousie as a "punishment" for questioning imperial decrees. Tytler, *An Englishwoman in India: Memoirs, 1828–1858*, ed. Anthony Sattin (Oxford: Oxford University Press, 1986), 81–82.

30. Kipling, *Something of Myself*, ed. Thomas Pinney. Concerning Kipling's many "ruthless omissions," Pinney notes, "Indeed a part of the method of *Something of Myself* is not just concealment and omission but repeated reminders to the reader that only certain things are to be talked of" (viii, xxv).

31. In Kipling, *War Stories and Poems*, 328.

32. See Kipling, "Under the Deodars" (1888), collected in *Wee Willie Winkie*.

33. Sigmund Freud, "The Theme of the Three Caskets," in Freud, *Character and Culture* (New York: Macmillan, 1963), 71.

34. I read this tale as an allegory of the mutilation of text and writer—both lovers lose body parts that are associated with writing or generation: Bisesa's hands are cut off (presumably by her family), and Trejago is almost castrated. However, it is more often read as a warning against the dangers of interracial sexuality. Also see Hubel, "Bride of His Country"; and Moore-Gilbert, *Writing India*, 14–16.

35. Hai, "On Truth and Lie."

36. See Pinney's discussion in Kipling, *Something of Myself*, xxiii–xxiv; and Kipling's account in that autobiography, 31–32. Too progressive for its time, the Ilbert Bill allowed Indian judges (educated in the British system) to hear charges against Europeans in their

jurisdiction and aroused immense irritation among the latter. Of his newspaper's sudden editorial switch from protest to approbation of the bill, Kipling writes, "I followed . . . the many pretty ways by which a Government can put veiled pressure on its employees" (32). (The bill was subsequently amended to reinstate the racially discriminatory practice of not allowing even qualified Indians to preside over Europeans in court.)

37. See Margarita Barns's detailed account, *The Indian Press: A History of the Growth of Public Opinion in India* (London: Allen and Unwin, 1940), 241–47; and Gerald N. Barrier, *Banned: Controversial Literature and Political Control in British India, 1907–1947* (Columbia: University of Missouri Press, 1974), 1–10.

38. Barns, *Indian Press*, 93–110.

39. Quoted in Barns, *Indian Press*, 136.

40. Quoted in Barns, *Indian Press*, 255.

41. Kipling, *Something of Myself*, 3, 10. It was later accepted by *The Englishman*.

42. Quoted in Barns, *Indian Press*, 269.

43. Barrier, *Banned*, 5; see also Barns, *Indian Press*, 262–68.

44. Thomas, *Long Time Burning*, 296. For discussions of more-recent forms of censorship under the Official Secrets Act in Britain, especially under Margaret Thatcher, see Robert Emmet Long, ed., *Censorship*, The Reference Shelf, vol. 61, no. 3 (New York: Wilson, 1990); and Paul O'Higgins, *Censorship in Britain* (London: Nelson, 1972).

45. It is worth distinguishing between Kipling the "author" and the Kipling "narrator," a textual construct—a persona that can be manipulated, used, or ironized by Kipling. For an account of the slipperiness and instability of this narrative voice, see Sullivan, *Narratives of Empire*, chapter 3.

46. The title is ambiguous, since it may refer both to the tale itself, as that which must be filed for reference, and to the tale *within* the tale, the manuscript that stores Indian secrets and, as Kipling suggests, has become *his* file for reference.

47. Koestenbaum writes, "Looking at a variety of the specimens of 'double talk,' I apply to each the same paradigm, which is, bluntly stated, that men who collaborate engage in a metaphoric sexual intercourse, and that the text they balance between them is alternately the child of their sexual union, and a shared woman" (*Double Talk*, 3).

48. Sullivan reads this story as Kipling's cautionary account of the relation between colonial knowledge and failure (*Narratives of Empire*, 111–13). However, where she focuses on the deterioration and death of McIntosh the writer as the key to the story, I locate its interest in Kipling's emphasis on the "baby" and narrator left behind, which is indicative of Kipling's intertwined concerns with censorship, textual hybridity, and power.

49. Carrington, *Rudyard Kipling*, 284, 424; Martin Seymour-Smith, *Rudyard Kipling: A Biography* (New York: St. Martin's Press, 1989), 77–78; and Angus Wilson, *The Strange Ride of Rudyard Kipling* (New York: Penguin, 1977), 63. Sullivan also cites this as an example of familial censorship: Kipling was discouraged from publishing it by his parents, thereby being "censored by his most beloved authority Figures" (*Narratives of Empire*, 112).

50. On the controls that contemporary reviewers imposed on the content and ideological possibilities of Kipling's writings, see also Sandra Kemp, *Kipling's Hidden Narratives* (London: Blackwell, 1988), 1; and Ann Parry, "Reading Formations in the Victorian Press: The Reception of Kipling, 1888–1891," *Literature and History* 2 (1985): 256.

51. The earliest form of this law was first enacted in 1823, after the deportation of Buckingham: "The first and last pages of books and papers printed at a licensed press, to contain certain specifications," which included the name of the printer, the place of publication, and a list of all other books and papers printed at that press (Barns, *Indian Press*, 121–22).

52. Kipling's preface to *Life's Handicap*, for instance, insists that all his tales in that volume come from an Indian one-eyed holy mendicant named Gobind (who also instructs him to seek the poor for more "authentic" stories, because they keep their "ear to the ground"). Similarly, the preface to *The Jungle Book* solemnly thanks his sundry animal "informants," as if an Anglo-Indian could tell Indian tales only by repudiating his own creativity. *In Black and White* is a collection of native stories, in some of which Kipling tries to create a native speaking voice. But its preface is purportedly written by his domestic (native) servant, who inserts his prior claim to the stories collected or "written" by his white master, Kipling, who has stolen credit as author.

53. Teresa Hubel, *Whose India? The Independence Struggle in British and Indian Fiction and History* (Durham, NC: Duke University Press, 1996); and Edward Said, *Culture and Imperialism*, 11, emphasis in original. As William Blake wrote, "The Foundation of Empire is Art and Science. Remove them or Degrade them and the Empire is no more. Empire follows Art and not vice versa" (quoted in Said, *Culture and Imperialism*, 13).

54. See my discussion of his "Biggest Liar in Asia" in Hai, "On Truth and Lie."

55. Cleanth Brooks has memorably argued that Macbeth kills Macduff's children because he has none of his own: a lack of posterity renders useless Macbeth's murderous rise to power, for his name will not live (Brooks, "The Naked Babe and the Cloak of Manliness," in Brooks, *The Well-Wrought Urn* [New York: Harcourt, Brace, 1947]).

56. Gauri Viswanathan argues, "In the psychodrama of the British presence in India, . . . the loss of children in the unfamiliar climate of the tropics brought out the deepest insecurity in the British male colonizer, his apparent power and authority in the military and political sphere undermined by his inability to ensure the continuity of his biological line" (Viswanathan, "Yale College and the Culture of British Imperialism," *Yale Journal of Criticism* 7, no. 1 [1994]: 7).

57. In his 1893 story "One View of the Question," Kipling suggests that Indians are not invested in fighting off the British, because this empire cannot sustain itself anyway: a Rajah's minister writes that he would be happy to fight the colonizers for their posterity's rule "if the Sahibs in India could breed sons who lived so that their houses might be established . . . but the Sahibs die out at the third generation in our land" (Kipling, *Many Inventions* [New York: D. Appleton, 1893], 93).

Chapter Two: The Doubleness of Writing (in) Kim

1. Rudyard Kipling, *Kim* (New York: Penguin, 1987), 49, 52.
2. See, for example, Mark Kinkead-Weekes, "Vision in Kipling's Novels," in Rutherford, *Kipling's Mind and Art*, 216. By contrast, Zohreh Sullivan notes the opposition be-

tween the initial "rejection of authority" and the subsequent "new image of authority —the boy in control of the gun" (*Narratives of Empire*, 149).

3. Many critics, such as Irving Howe, have pointed out that Kim's magical propensities and ease in the Indian bazaar are Kipling's wholly unreal fantasy (Howe, "The Pleasures of Kim" [1977]; reprinted in *Kim: Modern Critical Interpretations*, ed. Harold Bloom [New York: Chelsea House, 1987], 37. I would add that the fantasy also acknowledges and explores the illicit power that prevails in the text. "The men of the city" do not "smile" when Kim "sidles up . . . knowing that they will hear something clever or mischievous or . . . enjoy his command of the Indian art of cursing" (Howe, "Pleasures of Kim," 37). They are silenced by a power that they are forced to recognize is superior.

4. For an account of fiction as a truth-telling lie for Kipling, see Hai, "On Truth and Lie."

5. The term *Great Game* refers to the competition between Britain and Russia for imperial power in the late nineteenth century.

6. The history of the reception of *Kim* tells us how it may have been used to serve in the imperial game, that is, how the writing of empire indeed can enable empire to write itself on the world. Michael Rosenthal describes how British statesman Robert Baden-Powell's invention of scouting—as an institution for training boys to become tools of empire—was inspired by his reading of *Kim* (Rosenthal, *The Character Factory: Baden-Powell's Boy Scouts and the Imperatives of Empire* [New York: Pantheon, 1986], 108–9, 165).

7. Said, "The Pleasures of Imperialism," in *Culture and Imperialism*, 144.

8. S. P. Mohanty, "Kipling's Children and the Colour Line," *Race and Class* 31 (1989): 21–40.

9. Even critics who have studied Kipling's figurations of the artist have ignored *Kim*. In "Kipling's Portraits of the Artist," David H. Stewart lists artists or writers in Kipling's writing but omits *Kim* (Stewart, "Kipling's Portraits of the Artist," *English Literature in Transition: 1880–1920* 31, no. 3 [1988]: 265–83). Edward Said has argued that *Kim* is a lapsed bildungsroman that does not lead to the protagonist's moral education, for no "awakening" is to be found for Kim (Said, *Culture and Imperialism*, 156). However, we might instead see *Kim* as a text that inverts not only the bildungsroman but also the *künstlerroman* (artist-novel). It tells a very canny story of the destruction of the artist, for it tells the story of a mutilated artist and art, a story not of the growth but of the decline of an artist under the force of empire. Perhaps an awakening *is* to be found in *Kim*—an awakening not of the character but of the writer—a knowledge of the costs of empire that the text may only intimate.

10. Suleri, *Rhetoric of English India*, 125.

11. Bhabha, "Signs Taken for Wonders," in Bhabha, *Location of Culture*.

12. Brooks, *Body Work*, 3.

13. In a rare moment, Kipling takes the reader aside: "But Kim did not suspect [yet] that Mahbub Ali, . . . a wealthy and enterprising trader, . . . was registered in one of the locked books of the Indian Survey department as C25IB" (69).

14. See, for example, J. M. S. Tompkins, *The Art of Rudyard Kipling* (Lincoln: University of Nebraska Press, 1965), 22.

15. Mohanty, "Kipling's Children," 24, 35.

16. It is worth comparing Kim's initial namelessness with the problem of *Gora*, Rabindranath Tagore's novel, which was modeled on *Kim* (trans. Surendranath Tagore [Madras: Macmillan, 1924]). Like Kim, Gora, the protagonist of the novel, is white, of Irish background, but unlike Kim, he thinks he *is* Indian and has no idea of his original parentage. Only at the very end of the novel does Gora discover that he is the child of white parents killed during the "Mutiny" of 1857. But when his Bengali foster-father tries to return to him the identity hidden for twenty-four years, Gora refuses it: "Your father had been killed the previous day. . . . His name was—" "There is no need to hear his name!" roared Gora. "I don't want to know his name" (402). Born of the Mutiny, with "no mother, no father, no country, no nationality, no God even," Gora claims that he has now become a "real Indian," free from the binds of caste and of "opposition between Hindu, Muslim and Christian" (402–6). Whereas Kim's freedom ends with the discovery of his parentage, Gora's freedom—and by implication the postcolonial nation's—begins with the loss of his adopted father's name and the rejection of his biological one's. For both Kim and Gora, anonymity (or self-naming) constitutes freedom from the entrapment of signification.

17. Kipling, "How the First Letter was Written," in *Just So Stories* (London: Macmillan, 1902), 83–96.

18. Kipling, "The Conversion of Aurelian McGoggin," in *Plain Tales*, 83.

19. Suleri, *Rhetoric of English India*, 116–17.

20. Ian Baucom, *Out of Place: Englishness, Empire, and the Locations of Identity* (Princeton, NJ: Princeton University Press, 1999), 94. There is now a growing literature on imperial geography and the politics of map making. See, for instance, Paul Carter, *The Road to Botany Bay: An Exploration of Landscape and History* (New York: Knopf, 1988); and Benedict Anderson on the role of European map making in the colonization of Asia (Anderson, *Imagined Communities: Reflections on the Origin and Spread of Nationalism* [New York: Verso, 1991], 170–78). Baucom elaborates: "The mapping of India . . . was a vital element in the English attempt to control the empire less by occupying it than by knowing it, classifying it, and rendering it visible" (*Out of Place*, 93).

21. Much anthropological and cultural criticism has examined the ideological underpinnings of museums, which institutionalize the death of cultural forms and indeed participate in killing them as living forms: preservation suggests death. See, for instance, James Clifford on the politics of the collection of the art of "tribal cultures" (Clifford, *The Predicament of Culture: Twentieth Century Ethnography, Literature and Art* [Cambridge, MA: Harvard University Press, 1988], 189–251).

22. See, for instance, Said, *Culture and Imperialism*, 139.

23. Ian Baucom has read this moment as an anomalous instance of the lama's "civil insubordination and sly mockery" (*Out of Place*, 97). But this is not substantiated by the text. The lama's deconstruction of imperial cartography is entirely and typically guileless.

24. A good example is James Mill's highly influential text, *The History of British India*, abridged and with an introduction by William Thomas (Chicago: University of Chicago Press, 1975), 27.

25. E. M. Forster, *A Passage to India* (New York: Harcourt, Brace and Jovanovich, 1965), 13.

26. Suvir Kaul, "*Kim*, or How to Be Young, Male, and British in Kipling's India," in *Kim*, ed. Zohreh Sullivan (New York: Norton, 2002), 436.

27. Mohanty, "Kipling's Children," 24–25.

28. Deirdre David, "Children of Empire: Victorian Imperialism and Sexual Politics in Dickens and Kipling," in *Gender and Discourse in Victorian Literature and Art*, ed. Antony H. Harrison and Beverly Taylor, 135, 137 (DeKalb: Northern Illinois University Press, 1992).

29. Sullivan, *Narratives of Empire*, 176).

30. Suleri and Baucom also note the debilitation of Kim: "Creighton erases [Kim] until he exists as nothing other than a code name" (Baucom, *Out of Place*, 95); "As Kim is inexorably reduced to the sum of his utility, his power as a cultural reader is simultaneously curtailed" (Suleri, *Rhetoric of English India*, 127).

31. Definitions of "doctor," in *Webster's New World Dictionary*.

32. Said, *Culture and Imperialism*, 142–43.

33. Some critics have read this ending as the lama's appropriation "into the values of action" of the Game, giving up his values of "vision, repose and nonaction" to "postpone his entry into Nirvana" for Kim's sake (Sullivan, *Narratives of Empire*, 177). In either case, as the text makes clear, he remains deluded.

Chapter Three: Forster's Crisis

1. E. M. Forster, "Liberty in England" (1935), an essay reprinted in his collection *Abinger Harvest* (New York: Harcourt, Brace, 1936), 68–69.

2. Forster began his first novel in 1902 (*Lucy*, later published as *A Room with a View* in 1908), but his first published novel was *Where Angels Fear to Tread* (1905), followed by *The Longest Journey* (1907) and *Howards End* (1910). In 1911 he published a group of previously published short stories under the title *The Celestial Omnibus, and Other Stories*.

3. As Adela toils up the mountain with Aziz, her progress is halted, her "rope broken" by her sudden realization that she does not love her fiancé (E. M. Forster, *A Passage to India* [New York: Harcourt, Brace and Jovanovich, 1965], 168; hereafter cited as *PI*). What stalled Forster at this point was the crucial event of the novel: he knew that something catastrophic needed to happen in the caves, but he could not give it shape. See Oliver Stallybrass, introduction to *A Passage to India* (Abinger Edition, vol. 6, 1978) and introduction to *The Manuscripts of "A Passage to India,"* Abinger Edition, vol. 6a (London: Edward Arnold, 1978), xiii; hereafter cited as *MPI*. Of existing manuscripts, the greatest number of abandoned versions are of the caves episode. Stallybrass speculates that there were still more chapters or fragments, probably destroyed by Forster before he could resume the novel (*MPI*, xiii).

4. Mary Lago and P. N. Furbank, eds., *Selected Letters of E. M. Forster*, vol. 1, 1879–1920 (Cambridge, MA: Harvard University Press, 1983), 302; hereafter cited as *Letters*, with volume number indicated.

5. Lago and Furbank, introduction to *Letters*, 1:x. See also David Bradshaw's introduction to *The Cambridge Companion to E. M. Forster* (Cambridge: Cambridge University Press, 2007), 2–3.

6. P. N. Furbank, *E. M. Forster: A Life* (London: Cardinal, 1977, 1978), 1:191, 197, 255; 2:132. Hereafter cited as *A Life*.

7. In Britain, from 1885 onwards, the Labouchere Amendment legally criminalized "gross indecency" between men. Only in 1967, ten years after the Wolfenden Report, was male homosexuality partially decriminalized between consenting adults. See also Jeffrey Meyers's introduction to his *Homosexuality and Literature, 1890–1930* (Montreal: McGill-Queen's University Press, 1977) for an account of the negative consequences for some of Forster's contemporaries upon discovery of their homosexuality.

8. He did find a partial solution in the form of the fantastic short story, as I elaborate in Hai, "Forster and the Fantastic: The Covert Politics of *The Celestial Omnibus*," *Twentieth-Century Literature* 54, no. 2 (Summer 2008): 217–46. But this did not work for the novel form.

9. For brief accounts, see the introduction to Robert K. Martin and George Piggford, eds., *Queer Forster* (Chicago: University of Chicago Press, 1997), 18–21; and Matthew Curr, "Recuperating E. M. Forster's *Maurice*," *Modern Language Quarterly* 62, no. 1 (2001): 53–69.

10. See, for instance, the work of Robert K. Martin, Sara Suleri, and Ian Baucom, as well as the important anthology of critical essays, *Queer Forster*, ed. Martin and Piggford.

11. Egypt was then part of the British Empire. The scion of an affluent Indian Muslim family, Masood was Forster's pupil at Cambridge, with whom he had fallen in love, to whom he would dedicate *A Passage to India*, and on whose behest Forster had been on a six-month traveling tour to India in 1912–13.

12. Eve Kosofsky Sedgwick, *The Epistemology of the Closet* (Berkeley: University of California Press, 1990), 19–21.

13. On the continuity between the homosocial and homosexual, see Eve Kosofsky Sedgwick, *Between Men: English Literature and Male Homosocial Desire* (New York: Columbia University Press, 1985), 1–5.

14. The censor's letter makes no allowance for the possibility that Forster's objections to conscription were a matter of conscience. As Forster explained to the chief commissioner later, "It was a matter of . . . a very profound instinct which he could only call conscience and which presented the taking of life of a fellow creature as the most horrible thing he could do" (Furbank, *A Life*, 2:26). This later developed into his famous 1938 statement in "What I Believe": "I hate the idea of causes, and if I had to choose between betraying my country and my friend I hope I should have the guts to betray my country" (Forster, "What I Believe," in Forster, *Two Cheers for Democracy* [New York: Harcourt, Brace Jovanovich, 1951], 68).

15. I use the term *queer* as Martin and Piggford define it, as that which "seeks to disrupt the economy of the normal" (Martin and Piggford, introduction to *Queer Forster*, 4).

16. In *The Ruling Passion: British Colonial Allegory and the Paradox of Homosexual Desire* (Durham, NC: Duke University Press, 1995), Christopher Lane argues that homosexuality in fact cemented colonial power, but coexisted with the broadly held understanding that such irregularity could only undermine that power.

17. Quoted in Furbank, *A Life*, 1:199.

18. Quoted by Elizabeth Heine and Oliver Stallybrass, in their introduction to Forster, *Arctic Summer* (London: Edward Arnold, 1980), xvi.

19. Debrah Raschke, "Breaking the Engagement with Philosophy: Re-envisioning Hetero-Homo Relations in *Maurice*," in Martin and Piggford, *Queer Forster*, 153–54, 162.

20. Unpublished until after his death, the novel was circulated only among intimate and sympathetic friends. Sassoon had read and liked it.

21. As we know from his diary, Forster sought models of implicitly homoerotic writing by making a list of possible writers that included Shakespeare, Housman, Whitman, and Carpenter. See Furbank, *A Life*, 1:159n1.

22. His caustic reply to D. H. Lawrence's attempts to conscript him into Lawrence's sexual revolution suggests a similar disinclination toward the explicit: "I do not like the deaf imperciplent fanatic who has nosed over his own little sexual round until he believes that there is no other path for others to take" (February 12, 1915; *Letters*, 1:219). Repudiating both Lawrence's social program and the explicit sexuality of Lawrence's art, Forster implies that the "fanatic" who cannot perceive the subtlety of politics other than his own may be equally blind to other artistic approaches to the body or sexuality.

23. See also Eric Haralson, "'Thinking about Homosex' in Forster and James," in Martin and Piggford, *Queer Forster*, 59–74.

24. According to the *Oxford English Dictionary*, the earliest use of the word *fairy* for "homosexual" occurred in 1895, in the *American Journal of Psychology*, and by 1945 had become current.

25. To Malcolm Darling, December 1, 1916; *Letters*, 1:246.

26. I elaborate on this in my essay, "Forster and the Fantastic."

27. Forster, "Edward Carpenter," in Forster, *Two Cheers for Democracy*, 207.

28. Forster, *The Hill of Devi, and Other Indian Writings*, ed. Elizabeth Heine, Abinger Edition, vol. 14 (London: Edward Arnold, 1983), 164; hereafter cited as *HDI*.

29. Even when he is repelled by phenomena he observes in India, he manifests the same attentiveness to the body in a new space. His reaction to the sight of Muslims praying together in a mosque, for instance, expresses an orientalist compulsion and repulsion: "I then saw the Friday prayers—impressive but ridiculous to see hundreds of people [men] squatting at once, with their faces on the ground" (to Florence Barger, November 2, 1912; *Letters*, 1:147). Yet Forster singles out this act for comment, possibly because it emphasizes a disturbing configuration of the relation between the body and individual identity—conformity and submission.

30. E. M. Forster, *The Hill of Devi* (New York: Harvest/HBJ, 1953), 33–34; hereafter cited as *HD*.

31. Yonatan Touval, "Colonial Queer Something," in Martin and Piggford, *Queer Forster*, 237.

32. "The Poetry of C. P. Cavafy," in Forster, *Pharos and Pharillon* (New York: Knopf, 1961), 91. Tellingly, Forster adds that "either life entails courage, or it ceases to be life" (97). See also Furbank, *A Life*, 2:31–32. In an interesting echo, Rushdie uses the same phrase later: "My story, my fictional country exist, like myself, at a slight angle to reality. I have found this off-centering to be necessary" (Salman Rushdie, *Shame* [New York: Aventura, 1983], 24). Here, both postcolonial subject and writer must be positioned in such a way as to see anew.

33. Joseph Bristow, *Effeminate England: Homoerotic Writing after 1885* (New York: Columbia University Press, 1995), 3.

34. E. M. Forster, *Maurice* (New York: Norton, 1971), 91.

35. This chance encounter with Risley also dissuades Maurice from posing as heterosexual when he learns of Tchaikovsky's artistic and psychic breakdown when attempting the same. Risley thus not only warns Maurice but also helps him to consolidate his affinities with other homosexual men.

36. Lago and Furbank, *Letters*, 1:141n3. See also Forster's *Indian Journal*: "The minorite [i.e., homosexual] story of S's. Amazing conversation. His diary" (*HDI*, 122).

37. Furbank, *A Life*, 1:255.

38. See also Baucom's reading of Forster's letters and travel diary in *Out of Place*, 116–30.

39. A good example of the latter is Kipling's story "His Chance in Life," which presents the Eurasian as a weak, pretentious, opportunistic "half-breed" (in Kipling, *Plain Tales*), 59–64.

40. It might be useful to recall Forster's itinerary and unusually intimate experience with at least three different groups in this six-month trip: Indian Muslims, British officials, and Hindus. Upon arriving in Bombay, he separated from G. L. Dickinson and his English fellow-travellers and plunged into Masood's Muslim circle in Aligarh and Old Delhi, where he stayed with M. S. Ansari, "one of the moderate leaders of the ... future Muslim separatist movement" (*Letters*, editors' note, 1:137). His next experience was of Lahore, where he saw the British in India and observed the festering resentments there while staying with his English friends, the Darlings. After a brief sightseeing tour in the north—including the historic Khyber Pass, the Himalayas, and Simla—he rejoined his English friends to visit the Hindu states of Chhatarpur and Dewas, where he witnessed the tensions of British surveillance over an "independent" native state. Then he visited Masood in Bankipore—the basis for Chandrapore—and noted the particularly ugly prejudice of Anglo-Indians toward educated Indians. Finally, Forster returned to Bombay, via Patiala, Jaipur, and (predominantly Muslim) Hyderabad.

41. Malcolm Darling had been the Rajah's tutor.

42. On the performative in gender and sexuality, see Judith Butler, *Gender Trouble*, 128–41.

43. Mary Louise Pratt, *Imperial Eyes: Travel Writing and Transculturation* (New York: Routledge, 1992).

44. See, for instance, George Steiner, who argues that the model of true friendship between Fielding and Aziz replaces Alec and Maurice's "unresolved homosexual intimacy" (Steiner, "Under the Greenwood Tree," *New Yorker* 47 [October 9, 1971], 158–69).

45. See Furbank, *A Life*, 1:256–59.

46. Forster's jubilation was mixed with anxiety about its reception, for *Maurice* functioned as a coming-out occasion even among friends he could trust. To Forrest Reid, he wrote defensively, hoping that Reid's feelings toward Forster would not alter: "I have not written one word of which I am ashamed" (January 23, 1915; *Letters*, 1:217).

47. In the same letter, Forster comments, "Whitman nearly anticipated me but didn't really know what he was after, or only half knew—and shirked, even to himself, the statement"; and on Lawrence's *The White Peacock*, Forster notes, "The whole book is the queerest product of subconsciousness that I have yet struck—he has not a glimmering from first to last of what he's up to."

48. Robert K. Martin, "The Double Structure of *Maurice*," in *E. M. Forster: New Casebooks*, ed. Jeremy Tambling (New York: St. Martin's, 1995), 100–114.

49. Quentin Bailey gestures insistently toward links between *Maurice* and *A Passage to India* but does not specify what those links are, other than a similar underlying system of racial and class education for Britain's middle and ruling classes. Ultimately, he criticizes Forster for subsuming, even sacrificing, imperial issues to domestic ones, a reading with which I clearly disagree, for I find the two necessarily intertwined and mutually enabling (Bailey, "Heroes and Homosexuals: Education and Empire in E. M. Forster," *Twentieth-Century Literature* 48, no. 3 [2002]: 324–48).

50. In the same letter, Forster adds that he is afraid to send her the novel, for reading it might render him "remote" to Florence—although, he hopes, not "repellant."

51. For an excellent account of the country house tradition and its links to imperialism, see Baucom, *Out of Place*, chapter 5.

52. See Matthew Curr for a different but positive reading of the novel, though one that does not locate it in relation to empire. Curr, "Recuperating E. M. Forster's Maurice," *Modern Language Quarterly* 62, no. 1 (2001): 53–69.

53. Forster, "The Other Boat," posthumously published in *The Life to Come, and Other Stories*, ed. Oliver Stallybrass (London: Edward Arnold, 1972), 166–97.

54. Forster became the first president of the National Council for Civil Liberties in 1934 (Furbank, *A Life*, 2:186–91). In 1928, Forster had taken a stand on the *Well of Loneliness* case, Radclyff Hall's lesbian novel. Unable to praise it but clear about the wrongness of its being prosecuted, he published an anonymous article entitled "The New Censorship," then co-signed a joint letter with Virginia Woolf protesting its suppression (Furbank, *A Life*, 2:153–55). In 1945, he wrote an essay on Milton's *Areopagitica* and frequently used his position as an eminent writer to take positions and urge action against suppressive bills (Furbank, *A Life*, 2:189).

55. For the complicated publication history of *Alexandria*, see Furbank, *A Life*, 2:44, 57, 109, 113.

56. Forster's introduction explains the title with characteristic self-deprecation: "Pharos, the vast and heroic lighthouse that dominated the first city—under Pharos I have grouped a few antique events; to modern events and to personal impressions I have given the name of Pharillon, the obscure successor of Pharos, which clung for a time to the low rock of Silsileh and then slid unobserved into the Mediterranean" (12). Like Pharillon, he suggests, his writing too might provide a kind of light before it slides into the sea.

57. Much had occurred in the meantime to increase Indian resistance and British nervousness, including the Rowlatt Act, the Amritsar massacre, and Gandhi's non-cooperation movement.

58. In his reading of this letter as exemplifying the dangers of colonial intimacy, Gregory Bredbeck assumes that the couple is British. But there is no such indication in the text. This account is not about interracial homoerotic exchange or xenophobia, as Bredbeck argues. Rather, it suggests that Forster saw Indian men as enacting a form of heterosexuality among themselves that incorporated homophobic jokes about homosexuality as well as a permissiveness about homosexuality legitimized by the open joking (Bredbeck, "'Queer Superstitions': Forster, Carpenter, and the Illusion of [Sexual] Identity," in Martin and Piggford, *Queer Forster*, 29–32).

59. See, for instance, Lane, *Ruling Passion*, 145–75.

60. Christopher Lane also sees a split in Forster's public and private writing, which Lane identifies as a dissonance between a public liberal politics of homophilia ("only connect" from *Howards End* to "What I Believe") and a private unconscious ambivalence about interracial homosexuality. The split I see is different: between that public politics and a private but *conscious* understanding of sexual erotics that developed later, after 1922.

61. Christopher Lane, "Volatile Desire: Ambivalence and Distress in Forster's Colonial Narratives," in Moore-Gilbert, *Writing India*, 188–89.

62. Young, *Colonial Desire*, 149. See also Peter Stallybrass and Allon White, *The Politics and Poetics of Transgression* (Ithaca, NY: Cornell University Press, 1984) on the conjoining of desire with disgust in the structure of bourgeois repression.

63. See Forster, *Two Cheers for Democracy*, 67–76.

64. For a lengthier discussion of this strategy in Orwell and Forster, see Hai, "'Out in the Woods': E. M. Forster's Spatial Allegories of Property, Sexuality, Colonialism," *Literature, Interpretation, Theory* 14, no. 4 (October–December 2003): 317–55.

65. Forster, "Kanaya," in *HDI*, 310–25. See also the editor's note on page 310.

66. Ian Baucom reads this episode as cementing the homoerotic intimacy between the Rajah and Forster over the body of Kanaya, in an analogous structure to Fielding and Aziz cementing their relationship over the body of Adela (*Out of Place*, 129–30). However, for Forster, any romantic charge that may have existed between them was trumped by exasperation and disappointment. Forster's public support of the Rajah, in gratitude for his kindness and tactful treatment of Forster's homosexuality, was mitigated by private reflections such as the following in a letter to Dickinson: "I am supposed to read aloud to him once a day. I read aloud to him once a month." Complaining about how H.H. misapprehends and cheapens what he reads, Forster adds, "Thus is his mind constituted. The intellect is in splendid condition but he does not want to use it, cannot see why it should be used" (August 6, 1921; *Letters*, 2:10).

67. See, for instance, Forster's account of his sexual arousal by a palace servant despite his inability to tell "these little Indians apart" (*HDI*, 317).

68. Some critics have read this episode as straightforward proof of the colonial exploitation of an underclass. Revathi Krishnaswamy, for example, rightly notes that "Kanaya" "reverses the colonial myth of the lascivious Oriental and replaces it with the colonial reality of the lascivious European" (Krishnaswamy, *Effeminism: The Economy of Colonial Desire* [Ann Arbor: University of Michigan Press, 1998], 161). But she reads Kanaya as simply an "abject figure of the subaltern Indian male, serially victimized by Indian feudalism and English colonialism" (161). Undoubtedly, a court servant such as Kanaya had no choice but to accede to the Rajah's demand that he satisfy an Englishman's depersonalized lust, nor could he resist Forster's vindictive violence, but he is not wholly without agency even as Forster describes him: instead of maintaining the silence of subjection, he chooses to aggrandize his prestige by boasting of his relations with Forster, and then to blackmail the Rajah. Moreover, such a narrative needs to be read not only as a mode of access to historical or cultural reality but also as a rhetorically crafted mode of representation and confession that complicates our understanding of the writer's consciousness of his own location in the structures of colonial desire and power.

69. April 8, 1922; quoted in the introduction to Forster, *Life to Come*, xii.
70. The story was posthumously published in Forster, *Life to Come*.

Chapter Four: At the Mouth of the Caves

1. E. M. Forster, "Pan," in *Abinger Harvest* (New York: Harcourt Brace, 1936, 1964), 318–24.
2. For a detailed discussion of this and other stories, see Hai, "Forster and the Fantastic," in which I argue that Forster used the genre of the fantastic as a mode to advance a queer, liberatory politics, despite the difficulties he faced in writing about homosexuality.
3. Quoted in Furbank, *A Life*, 2:106.
4. Forster began writing *A Passage To India* upon his return from India in 1913, but after a few chapters, he found himself "stalled" (Furbank, *A Life*, 1:255). After a long gap, interrupted by the war and his sojourn in Alexandria, he resumed it upon his return from his second trip to India, in 1922 (Furbank, *A Life*, 2:106). Oliver Stallybrass argues that Forster wrote the novel in two stages: roughly July 1913 to June 1914 and April or May 1922 to January 1924 (Stallybrass, introduction to *MPI*, xii). The surviving manuscripts show intense revision but also indicate that others may have been lost. For Stallybrass's detailed attempts to date the manuscripts, see *MPI*, xii–xii.
5. Among the earlier, influential readings of Forster were Lionel Trilling's *E. M. Forster* (New York: New Directions, 1943), which established Forster as a liberal humanist, and Wilfrid Stone's magisterial study, *The Cave and the Mountain* (Stanford, CA: Stanford University Press, 1965). For representative selections of subsequent criticism, see Harold Bloom, ed., *E. M. Forster's* A Passage to India: *Modern Critical Interpretations* (New York: Chelsea House, 1987); and Jeremy Tambling, ed., *E. M. Forster: New Casebooks* (New York: St. Martin's, 1995).
6. Judith Scherer Herz, "Listening to Language," in J. Beer, *Passage to India*, 59. See also Gillian Beer, "Negation in *A Passage to India*," in J. Beer, *Passage to India*, 44–58; Molly Tinsley, "Muddle *et cetera*: Syntax in *A Passage to India*," in J. Beer, *Passage to India*, 71–80; and Michael Orange, "Language and Silence in *A Passage to India*," in Bloom, *E. M. Forster's*, 57–74. For a feminist reading of rape as the unsayable, see Brenda Silver, "Periphrasis, Power, and Rape in *A Passage to India*," *Novel* 22 (Fall 1988): 86–105.
7. Of course, these two mutually exclusive possibilities—the ultimate failure or success of language—produce an inevitable instability. Herz's optimistic affirmation of the triumph of art can be revoked if we push the implications of her argument further: if the novel tries to present some form of understanding while concurrently undermining the possibility of the effectiveness of language, then, by the same token, its own act of language may be equally futile.
8. John Colmer, *E. M. Forster: The Personal Voice* (London: Routledge, 1975), 168.
9. Orange, "Language and Silence," 58.
10. Tinsley, "Muddle *et cetera*," 258, 266.
11. This is not to deny that some differences (such as, for example, Aziz's and his friends' different ways of hearing poetry) are due to history.

12. For instance, Herz reads the Bhattacharya's invitation to visit (which fails to materialize in the promised carriage) as simply a "time-filler" with "no meaning" ("Listening to Language," 67). But it does have a meaning: the invitation (like Aziz's later) is ingratiatingly given with the conviction that no English lady would really deign to accept: a political reality of Anglo-India that Bhattacharya knows and that both Mrs. Moore and Adela, looking for the "real India," fail to see.

13. Benita Parry, "The Politics of *A Passage to India*," in J. Beer, *Passage to India*, 28–30. In Parry's important reading, the novel's coincidence with colonial discourse lies in both the racial generalizations about the "fixed characteristics" of Orientals, especially Aziz, and its understanding of imperialism as merely socially pernicious, rather than an economic, capitalist, and political system. Its counterdiscourse, according to her, consists in its exposure of the failure of liberalism, the impossibility of friendship, compromise, or dialogue in a context of colonialism (34); and in its revocation of colonial stereotypes, replacing the exotic with the formless, the knowable and inferior with the remote but "original system of knowledge and alternative world view"(29). For other influential postcolonial readings of Forster's ideology, see Abdul JanMohamed, who finds Forster more impeded, despite his best efforts, by imperial ideology (*Manichean Aesthetics*, 92–96), and Edward Said, who finds the novel "remarkable" for its liberal critique but faults Forster for evading the reality of Indian nationalism (*Culture and Imperialism*, 200–206).

14. Suleri, *Rhetoric of English India*, 132–48.

15. On representation as violence, see Nancy Armstrong and Leonard Tennenhouse, eds. *The Violence of Representation: Literature and the History of Violence* (New York: Routledge, 1989).

16. E. M. Forster, *A Passage to India* (New York: Harcourt Brace, 1924, 1965), 12; hereafter cited as *PI*.

17. In an more telling earlier version, finally excluded perhaps because it made Aziz too ridiculous, Forster included another instance, in which Mrs. Moore writes Aziz a letter accepting his invitation to the Marabar Caves, which he then excitedly displays "to all his friends" (174). "Mrs. Moore wrote Aziz a . . . \gracious/ line of acceptance — the first \letter/ he had ever received from an English woman. . . . [I]t moved him deeply." The letter is passed around from hand to hand, a material object of marvel and pride, spelling proximity to the forbidden and distant (*The Manuscripts of "A Passage to India*," ed. Oliver Stallybrass, Abinger Edition, vol. 6a [London: Edward Arnold, 1978], 172, hereafter cited as *MPI*). In quoting from these earlier manuscripts, I follow the editor's convention of indicating Forster's additions by \. . ./ and deletions by <. . .>.

18. From the rationalist viewpoint of Fielding, Aziz misreads Mrs. Moore, who made no effort to help him. But if seen through the lens of memory and emotional truth, Aziz's gratitude seems less absurd. "During the shouting of her name in court I fancied she was present," he reports (282). This is validated by Adela's recantation and the textual hints of Mrs. Moore's ghost flying back from her ship at the same time (284), suggesting that the evocation of her name has a material effect on Adela, jogging her memory and recalling Mrs. Moore's conviction of his innocence (227), which results in the clearing of Aziz's name.

19. Fielding's remark is a crucial one, but it disappears from the final text of *Passage*, probably for two reasons: first, Forster preferred to show rather than state such a point; and second, it goes verbatim into *Maurice* (32).

20. Adela Quested's name is usually read as indicative of her *questing* urge to see the "real India," for which she is well and truly punished—by India and by Forster's narrative. But her name also suggests her *questioning* feistiness, a resistant irrepressibility for which she is punished by *Anglo*-India.

21. In phrases such as "the shawl of night," Forster's language may echo the poetic mode of writers such as Edward Fitzgerald and other Urdu and Persian poets whose work he would have heard recited and translated during his sojourns in India.

22. This is a good example of what Frantz Fanon has called "third-person consciousness" (Fanon, *Black Skin, White Masks*, trans. Charles Lam Markmann [New York: Grove Press, 1967], 110).

23. The language of Christina Rossetti's brilliant poem "Goblin Market" suggests that the forbidden goblin bodiliness prohibited by "good" society includes both (homo)sexuality and the foreign produce of colonial lands that may infect English purity.

24. For a foundational discussion of naming as a mode of exerting colonial control, see Paul Carter, *The Road to Botany Bay: An Exploration of Landscape and History* (New York: Knopf, 1988), esp. 1–34. The naming of landscape, the transformation of "space" into "place," Carter writes, "embodied the traveler's directional and territorial ambition: his desire to possess where he had been as a preliminary to going on" (48).

25. See Jenny Sharpe, *Allegories of Empire: The Figure of Woman in the Colonial Text* (Minneapolis: University of Minnesota Press, 1993), 113–36.

26. By deconstruction, I do not mean that I as critic destroy another's meanings (or that Forster as writer does so); instead, I show how the text (of Ronny's words) deconstructs itself, to reveal its own fundamental contradictions. As Barbara Johnson notes, *deconstruction* is etymologically related to *analysis*, which means to "undo": "The de-construction of a text does not proceed by random doubt or arbitrary subversion, but by the careful teasing out of warring forces of signification within the text itself" (Johnson, *Critical Difference*, 5). Forster functions as a deconstructive reader and critical worker in that he shows (e.g., through Mrs. Moore, a reader internal to the text) how colonial language (e.g., Ronny's) undoes itself.

27. Francis Barker, *The Tremulous Private Body: Essays on Subjection* (London: Methuen, 1984), 63.

28. E. M. Forster, "The Celestial Omnibus," in Forster, *Celestial Omnibus*, 62.

29. I discuss this at more length in Hai, "Out in the Woods."

30. For a detailed reading of the punkah-wallah along these lines, see Charu Malik, "To Express the Subject of Friendship: Masculine Desire and Colonialism in A *Passage to India*," in Martin and Piggford, *Queer Forster*, 221–36.

31. On the occasion of a speech he gave in Italy in 1959, Forster chose to read from *Passage* the central description of the caves, which, his comment suggests, is basic to the action or sequence of events but also initiates the action, or is the agent of the narrative (Forster, "Three Countries," in Forster, *The Hill of Devi*, 298).

32. See *MPI*, xii and 165–360.

33. In 1756, a small English army at Fort William, the English garrison in Calcutta, was attacked and defeated by Siraj-ud-daula, the Nawab of Bengal. Unknown to the Nawab, some English prisoners (the exact numbers are disputed) were placed in a dungeon, the proverbial "Black Hole," where they died of suffocation. The incident aroused tremendous indignation in Britain and became a legendary moment in British-Indian relations. See Stanley Wolpert, *A New History of India*, 5th ed. (Oxford: Oxford University Press, 1997), 179.

34. Stallybrass and White, *Politics and Poetics*, 19, 53.

35. Jo Ann Hoeppner Moran, "E. M. Forster's *A Passage to India*: What Really Happened in the Caves," *Modern Fiction Studies* 34, no. 4 (Winter 1988): 596–604.

Chapter Five: From a Full Stop to a Language

1. Salman Rushdie, "Outside the Whale," in *Imaginary Homelands* (New York: Viking Penguin, 1991), 100; hereafter cited as *IH*.

2. Saleem the narrator often shares narratival strategies—but is not to be confused—with Salman Rushdie the author. Like Rushdie, he aspires to write a history of the nation that will help rebuild that nation, but, as Rushdie points out, Saleem is also a tool of the author: he is an unreliable narrator whose megalomania and limitations Rushdie foregrounds to inculcate readerly skepticism of any claims to truth (Rushdie, "Errata; or, Unreliable Narration in Midnight's Children," *IH*, 24).

3. Rushdie, *Midnight's Children* (New York: Viking Penguin, 1981), 115; hereafter cited as *MC*.

4. Anderson, *Imagined Communities*, 6–7.

5. Ferdinand Saussure, *Course on General Linguistics* (1915), excerpted in *The Norton Anthology of Theory and Criticism*, ed. Vincent B. Leitch et al., 956–76 (New York: Norton, 2001). Languages, of course, also have their limiting frameworks, syntactic and semantic boundaries, and implicit worldviews that are dependent on specific cultural histories.

6. Rushdie's early essay "The Empire Writes Back with a Vengeance" (*London Times* [July 3, 1982], 8) was the first use of this characteristically witty, now frequently quoted phrase.

7. Rushdie's political work and its efficacy have been understandably a matter of critical controversy, depending in part on how his location is read: as a metropolitan cosmopolitan writer (see Timothy Brennan, *Salman Rushdie and the Third World: Myths of the Nation* [New York: St. Martin's, 1989]); as a diasporic Indian (see Anuradha Dingwaney Needham, *Using the Master's Tools: Resistance and the Literature of the African and South Asian Diasporas* [New York: St. Martin's, 2000]); reclaimed as an indigenous Indian elite (Bishnupriya Ghosh, *When Borne Across: Literary Cosmopolitics in the Contemporary Indian Novel* [New Brunswick, NJ: Rutgers University Press, 2004]); and now as an immigrant American. For a brief account of some of these debates, see M. Keith Booker, introduction to *Critical Essays on Salman Rushdie*, ed. Booker (New York: G. K. Hall, 1999), 1–15. For an updated chronology of Rushdie's life, see Abdulrazak Gurnah, *The Cambridge Companion to Salman Rushdie* (Cambridge: Cambridge Uni-

versity Press, 2007), xi–xiv. I read Rushdie as doing multiple kinds of political work, as I specify in each instance, and addressing multiple audiences while being enabled rather than limited by his location.

8. Gilles Deleuze and Félix Guattari, *Kafka: Toward a Minor Literature* (1975), excerpted in Leitch et al., *Norton Anthology of Theory and Criticism*, 1593–1601.

9. As Dennis Brutus notes, this was also an explicit concern for South African writers in the new post-apartheid South Africa: how they would contribute to "the construction of a new, non-racial, and democratic society. . . . [W]hat they should write about, how they should write, and where they should direct their energies" (Brutus, "Literature and Change in South Africa," *Research in African Literatures* 24 [Fall 1993]: 102).

10. *Midnight's Children* in particular provided a new language for South Asian writers in English, legitimating all kinds of new stories of selfhood and community and opening up new stylistic and discursive possibilities that made an almost complete break from the first generation of Indian English writers. See Josna Rege, "Victim into Protagonist? *Midnight's Children* and the Indian National Narrative of the 1980s," reprinted in Booker, *Critical Essays*, 250–82. Among other examples, Rege reports Anita Desai describing how her fiction too was enabled by Rushdie's new idiom (272).

11. For a handy collection of such introductory critical essays on Rushdie's work, see D. M. Fletcher, ed., *Reading Rushdie: Perspectives on the Fiction of Salman Rushdie* (Amsterdam: Rodopi, 1994); and the later collection edited by Booker, *Critical Essays*. Important early critical introductions include James Harrison's *Salman Rushdie* (New York: Twayne, 1992); and D.C.R.A. Goonetilleke's *Salman Rushdie* (New York: St. Martin's, 1998). Timothy Brennan's *Salman Rushdie and the Third World* (New York: St. Martin's, 1989) was the first monograph to be published on Rushdie's work.

12. See, for instance, Needham, *Using the Master's Tools*; and Ghosh, *When Borne Across*. Booker (in the introduction to *Critical Essays*, 13) accuses Rushdie of anticommunism, Bahri (in *Native Intelligence*) of failure to address subalternity adequately.

13. Examples of the former include Lisa Appignanesi and Sara Maitland, eds., *The Rushdie File* (Syracuse, NY: Syracuse University Press, 1990); Akeel Bilgrami, "Rushdie and the Reform of Islam," *Grand Street* 8, no. 4 (Summer 1989): 170–84; Feroza Jussawalla, "Rushdie's *Dastan-e-Dilruba*: The Satanic Verses as Rushdie's Love Letter to Islam," *Diacritics* 26, no. 1 (Spring 1996): 50–73; and of the latter (on *The Satanic Verses*) in particular, Gayatri Spivak, *Outside in the Teaching Machine* (New York: Routledge, 1993), 217–42; Suleri, *Rhetoric of English India*, 174–206; Sara Suleri, "Whither Rushdie?" *Transition* 51 (1991): 198–212; Michael Gorra, *After Empire: Scott, Naipaul, Rushdie* (Chicago: University of Chicago Press, 1997), 149–56; Ian Baucom, *Out of Place*, 190–218; and Srinivas Aravamudan, "'Being God's Postman Is No Fun, Yaar': Salman Rushdie's *The Satanic Verses*," *Diacritics* 19, no. 2 (1989): 3–20.

14. Deepika Bahri, for instance, argues that postcolonial novels such as Rushdie's and Arundhati Roy's must be read recuperatively with attention to their aesthetics, in which is located a necessary politics, despite their commercial, global success. See also Madalena Gonzalez, *Fiction after the Fatwa: Salman Rushdie and the Charm of Catastrophe* (Amsterdam: Rodopi, 2005).

15. Fletcher, *Reading Rushdie*, 3.

16. Josna Rege, *Colonial Karma: Self, Action and Nation in the Indian English Novel* (New York: Palgrave Macmillan, 2004); John Clement Ball, *Satire and the Postcolonial Novel: V. S. Naipaul, Chinua Achebe, Salman Rushdie* (New York: Routledge, 2003).

17. Rege, for instance, argues that the problem of acting without concern for self or consequences (karma) is endemic to Indian nationalist and novelistic discourses, but Rege finds that the novelists' middle-class basis ultimately produces failure to act: "Identifying with the downtrodden, their characters tend to gravitate toward revolutionary action; but, constrained by self-interest, they pull back at the eleventh hour, . . . Action fails to be carried out in the novel's resolution, or else it is compromised, privatized" (*Colonial Karma*, 9–10). My concern is with how both colonial and postcolonial literatures chart the constraints and possibilities of their own agency and do succeed in achieving agency, in however varied or attenuated a form.

18. Bakhtin's work is the basis for Ball's reading of Rushdie. See also M. Keith Booker, "'Beauty and the Beast': Dualism as Despotism in the Fiction of Salman Rushdie," *ELH* 57, no. 4 (Winter 1990): 980; and Abdulrazak Gurnah, "Themes and Structures in *Midnight's Children*," in Gurnah, *Cambridge Companion*, 97.

19. Mikhail Bakhtin, *Rabelais and His World*, trans. Helene Iswolsky (Bloomington: Indiana University Press, 1984), 11–12.

20. Though the novel has often been regarded as limited to or even culpable for Saleem's upper-class perspective, we can read it rather differently if we recognize Saleem's positionality as ironized by the narrative. When Saleem first encounters Shiva via telepathic communication, for instance, Saleem's youthful intellectualism and democratic idealism are scorned by Shiva, "the rat-faced youth with filed-down teeth" whose life on the street has understandably taught him a brutal law of gangsterhood and tyranny as a means of survival. "'Rich kid,' Shiva yelled, 'you don't know one damn thing! What *purpose*, man? What thing in the whole sister-sleeping world got *reason*, yara? For what reason you're rich and I'm poor? Where's the reason in starving, man? God knows how many millions of damn fools living in this country, man, and you think there's a purpose! Man, I'll tell you—you got to get what you can, do what you can with it, and then you got to die'" (*MC*, 262–64; italics in original). The twin principles of brutality and intellect, tyranny and communality that these children of midnight represent are not simple binarisms but are instead produced by their material locations. In Book 3, Saleem must learn, by becoming dispossessed, Shiva's position, just as Shiva learns about power and privilege. At the same time, the text clearly chooses Saleem's constructive agency over Shiva's destructiveness, regardless of their class position.

21. Rushdie, *Shame*, 313–14.

22. Katherine Rowe, *Dead Hands: Fictions of Agency, Renaissance to Modern* (Stanford, CA: Stanford University Press, 1999).

23. Though Rowe does not discuss postcolonial literature or literary agency, my thinking in this section is much indebted to her work.

24. Literary examples abound: although Macbeth is literally the hand (instrument) that kills Duncan, it is Lady Macbeth, the instigator of his action and the agent of responsibility, whose stained hands cannot be washed clean.

25. The repressive Rowlatt Act was passed in March 1919, denying constitutional rights to Indians and occasioning severe protests. Mahatma Gandhi called for civil dis-

obedience, in response to which British colonial authorities banned all public meetings. On April 13, 1919, General Dyer ordered the military to fire on an unarmed crowd of ten thousand peasant festivalgoers trapped in Jallianwallah Bagh in Amritsar, resulting in a massacre that became pivotal in inciting further nationalist sentiment. See Wolpert, *New History of India*, 298–300.

26. See, for example, Jean M. Kane, "The Migrant Intellectual and the Body of History: Salman Rushdie's *Midnight's Children*," *Contemporary Literature* 37, no. 1 (Spring 1996): 94–118.

27. See, for example, Rudolf Bader, "On Blood and Blushing: Bipolarity in Salman Rushdie's *Shame*," *International Fiction Review* 15, no. 1 (1998): 30–34.

28. In *Shame*, for instance, the murderous hatred between Haroun Harappa and his father (Little Mir) is acted out upon the impotent body of a pet dog that leaks a thin yellow liquid as it starves to a putrefying death (159–61). In *Midnight's Children*, the overfed goldfish of the departed British explode to float belly up, with their ruptured insides, in Saleem's pond; Ahmed Sinai's obdurate irascibility makes a pet dog's bowels explode; this is mirrored later in the Bangladesh war, when Saleem's childhood friends reappear as a pyramid of dying intermingled body parts.

29. For an excellent analysis of the meanings and functions of excrement in African and Irish postcolonial fiction of nationalist disillusionment in relation to this tradition, see Joshua D. Esty, "Excremental Postcolonialism," *Contemporary Literature* 40, no. 1 (Spring 1999): 22–59. Whereas Esty reads "the rich life of scatology" in Ayi Kwei Armah, Wole Soyinka, Samuel Beckett, and James Joyce as a negative mode of postcolonial satire, self-implication, or counterdiscourse, I read it in Rushdie (whom he does not mention) as a positive, regenerative trope for the salutary and subversive effects of Rushdie's writing as it circulates in the body politic. Esty usefully identifies two registers through which "shit" has been read—the private, psychological but transcultural and transhistorical versus the public, political but topical—and addresses how they intersect ("Excremental Postcolonialism," 26). My reading of bodily effluvia in Rushdie obviates both the psychoanalytic (of infantile sexuality and so forth) and literal (identifying specific historical detail), to read it as political in its more general effort to disrupt social hierarchies and boundaries of pollution and purity.

30. In terms of chronological revelation, these are therefore the first words of the Quran. See N. J. Dawood, introduction to *The Koran*, trans. Dawood (London: Penguin, 1990), 2; and Marmaduke Pickthall, introduction to *The Meaning of the Glorious Koran* (New York: Penguin, Mentor Book, n.d.), x. The now standardized nonchronological rearrangement of the verses of the Quran (from longest to shortest *suras*) occurred after Muhammad's death, for reasons that scholars can only hypothesize.

31. Though derived from the Judeo-Christian tradition, this Quranic statement is not quite the same as the biblical saying that God created man in his own image: to create man from "clots of blood" implies a palpable bodily relation between creator and creation, not a mimetic one. It also calls for a different poetics of representation.

32. Other references in the Quran suggest that the clot of blood refers literally to the fertilized embryo, which grows from a "living germ" or "a drop of ejaculated semen" into a "lump of flesh." Elsewhere, in describing the divine creation of Man, the Quran

also uses the terms *dust* and *clay*, into which life-spirit was blown (Dawood, *The Koran*, 22:5, 75:38; see also 23:10).

33. In the most everyday examples, for instance, members of the same community —colleagues, friends, or families—start talking like each other, picking up each other's mannerisms, and using the same expressions and, eventually, with more important effects, the same structures of thought.

34. Language literally enters our bodies when we hear or read it; it impinges on our sensory receptors. These inaugurating words of the affirmation of faith require the Prophet, and then all believers, to "recite" the words they hear: they must, in other words, take the words of God into their bodies, subordinating their bodies to their power, and by reciting those words orally, they must enact that belief, so that those words make the human body into their agent. (The heavy emphasis on Quranic recitation—with correct Arabic accent and inflection and often without any idea of the meaning of the words—remains a central feature of South Asian Islamic devotional practice.)

35. Michael Gorra observes that it is hard to care about the individual characters in Rushdie's novels because they are "too firmly under the thumb of his self-regarding style" (*After Empire*, 144–47). But Rushdie is not writing a realist novel in the bourgeois European tradition. What he asks us to care about is the political urgency of the history and ideas he explores, as is clear from the passion and emotional intensity of his writing.

36. Rushdie thus brilliantly conflates the totalitarianism of Indira Gandhi's regime (because it metaphorically kills the future) with the literal birth control program of forcible sterilization of the poor, disabling them from reproducing more children.

37. In fact, as we learn later, it is Shiva's body in Amina's womb, but Saleem's narrative suggests that this does not matter, because Saleem the substitute baby inherits that very same history.

38. For a more detailed account of this in contemporary culture, see Laura Kipnis, "(Male) Desire and (Female) Disgust: Reading *Hustler*," in *Cultural Studies*, ed. Lawrence Grossberg et al., 373–91 (New York: Routledge, 1992).

39. W. B. Yeats, "Crazy Jane Talks with the Bishop" (1933); reprinted in *Norton Anthology of Modern Poetry*, 2nd edition, ed. Richard Ellman and Robert O'Clair (New York: Norton, 1988), 179.

40. For a more detailed discussion of Padma's formative role in co-producing Saleem's narrative, see Hai, "Marching In from the Peripheries: Rushdie's Feminized Artistry and Ambivalent Feminism," in Booker, *Critical Essays*, 26.

41. A *chapati* is the most common form of Indian bread.

42. Naipaul, *Area of Darkness*, 73–76.

43. Mary Douglas, *Purity and Danger: An Analysis of the Concept of Pollution and Taboo* (New York: Routledge, 1984), esp. chapter 7.

44. Saleem has married Parvati, who is pregnant by Shiva, the biological son of Saleem's adoptive parents, so that, through a double twist of fate, their child, Aadam, is the biological grandchild of Amina and Ahmed Sinai.

45. Spiderwebs are built by beginning, emblematically, in the middle, around which larger networks are constructed as extensions. Moreover, this structure is not

static but dynamic: it moves, readjusts, and is subject to damage and repair (as long as the spider survives) so that the web is continually reconstructed in new patterns in response to exigencies of time and chance.

46. James Joyce, *A Portrait of the Artist as a Young Man* (1916), ed. Chester G. Anderson (New York: Viking Penguin, 1968), 253.

47. The only critic I have seen address this episode is David Price, who examines it as an example of *fantasia* (Price, *History Made, History Imagined: Contemporary Literature, Poiesis, and the Past* [Chicago: University of Illinois Press, 1999], 147–51). I likewise read the episode as an account of art, of truthful and therapeutic historiography; however, I see it not as a retreat but as a crucial form of political engagement.

48. For a concise account, see Wolpert, *New History of India*, 386–90.

49. Bhutto became the president of Pakistan until the army took over again in 1977: he was hanged in 1979. Mujib ruled as prime minister and president of the newly independent Bangladesh from 1972 until he was assassinated in 1975. See Sugata Bose and Ayesha Jalal, *Modern South Asia: History, Culture, Political Economy* (New York: Routledge, 1998), 236.

50. Linda Hutcheon, keynote address, Postcolonial Conference, University of Southern Georgia, Savannah, 1998.

51. Ashis Nandy, keynote address, South Asia Conference at the University of Wisconsin–Madison, October 14, 2000.

52. There are, of course, widening circles of complicity: Richard Nixon, the U.S. president at the time, was a strong ally of Pakistan and was well informed about the Pakistani army's action in East Bengal but chose not to exert pressure to stop it.

53. It is through passages of such passionate intensity that we come to care about the characters and what happens to them, even if we do not know their names. See note 35 above.

Chapter Six: When Truth Is What It Is Told to Be

1. Rushdie, "Outside the Whale," in *Imaginary Homelands*, 100.

2. The fisherman (like Tai) directs his young listener, Sir Walter Raleigh (and Saleem), to "something" beyond the horizon. This image haunts Saleem's sleep and, as a text, replicates itself in his life when his mother has a suit of clothes designed for him that is copied from the suit worn by the boy in the picture. For an important reading of this painting as postcolonial ekphrasis, see Neil Ten Kortenaar, "Postcolonial Ekphrasis: Salman Rushdie Gives the Finger Back to the Empire," *Contemporary Literature* 38, no. 2 (1997): 232–59.

3. In fact, Pakistani families do not draw up their family trees, least of all in the Quran, which in Muslim tradition is too sacred a text to be violated by human inscription.

4. The Mohajir Qaumi Movement (MQM) was formed in Pakistan in the 1980s to unify (and arm some) mohajirs against state repression and to redress the various forms of discrimination faced by mohajirs in arenas such as education, employment, and business.

5. For Rushdie to suggest that Bhutto and Zia come from the same family is not historically true, but it suggests that they are akin, both men who abused power in Pakistan—one a military commander and Islamic fundamentalist, the other a feudal landlord, quasi-socialist, and dictator—and manifested the same traits of brutality, corruption, and destruction of the nation.

6. For a discussion of Rushdie's ambivalent representation of women and their artistic powers, see Hai, "Marching In from the Peripheries."

7. As the *Oxford English Dictionary* shows, the etymology of the word *matrix* reveals its development from the female site of reproduction to that which gives form, structure, and unity: uterus, womb; place or medium in which something is bred or produced; mold in which something is cast or reshaped.

8. Anderson, *Imagined Communities*, 187–206. Thus, all self-construction is necessarily predicated on some forms of erasure, indeed, on (self-)censorship. See also Eric Hobsbawm and Terence Ranger's important edited collection, *The Invention of Tradition* (Cambridge: Cambridge University Press, 1983).

9. I can testify personally to how, after both my parents' families migrated to Pakistan from India in 1947 and left behind members of their extended families, I grew up in Pakistan with little sense of how those parts of their now-Indian families still belonged, for they seemed no longer related to "us." As older generations lost touch and letters or visits became increasingly rare, that other "family" quietly dropped out of our familial memories and discourses of selfhood.

10. In talking of the "sacred text" of the story that eventually becomes the congealed final acceptable version, Rushdie is implicitly (at another level, of course) already telling another story here, the story of the construction—by elimination of variety—of another sacred text, the Quran, a story he would tell only too well in *The Satanic Verses*.

11. In his essay "Censorship," Rushdie writes that "the most insidious effect of censorship is that, in the end, it can deaden the imagination. Where there is no debate, it is hard to go on remembering, every day, that there is a suppressed side to every argument. It becomes almost impossible to conceive of what the suppressed things might be" (*Imaginary Homelands*, 39). The existence of such total censorship vitiates an entire people, nullifying their capacity to even imagine alternatives, producing such deep cynicism and mind-numbing helplessness that its citizens no longer know what truth or rights are, nor can they imagine what political accountability or agency might be.

12. See also Rushdie's subsequent explanation of Saleem's unreliable narration in "'Errata'; or, Unreliable Narration in *Midnight's Children*" (1983), in *Imaginary Homelands* (22–25): "As I worked, I found that what interested me was the process of filtration itself" (24). To make the mistakes Saleem does is not only to represent the problematics of representation and historiography but also "a way of telling the reader to maintain a healthy distrust" (25). Rushdie concludes that "the reading of Saleem's unreliable narration might be, I believed, a useful analogy for the way in which we all, every day, attempt to 'read' the world" (25).

13. For instance, my prescribed school textbooks on the history of Pakistan (written in English by nationalist historians) enacted a peculiar disjunction: because Pakistan did not exist before 1947, they would recount the history of the subcontinent as a glorious (Indian) tradition that began with the civilizations of Mohenjodaro and Harappa, but

after 1947 we only got the history of the nation of Pakistan, as if the remaining South Asian land mass had suddenly evaporated from the earth. See, for example, M. Kabir, *A Short History of Pakistan*, general editor I. H. Qureshi, vols. 1–4 (Karachi: University of Karachi, 1967). The general editor's preface revealingly asks, "Is it possible to write the history of Pakistan at all? Can it be disentangled sufficiently from the history of India to stand by itself?" (vii).

14. For powerful fictional accounts of the massacres of Hindus, Sikhs, and Muslims by each other, see Khushwant Singh, *Train to Pakistan* (New York: Grove Press, 1956); and Bapsi Sidhwa, *Cracking India* (Minneapolis: Milkweed, 1991), originally published in 1988 as *The Ice-Candy Man*. See also Rob Nixon, "Of Balkans and Bantustans: The Discourse of 'Ethnic Cleansing' and the Crisis of National Legitimation," *Transition* 60 (1993): 4–26.

15. Spivak, *Outside in the Teaching Machine*, 217–42.

16. Mark Johnson and George Lakoff, *Philosophy in the Flesh: The Embodied Mind and Its Challenge to Western Thought* (New York: Harper Collins, 1999).

17. Salman Rushdie, *The Satanic Verses* (New York: Penguin, 1989), 110; hereafter cited in the text as *SV*.

18. Spivak reads this omnipresence of dreams, or "the dream as legitimizing matrix," in *The Satanic Verses* in terms of the "staging of the author" and the problem of the artist's identity: "The multiple dreams, carried to absurdity, support as they take away the power of this planning genius" (*Outside in the Teaching Machine*, 224–26). While these dreams grant a "peculiar authority" to the dreamer (Gibreel), Spivak argues, they also represent a structure of postcolonial schizophrenia, "because empire messes with identity" (226).

19. In 1983, when *Shame* was published, Zia, erstwhile martial law administrator, was at the peak of his powers as military dictator and president of Pakistan, and Benazir Bhutto was under house arrest, from which she issued ineffectual challenges. Rushdie's prediction that she would replace and mirror Zia's regime was borne out by subsequent Pakistan history. Zia's death and dismemberment in a sabotaged airplane explosion in 1988 was no less phantasmagoric than any prefiguration that Rushdie could dream up. And the story of Benazir's marriage, prime ministership (1988–90), and dismissal on charges of corruption (1990), followed by the familial melodrama of her re-election amidst violent opposition by her mother and the rivalry of her brother (1993–94) almost uncannily confirms Omar's dream and Rushdie's narrative.

20. In the 1970s and 1980s, it was not uncommon for political terrorists in Pakistan to throw acid on women's faces, both to sabotage the work of universities (which were taken over by such male political agents) and to keep women in their place at home. This political intimidation through painful physical disfigurement may well be a subtext for Rushdie's images.

21. Northrop Frye, *The Anatomy of Criticism: Four Essays* (Princeton, NJ: Princeton University Press, 1957), 163–71.

22. I use the term *ending* instead of *closure*, because the former is a more inclusive term that maintains the tension, integral to the dilemma that Rushdie confronts, between a sense of arbitrary or inevitable termination and a sense of the conclusion that one arrives at by design and which reveals or rounds off the implications of all that led

up to it. *Closure*, in contrast, is limited to the latter sense alone, for which it is preferred by D. A. Miller in his study of the incapability of novelistic closure to contain what precedes it: "[Closure] refers us better, I think, to the functions of an ending: to justify the cessation of narrative and to complete the meaning of what has gone before" (Miller, *Narrative and Its Discontents: Problems of Closure in the Traditional Novel* [Princeton, NJ: Princeton University Press, 1981], p. xi, note 2). For an earlier discussion of closure, see Barbara Hernstein Smith, *Poetic Closure: A Study of How Poems End* (Chicago: University of Chicago Press, 1968). Smith classifies various kinds of closure and their functions in poetry, avoiding "psychological speculation" on why closure satisfies or why there may be a resistance to it. See also I. A. Richards, "How Does a Poem Know When It Is Finished?" in *Parts and Wholes*, ed. Daniel Lerner (New York: Free Press of Glencoe, 1963), 163–74.

23. Smith, *Poetic Closure*, 2.

24. Frank Kermode, *The Sense of an Ending: Studies in the Theory of Fiction* (New York: Oxford University Press, 1966).

25. Peter Brooks, *Reading for the Plot: Desire and Intention in Narrative* (Cambridge, MA: Harvard University Press, 1984), 94–96.

26. Nancy Batty discusses Rushdie's narrative techniques of creating suspense, but this is still in aid of achieving a greater "fulfillment" (Batty, "The Art of Suspense: Rushdie's 1001 [Mid]Nights," *Ariel* 18, no. 3 [1987]: 49–65). What I identify as Rushdie's avoidance of ending has little to do with suspense, for it is built on avoiding that satisfaction of closure and the culmination of meaning in the end.

27. See, for example, Aijaz Ahmad, "Salman Rushdie's *Shame*," in Ahmad, *In Theory: Classes, Nations, Literatures* (New York: Verso, 1992), 145–52. See also Inderpal Grewal, "Salman Rushdie: Marginality, Women, and *Shame*," *Genders* 3 (Fall 1988): 24–42.

28. For a reading of this episode as a feminization of prophetic leadership, see Suleri, *Rhetoric of English India*, 202–5.

29. For her dissatisfaction with this ending, which she reads as a failed feminism and final turn to "casual urban fucking," see Spivak, *Outside in the Teaching Machine*, 223; see also interview with Afsaneh Najmabadi, *Social Text* 28 (1991): 132–34.

30. *Haroun* appeared in 1990, a year after the fatwa was declared against Rushdie's life by Khomeini, the figure of darkness who is represented in the figure of Khattam-Shud (as well as in the exiled imam of *The Satanic Verses*). It was written at the beginning of Rushdie's life of incarceration, explicitly for *his* son, soon after Rushdie's second wife, Marianne Wiggins, had left him.

31. The ominous, totalizing control of Khattam-Shud is suggested in the translation of *Chup* as "silence" and *Bezaban* as "tongueless." The chilling nature of this realm of the tongueless is rendered by its physical coldness and absence of light.

32. Deconstructive analysis discloses what binary divisions conceal: differences *within* supposedly homogenous entities and also similarities *across* opposed ones. For example, in the binary man/woman, there are differences within (men as well as women are divided by differences of race, class, nationality, religion, and so forth) and similarities across (men as well as women are connected with each other by religion, race, political affiliation, and so forth, often more so than with others of their own gender).

33. Samuel Beckett, *Waiting for Godot* (New York: Grove Press, 1954), 10, 54, 61.

Epilogue: The Body as the Basis for Literary Agency

1. I borrow the term from Jahan Ramazani, *The Hybrid Muse: Postcolonial Poetry in English* (Chicago: University of Chicago Press, 2001), 19, preferring it to the singularity of terms such as *subject position*.
2. Chinua Achebe, *Things Fall Apart* (New York: Anchor Doubleday, 1959, 1994). Originally published in 1959.
3. Ramazani, *Hybrid Muse*. See in particular chapter 3, "The Wound of Postcolonial History: Derek Walcott's *Omeros*."
4. Derek Walcott, "A Far Cry from Africa," *Collected Poems, 1948–1984* (New York: Noonday–Farrar, Strauss and Giroux, 1986), 17–18. For the early date, see Ramazani, *Hybrid Muse*, 194n.3.
5. Derek Walcott, "The Muse of History: An Essay," in *Is Massa Day Dead? Black Moods in the Caribbean*, ed. Orde Coombs (New York: Doubleday, 1974), 6.
6. Grace Nichols, "Epilogue," in *I Is a Long-Memoried Woman* (London: Karnak House, 1983), 80.
7. Edward Kamau Brathwaite, "Nation Language," in *The Post-Colonial Studies Reader*, ed. Bill Ashcroft et al. (New York: Routledge, 1995), 309–13.
8. Wilson Harris, "The Limbo Gateway" (1981), in *The Post-Colonial Studies Reader*, ed. Bill Ashcroft et al. (New York: Routledge, 1995), 378.
9. *Foe* also incorporates other Defoe novels, particularly *Roxana*. See Gayatri Spivak, "Theory in the Margin: Coetzee's *Foe* reading Defoe's *Crusoe/Roxana*," in *Consequences of Theory*, ed. Jonathan Arac and Barbara Johnson, 154–80 (Baltimore, MD: Johns Hopkins University Press, 1991).
10. J. M. Coetzee, *Foe* (New York: Penguin, 1987). "Cruso" is Coetzee's spelling.
11. J. Coetzee, *Waiting for the Barbarians* (New York: Penguin, 1982).
12. For some of the debates surrounding Coetzee's notoriously elusive fiction both in South Africa and internationally, see especially the introduction by Sue Kossew, ed., *Critical Essays on J. M. Coetzee* (New York: G. K. Hall, 1998), 1–17; and Dominic Head, *J. M. Coetzee* (Cambridge: Cambridge University Press, 1997). For an excellent recent study, see Derek Attridge, *J. M. Coetzee and the Ethics of Reading* (Chicago: University of Chicago Press, 2004).
13. Sara Suleri, *Meatless Days* (Chicago: University of Chicago Press, 1989).
14. It is perhaps no accident that Suleri is quite familiar with the three writers discussed in this book, for while writing her memoir, Suleri was also writing about them, among others, in her scholarly work, *The Rhetoric of English India*.
15. For a quick overview of French feminist theory, see Toril Moi, *Sexual/Textual Politics: Feminist Literary Theory* (London: Methuen, 1985).
16. Michelle Cliff, *Abeng* (New York: Penguin, Plume, 1984), 165–66.
17. Jean Rhys, *Wide Sargasso Sea* (1966), ed. Judith L. Raiskin (New York: Norton, 1999), 27.
18. As Cliff explains, "*Abeng* is an African word meaning conch shell," which had a double purpose, for it was an "instrument" used both by the overseer to call "slaves to the cane fields in the West Indies" and by the rebel "Maroon armies to pass their messages and reach one another" (vi). By using the word as the title of her novel, Cliff also

suggests self-referentially that (her) writing likewise embodies the dualities of agency: it can be used either by those in power to maintain power over the oppressed, or as a counterhegemonic tool to build networks among the oppressed, to fight on their side. This is the choice that Clare faces at the end of the novel.

    19. Shani Mootoo, "Sushila's Bhakti," in Mootoo, *Out on Main Street, and Other Stories* (Vancouver, BC: Press Gang Publishers, 1993), 58–67.

BIBLIOGRAPHY

Achar, Radha. "The Child in Kipling's Fiction: An Analysis." *Literary Criterion* 22, no. 4 (1987): 46–53.
Achebe, Chinua. *Things Fall Apart* (1959). New York: Anchor Doubleday, 1994.
Ahmad, Aijaz. *In Theory: Classes, Nations, Literatures*. New York: Verso, 1992.
Anderson, Benedict. *Imagined Communities: Reflections on the Origin and Spread of Nationalism*. New York: Verso, 1991.
Anderson, Perry. *Arguments within English Marxism*. London: Verso, 1980.
Appignanesi, Lisa, and Sara Maitland, eds. *The Rushdie File*. Syracuse, NY: Syracuse University Press, 1990.
Aravamudan, Srinivas. "'Being God's Postman Is No Fun, Yaar': Salman Rushdie's *The Satanic Verses*." *Diacritics* 19, no. 2 (1989): 3–20.
———. *Tropicopolitans: Colonialism and Agency*. Durham, NC: Duke University Press, 1999.
Armstrong, Nancy, and Leonard Tennenhouse, eds. *The Violence of Representation: Literature and the History of Violence*. New York: Routledge, 1989.
Ashcroft, Bill, Gareth Griffiths, and Helen Tiffin. *The Empire Writes Back: Theory and Practice in Postcolonial Literatures*. London: Routledge, 1989.
Attridge, Derek. *J. M. Coetzee and the Ethics of Reading*. Chicago: University of Chicago Press, 2004.
———. *The Singularity of Literature*. New York: Routledge, 2004.
Austen, Jane. *Mansfield Park* (1814). Edited by Tony Tanner. London: Penguin, 1985.
Bader, Rudolf. "On Blood and Blushing: Bipolarity in Salman Rushdie's *Shame*." *International Fiction Review* 15, no. 1 (1998): 30–34.
Bahri, Deepika. *Native Intelligence: Aesthetics, Politics and Postcolonial Literature*. Minneapolis: University of Minnesota Press, 2003.
Bailey, Quentin. "Heroes and Homosexuals: Education and Empire in E. M. Forster." *Twentieth-Century Literature* 48, no. 3 (2002): 324–48.
Bakhtin, Mikhail. *Rabelais and His World* (1965). Translated by Helene Iswolsky. Bloomington: Indiana University Press, 1984.
Ball, John Clement. *Satire and the Postcolonial Novel: V. S. Naipaul, Chinua Achebe, Salman Rushdie*. New York: Routledge, 2003.
Barker, Francis. *The Tremulous Private Body: Essays on Subjection*. London: Methuen, 1984.
Barns, Margarita. *The Indian Press: A History of the Growth of Public Opinion in India*. London: Allen and Unwin, 1940.
Barrier, Gerald N. *Banned: Controversial Literature and Political Control in British India, 1907–1947*. Columbia: University of Missouri Press, 1974.
Batty, Nancy. "The Art of Suspense: Rushdie's 1001 (Mid)Nights." *Ariel* 18, no. 3 (1987): 49–65.

Baucom, Ian. *Out of Place: Englishness, Empire, and the Locations of Identity*. Princeton, NJ: Princeton University Press, 1999.
Beer, Gillian. "Negation in *A Passage to India*." In J. Beer, *Passage to India*, 44–58.
Beer, John, ed. *A Passage to India: Essays in Interpretation*. New Jersey: Barnes and Noble Books, 1986.
Bhabha, Homi. *The Location of Culture*. New York: Routledge, 1994.
Bilgrami, Akeel. "Rushdie and the Reform of Islam." *Grand Street* 8, no. 4 (Summer 1989): 170–84.
Bloom, Harold. *The Anxiety of Influence: A Theory of Poetry*. New York: Oxford University Press, 1973.
———, ed. *E. M. Forster's* A Passage to India: *Modern Critical Interpretations*. New York: Chelsea House, 1987.
———, ed. *Kim: Modern Critical Interpretations*. New York: Chelsea House, 1987.
Booker, M. Keith. "'Beauty and the Beast': Dualism as Despotism in the Fiction of Salman Rushdie." *ELH* 57, no. 4 (Winter 1990): 977–97.
———, ed. *Critical Essays on Salman Rushdie*. New York: G. K. Hall, 1999.
Bose, Sugata, and Ayesha Jalal. *Modern South Asia: History, Culture, Political Economy*. New York: Routledge, 1998.
Bourdieu, Pierre. *In Other Words: Essays Towards a Reflexive Sociology*. Stanford, CA: Stanford University Press, 1990.
Bradshaw, David, ed. *The Cambridge Companion to E. M. Forster*. Cambridge: Cambridge University Press, 2007.
Brathwaite, Edward Kamau. "Nation Language." In *The Post-Colonial Studies Reader*, ed. Bill Ashcroft et al., 309–13. New York: Routledge, 1995.
Bredbeck, Gregory W. "'Queer Superstitions': Forster, Carpenter, and the Illusion of (Sexual) Identity." In Martin and Piggford, *Queer Forster*, 29–58.
Brennan, Timothy. *Salman Rushdie and the Third World: Myths of the Nation*. New York: St. Martin's Press, 1989.
Bristow, Joseph. *Effeminate England: Homoerotic Writing after 1885*. New York: Columbia University Press, 1995.
Brooks, Cleanth. *The Well-Wrought Urn*. New York: Harcourt, Brace and Co., 1947.
Brooks, Peter. *Body Work: Objects of Desire in Modern Narrative*. Cambridge, MA: Harvard University Press, 1993.
———. *Reading for the Plot: Desire and Intention in Narrative*. Cambridge, MA: Harvard University Press, 1984.
Brutus, Dennis. "Literature and Change in South Africa." *Research in African Literatures* 24 (Fall 1993): 101–4.
Burke, Kenneth. *Language as Symbolic Action: Essays on Life, Literature, and Method*. Berkeley: University of California Press, 1966.
Butler, Judith. *Gender Trouble: Feminism and the Subversion of Identity*. New York: Routledge, 1990.
Callon, Michael, and John Law. "Agency and the Hybrid Collectif." *South Atlantic Quarterly* 94, no. 2 (Spring 1995): 481–508.
Care, Norman S., and Charles Landesman, eds. *Readings in the Theory of Action*. Bloomington: Indiana University Press, 1968.

Carrington, John. *Rudyard Kipling: His Life and Work.* London: Macmillan, 1955.
Carter, Paul. *The Road to Botany Bay: An Exploration of Landscape and History.* New York: Knopf, 1988.
Cliff, Michelle. *Abeng.* New York: Penguin, Plume, 1984.
Clifford, James. *The Predicament of Culture: Twentieth Century Ethnography, Literature and Art.* Cambridge, MA: Harvard University Press, 1988.
Coetzee, J. M. *Foe.* New York: Penguin, 1987.
———. *Waiting for the Barbarians.* New York: Penguin, 1982.
Colmer, John. *E. M. Forster: The Personal Voice.* London: Routledge, 1975.
Curr, Matthew. "Recuperating E. M. Forster's *Maurice.*" *Modern Language Quarterly* 62, no. 1 (2001): 53–69.
David, Deirdre. "Children of Empire: Victorian Imperialism and Sexual Politics in Dickens and Kipling." In *Gender and Discourse in Victorian Literature and Art,* edited by Antony H. Harrison and Beverly Taylor, 124–42. DeKalb: Northern Illinois University Press, 1992.
Davis, Rocío, and Sue-Im Lee, eds. *Literary Gestures: The Aesthetic in Asian American Writing.* Philadelphia: Temple University Press, 2006.
Dawood, N. J. Introduction to *The Koran* (1956). Translated by N. J. Dawood. London: Penguin, 1990.
Deleuze, Gilles, and Félix Guattari. *Kafka: Toward a Minor Literature* (1975). Excerpted in *The Norton Anthology of Theory and Criticism,* edited by Vincent B. Leitch et al., 1593–1601. New York: Norton, 2001.
Desai, Gaurav. *Subject to Colonialism: African Self-Fashioning and the Colonial Library.* Durham, NC: Duke University Press, 2001.
Douglas, Mary. *Purity and Danger: An Analysis of the Concept of Pollution and Taboo.* New York: Routledge, 1984.
Esty, Joshua D. "Excremental Postcolonialism." *Contemporary Literature* 40, no. 1 (Spring 1999): 22–59.
Fanon, Frantz. *Black Skin, White Masks.* Translated by Charles Lam Markmann. New York: Grove Press, 1967.
Fish, Stanley. "Literature in the Reader: Affective Stylistics." In *Reader-Response Criticism: From Formalism to Post-Structuralism,* edited by Jane Tompkins, 70–100. Baltimore, MD: Johns Hopkins University Press, 1980.
Fletcher, D. M., ed. *Reading Rushdie: Perspectives on the Fiction of Salman Rushdie.* Amsterdam: Rodopi, 1994.
Forster, E. M. *Abinger Harvest.* New York: Harcourt, Brace, 1936.
———. *Arctic Summer.* Edited by Elizabeth Heine and Oliver Stallybrass. Abinger Edition, vol. 9. London: Edward Arnold, 1980.
———. *Aspects of the Novel* (1927). Edited by Oliver Stallybrass. Harmondsworth, UK: Penguin, 1974.
———. *The Celestial Omnibus, and Other Stories.* London: Sidgwick and Jackson, 1911. Reprinted in *The Collected Tales of E. M. Forster.* New York: Knopf, 1946.
———. *The Hill of Devi.* New York: Harvest/HBJ, 1953.
———. *The Hill of Devi, and Other Indian Writings.* Edited by Elizabeth Heine. Abinger Edition, vol. 14. London: Edward Arnold, 1983.

———. *The Life to Come, and Other Stories*. Edited by Oliver Stallybrass. Abinger Edition, vol. 8. London: Edward Arnold, 1972.
———. *Maurice* (1914). New York: Norton, 1971.
———. *A Passage to India* (1924). New York: Harcourt, Brace and Jovanovich, 1965.
———. *Pharos and Pharillon* (1923). New York: Knopf, 1961.
———. *Selected Letters of E. M. Forster*, vol. 1, 1879–1920. Edited by Mary Lago and P. N. Furbank. Cambridge, MA: Harvard University Press, 1983.
———. *Selected Letters of E. M. Forster*, vol. 2, 1921–1970. Edited by Mary Lago and P. N. Furbank. Cambridge, MA: Harvard University Press, 1985.
———. *Two Cheers for Democracy*. New York: Harcourt, Brace and Co., 1951.
Foucault, Michel. *Discipline and Punish: The Birth of the Prison*. Translated by Alan Sheridan. New York: Vintage, 1977.
———. "Truth and Power." In Foucault, *Power/Knowledge: Selected Interviews and Other Writings, 1972–1977*. Edited by Colin Gordon. New York: Pantheon, 1980.
Freud, Sigmund. "The Theme of the Three Caskets." In Freud, *Character and Culture* (1913). New York: Macmillan, 1963.
Frye, Northrop. *The Anatomy of Criticism: Four Essays*. Princeton, NJ: Princeton University Press, 1957.
Furbank, P. N. *E. M. Forster: A Life*. Vols. 1 and 2. London: Cardinal, 1977, 1978.
Ghosh, Bishnupriya. *When Borne Across: Literary Cosmopolitics in the Contemporary Indian Novel*. New Brunswick, NJ: Rutgers University Press, 2004.
Giddens, Anthony. *Central Problems in Social Theory: Action, Structure and Contradiction in Social Analysis*. Berkeley: University of California Press, 1979.
———. *Modernity and Self-Identity: Self and Society in the Late Modern Age*. Stanford, CA: Stanford University Press, 1991.
Gikandi, Simon. *Maps of Englishness: Writing Identity in the Culture of Colonialism*. New York: Columbia University Press, 1996.
Gonzalez, Madalena. *Fiction after the Fatwa: Salman Rushdie and the Charm of Catastrophe*. Amsterdam: Rodopi, 2005.
Goonetilleke, D.C.R.A. *Salman Rushdie*. New York: St. Martin's, 1998.
Gorra, Michael. *After Empire: Scott, Naipaul, Rushdie*. Chicago: University of Chicago Press, 1997.
Grewal, Inderpal. "Salman Rushdie: Marginality, Women, and *Shame*." *Genders* 3 (Fall 1988): 24–42.
Gurnah, Abdulrazak, ed. *The Cambridge Companion to Salman Rushdie*. Cambridge: Cambridge University Press, 2007.
———. "Themes and Structures in *Midnight's Children*." In Gurnah, *Cambridge Companion*, 91–108.
Hai, Ambreen. "Forster and the Fantastic: The Covert Politics of *The Celestial Omnibus*." *Twentieth-Century Literature* 54, no. 2 (Summer 2008): 217–46.
———. "'Marching In from the Peripheries': Rushdie's Feminized Artistry and Ambivalent Feminism." In *Critical Essays on Salman Rushdie*, edited by Booker, 16–50. New York: G. K. Hall, 1999.
———. "On Truth and Lie in a Colonial Sense: Kipling's Tales of Tale-Telling." *English Literary History* 64, no. 2 (Summer 1997): 599–625.

———. "'Out in the Woods': E. M. Forster's Spatial Allegories of Property, Sexuality, Colonialism." *Literature, Interpretation, Theory* 14, no. 4 (October–December 2003): 317–55.

Haralson, Eric. "'Thinking about Homosex' in Forster and James." In Martin and Piggford, *Queer Forster*, 59–74.

Harris, Wilson. "The Limbo Gateway" (1981). In *The Post-Colonial Studies Reader*, edited by Bill Ashcroft et al. (New York: Routledge, 1995), 378–82.

Harrison, James. *Salman Rushdie*. New York: Twayne, 1992.

Head, Dominic. *J. M. Coetzee*. Cambridge: Cambridge University Press, 1997.

Herz, Judith Scherer. "Listening to Language." In J. Beer, *Passage to India*, 59–70.

Hobsbawm, Eric, and Terence Ranger, eds. *The Invention of Tradition*. Cambridge: Cambridge University Press, 1983.

Howe, Irving. "The Pleasures of Kim." In Bloom, *Kim*, 31–42.

Hubel, Teresa. "'The Bride of His Country': Love, Marriage, and the Imperialist Paradox in the Indian Fiction of Sara Jeannette Duncan and Rudyard Kipling." *Ariel* 22, no. 4 (1987): 3–19.

———. *Whose India? The Independence Struggle in British and Indian Fiction and History* Durham, NC: Duke University Press, 1996.

Iser, Wolfgang. "The Play of the Text." In *Languages of the Unsayable: The Play of Negativity in Literature and Literary Theory*, edited by Sanford Budick and Wolfgang Iser. Stanford, CA: Stanford University Press, 1987.

James, Henry. Introduction to *Mine Own People*, by Rudyard Kipling, vii–xxvi. New York: Lovell, Coryell and Co., 1891.

JanMohamed, Abdul R. *Manichean Aesthetics: The Politics of Literature in Colonial Africa*. Amherst: University of Massachusetts Press, 1983.

Jewett, William. *Fatal Autonomy: Romantic Drama and the Rhetoric of Agency*. Ithaca, NY: Cornell University Press, 1997.

Johnson, Barbara. *The Critical Difference: Essays in Contemporary Rhetoric of Reading*. Baltimore, MD: Johns Hopkins University Press, 1980.

Johnson, Mark. *The Body in the Mind: The Bodily Basis of Meaning, Imagination, and Reason*. Chicago: University of Chicago Press, 1990.

Johnson, Mark, and George Lakoff. *Philosophy in the Flesh: The Embodied Mind and Its Challenge to Western Thought*. New York: Harper Collins, 1999.

Joyce, James. *A Portrait of the Artist as a Young Man* (1916). Edited by Chester G. Anderson. New York: Viking Penguin, 1968.

Jussawalla, Feroza. "Rushdie's *Dastan-e-Dilruba: The Satanic Verses* as Rushdie's Love Letter to Islam." *Diacritics* 26, no. 1 (Spring 1996): 50–73.

Kabir, M. *A Short History of Pakistan*. General editor, I. H. Qureshi, vols. 1–4. Karachi: University of Karachi, 1967.

Kane, Jean M. "The Migrant Intellectual and the Body of History: Salman Rushdie's *Midnight's Children*." *Contemporary Literature* 37, no. 1 (Spring 1996): 94–118.

Katrak, Ketu. *Politics of the Female Body: Postcolonial Women Writers of the Third World*. New Brunswick, NJ: Rutgers University Press, 2006.

Kaul, Suvir. "*Kim*, or How to Be Young, Male, and British in Kipling's India." In *Kim*, edited by Zohreh Sullivan, 426–36. Norton Critical Edition. New York: Norton, 2002.

Kemp, Sandra. *Kipling's Hidden Narratives*. London: Blackwell, 1988.
Kermode, Frank. *The Sense of an Ending: Studies in the Theory of Fiction*. New York: Oxford University Press, 1966.
Kipling, Rudyard. *A Book of Words: Selections from Speeches and Letters Delivered between 1906 and 1927*. New York: Doubleday, 1928.
———. *In Black and White* (1889). Reprinted in *Selected Prose and Poetry of Rudyard Kipling*. Authorized edition. New York: Garden City Publishing, 1937. Originally published in 1893.
———. *Just So Stories*. London: Macmillan, 1902.
———. *Kim* (1901). Introduction and notes by Edward Said. New York: Penguin, 1987.
———. *Land and Sea Tales for Scouts and Guides*. Vol. 35. New York: Charles Scribner's and Sons, 1923.
———. *Life's Handicap* (1891). Edited by P. N. Furbank. New York: Penguin, 1987.
———. *The Man Who Would Be King, and Other Stories*. Edited by Louis Cornell. Oxford: Oxford University Press, 1987.
———. *Many Inventions*. New York: D. Appleton and Co., 1893.
———. *Mine Own People*. Introduction by Henry James. New York: Lovell, Coryell and Co., 1891.
———. *Plain Tales from the Hills* (1888). Edited by Andrew Rutherford. Oxford: Oxford University Press, 1987.
———. *Rudyard Kipling: Something of Myself and Other Autobiographical Writings*. Edited by Thomas Pinney. Cambridge: Cambridge University Press, 1990.
———. *Selected Prose and Poetry of Rudyard Kipling*. Authorized edition. New York: Garden City Publishing, 1937.
———. *War Stories and Poems*. Edited by Andrew Rutherford. London: Oxford University Press, 1987.
———. *Wee Willie Winkie* (1889). Edited by Hugh Haughton. London: Penguin, 1988.
Kipnis, Laura. "(Male) Desire and (Female) Disgust: Reading *Hustler*." In *Cultural Studies*, edited by Lawrence Grossberg et al., 373–91. New York: Routledge, 1992.
Koestenbaum, Wayne. *Double Talk: The Erotics of Male Literary Collaboration*. New York: Routledge, 1989.
Kortenaar, Neil Ten. "Postcolonial Ekphrasis: Salman Rushdie Gives the Finger Back to the Empire." *Contemporary Literature* 38, no. 2 (1997): 232–59.
Kossew, Sue, ed. *Critical Essays on J. M. Coetzee*. New York: G. K. Hall, 1998.
Krishnaswamy, Revathi. *Effeminism: The Economy of Colonial Desire*. Ann Arbor: University of Michigan Press, 1998.
Kureishi, Hanif. *The Buddha of Suburbia*. New York: Penguin, 1990.
Lago, Mary, and P. N. Furbank, eds. *Selected Letters of E. M. Forster*, vol. 1, 1879–1920. Cambridge, MA: Harvard University Press, 1983.
———. *Selected Letters of E. M. Forster*, vol. 2, 1921–1970. Cambridge, MA: Harvard University Press, 1985.
Lakoff, George. *Philosophy in the Flesh: The Embodied Mind and Its Challenge to Western Thought*. New York: Harper Collins, 1999.
Lane, Christopher. *The Ruling Passion: British Colonial Allegory and the Paradox of Homosexual Desire*. Durham, NC: Duke University Press, 1995.

———. "Volatile Desire: Ambivalence and Distress in Forster's Colonial Narratives." In Moore-Gilbert, *Writing India*, 188–212.

Lauritzen, Paul. "Arguing with Life Stories: The Case of Rigoberta Menchu." In *The Ethics of Life-Writing*, edited by Paul John Eakin, 19–39. Ithaca, NY: Cornell University Press, 2004.

Locke, John. *The Second Treatise of Civil Government* (1690). Edited by C. B. Macpherson. Indianapolis: Hackett Publishing, 1980.

Long, Robert Emmet, ed. *Censorship*. The Reference Shelf, vol. 61, no. 3 New York: Wilson, 1990.

Loomba, Ania. *Colonialism/Postcolonialism*. New York: Routledge, 1998.

Macaulay, Thomas. "Minute on Indian Education" (1835). In Macaulay, *Selected Writings*, edited by John Clive and Thomas Pinney, 235–51. Chicago: University of Chicago Press, 1972.

Macpherson, C. B. *The Political Theory of Possessive Individualism: Hobbes to Locke*. Oxford: Oxford University Press, 1962.

Malik, Charu. "To Express the Subject of Friendship: Masculine Desire and Colonialism in *A Passage to India*." In Martin and Piggford, *Queer Forster*, 221–36.

Martin, Graham Dunstan. *Language, Truth and Poetry: Notes Towards a Philosophy of Literature*. Edinburgh: Edinburgh University Press, 1975.

Martin, Robert K. "The Double Structure of *Maurice*." In *E. M. Forster: New Casebooks*, edited by Jeremy Tambling, 100–114. New York: St. Martin's, 1983, 1995.

———, and George Piggford, eds. *Queer Forster*. Chicago: University of Chicago Press, 1997.

McGann, Jerome. *Towards a Literature of Knowledge*. Chicago: University of Chicago Press, 1989.

Meyers, Jeffrey. *Homosexuality and Literature, 1890–1930*. Montreal: McGill-Queen's University Press, 1977.

Mill, James. *The History of British India*. Abridged and with an introduction by William Thomas. Chicago: University of Chicago Press, 1975.

Miller, D. A. *Narrative and Its Discontents: Problems of Closure in the Traditional Novel*. Princeton, NJ: Princeton University Press, 1981.

Minh-ha, Trinh. *When the Moon Waxes Red: Representation, Gender and Cultural Politics*. New York: Routledge, 1991.

Mohanty, S. P. "Kipling's Children and the Colour Line." *Race and Class* 31 (1989): 21–40.

Moi, Toril. *Sexual/Textual Politics: Feminist Literary Theory*. London: Methuen, 1985.

Montrose, Louis. "The Elizabethan Subject and the Spenserian Text." In *Literary Theory/Renaissance Texts*, edited by Patricia Parker and David Quint, 303–40. Baltimore, MD: John Hopkins University Press, 1986.

———. "Professing the Renaissance: The Poetics and Politics of Culture." In *The New Historicism*, edited by H. Aram Veeser, 15–36. New York: Routledge, 1989.

Moore-Gilbert, Bart, ed. *Writing India, 1757–1990: The Literature of British India*. Manchester, UK: Manchester University Press, 1996.

Mootoo, Shani. "Sushila's Bhakti." In Mootoo, *Out on Main Street, and Other Stories*, 58–67. Vancouver, BC: Press Gang Publishers, 1993.

Moran, Jo Ann Hoeppner. "E. M. Forster's *A Passage to India*: What Really Happened in the Caves." *Modern Fiction Studies* 34, no. 4 (Winter 1988): 596–604.
Naipaul, V. S. *An Area of Darkness* (1964). New York: Vintage, 1981.
Needham, Anuradha Dingwaney. *Using the Master's Tools: Resistance and the Literature of the African and South Asian Diasporas*. New York: St. Martin's Press, 2000.
Nichols, Grace. "Epilogue." In Nichols, *I Is a Long-Memoried Woman*, 80. London: Karnak House, 1983.
Nietzsche, Friedrich. *The Portable Nietzsche*. Edited and translated by Walter Kaufman. New York: Viking Penguin, 1954.
Nixon, Rob. "Of Balkans and Bantustans: The Discourse of 'Ethnic Cleansing' and the Crisis of National Legitimation." *Transition* 60 (1993): 4–26.
Norris, Christopher. *Reclaiming Truth: Contribution to a Critique of Cultural Relativism*. Durham, NC: Duke University Press, 1996.
O'Higgins, Paul. *Censorship in Britain*. London: Nelson, 1972.
Orange, Michael. "Language and Silence in *A Passage to India*." In Bloom, *E. M. Forster's* A Passage to India, 57–74.
Parry, Ann. "Reading Formations in the Victorian Press: The Reception of Kipling, 1888–1891." *Literature and History* 2 (1985): 254–63.
Parry, Benita. *Delusions and Discoveries: Studies on India in the British Imagination, 1880–1930*. Berkeley: University of California Press, 1972.
———. "The Politics of *A Passage to India*." In J. Beer, *Passage to India*, 27–43.
Pickthall, Marmaduke. Introduction to *The Meaning of the Glorious Koran*. Translated by Marmaduke Pickthall. New York: Penguin, Mentor Book, n.d.
Pinney, Thomas, ed. *Rudyard Kipling: Something of Myself and Other Autobiographical Writings*. Cambridge: Cambridge University Press, 1990.
Plato. *The Republic*. Translated by Francis Cornford. New York: Oxford University Press, 1941.
Pratt, Mary Louise. *Imperial Eyes: Travel Writing and Transculturation*. New York: Routledge, 1992.
Price, David. *History Made, History Imagined: Contemporary Literature, Poiesis, and the Past*. Chicago: University of Illinois Press, 1999.
Ramazani, Jahan. *The Hybrid Muse: Postcolonial Poetry in English*. Chicago: University of Chicago Press, 2001.
Raschke, Debrah. "Breaking the Engagement with Philosophy: Re-envisioning Hetero-Homo Relations in *Maurice*." In Martin and Piggford, *Queer Forster*, 151–66.
Reder, Michael, ed. *Conversations with Salman Rushdie*. Jackson: University Press of Mississippi, 2000.
Rege, Josna. *Colonial Karma: Self, Action and Nation in the Indian English Novel*. New York: Palgrave Macmillan, 2004.
———. "Victim into Protagonist? *Midnight's Children* and the Indian National Narrative of the 1980's." In Booker, *Critical Essays*, 250–82.
Rhys, Jean. *Wide Sargasso Sea* (1966). Edited by Judith L. Raiskin. Norton Critical Edition. New York: Norton, 1999.
Richards, I. A. "How Does a Poem Know When It Is Finished?" In *Parts and Wholes*, edited by Daniel Lerner, 163–74. New York: Free Press of Glencoe, 1963.

Riffaterre, Michael. *Fictional Truth.* Baltimore, MD: Johns Hopkins University Press, 1990.
Robbins, Bruce. "The Butler Did It: On Agency in the Novel." *Representations* 6 (Spring 1984): 85–97.
Rosenthal, Michael. *The Character Factory: Baden-Powell's Boy Scouts and the Imperatives of Empire.* New York: Pantheon, 1986.
Rowe, Katherine. *Dead Hands: Fictions of Agency, Renaissance to Modern.* Stanford, CA: Stanford University Press, 1999.
Rushdie, Salman. "The Empire Writes Back with a Vengeance." *London Times* (July 3, 1982), 8–9.
———. *The Ground Beneath Her Feet.* New York: Henry Holt, 1999.
———. *Haroun and the Sea of Stories.* New York: Penguin, 1990.
———. *Imaginary Homelands.* New York: Viking Penguin, 1991.
———. *Midnight's Children.* New York: Viking Penguin, 1981.
———. *The Moor's Last Sigh.* New York: Pantheon, 1995.
———. *The Satanic Verses* (1988). New York: Penguin, 1989.
———. *Shame.* New York: Aventura, 1983.
Rutherford, Andrew, ed. *Kipling's Mind and Art.* Stanford, CA: Stanford University Press, 1964.
Sabin, Margery. *Dissenters and Mavericks: Writings about India in English, 1765–2000.* New York: Oxford University Press, 2002.
Said, Edward. *Culture and Imperialism.* New York: Knopf, 1993.
———. *Orientalism.* New York: Vintage, 1979.
Saussure, Ferdinand. *Course on General Linguistics* (1915). Excerpted in *The Norton Anthology of Theory and Criticism,* edited by Vincent B. Leitch et al., 956–76. New York: Norton, 2001.
Scarry, Elaine. *The Body in Pain.* New York: Oxford University Press, 1985.
———, ed. *Literature and the Body.* Baltimore, MD: Johns Hopkins University Press, 1988.
Sedgwick, Eve Kosofsky. *Between Men: English Literature and Male Homosocial Desire.* New York: Columbia University Press, 1985.
———. *The Epistemology of the Closet.* Berkeley: University of California Press, 1990.
Seymour-Smith, Martin. *Rudyard Kipling: A Biography.* New York: St. Martin's Press, 1989.
Sharpe, Jenny. *Allegories of Empire: The Figure of Woman in the Colonial Text.* Minneapolis: University of Minnesota Press, 1993.
Sidhwa, Bapsi. *Cracking India.* Minneapolis: Milkweed, 1991.
Sidney, Philip. "An Apology for Poetry." Excerpted in *The Norton Anthology of Theory and Criticism,* edited by Vincent B. Leitch et al., 323–62. New York: Norton, 2001.
Silver, Brenda. "Periphrasis, Power, and Rape in *A Passage to India.*" *Novel* 22 (Fall 1988): 86–105.
Singh, Khushwant. *Train to Pakistan.* New York: Grove Press, 1956.
Sirhandi, Marcella Nesom. *Contemporary Painting in Pakistan.* Lahore, Pakistan: Ferozesons, 1992.
Smith, Barbara Hernstein. *Poetic Closure: A Study of How Poems End.* Chicago: University of Chicago Press, 1968.

Smith, Paul. *Discerning the Subject*. Minneapolis: University of Minnesota Press, 1988.
Spivak, Gayatri Chakravorty. *In Other Worlds: Essays in Cultural Politics*. New York: Routledge, 1988.
———. *Outside in the Teaching Machine*. New York: Routledge, 1993.
———. "Theory in the Margin: Coetzee's *Foe* reading Defoe's *Crusoe/Roxana*." In *Consequences of Theory*, edited by Jonathan Arac and Barbara Johnson, 154–80. Baltimore, MD: Johns Hopkins University Press, 1991.
Stallybrass, Peter, and Allon White. *The Politics and Poetics of Transgression*. Ithaca, NY: Cornell University Press, 1984.
Steele, Meili. *Theorizing Textual Subjects: Agency and Oppression*. Cambridge: Cambridge University Press, 1997.
Steiner, George. "Under the Greenwood Tree." *New Yorker* 47 (October 9, 1971), 158–69.
Stewart, David H. "Kipling's Portraits of the Artist." *English Literature in Transition: 1880–1920* 31, no. 3 (1988): 265–83.
Stone, Wilfrid. *The Cave and the Mountain*. Stanford, CA: Stanford University Press, 1965.
Suleri, Sara. *Meatless Days*. Chicago: University of Chicago Press, 1989.
———. *The Rhetoric of English India*. Chicago: University of Chicago Press, 1992.
———. "Whither Rushdie?" *Transition* 51 (1991): 198–212.
Sullivan, Zohreh. *Narratives of Empire: The Fictions of Rudyard Kipling*. Cambridge: Cambridge University Press, 1993.
Tagore, Rabindranath. *Gora*. Translated by Surendranath Tagore. Madras: Macmillan, 1924.
Tambling, Jeremy, ed. *E. M. Forster: New Casebooks*. New York: St. Martin's, 1995.
Thomas, Donald. *A Long Time Burning: The History of Literary Censorship in England*. London: Routledge, 1969.
Tiffin, Chris, and Alan Lawson. *De-Scribing Empire: Post-Colonialism and Textuality*. London: Routledge, 1994.
Tinsley, Molly. "Muddle *et cetera*: Syntax in *A Passage to India*." In J. Beer, *Passage to India*, 71–80.
Todorov, Tzetvan. "Fictions and Truths." In *Critical Reconstructions: The Relationship of Fiction and Life*, edited by Robert M. Polhemus and Roger B. Henkle, 21–51. Stanford, CA: Stanford University Press, 1994.
Tompkins, J. M. S. *The Art of Rudyard Kipling*. Lincoln: University of Nebraska Press, 1965.
Tompkins, Jane. *Sensational Designs: The Cultural Work of American Fiction, 1790–1860*. Oxford: Oxford University Press, 1985.
Touval, Yonatan. "Colonial Queer Something." In Martin and Piggford, *Queer Forster*, 237–54.
Trilling, Lionel. *E. M. Forster*. New York: New Directions, 1943.
Tytler, Harriet. *An Englishwoman in India: Memoirs, 1828–1858*. Edited by Anthony Sattin. Oxford: Oxford University Press, 1986.
Viswanathan, Gauri. "The Beginnings of English Literary Study in British India." *Oxford Literary Review* 9 (1987): 2–26.

———. "Yale College and the Culture of British Imperialism." *Yale Journal of Criticism* 7, no. 1 (1994) 7.
Walcott, Derek. *Collected Poems, 1948–1984*. New York: Noonday–Farrar, Strauss and Giroux, 1986.
———. "The Muse of History: An Essay." In *Is Massa Day Dead? Black Moods in the Caribbean*, edited by Orde Coombs, 1–28. New York: Doubleday, 1974.
Wilson, Angus. *The Strange Ride of Rudyard Kipling*. New York: Penguin, 1977.
Wilson, Edmund. "The Kipling that Nobody Read." In Rutherford, *Kipling's Mind and Art*, 17–69. Stanford, CA: Stanford University Press, 1964.
Wolpert, Stanley. *A New History of India*. 5th ed. Oxford: Oxford University Press, 1997.
Young, Robert. *Colonial Desire: Hybridity in Theory, Culture and Race*. New York: Routledge, 1995.

INDEX

Achar, Radha, 334n7
Achebe, Chinua, 328n10; *Things Fall Apart*, 314–15
agency, 8–10; and the body, 3, 6, 8–9, 326; literary, 6–7, 9–11, 13–17, 18, 26, 27–28, 312–26. *See also under* Forster, E. M.; Kipling, Rudyard; Rushdie, Salman
Althusser, Louis, 16, 61, 72
Anderson, Benedict, 11, 249, 270, 340n20, 356n8
Anderson, Perry, 16, 330n45
Appignanesi, Lisa, 251n13
Aravamudan, Srinivas, 10, 330n46, 351n13
Armstrong, Nancy, 348n15
Arnold, Matthew, 105
Ashcroft, Bill, 10
Attridge, Derek, 11–12, 359n12
Austen, Jane: *Mansfield Park*, 13–14

Bader, Rudolf, 353n27
Bahri, Deepika, 329n35, 351n12, 351n14
Bailey, Quentin, 345n49
Bakhtin, Mikhail, 9, 23, 25, 214–18, 227, 240, 352n18
Ball, John Clement, 214, 352n16, 352n18
Barker, Francis, 25, 179, 181
Barns, Margarita, 48, 337n37, 338n51
Barrier, Gerald, 50
Batty, Nancy, 358n26
Baucom, Ian, 81, 340n20, 340n23, 341n30, 342n10, 344n38, 345n51, 346n66, 351n13
Beckett, Samuel, 311, 358n33
Beer, Gillian, 347n6
Beer, John, 347n6
Bhabha, Homi, 11, 37, 61, 177, 329n28
Bilgrami, Akeel, 351n13
Blake, William, 10, 338n53
Bloom, Harold, 333n3, 347n5
body: as basis for agency, 2–9, 312–26; as interrelational with world, 25–26; as site of power and resistance, 25; and words, or language, 1–2, 5, 18, 19, 22–28. *See also under* Forster, E. M.; Kipling, Rudyard; Rushdie, Salman
Booker, M. Keith, 350n7, 351n12, 352n18
Bose, Sugata, 355n49
Bourdieu, Pierre, 330n42
Bradshaw, David, 341n5
Brathwaite, Edward Kamau, 317
Bredbeck, Gregory, 345n58
Brennan, Timothy, 350n7, 351n11
Bristow, Joseph, 343n33
Brooks, Cleaneth, 338n55
Brooks, Peter, 23, 24, 297, 300, 307; *Body Work*, 22, 64
Brutus, Dennis, 351n9
Burke, Kenneth, 17
Butler, Judith, 23, 344n42

Callon, Michel, 330n47
Care, Norman, 8
Carrington, John, 333n4, 337n49
Carter, Paul, 340n20, 349n24
Cavafy, C. P., 117, 343n32
Cliff, Michelle, 319
  Abeng, 323–25, 359n18
Clifford, James, 340n21
cultural work, 16–17. *See also* agency
Coetzee, J. M., 317, 323; *Foe*, 318, 325, 359nn9–10, 359n12; *Waiting for the Barbarians*, 318–19
Coleridge, Samuel Taylor: *The Rime of the Ancient Mariner*, 255
Colmer, John, 157
Conrad, Joseph, 54, 61,178, 328n10; *Heart of Darkness*, 254
Curr, Matthew, 342n9, 345n52

David, Deirdre, 88
Davis, Rocío, 329n30
Dawood, N. J., 353n30
Deleuze, Gilles, 210
Derrida, Jacques, 22, 75
Desai, Anita, 351n10

373

Desai, Gaurav, 11, 330n46
Douglas, Mary, 28, 212, 239, 240, 279, 354n43

Esty, Joshua D., 353n29

Fanon, Frantz, 36, 349n22
Fish, Stanley, 328n13
Fletcher, D. M., 214, 351n11
Forster, E. M.
  anticolonialism of, 7, 27, 109, 110–11, 121, 123–25, 136, 144, 146, 153–54
  and the body, 103–10, 112–14, 120, 122, 135, 150
  body as landscape in, 164, 178–87, 190–91
  caves in, significance of, 26–27, 98, 160, 184–85, 187–202, 341n3, 349n31
  and censorship, 7–8, 19, 100–102, 121, 133, 135, 345n54
  colonial surveillance of, 101–2, 144
  crisis of writing of, 97–100, 102, 104, 109
  critical reception of, 99–100, 105, 156–58, 344n46
  cross-dressing in, 125–26, 139
  homosexuality in, 8, 19, 98–109, 111, 115–18, 130–33, 135–36, 141–42, 150, 342n7, 342n16, 345n58, 346n66, 347n2
  Indian letters and journal of, 99–129, 136–41
  interracial desire in, 27, 99, 103, 134, 136, 141–42, 144–46, 149, 155, 157, 192, 345n58
  and literary agency, 6, 27, 99–100, 103–4, 110–11, 129, 134–35, 155–56, 160, 203, 313–14, 326
  location as colonial writer, 6–7, 129, 135, 314
  and manuscripts of A Passage to India (MPI), 163, 170–72, 176–77, 198, 202
  Masood, Syed Ross, relationship with, 100–102, 110, 111–13, 116, 121, 123, 127, 137, 155, 175, 180
  problems of colonial language in, 99, 137, 152, 154, 156–75, 177–78
  queer/ que(e)ry, 113, 116–19, 123, 125, 127, 132, 140, 153, 165, 185, 342n15, 347n2
  revisions of, 98, 156, 175–76, 187, 347n4
  Sassoon, Siegfried, letters to, 98, 106, 346n60
  sexual politics of, 27, 103, 111, 117–19, 127, 151, 154–55, 158, 173
  trips to India of, 109–29, 134–50, 344n40
Works:
  Abinger Harvest, 97
  Alexandria: A History and Guide, 135, 345n55
  Arctic Summer, 97, 105, 108, 132, 342n18
  Aspects of the Novel, 107
  The Celestial Omnibus, 107, 109, 192, 341n2
  "The Celestial Omnibus," 180
  "The Curate's Friend," 107
  "Edward Carpenter," 109
  The Hill of Devi, 119, 136, 138, 140, 144, 187
  Howard's End, 98, 109, 142, 341n2, 346n60
  "Kanaya," 115, 143–46, 149, 346n66, 346n68
  "Liberty in England," 341n1
  "The Life to Come," 99, 143, 146–49, 151, 152, 157, 192, 345n53
  The Longest Journey, 341n2
  Maurice, 27, 98, 99, 105–6, 111, 118–19, 129–34, 149, 150, 344n35, 344n44, 344n46, 345n49, 349n19
  "The Other Boat," 133, 157
  "Other Kingdom," 172, 183, 192
  "Pan," 151–55
  A Passage to India, 26, 27, 97–98, 99, 102–3, 117, 123, 129, 136, 137, 149, 150, 151, 154–203, 204, 341n3, 342n11, 345n49, 347n4
  Pharos and Pharillon, 135, 345n56
  "The Story of a Panic," 27, 151
  "Three Countries," 349n31
  "What I Believe," 142, 342n14, 346n60
  Where Angels Fear to Tread, 341n2
Foucault, Michel, 21–23, 329n20, 332n63
Freud, Sigmund, 15, 44, 189, 283; "The Uncanny," 90
Frye, Northrop, 295
Furbank, P. N., 117, 134, 343n32

Ghosh, Bishnupriya, 350n7, 351n12
Giddens, Anthony, 8, 12, 15–16, 330n42, 330n47
Gikandi, Simon, 330n46
Gonzalez, Madalena, 351n14
Goonetilleke, D.C.R.A., 351n11
Gorra, Michael, 351n13, 354n35
Grewal, Inderpal, 358n27
Guattari, Félix, 210
Gurnah, Abdulrazak, 350n7, 352n18

Haralson, Eric, 343n23
Harris, Wilson, "The Limbo Gateway," 317
Harrison, James, 351n11
Head, Dominic, 359n12
Heine, Elizabeth, 108, 342n18
Herz, Judith Scherer, 156–57, 347nn6–7, 348n12

Hobbes, Thomas, 8–9
Hobsbawm, Eric, 356n8
Hubel, Teresa, 55, 333n2, 336n34, 338n53
Hutcheon, Linda, 256

Indian Emergency, 209 278–79, 282, 300–301
Iser, Wolfgang, 331n52

Jalal, Ayesha, 355n49
James, Henry, 106–7, 118, 333n4
JanMohamed, Abdul, 11, 329n28, 348n13
Jewett, William, 23
Johnson, Barbara, 330nn36, 349n26
Johnson, Mark, 283, 332n71
Joyce, James, 214, 353n29; *A Portrait of the Artist as a Young Man*, 253
Jussawalla, Feroza, 351n13

Kabir, M., 356–57n13
Kane, Jean M., 353n26
Katrak, Ketu, 10, 329n27
Kaul, Suvir, 87
Keats, John, 106, 128, 152, 333n3
Kemp, Sandra, 337n50
Kermode, Frank, 297–98
Kinkead-Weekes, Mark, 338n2
Kipling, Rudyard
  and agency of literature, 6, 11, 18, 26, 313, 326,
  breast-feeding as bodily/linguistic relation in, 34–38, 313, 322
  and censorship, 7, 17–19, 26, 41–43, 46–50, 57, 80, 313
  censorship as death in, 31, 41–47, 53–54, 56
  critical reception of, 31–32
  fiction as lies in, 47, 59
  hybrid children in, 38–41, 50, 53–57
  and hybrid interracial production, 29–38, 51–52
  and hybrid language, 32–38, 53
  and *Macbeth*, 55–56, 338n55, 352n55
  location as colonial writer of, 7, 314
  map making and magic in, 80–92
  and silence, 42–44, 46–47, 74, 79–80
  trope of family in, 30, 32, 36, 39
  and writing as empire making, 30–32, 55–56, 75, 339n6
Works:
  "Beyond the Pale," 45
  "A Conference of the Powers," 331n55, 335n20
  "The Conversion of Aurelian McGoggin," 35, 46–47, 78
  "The Drums of the Fore and Aft," 43
  A Fleet in Being, 19, 50
  "His Chance in Life," 344n39
  In Black and White, 338n52
  "In Error," 46
  "The Islanders," 44
  "The Judgment of Dungara," 41
  The Jungle Book, 35, 338n52
  Just So Stories, 75
  Kim, 26, 33–34, 52–53, 58–96, 254, 339n9, 340n16
    damage to Kim, 26, 80, 85–96
    Great Game, 26, 59–60, 63, 65–68, 70, 72, 73, 75–80, 85, 88–91, 341n33
    Kim's body as written upon, 59–67
    Kim's fall into writing, 73–80
    Kim's freedom with language, 33, 59, 66, 68–73
    map making and magic in, 80–92
    subversiveness of Kim, 58, 96
  Life's Handicap, 333n2
  The Man Who Would Be King, and Other Stories, 41, 122
  "My First Book," 29–31, 333n1
  "The Native Born," 36
  "One View of the Question," 338n57
  "Only a Subaltern," 44
  "The Other Side of the Question," 49
  Plain Tales from the Hills, 32, 333n2
  Soldiers Three, 254
  Something of Myself, 32, 42, 47, 67, 333n1
  "The Son of His Father," 35, 41
  "The Story of Muhammed Din," 45
  "To Be Filed for Reference," 51–55, 62
  "Tods' Amendment," 38–41, 43
  War Stories, 43
  "Wee Willie Winkie," 33–34, 41, 43
  "The White Man's Burden," 43, 336n28
  "Without Benefit of Clergy," 333n2
Kipnis, Laura, 354n38
Koestenbaum, Wayne, 52, 333n3, 337n47
Kortenaar, Neil Ten, 355n2
Krishnaswamy, Revathi, 346n68
Kureishi, Hanif, 332n61; *The Buddha of Suburbia*, 14

Lacan, Jacques, 24, 76
Lakoff, George, 332n71, 357n16

Landesman, Charles, 8
Lane, Christopher, 142, 342n16, 346n60, 346n61
Lauritzen, John, 331n56
Law, John, 330–31n47
Lawrence, D. H., 130, 343n22; *The Rainbow*, 135
Lawson, Alan, 10
Lee, Sue-Im, 329n30
Locke, John, 8–9, 329n19
Loomba, Ania, 328n10

Macaulay, Thomas, 48, 335n25
Macpherson, C. B., 328n18
Maitland, Sara, 351n13
Malik, Charu, 349n30
Martin, Graham Dunstan, 20
Martin, Robert K., 117, 130, 342nn9–10, 342n15
Marx, Karl, 15
McGann, Jerome, 10; *Towards a Literature of Knowledge*, 17
Melden, A. I., 8
Merleau-Ponty, Maurice, 23, 283
Meyers, Jeffrey, 342n7
Mill, James, 340n24
Miller, D. A., 357–58n22
Minh-ha, Trinh, 7, 328n11
Mira, Afzal, 327n5
Mistry, Rohinton, 213
Mohanty, S. P., 61, 70–71, 87, 334n7
Moi, Toril, 359n15
Montrose, Louis, 12–13, 16–17
Moore-Gilbert, Bart, 13, 336n34
Mootoo, Shani, 325–26
Moran, Jo Ann Hoeppner, 350n35

Naipaul, V. S., 215, 235; *An Area of Darkness*, 327–28n7
Najmabadi, Afsaneh, 358n29
Nandy, Ashis, 256
Needham, Anuradha Dingwaney, 350n7, 351n12
Nichols, Grace, 316–17, 325
Nietzsche, Friedrich, 20–21, 292
Nixon, Rob, 357n14
Norris, Christopher, 22

Orange, Michael, 157, 347n6
Orwell, George, 31, 346n64

Parry, Ann, 337n50
Parry, Benita, 31, 157–58, 348n13
Partition, 224, 265, 268, 270–72, 280–81, 313, 356n9, 356–57n13
Pickthall, Mohammed Marmaduke, 353n30
Piggford, George, 117, 342n9, 342n15
Pinney, Thomas, 333n1, 336n30, 336n36
Plato, 20, 331n58
Pratt, Mary Louise, 129
Price, David, 355n47

Ramazani, Jahan, 315–16, 328n10, 359n1, 359nn3–4
Ramay, Haneef, 1–4, 229, 327n3, 327n5
Ranger, Terrence, 356n8
Raschke, Debrah, 105
Rege, Josna, 214, 351n10, 352nn16–17
Rhys, Jean: *Wide Sargasso Sea*, 324–25
Richards, I. A., 357–58n22
Riffaterre, Michael, 21
Robbins, Bruce, 10
Rosenthal, Michael, 339n6
Rossetti, Christina: *Goblin Market*, 349n23
Rowe, Katherine: *Dead Hands*, 220
Roy, Arundhati, 213, 351n14
Rushdie, Salman
  body as dirt in, 28, 234–36, 239–41, 280, 313
  body and dreams in, 283–86, 294
  and the body in relation to language, 3–5, 205–8, 211–12, 214, 216–18, 225–44, 247–48, 257–60, 271–72, 278, 295, 305–6, 323
  chutnifying or pickling history in, 4, 280
  and constructing a new postcolonial language, 205–10, 264, 313
  critical reception of, 20, 213–14
  dreams as narrative mode in, 267, 282–94, 302–4, 307–11
  familial as national narration in, 246, 268–72, 296
  fatwa against, 5–6, 8, 213, 304, 358n30
  genealogy and historical repetition in, 244–53
  and halal/haram flesh, 3–4, 240, 272, 279, 327n7
  the human hand in, significance of, 219–25
  and literary agency and cultural work, 3–6, 206, 209–10, 212, 219–25, 248–49, 253, 256, 266, 313, 326
  and migrancy, 268–72, 278, 281

376

postcolonialism of, 208–10, 213, 273
problem endings or resistance to closure in, 294–311
purity/impurity in, significance of, 280–81
on the Sundarbans, the dream-forest, 254–64
and synesthesia, 241–44, 257
trauma and collective memory in, 255–57
on truth and censorship, 5, 8, 20, 265–67, 273–81, 287–94, 313–14
Works:
"Censorship," 356n11
The Ground beneath Her Feet, 220
Haroun and the Sea of Stories, 220, 304–8, 334n18, 358n30
Imaginary Homelands, 209–10, 334–35n14, 356nn11–12
Midnight's Children, 3–5, 26–27, 205–8, 212–13, 216–17, 219–38, 244–64, 273–87, 290–96, 299–301, 309–11, 319, 334n18, 350n2, 351n10, 353n28, 356n12
The Moor's Last Sigh, 5, 220
"Outside the Whale," 204, 210, 265
The Satanic Verses, 5, 20, 208–9, 213, 215–16, 231–32, 251, 281, 283, 285–86, 298, 303–4, 306, 356n10, 357n18, 358n30
Shame, 213, 251–52, 286–90, 313
Rutherford, Andrew, 43, 54–55

Sabin, Margery, 12–13
Said, Edward, 11, 14, 55, 61, 338n53, 339n9, 348n13
Sandison, Alan, 31, 334n10
Sassoon, Siegfried, 101, 343n20; letters from E. M. Forster, 98, 106
Saussure, Ferdinand, 15, 207, 350n5
Scarry, Elaine, 9, 23–24
Sedgwick, Eve Kosofsky, 342n13
Selvadurai, Shyam, 213
Seymour-Smith, Martin, 337n49
Shakespeare, William: *Coriolanus*, 239; *Hamlet*, 250; *Macbeth*, 55–56, 338n55, 352n55
Sharpe, Jenny, 197, 349n25
Shelley, Percy Bysshe, 17
Sidhwa, Bapsi, 357n14
Sidney, Sir Philip, 20, 332n59
Silver, Brenda, 347n6
Singh, Khushwant, 357n14

Smith, Barbara Hernstein, 297, 357n22
Smith, Paul, 13, 15
Spivak, Gayatri, 283, 335n21, 351n13, 357n18, 358n29, 359n9
Stallybrass, Oliver, 341n3, 347n4
Stallybrass, Peter, 193, 346n62
Steele, Meili, 16
Steiner, George, 344n44
Sterne, Lawrence, 333n3
Stewart, David H., 339n9
Stone, Wilfrid 347n5
Suleri, Sara, 11, 31, 61, 78, 91, 150, 158, 287, 319–22, 329nn28–29, 335n21, 341n30, 342n10, 351n13, 358n28, 359n14
Sullivan, Zohreh, 30, 31, 61, 76, 88, 95, 334n11, 337n45, 337nn48–49, 338–39n2

Tagore, Rabindranath, 340n16
Tambling, Jeremy, 347n5
Tennenhouse, Leonard, 348n15
Tiffin, Chris, 10
Tinsley, Molly, 157, 347n6
Todorov, Tzvetan, 20
Tompkins, Jane (J.M.S.), 339n14
Touval, Yonatan, 117
Trilling, Lionel, 347n5
truth: and censorship, 7, 18; and unspeakability, 3, 17–22. *See also under* Forster, E. M.; Kipling, Rudyard; Rushdie, Salman
Turner, Victor, 60–61
Tytler, Harriet, 336n29

Viswanathan, Gauri, 40, 338n56

Walcott, Derek, 323, 328n10; "A Far Cry from Africa," 316; "The Muse of History," 249; *Omeros*, 315–16
Wheeler, Stephen, 49
White, Allon, 193, 346n62
Wilson, Angus, 337n49
Wilson, Edmund, 31, 334n8
Wolpert, Stanley, 350n33, 352–53n25, 355n48
Wright, Richard, 209

Yeats, W. B., 234
Young, Robert, 37, 142

Zia-ul-Haq, Mohammad, 269